Histoires Pour Enfant .... Stravinsky
and songs by Purcell and Barber.

FEBRUARY 22:
UBC UNIVERSITY CHAMBER SINGERS (Cortland Hultberg, Director)
Program: Ravel, Elliot Carter, and Istvan Anhalt's new composition, **A Cento on Eldon Grier's "An Ecstasy,"** commissioned for the Centennial Year by the University Chamber Singers.

MARCH 1:
CASSENTI PLAYERS (Conrad Crocker, flute; Warren Stannard, oboe; George Zukerman, bassoon; and Harold Brown, piano)
Bachiana Brasilieras No. 2 (flute and bassoon) .... Villa-Lobos
Quartet (1924) .... Rietti

MARCH 8: To be announced.

MARCH 15:
UBC TRIO (John Loban, violin; Hans-Karl Piltz, viola; and Eugene Wilson, cello)
They will perform Trio con Alea (1966) by Vancouver composer Barbara Pentland, whose opera, orchestra works, chamber music, piano and vocal works and scores for ballet, film and radio have firmly established her in Canada, the U.S. and Europe as one of Canada's foremost composers.

MARCH 22:
MUSIC OF TOKUGAWA JAPAN performed by **ELLIOTT WIESGARBER, shakuhachi** (vertical flute) and **MIYOKO KOBAYASHI, koto.** Mr. Weisgarber is a composer and ethnomusicologist at UBC. His partner, born in Hiroshima and brought up in Manchuria, is now making her home in Vancouver.

MARCH 29:
L'HISTOIRE DU SOLDAT .... Stravinsky
Norman Nelson, violin; Ronald de Kant, clarinet; and Elizabeth Winship, piano; with soldier, devil and narrator.

APRIL 5:
VICTORIA SCHOOL OF MUSIC TRIO
Robin Wood, piano; Jean Angers, violin; Hans Siegrist, cello.
Trio in D Minor .... Mendelssohn

February 2, 3, 4
All seats reserved. $1.25 (Students 75c).
Tickets now on sale — 291-3514.

SOME EARLY AND RECENT WORK BY

TONI ONLEY

Eighteen watercolours, collages and other works ranging from delicate, impressionistic landscapes of the Isle of Man twenty years ago to the abstract landscapes he paints today. A similar exhibition was held in October 1965 at the New Design Gallery.

February 25 - March 17 in the Foyer.

N. E. BAXTER THING CO.

Iain Baxter, President

and

four acquatex on canvas by

GARY LEE-NOVA

An exhibition of recent works by two young Vancouver artists, who were represented in **PAINTING '66.** Iain Baxter's bagged landscape, which shared the Centennial Prize, will become part of the Vancouver Art Gallery's permanent collection.

Iain Baxter, University Lecturer in Visual Arts at SFU, has had one-man shows this year in Regina, Toronto, Vancouver, Victoria and Los Angeles.

The work of **Gary Lee-Nova** has been seen in Toronto, Vancouver and Ottawa shows this year. He has recently become interested in experiments with 8mm and 16mm film, worked the light show for Canada's first "Trips Festival" last summer, and is associated with WECO Pop Art Multi Projection Co. in Vancouver.

February 1 - 22 in the Foyer.

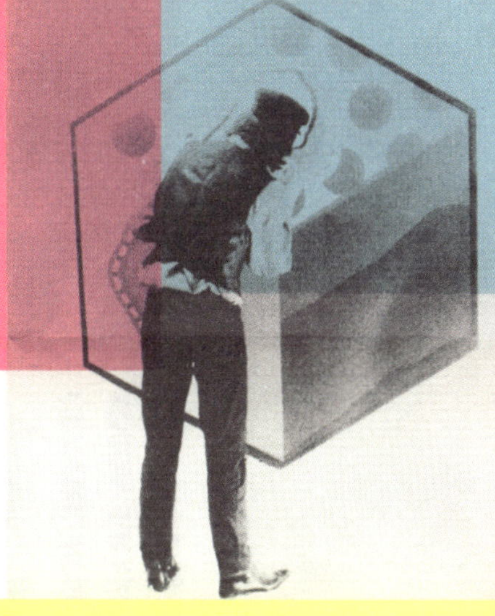

THE CENTRALIA INCIDENT

an original production
by the
SFU THEATRE WORKSHOP
Directed by Michael Bawtree

Using initially the techniques developed by Joan Littlewood of the London Theatre Workshop, the SFU Theatre Workshop began in September to create a piece of theatre suggested by an incident that took place in 1919 in Centralia, Washington.

The Workshop absorbed the atmosphere of post-war hysteria in America from personal memoirs, books, magazines and newspapers, photographs, posters and handouts, contemporary songs and marches. An expedition into Washington produced further photographs of Centralia today.

Using the background material, the Workshop discussed and then improvised sections of the story. These improvisations were taped and transcribed, and a plot line developed. From these sessions a script-writing group assembled the basic script of **The Centralia Incident.**

Wednesday through Saturday
March 1, 2, 3, 4, at 8:30 p.m.

All seats reserved. $1.25 (Students 75c).
Tickets on sale February 6.

The Canadian Broadcasting Corporation
in association with
Simon Fraser University
presents a

CBC CELEBRITY CONCERT

DONALD BELL
Baritone

Donald Bell, well-known opera, concert and recording star, is a native of Burnaby.

Now principal baritone with the Dusseldorf Opera, he has sung at many of the leading European festivals, toured the Soviet Union, Israel, and the United States, and is a regular performer with leading British Orchestras.

He was chosen by Leonard Bernstein as one of the soloists for the opening concert of Philharmonic Hall at Lincoln Center in New York; among his recordings are Belshazzar's Feast by Sir William Walton with the composer conducting and a lieder album for Columbia.

His program at SFU will include songs by Oskar Morawetz, commissioned with a grant from the Centennial Commission. Phyllis Schuldt will be at the piano.

Monday, February 13, at 8:30 p.m.

Unreserved seat tickets for this concert are available without charge at the SFU Theatre. They will be honored until 8:15 p.m. on the evening of the concert.

The Department of English
in co-operation with the
Centre for Communications and the Arts
presents

POETS and WRITERS

a series of readings by poets, playwrights and novelists of their own works and of lectures on literature.
Each Thursday at 12:45 p.m.

January 19: **Gabriel Fielding,** British author of **The Birthday King** and five other novels, currently writer-in-residence at Washington State University at Pullman, will speak on "The Class Structure in the Modern British Novel."

Special: Friday, January 20, at 12:45 p.m. Playwright **Jack Winter** will lecture on his Theatre Workshop in Toronto.

January 26: Recordings of Poetry.

February 2: **Stephen Black** of SFU reading his fiction; **Fred Candelaria** of SFU reading his poetry.

February 9: **Seymour Mayne** and **Pat Lane** of Vancouver reading their poetry.

February 16: **John Newlove** and **Milton Acorn** of Vancouver reading their poetry.

February 23: The well-known California poet **Elizabeth Bartlett,** poetry editor of ETC, author of four books of poetry and editor of ten anthologies, the most recent of which is "Where Is Viet Nam?" She will read her poetry.

March 2: **Stanley Cooperman** of SFU reading his poetry.

March 9: **John Mills** of SFU will read another excerpt from his novel in progress, **Seance on a Black Afternoon.**

March 16: The well-known Canadian poet and novelist **Earle Birney** reading his poetry.

March 23: **Roy Daniells** of UBC will lecture on Milton's **Paradise Lost.**

March 30: Yale Younger Poet of the Year (1967) **James Tate** reading his poetry. Yale will publish his volume of Poetry, **The Lost Pilot,** in January, 1967. He is a member of the Creative Writing Workshop at the University of Iowa.

April 6: To be announced.

The **Simon Fraser Film Society** in co-operation with the Centre for Communications and the Arts announces

SCOPE '67

SPRING FILM SERIES
Tuesday evenings at 8 p.m.

January 17: **Last Year at Marienbad.** France, 1961. Directed by Alain Resnais.

January 31: ***The Island.** Japan, 1961. Directed by Kanato Shindo.

February 14: **Lesson in Love.** Sweden, 1953. Directed by Ingmar Bergman.

February 21: **Billy Liar.** England, 1963. Directed by John Schlesinger.

March 7: ***Bell Antonio.** Italy, 1961. Directed by Mauro Bolognini.

March 14: ***Passion de Jeanne D'Arc.** France, 1926-27. Directed by Carl Dreyer.

March 28: **The Cabinet of Doctor Caligari.** Germany, 1919. Classic silent horror film, directed by Robert Wiene.

April 4: **The White Sheik.** Italy, 1956. Directed by Federico Fellini.

Film Society memberships at $3.75 each are now on sale at the Theatre.

*—Bookings not confirmed by press time.

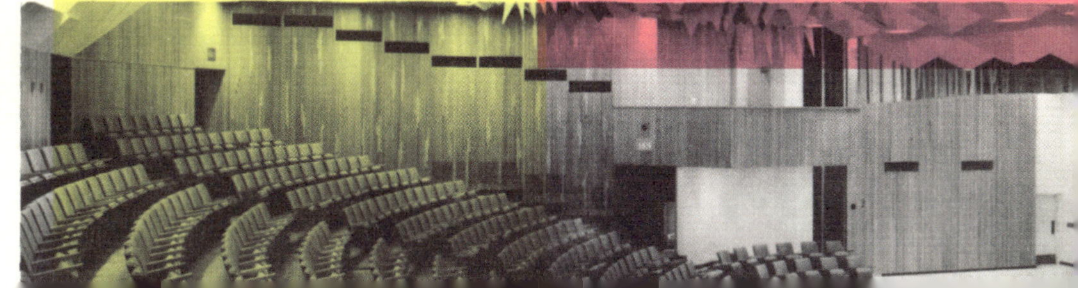

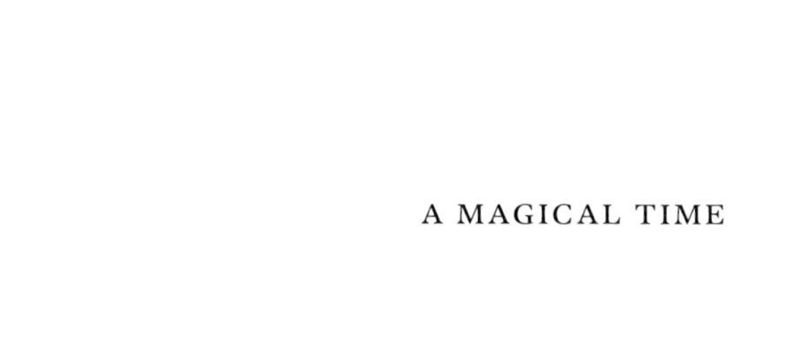

A MAGICAL TIME

A Magical Time

THE EARLY DAYS OF THE ARTS AT SIMON FRASER UNIVERSITY

Francis Mansbridge, Christine Hearn, Tessa Perkins Deneault, Carole Gerson, Bill Jeffries and Ann Cowan, with an introduction by Max Wyman

---

Project leader and photo management: Frances Atkinson

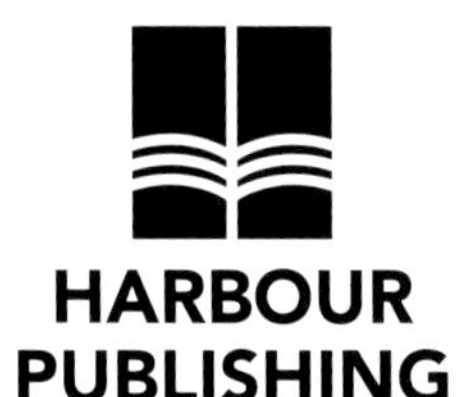

1 2 3 4 5 — 29 28 27 26 25

Harbour Publishing Co. Ltd.
P.O. Box 219, Madeira Park, BC, V0N 2H0
www.harbourpublishing.com

Edited by Christine Hearn, Francis Mansbridge and Pam Robertson
Indexed by Jessica Dee Humphreys
Text design by Libris Simas Ferraz / Onça Publishing
Front cover image: SFU Archives
Back cover image: Detail from *Theatres of the World* mural by Buell Mullen, photo by Ron Long
Printed and bound in South Korea

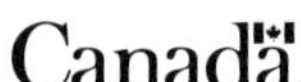

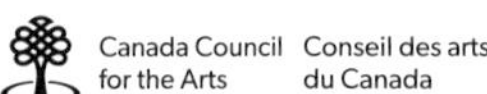

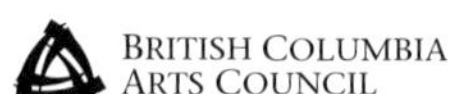

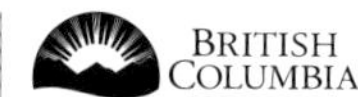

Harbour Publishing acknowledges the support of the Canada Council for the Arts, the Government of Canada, and the Province of British Columbia through the BC Arts Council.

Library and Archives Canada Cataloguing in Publication

Title: A magical time : the early days of the arts at Simon Fraser University / Francis Mansbridge, Christine Hearn, Tessa Perkins Deneault, Carole Gerson, Bill Jeffries and Ann Cowan ; with an introduction by Max Wyman ; project leader and photo management: Frances Atkinson.
Names: Atkinson, Frances (President of SFURA), project leader. | Simon Fraser University Retirees Association, issuing body.
Description: "Simon Fraser University Retirees Association"--Cover. | Barry Truax, Hildegard Westerkamp, Sandy Wilson, Tony Westman, contributors. | Includes bibliographical references and index.
Identifiers: Canadiana (print) 20240503872 | Canadiana (ebook) 20240495225 | ISBN 9781998526062 (hardcover) | ISBN 9781998526079 (EPUB)
Subjects: LCSH: Simon Fraser University—History. | LCSH: Arts—Study and teaching (Higher)—British Columbia—Burnaby—History.
Classification: LCC N331.C33 B87 2025 | DDC 707.1/171133—dc23

Table of Contents

Preface

by Frances Atkinson

SIMON FRASER UNIVERSITY WENT FROM AN IDEA IN 1963 TO OPENING ITS doors in 1965, a feat that led it to be dubbed the instant university. Building the physical university in two years was a major challenge. Equally demanding was deciding what would be taught, by whom, and how. The first academic planners, notably Ron Baker and Gordon Shrum, believed it was time to rethink the academy and break down barriers between disciplines so there could be a flow of ideas as fluid as the corridors of the new academic quadrangle. Meanwhile, a brand-new theatre built right in the centre of campus quickly enticed young innovators to experiment with new forms of artistic expression in theatre, music, film, dance, visual arts and the literary arts, discarding the traditional for the contemporary and unconventional.

To give focus to the growing range of artistic activities, a non-credit unit known as the Centre for Communications and the Arts (CCA) was established in the Faculty of Education under Dean Archie McKinnon, with UC Berkeley graduate Nini Baird hired as a publicist. Showing significant entrepreneurial skills from the outset, Baird quickly became the manager in charge of scheduling a formidable array of events while also raising funds both from internal sources and various arts-granting bodies across Canada. Students congregated with resident artists and visiting professionals in a buzz of creativity that attracted the general public, generated much attention from Vancouver newspapers and arts critics, and launched the careers of many.

This multi-authored book captures the excitement of that first decade of the arts at SFU. It chronicles the bold experiment represented by the CCA from 1965 until the early 1970s, when the transition to more traditional credit-granting arts programs began.

The introduction and first chapter of this book set the scene: the arts in Canada were blossoming; the university was new and unformed; non-traditional students from rural areas or working-class families had few preconceptions and were ready for something new; newly hired resident artists generated an explosion of new artistic opportunities centred in the new theatre. We discuss external influences, such as the Bauhaus movement and Black Mountain College, on the formation of the CCA. We introduce the leading resident artists who created great innovations, and we explore the personality clashes and tensions that eventually pulled the Centre apart.

In chapter two, we review the campus scene experienced by students both as receptive audience members and budding artists. We delve into the extensive range of plays and shows that were put on every week by student performers and let the heady excitement shine through. We highlight the Simon Fraser Student Society's role in bringing many mainstream rock, folk and jazz acts to campus, as well as professional performances arranged by the CCA. And we examine how the concerts and performances were promoted and critiqued by students writing for *The Peak* newspaper, which launched many careers in journalism.

In chapters three through eight we discuss each of the major artistic disciplines—theatre, dance, music, film, literary arts and visual arts—in turn. The chapters vary in approach, with some probing the highs and lows of leading figures, others focusing mainly on key students, and some containing excerpts from archival materials or previously published sources. Chapters three, five and six include stories from contributors who were students in the early days.

In the last chapter, we trace how the spirit of artistic innovation and the core belief in interdisciplinarity shaped events over the next six decades at SFU, including the formation of SFU's School for the Contemporary Arts and its move to downtown Vancouver. Last but not least, we link the legacy of the early days to the gift from Marianne and Edward Gibson, founding members of the university community, to create a free-standing gallery that offers a new gathering space in which to celebrate creativity in the arts on SFU's Burnaby campus once again.

Research sources for this book include materials from the SFU Archives, SFU Library and several public libraries, SFU Special Collections, *The Peak* student newspaper, interviews with key participants, and written pieces from contributors who were students or faculty at the time.

There is a risk in writing about a period that decades later still looms large and memorable in many minds in myriad and sometimes controversial ways. As Thomas J. Mallinson remarks, "Over the years, many accounts, histories and reminiscences have appeared by faculty members and students about the early days of SFU. In almost every case I have found myself wondering if the author and I were both here at the same time."[1] These other accounts vary, focusing on different aspects of the SFU experience, and particularly on the political upheaval of the time. This account is about the arts. Recognizing that it was not possible to represent all viewpoints, we have made every effort to be true to available archival and interview sources, while focusing on key figures and other participants at the centre of events.

True to its radical nature, SFU developed Canada's first academic women's studies program, and its Department of Women's Studies was one of the country's first. Yet many chapters in this book are dominated by male names, even though the SFU student body was over one-third female during the years covered by this book. Other than Phyllis Mailing in music and Iris Garland in dance, very few female artists were acknowledged as leaders. If they were mentioned at all, it was often tangentially, as the girlfriend of a named man. Only occasionally were they identified by their own name. In theatre, young women were involved in every aspect of production—costume making, set design, stage management and other backstage work—as well as performing on stage, but these accomplishments are not well represented in archival records. The visual arts were similarly unbalanced. We have acknowledged as many female participants as possible from available sources.

Those who may be looking for significant Indigenous content in this book will be disappointed. Other than projects relating to education or anthropology, SFU in general and the CCA in particular reflected the focus of the time on cultural issues that connected Canada with major artistic movements in the US and Europe. Occasionally, the campus was alerted to Indigenous concerns. For example, in April 1967, *The Peak* published a "Symposium on the Canadian Indian" that addressed matters of discrimination and education, including a stirring contribution by Shuswap leader George Manuel on the importance of preserving Canada's Indigenous heritage.[2] The following September, Chief Dan George addressed incoming students on the need for "unity, understanding and charity."[3] However, with a few notable exceptions, these issues seldom influenced the arts directly. In this book, Indigenous writers and actors appear in the corresponding chapters, as does a brief discussion of Indigenous art. A film project in Bella Coola that resulted in the award-winning film *Noohalk* is discussed in chapter six. (An archived collection of Bella Coola photographs can be found in our companion website, https://www.sfu.ca/earlyarts.)

We hope you enjoy our efforts to illustrate this exciting artistic period in SFU's beginnings. We have tried to capture the radical and open spirit of the time and the new university's responsiveness, allowing creative people to experiment and take risks. There is much to appreciate about the energy and inclusivity that marked the early years of the "instant university." It has been our great pleasure to try to bring it all to life.

Acknowledgements

FUNDING FOR THIS PROJECT CAME FROM SEVERAL SFU SOURCES. WE ARE especially indebted to SFU presidents Andrew Petter and Joy Johnson, Vice President External Relations Joanne Curry, Vice President Advancement and Alumni Engagement Erin Morantz, the Faculty of Arts and Social Sciences, and the Faculty of Communication, Art and Technology for generously funding the work on this book. We very much appreciate their unwavering support.

We are immensely grateful to our research assistant Casey McCarthy, who, while a student in SFU's Masters in Publishing program, worked for us for five months in 2021 after the COVID-19 pandemic eased. After retrieving a trove of archival material from the SFU Archives, Casey created a website (www.sfu.ca/earlyarts) that enabled a core team to promote the project and elicit contributions from charter students and resident artists, and write this book that includes about one hundred images. Many thanks also to SFU's archivists, especially Matthew Lively and Melanie Hardbattle, for their enthusiastic collaboration; to the university's copyright officer, Don Taylor, for his advice and counsel on copyright issues; to the staff of SFU Library Special Collections & Rare Books for their help finding additional materials and images; and to numerous interviewees and contributors noted throughout the book. We thank editor Wendy Plain for her excellent editing skills and constructive comments.

Thank you to the entire team at Harbour Publishing, especially editor Pam Robertson, designer Libris Simas Ferraz who worked on the cover art and interior design, and production assistant Harry McKeown who made the whole process much easier than we imagined it might be.

Finally, a very special thanks to the team that has worked so long and diligently on this multi-authored book. They persevered through the difficult days of the Covid-19 pandemic, contributed their extensive skills and experience, and maintained their dedication throughout. The team membership evolved over the course of creating the book. The core team included Frances Atkinson (project leader, image management), Ann Cowan (writer), Carole Gerson (writer/editor), Christine Hearn (writer/editor), Bill Jeffries (writer), Francis Mansbridge (writer/editor) and Tessa Perkins Deneault (writer). We are also very grateful to Walter Piovesan, Marcia Toms, Gladys We, Tony Westman and Joanie Wolfe, who contributed in ways too numerous to list.

Frances Atkinson
President
Simon Fraser University Retirees Association (SFURA)

Introduction

by Max Wyman

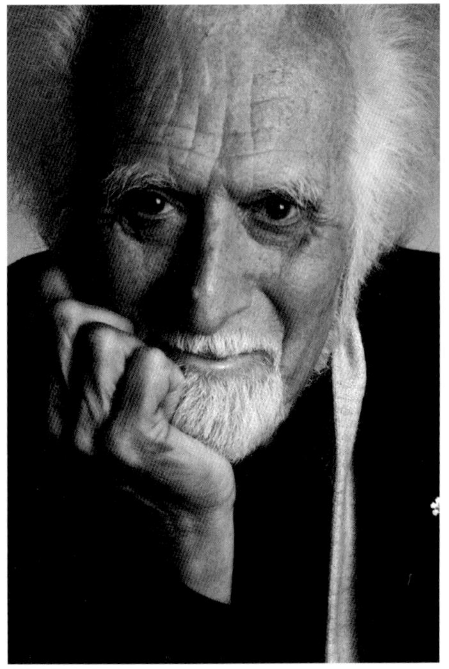
Max Wyman. *Yukiko Onley*

THE END OF THE 1960S AND MUCH OF THE 1970S SEEMS, IN retrospect, to have been a golden age for the arts in Canada. Liberated by the sixties spirit of adventure and social freedom, spurred on by the imaginative openness of Expo 67 and the celebration of the country's centennial that year, Canadians were waking from a long sleep under a shroud of colonial diffidence and Presbyterian temperance, and developing a taste for experiment and innovation in creative expression. Canada felt fresh, sometimes even—my giddy goodness!—saucy.

This sense of blossoming—of welcoming what might be possible—was reflected in the work of the country's artists. They were building a new cultural identity. In Vancouver in that period, the range and availability of music, dance and theatre at all levels of achievement and experimental outrageousness was probably not matched until half a century later. Simon Fraser University, the upstart newcomer with the sheen of youth on its face and the spirit of intelligent creative inquiry infusing its being, was at the pulsing, chaotic centre of it all.

The city's professional music scene had largely been developed by a generation of sophisticated Europeans driven to Canada in the 1930s and 1940s by war. Eager to recreate the standard of cultural life they had been used to and to help enrich the civilization of the place they now lived in, they gave generous support to the arts, particularly the opera and the symphony. The high-minded Vancouver International Festival, based on similar concert series in Europe, flamed out in the late 1960s in a blaze of debt after several seasons of glamorous international programming, but it left our audiences with a taste for quality in performance.

But if you were interested in the shock of the new, you had to go farther afield to the places where youth was flexing its imaginative muscles and the old ways were being challenged and supplanted by the experimental and the unconventional. Like the Vancouver Art Gallery, where director Tony Emery and events coordinator Marguerite Pinney welcomed a flood of unorthodox happenings from the city's creative community—a ferment of new music, theatre, dance, poetry—to augment the shows on the walls. Like the University of British Columbia, where from 1961 to 1971 the annual UBC Festival of the Contemporary Arts showcased new directions in artmaking.

And particularly like Arthur Erickson's concrete brutalist extravagance carved into the top of a mountain to the east of the city: Simon Fraser University. Here, from the mid-1960s on, innovation was the order of the day; nothing was sacrosanct. Visionaries and provocateurs from both sides of the border (many escaping the military draft to Vietnam) had flocked to the university when it opened in 1965, and over the next five years it became a hotbed of anarchy and experiment. The Centre for Communications and the Arts (CCA) became the place where that creative revolution was translated into cultural expression. As Michael Bawtree, the Centre's first resident in theatre, recalls in his memoir *The Best Fooling: Adventures in Canadian Theatre*, the Centre was to be a component of the Faculty of Education, which was being conceived on a wholly new and experimental principle.

Inspired by McLuhan's theories about communications, the Centre was deeply involved in experiments in the emerging field of multimedia. "Everything was to be invented fresh," Bawtree recalls, "with a new and brave cluster of buildings to house it all. Old modes of thinking were to be discarded. The talk was all of the world we were about to make: a new place of learning, new kinds of teaching, new ways of thinking about the arts, new colleagues. 'Creativity' was one of the watchwords."[1]

Initially the Centre had no intention of turning out new professionals in the arts, and until 1975 it was a non-credit affair (its teaching staff were untenured "residents") intended to sensitize the university community, through a wide program of workshops and performances, to the civilizing and educational aspects of contact with artistic expression. Says Bawtree: "I liked to say, not entirely jokingly, that our theatre work was not non-curricular but 'supra-curricular': far too important to be constrained within the curriculum."[2] However, the lines became blurred very quickly. Everyone who encountered the Centre and its inspirational faculty wanted to *make* art, and art that *meant* something. Its first director, the genial Tom Mallinson, called it "the new Bauhaus."

From the start, the people in charge—knowing how important it was to be seen to be in touch with the wider community—made sure the doors were open to all comers. The Centre played host to a broad range of professional performances from off-campus, sometimes very far off, and anyone prepared to

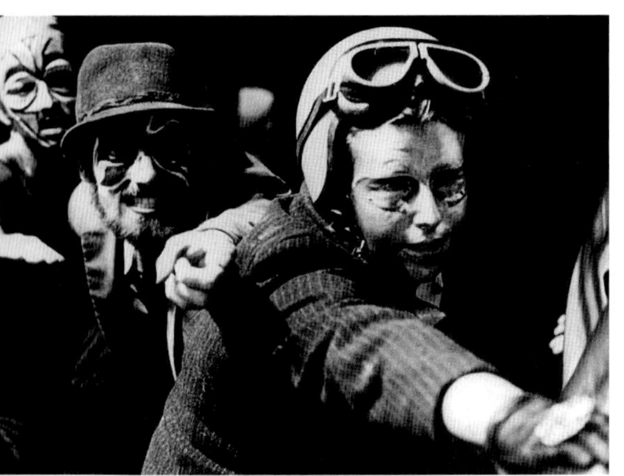

Actors from *Coriolanus*, the play that shook the SFU establishment in 1968. *SFU Archives*

make the trek up the mountain could expect to encounter edgy new work by visiting international musicians and choreographers and new experimental creations by the school's own often-fractious faculty and students.

It was the perfect microcosm of the messy, exciting, uproarious new world of contemporary art that was being shaped in those years in Canada and around the world. Lots happened on the hill that Vancouver otherwise would not have had a sniff at, and we have probably not experienced such rampant and rambunctious richness since.

Bawtree, an Oxford-educated Australian who had come to SFU's theatre department from a post as dramaturge at the Stratford Shakespeare Festival (its first), believed in fostering new ideas in a climate of collaboration. Out of this petri dish of experiment emerged John Juliani, the hot-eyed scourge of the theatrical bourgeoisie. Rhetoric, shock and violence were the essential elements of style of his Savage God ensemble, which he established soon after arriving on campus. He was on a search, he said, for a "meta-language of the theatre" that went beyond the norms of conventional drama. The process involved deep soul-searching and personal exposure for the performers, in the manner of European modernists like Alfred Jarry and adherents of the Grand Guignol and the Method school.

At the end of 1968, Juliani was rehearsing a modern-day production of Shakespeare's bloody military tragedy *Coriolanus* at the SFU Theatre when police were called to deal with a student occupation of the main administration building nearby. Among the *Coriolanus* production effects was the taped sound of gunfire broadcast from an amplifier on top of the theatre lobby. In full military makeup and costumes, the cast stood outside the theatre to watch the police reclaim the administration building from its occupiers as the fake gunfire echoed around the glassed-in SFU mall.

Not long after the *Coriolanus* incident, according to Juliani, he was told by Mallinson's successor, Patrick Lyndon: "Your career forms a great trajectory ahead of you. I want you to follow it by shooting like a rocket off this campus." That trajectory took Juliani into experimental movie-making, acting, broadcasting, teaching and actors-union activism, all of it fuelled by a strident Canadian nationalism. He famously challenged Robin Phillips to a duel to protest the Englishman's appointment as head of the Stratford Festival. And in the firm conviction that his life was his art, he arranged for his marriage to Donna Wong to be the climax of a *Savage God* performance at the Vancouver Art Gallery.

Bawtree himself returned to Stratford in 1969, became director of the Third Stage, and went on to a distinguished career across Canada as an actor, playwright, director and teacher. His Stratford productions included an opera, *Patria II: Requiems for the Party Girl*, written by his colleague Murray Schafer to feature the mezzo-soprano voice of his wife, Phyllis Mailing, another resident at the Centre.

In the dance department, Iris Garland was a Centre stalwart from the earliest years. A Chicago-born kinesiologist who had launched the SFU dance program in 1965, she saw the future, in dance terms at least, long before the rest of us, and took a chance on it. She was impatient to push her adopted country toward maturity, and dance became, as Evan Alderson once described it to researcher Alana Gerecke, the "lead card" for the Centre. Garland's joyful pioneering in the use of new technologies, and her consistent showcasing of performance and teaching by much of the cutting edge of New York new dance, helped shape the future of dance-making not only in BC but across Canada. Every time an SFU dance class graduated, we used to joke, three new dance companies sprang up.

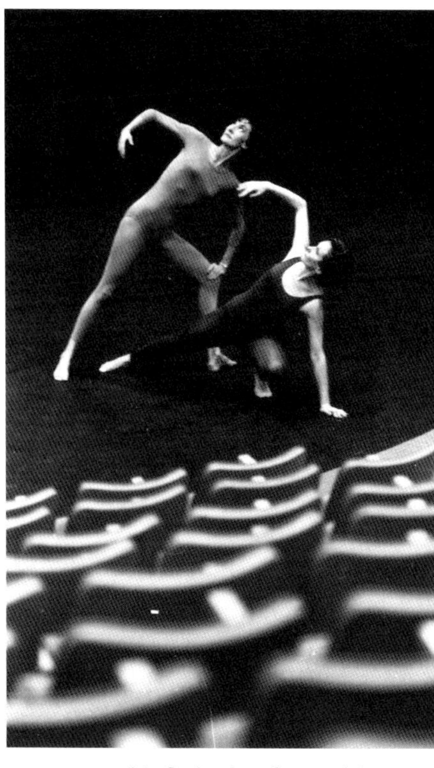

Iris Garland performs with a guest artist in the SFU Images Theatre in 1968. *IMC, SFU Archives*

Those were the days when the *Vancouver Sun* used to review student dance performances. As the paper's music and dance critic I spent so many lunchtimes and evenings in the little theatre on the mountain that for a while I had a designated parking spot in the lot under the mall, astonishing as such an idea might seem now. On one occasion I was snootier about an end-of-term show than I perhaps should have been, and Garland promptly loosed off a thunderbolt to the *Sun* letters page reminding "Mr. Wyman" in no uncertain terms that few choreographies "spring fully-formed from the brow of Zeus," and would he kindly learn to be more understanding. (When the place became a full-credit institution, a theatre faculty member persuaded those in charge that thenceforth student productions should not be reviewed, on the principle that critical assessment in the public media was incompatible with the freedom of students to learn by taking risks.) Garland eventually married James W. Felter, a Peace Corps alumnus who set up the SFU Gallery, and we all became great pals.

In the music faculty, the composer R. Murray Schafer was getting angry about sound pollution. With his tight little smile, his eyes alight, the hair around his mouth setting off his gleaming teeth, he warned us that we were all going to be deaf in thirty years. Wearing his professor-of-communications hat, he ran SFU's World Soundscape Project, which gathered and compared the sounds of different cities, and published *The Vancouver Soundscape*, a book and two LPs that included "ear-witness accounts" of the sound of the area in pre-city times—ship whistles, foghorns, cathedral bells. He lamented the way the sky was becoming "a sound sewer" and decried "insidiously abusive" wired background music, which "reduces a sacred art to a slobber." In the area of the sacred art itself, meanwhile, he was turning out some of the most interesting new music in the country, all of it recorded in written and illustrated scores that were works of art in themselves.

SFU's music department matched the Faculty of Dance in its determination to expose the university community, and the city, to the newest innovations in the art form. In 1970 we were visited by the British composer Cornelius Cardew, so far ahead of the game he made the avant-garde look prehistoric. He was looking, he said, for a return to "elemental simplicity" in our lives, and his music was a way for people to clear their minds. His recital, which started with an audience of thirty reduced by the end to twenty, included a piece consisting of a single note held for eight minutes on a cello and a work called *Stones*, by Christian Wolff, which consisted of Cardew tapping, scraping and hammering stones that he had hung from wires and a coat hanger. What sort of sound did they make? Well, you know—real rock music.

Christian Wolff himself arrived hard on the heels of Cardew to offer what he called a "continuous concert," with two pieces always on the go and most of them challenging the idea of what music is: not just the stones, for instance, but someone pouring water into a bucket from a stepladder, someone else rattling peas in a box then scattering them on the floor. "Music exists wherever anyone listens," he said. "It is anything you bring a disposition of attention to, and a disposition to sense harmoniousness." "Ho hum," an audience member shouted in the middle of it all, slamming his briefcase shut, snapping on the locks and walking out.

"Ho-hum" depended on your perspective, of course. The legacy for the arts in Canada of those years of experiment and provocation on the hill are extensive and indelible. Conceptual artist IAIN BAXTER& (Iain Baxter formally changed his name in 2005) called his years teaching at SFU, from 1966 to 1971, "one of the most important developmental stages of my career." One year, as he told Tessa Perkins Deneault for an article in *The Peak*, he taught his entire course in a consecutive twenty-six hours. That left him free to pursue his own creative interests, which included establishing, with his wife, Ingrid, the now-legendary N.E. Thing Co., one of the early investigators of conceptual art and a significant influence on the "Vancouver" school of photography that emerged in the following decades.

Meanwhile, the four front-desk string players at the VSO quit the orchestra to create the Purcell String Quartet and were in residence at the Centre for a decade from 1972, popping up all over campus, touring BC and eastern Canada under the SFU flag, and providing the music for a 1973 production of Purcell's opera *Dido and Aeneas* with the SFU Madrigal Singers under the direction of Phyllis Mailing.

The Centre in those years was a playground of almost inexhaustible riches. Murray Schafer and fellow composers Martin Bartlett (who founded the Electronic Music Studio), Phillip Werren and Bruce Davis; Juliani and fellow theatre innovators like mime and mask expert Wendy Gorling; dancer-choreographers such as Karen Jamieson (who was snatched away to dance in New York with modernist legends Alwin Nikolais and Merce Cunningham) and the team that created one of the seminal dance collectives of the era, Terminal City Dance. This was where they honed their craft, demonstrating, in the process, that everything was possible, however outrageous, as long as you had the vision and the conviction.

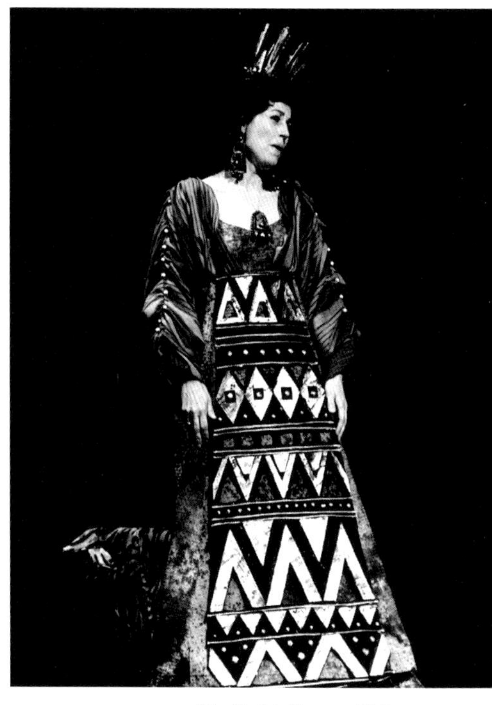

Phyllis Mailing as Dido in the opera *Dido and Aeneas* in 1973. *Peter Higdon, SFU Archives*

And this exuberance was not limited to the performing arts. Literary activity abounded as eager young poets and other writers were encouraged by faculty in the English department to produce their own periodicals, and international authors brought their words into the public realm with well-attended readings in the theatre and at other on-campus sites. Sharon Thesen, Sharon Riis, Brian Fawcett, Brian Brett and Allan Safarik were among writers who got their start in small SFU-based magazines such as *Iron*, *Blackfish*, *BallsOut* and the *West Coast Review*. It was a burgeoning time at the university, and the Centre in particular, but artistic output was not the only area in which SFU played an influential role on the BC cultural scene during those years. By the late 1960s, the simmering issue of cultural policy was coming to a boil. Advocacy networks at both the national and provincial levels were beginning to make serious noise about the need to bring more support and focus to a disorganized and underfunded segment of society. Both the Canada Council and the BC government responded to the mounting pressure by hiring specialists to come up with recommendations for change.

Early in 1972, Paul Schafer, the brother of composer Murray Schafer, delivered a report to the BC government on the best ways to develop the province's cultural facilities. Schafer, who was also advising UNESCO on cultural policy, framed the debate as a clash between technological materialists and cultural humanists: "value, once deliberately lodged in the material objects and technological extensions of man, is shifting to the subject, man himself," he said. It was this concern for "the state of the inner and outer environment of man, and the need for a total and creative man, that should guide all our thought and actions in the formulation and implementation of cultural policies." His ideas were music to the ears of many who endorsed the Centre's core philosophies.

Not everyone was in love with the Schafer report. One who opposed it was Peter Hay, who had been a resident in theatre at SFU during the turbulent late sixties and "left under a cloud," as he put it (he was a co-conspirator with John Juliani in the ongoing unrest on the hill), went to work as dramaturge at the Vancouver Playhouse (which he "left under a separate cloud" a year later), and moved on to work at the CBC and to launch the plays division at the pioneering literary publisher Talonbooks. The immigrant son of a Hungarian playwright who had been jailed for his beliefs, he was unashamedly outspoken in the European manner and made it his business to be a thorn in the side of the cultural establishment and any arts organization he felt wasn't doing its job properly.

The cultural deficiencies of the BC government brought out the bristling best in him. The Schafer report would leave control of cultural policy in the hands of "an interlocking corporate, self-perpetuating establishment," he fumed. If Schafer's recommendations were implemented, "this would simply enhance the neglect, persecution and betrayal of the BC artists who have been fighting this ingrown cultural establishment at the cost of their jobs, their health, their families and above all their creativity." What was needed was a full-scale government study outlining policy strategies and a detailed machinery for administering support, with thorough input from the arts community itself. "Artists are not, as they are often portrayed in popular myth, freaks or parasites on society, and they do not deserve to be treated as such."

The debate was loud and strong, and in the fall of 1973 the BC government organized a conference on provincial arts policy, choosing SFU as the place to hold it. Under the umbrella title of Arts Access, the gathering was coordinated by Nini Baird, at that time the director of the Centre and a Canada Council board member. It brought together around 1,000 individuals from the professional and non-professional arts scene for a weekend on the mountain to talk about the future.

What emerged was a 50,000-signature proposal to the premier echoing Schafer's calls for a new stand-alone agency, the development of a long-term cultural policy in BC, and more money for the arts. The following spring the BC government sent Baird around the province to check out public attitudes to cultural policy; her report led to the appointment of the BC Arts Board—a significant indication that the powers that be were taking the arts seriously at last.

Progress of a kind was in the air. The university had helped to foster it and would remain an integral part of it.

CHAPTER 1

Leap Before You Look

THE CENTRE FOR COMMUNICATIONS AND THE ARTS

by Francis Mansbridge

"[A] blank canvas on which we could do whatever we wanted."
—SFU photographer and film student Tony Westman

SIMON FRASER UNIVERSITY SPRANG TO LIFE AT ONE OF THOSE RARE MOMENTS in human history when a convergence of energies vibrated through every aspect of society, totally transforming the human landscape. It's also characteristic of these rare times that those who are fortunate to live in them often assume they will last forever—that the liberation of the human soul will permanently change the face of the world, making it a more humane and loving place. SFU was a place of intense excitement and celebration of life. A summer of love? More like a decade.

The Promise of a Mountaintop Eden

Reflecting the social vision of the time, SFU was imbued with the optimistic belief that people are basically good and, given the opportunity, will make the choices that will lead to a better, richer life for themselves and others. SFU was a mountaintop Eden, a place where there could be a fresh start, transcending the stale forms that had encrusted education elsewhere. Everyone was open to new ideas, at least in principle. Unfortunately, the world is complex, and not all

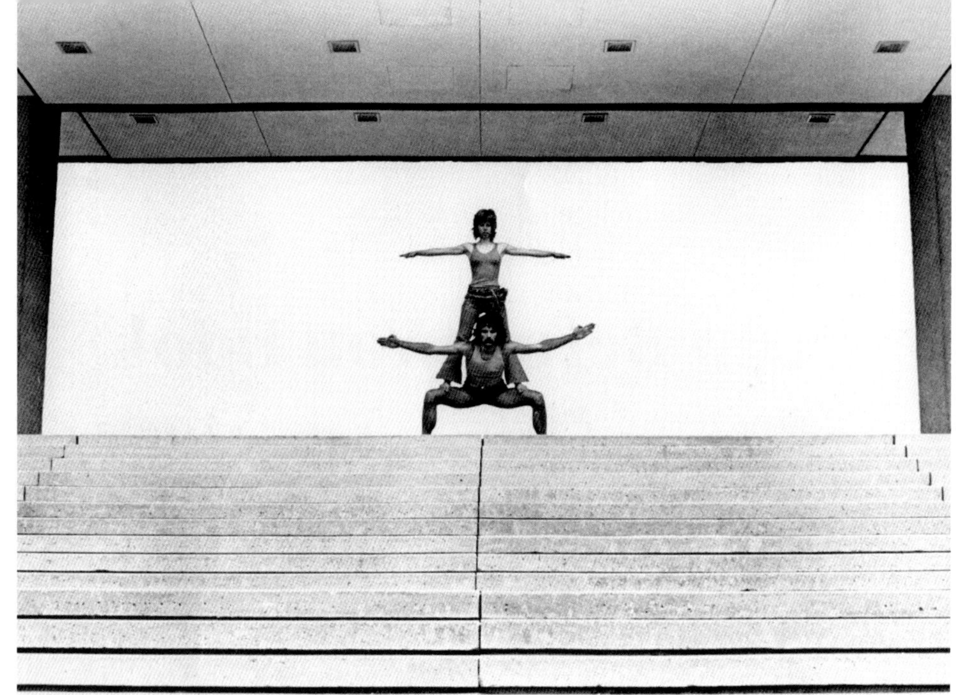

Two dancers from the SFU Dance Workshop perform on top of the academic quadrangle steps in 1972. *Peter Higdon, SFU Archives*

was peace and love. Confrontations among factions and people were frequent—occasionally even violent—and one incident with the police led to the arrest of students who had been occupying the SFU administration building.

But the excitement and celebration more than compensated for the difficulties. Few now would wish anything to have been different. The university's main architect, Arthur Erickson, had taught in an experimental program at the University of Oregon that emphasized interdisciplinary education and the Socratic method. The first president of SFU, Oxford graduate Dr. Patrick McTaggart-Cowan, was an enthusiastic supporter of and leader in new directions. And even the venerable chancellor, Gordon Shrum, was a brilliant advocate for the right type of innovation. Drawing on radical European and American thought, SFU became a home for educational innovation. And at SFU, the Centre for Communications and the Arts energized artistic experiment, creating a lively venue for students and faculty to stimulate each others' creativity while having a glorious time.

Bauhaus Ideals and Black Mountain College

The Bauhaus, one of the tributaries nourishing SFU, "was founded in 1919 in the city of Weimar by German architect Walter Gropius (1883–1969). Its core objective was a radical concept: to reimagine the material world to reflect the unity of all the arts."[1] When the political climate in Germany led to the Bauhaus shuttering in 1933, some of its adherents fled abroad to form Black Mountain College in North Carolina. Josef Albers, who had been a popular professor at the Bauhaus, became its rector. Key to its philosophy was the belief that the study and practice of art were indispensable aspects of a liberal arts education.

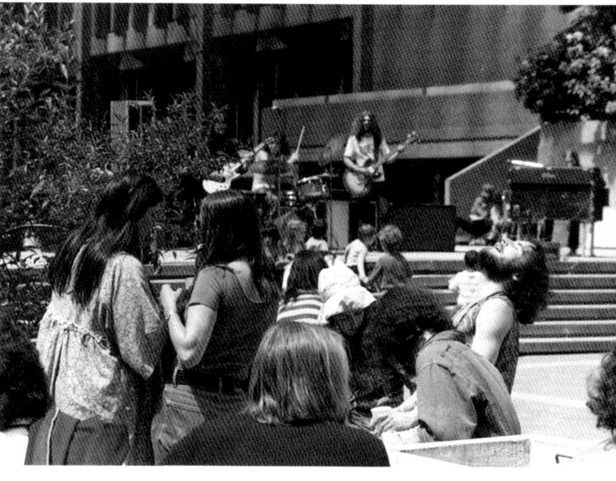

The first decade of SFU's existence was exhilarating for all. *IMC, SFU Archives*

Many creative artists found that the synergy of Black Mountain College created a congenial place in which to explore many of the ideas generated by the Bauhaus. Charles Olson, Robert Duncan and Robert Creeley (in poetry), John Cage (in music), Merce Cunningham (in dance) and futurist Buckminster Fuller were some of the North Americans who transformed art on this side of the Atlantic. Creeley, Fuller and the Merce Cunningham Dance Company with John Cage gave presentations at SFU, and several faculty members, including English professors Ralph Maud, Jerry Zaslove and Robin Blaser, helped their artistic spirit flourish on campus. Sound and music specialist Murray Schafer was particularly important in incorporating many of the transformative principles of the avant-garde into the university's programs.

A West Coast Avant-Garde

In the late fifties the centre of the American avant-garde moved to the West Coast, particularly Berkeley, California. Here Allen Ginsberg explored the dark side of the American dream in his enormously popular *Howl and Other Poems*, published in 1956 by Lawrence Ferlinghetti's City Lights Bookstore in San Francisco. With Gregory Corso, Gary Snyder and others, the "Beats" generally wrote in a much more accessible style than the Black Mountain poets, democratizing poetry and other arts, which flourished in the multitudes of coffee shops that sprang up throughout North America.

Mirroring Educational Philosophy in Architectural Design

While the aesthetic and political dimensions of the arts resonated in the marketplace, others were creating the conditions that would provide the infrastructure

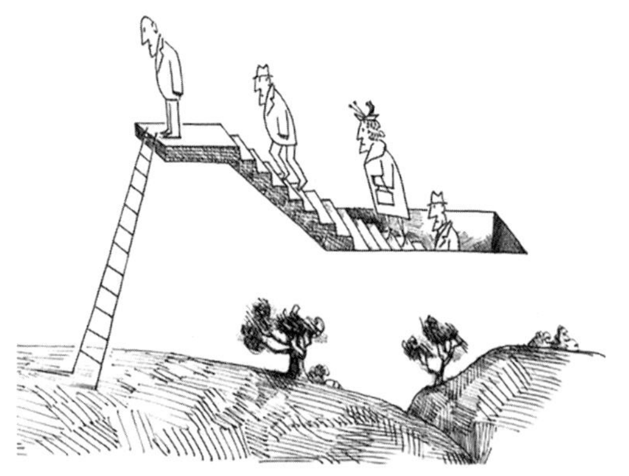

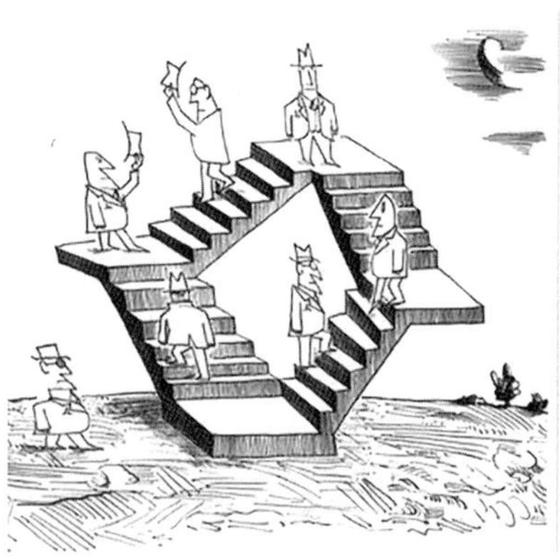

These cartoons circa 1965 were found in the SFU Archives along with professional architectural drawings of the new campus. Perhaps an anonymous draftsman was poking fun at all the lofty ideas that were circulating, or more prosaically at all the steps that were being built, seemingly going nowhere. (SFU's Burnaby campus has a great many steps at its centre.) *SFU Archives*

for this involvement. The competition for the building of SFU was announced late May 1963, with the entry deadline of July 30, a scant two months away. Arthur Erickson and Geoffrey Massey won the contest. The clean and elegant lines of their design owed much to modernism, so different from the ivy-covered castles that were more the rule in universities and elsewhere. The design of the university embodied a philosophy of education in which all knowledge was related and all its seekers were members of one community. Evoking the classic pattern of the monastery, with its covered arcade of rhythmic repetition, the new campus expressed the principle that knowledge was transferred as much outside the classroom as within.

The top five finishers in the architectural contest were each awarded a contract to design a section of the campus. Third place went to individual architect Zoltan Kiss. Kiss had fled Hungary in 1944, spending a year in Germany before reaching Denmark. He arrived in Canada on June 8, 1950, and as a painter, ceramicist and architect enjoyed a long and productive career in his adopted country. He lobbied successfully for his desired share of the project, the academic quadrangle. Designed as an expanse in which to stroll, talk and think—the heart of artistic expression and intellectual debate for a new generation—it was simply a large open space embraced on four sides by the library, classrooms and other academic structures.

Kiss had received his education at the Bauhaus-influenced Technical University of Budapest, which may have influenced this open mall as a place where students, faculty and others could intermingle. Christine Hearn, a student at that time, has noted, "You cross paths with everybody on the way to the library or on the way to the theatre. Or in the cafeteria."[2] Kiss later designed Vancouver's new airport terminal building, which opened in September 1968. Its modern design and clean functional lines echo those of SFU.

However, meaningful play was never far away. David Stouck describes Erickson's account of a 1966 enterprise to plant wild poppies in the slopes below the theatre:

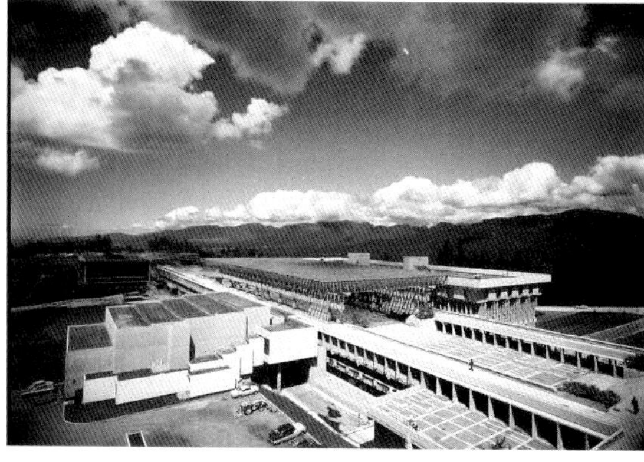

This view of the main campus shows the theatre as the staggered building on the left.
IMC, SFU Archives

> One evening in late April, he invited some colleagues from the office and several faculty and students to gather on the slopes below the theatre around Helen Goodwin, a dance teacher at UBC. They had 20 pounds of poppy seed and several bottles of Faisca. Each person was given a yard of red cotton to adorn themselves and a musical instrument, and in the delicate spring air and splendid colours of the evening, they danced through the fields, scattering the seeds, strips of red cloth flying and tambourines ringing. They were overcome with Bacchic exuberance. Then, forming a procession, they twirled and danced around the running track, up the stairs to the mall and across the mall to the foot of the Quadrangle. In Arthur's words, "It was a truly pagan rite, and just as the sun was lowering Helen mounted the Quad steps like a high priestess. Each one of us, without bidding, came forward silently to lay our instrument at her feet as she invoked the setting sun." Some bewildered tourists must have believed what they were seeing "were the ghosts of the original tribe that had built the mountain temple."[3]

This spontaneous delight in their world expressed much of the spirit of the new dawn at SFU and the hopes for a world shaped by love and art.

Creating the CCA

Chancellor Gordon Shrum promoted an original concept for the Centre for Communications and the Arts (CCA) that had communications as its binding principle, combining a tutorial system with teaching by residents, or specialists, and sought to expose all SFU students to creative opportunities beyond their own disciplines through non-credit courses. Archie MacKinnon, the dean of education, implemented these ideas.

At the beginning, each SFU student was required to take two non-credit courses in subject areas such as music, theatre, dance, sports, film and painting. The rationale behind these non-credit courses was that both students and faculty should be encouraged to broaden their knowledge and explore, in common, areas outside narrow disciplinary boundaries.

Wherever feasible, large lectures every week were supplemented by smaller classes taught by junior faculty or graduate students. Then-student Linda Johnston notes that as there were very few grad students, the role of teaching assistant was often played by the professors. "Having the tutorial discussions with 15 students and the head of the department was extraordinary."[4]

Talented specialists were hired to facilitate the large group lectures, mostly on short-term contracts; in the first year Iris Garland in the Physical Development Centre was the only faculty member in the CCA on tenure track. In addition, numerous events were organized in which visiting and local artists and thinkers provided stimulating presentations.

The intent of the CCA was to bring students directly into contact with their art, without the distractions of grading and marks, to make for a less adulterated educational experience. In "Brave New University," an unpublished essay, Tom Mallinson, the communications specialist in the CCA from 1966 to 1968, evokes the appeal of a world in which the absence of tradition and the dead weight of past practice made possible the implementation of utopian ideals. The "central focus" was "the exploration of both the contents and forms of human communication." It was "not intended for entertainment alone, but to provide opportunities to look at all facets of the creative and communicative process."[5] He recalls the intense energy, enthusiasm and vitality among students, staff and faculty. Michael Bawtree, hired as the first resident in the theatre, describes theatrical activity at his alma mater, Oxford, as run entirely by students, attracting actors, directors and theatre technicians from courses in physics to classics. Student control at SFU was not as complete, but faculty and students worked collaboratively to create exciting projects.

Brilliant minds, attracted by the spirit of artistic openness at SFU, created a rich and diverse atmosphere that caught the imaginations of the students. Jan Visscher became theatre manager; while the position was eliminated in the fall of 1966, he stayed on in the theatre program. Phyllis Mailing became a teaching assistant in music, and Iris Garland taught dance for the Department of Kinesiology. Summer 1966 additions included John Juliani in theatre and Iain Baxter in visual arts. Fall hires included Stan Fox and Adrienne Hunter in film, Paul Bettis in theatre, and Jack Behrens and Brian Carpenter in music and communications, respectively. Oxford graduate Peter Hay arrived in the fall of 1967 and soon became active in theatre and university politics.

Appointing the First Residents and Directors

Bruce Attridge was the first director of the Centre for Communications and the Arts, a part of the Department of Education. His first hire was Michael Bawtree as resident in theatre, whom he put in touch with Murray Schafer, who was being hired at the same time (the summer of 1965) as a resident in music. Schafer, "highly, intelligent and rebellious" in Bawtree's words,[6] was well known for his experimental music and provocative theories. Attridge made these appointments without going through a formal hiring process—no competition. Neither Bawtree nor Schafer had PhDs, which were fast becoming the academic union card in North American universities. This would later affect their academic life at SFU.

Attridge resigned from the directorship of the CCA for health reasons after only six weeks in his new job, and Tom Mallinson succeeded him. To Nini Baird, who came to the CCA in 1966, Mallinson was a "scientist and therapist, a research scientist on communication issues."[7] Bawtree found him "a very sweet-natured, nice guy who had no experience of the arts whatsoever... interpersonal communication is what he called it, but it was quite a different thing from the kind of communication that McLuhan was talking about." He added, "[W]e were always a little bit confused about what communications was" because it was "the glue between things rather than being something itself... There was never anyone to work it out with philosophical detail and accuracy."[8]

Many of the people who did the hiring had backgrounds at British universities, especially Oxford, which at this time favoured professors with a broad culture and humanistic interests rather than the technical and scientific specialization that characterized PhDs from most North American universities. Arvid Grantis, for example, while hired by Patrick McTaggart-Cowan as the founding Chair of Philosophy, had previously sung with the Riga Opera Company in Latvia, and pursued a career teaching flute and painting when he left SFU (he did not get tenure).

Patrick Lyndon was a graduate of Oxford and had been a close friend of Bawtree's in Toronto. He had also been a piano prodigy and gave a solo recital at Wigmore Hall, one of the world's great concert halls, when he was twelve. When Bawtree suggested he come to SFU to consider the directorship of the CCA, he responded enthusiastically. Hired in June 1968, he brought a focus on instilling order in the energized but chaotic scene he confronted. Not so easy.

More than anyone else, Bawtree said, Murray Schafer created a philosophical structure behind the CCA, although Bawtree felt that music, because

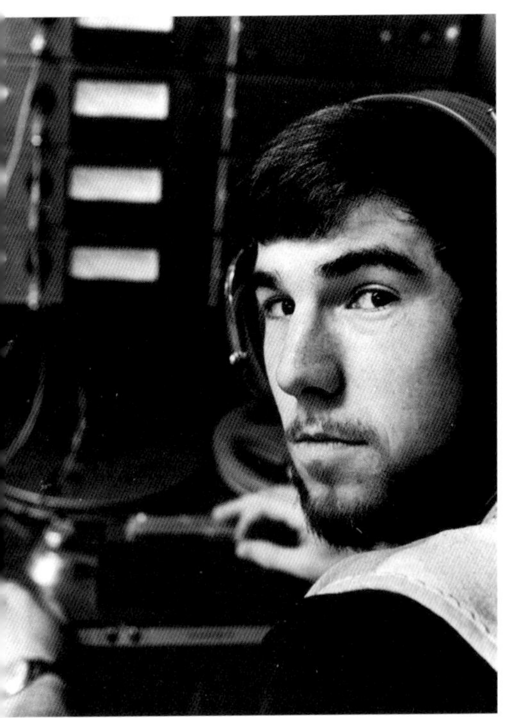

Student-director Wilfrid Mennell worked not only with music and sound, but also theatre productions on campus. *Tony Westman, SFU Archives*

it demanded the discipline needed to learn an instrument, did not benefit from a non-curricular approach in the same way as theatre. However, the innovative and interdisciplinary musical experiments of Wilfrid Mennell and Phillip Werren, who brought music and theatre together, suggest otherwise.

Schafer had a strong and consistent vision of where things should be going, which he discusses in a paper given in 1967 to the Royal Society of Canada on "The Future of Music in Canada":

> You cannot institutionalize the avant garde. Truly revolutionary activity cannot be bought. And this is what is needed: a healthy scattering of mercurial undertakings, individual enterprises or small co-operatives that will work merely as long as their organizers remain buoyant. It is in the conflictual abrasions of the establishments and the antiestablishment—those nervy Young-Turk activities—that truly significant cultures take shape.[9]

Schafer was sensitive to the dynamic nature of the new forms and their complex evolution with the establishment, as the two contended for dominant position.

Promoting CCA Artists and Events

Nini Baird first burst on the CCA scene in 1966, the only woman in a bevy of male administrators. She had graduated from UC Berkeley in 1955 with a degree in journalism, and for the next six years worked there for the Committee for Drama, Lectures and Music. She had first visited BC in 1958 with her husband, John, who wanted to see Nootka Sound, the subject of his MA thesis. While they didn't get to Nootka Sound, they travelled through BC, falling in love with the province's natural beauty. In January 1966 her husband accepted a position teaching history at SFU, and Tom Mallinson found work for Nini as a part-time publicity coordinator, starting on June 1, 1966. For Nini, it was "an exhilarating, exuberant time where everything seemed possible—the first task was not just publicity but creating a structure to present and promote Centre artists and events."[10] She moved up the ranks with impressive speed, becoming events manager and then theatre manager in the fall of 1968. Her role, as she said, was not to decide the artistic direction of the Centre, but to support it. When Patrick Lyndon resigned from the directorship of the CCA in 1970, the university residents universally recommended that she become general manager of the arts. Baird describes the CCA's core activities in an article published in *Communications*:

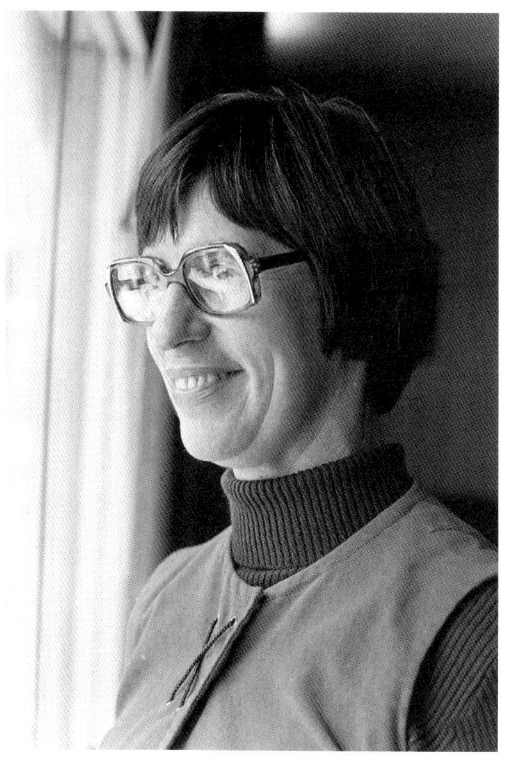

Nini Baird in 1975, the energetic animator who brought the cultural world to SFU during her years at the Centre for Communications. *Nini Baird*

> At the heart of the Centre's program are the workshops in which students are exposed to the fundamentals of the arts. The Centre does not intend to turn out professional artists but is primarily concerned with awakening in the students a sensitivity to the arts.
>
> During the 1969–70 academic year, the workshops have included beginning and advanced tape composition; beginning through advanced contemporary dance; an experiment in sound-dance improvisation; 8 mm and 16 mm film production; videotape techniques and program production for broadcast on an ETV channel; printmaking and other visual arts; colour photography and a theatre program emphasizing the "ensemble concept" in which student directors, actors, playwrights and technicians are encouraged to work together in creating a performance ensemble extending beyond any specific productions. Ensembles grow out of non-credit theatre workshops originated and guided by students.
>
> The more advanced students carry on individual work with elective credit ranging from five credit hours up to a full semester's credit. Such projects have included a full mime play, Aliice, based on Alice in Wonderland; a documentary film on the life of the Bella Coola Indians of BC's north coast [*Noohalk*] and a multi-media production of a contemporary play.[11]

Baird's insistent demand for programming, for concrete descriptions of casts and dates, provided the framework for a formidable range of events generated by resident artists or brought to campus from outside. The Centre appeared chaotic, but a lot of organization made the gears turn harmoniously. Artists were appreciative of her making sure that copies of their press materials were available. On November 5, 1967, Iris Garland sent her a memo thanking her for the publicity for the sold-out performances of the Anna Sokolow Dance Company. "Ron Baker, the stage manager, told us that the information received from you was the most helpful of all the universities on tour (including such bastions as UCLA, dance mecca of the West!)."[12]

Many artists appreciated the respect and care taken with their treatment.

The CCA Through Students' Eyes

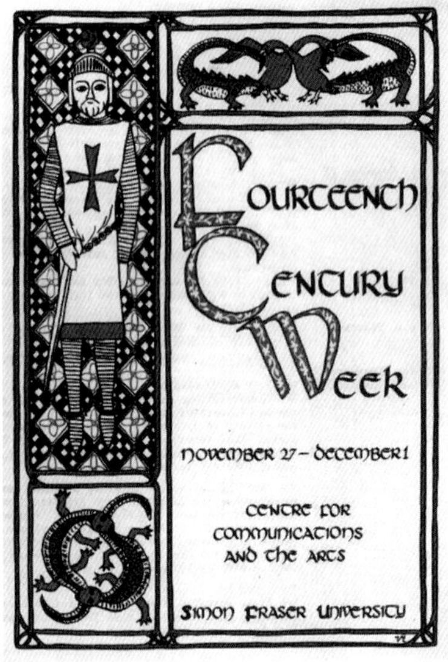

A poster announces Fourteenth Century Week, its events aimed at creating a mirror for our present age. *SFU Archives*

To students, the CCA provided the structure for them to develop their personalities in the context of modern art. Unlike at most universities, they were encouraged to learn how their art worked, not just study it from afar. In film workshops, for example, students didn't just learn about important filmmakers. They learned how to master the challenges of making films and produced some first-rate work. Many went on to have successful film careers.

"When I first got here to Simon Fraser, it was exciting, it was new," said Penn Lewis, a young undergraduate charter student, in an interview with Tessa Perkins Deneault. He had been accepted by universities in the UK and California, but SFU was the one he wanted to attend. Having been shy in his adolescence, he liked the concept of an original university with small class sizes and tutorials. "My parents had someone drive me here for the first month or two, and I got very annoyed at that," he said with a laugh. "You have to get away from that. I was seventeen and extremely shy. You would never have seen me without a jacket and tie and slacks."[13]

Among the original ideas students encountered were themed presentations such as Fourteenth Century Week in the fall of 1967, a brainchild of Murray Schafer, who believed that the fourteenth century was one of the last times when artists and craftsmen worked together, giving the presentations obvious links to the Bauhaus and to our modern age. Apocalyptic visions of the end of days were also a strong link. The Black Death, famine, and political and religious upheaval were recreated by the mime troupe in the *Dance of Death*. Vancouver's "official town fool" Joachim Foikis complemented it with the *Dance of Life*. Visual arts, film and lectures revealed many dimensions on the topic. Even the much-maligned CCA director Patrick Lyndon, who would receive an often rocky ride from those who did not appreciate his efforts to combine order with artistic innovation and spontaneity in the operations of the CCA, gave a talk on "Post-Television Media." "Bridges," organized by Michael

Bawtree in the spring of 1968, was another themed series representing the crossings necessary for effective communication—an apt theme for Vancouver. A second Bridges series, "Man to Man," explored the evolution of the individual as a factor in the evolution of society.

Especially attractive to students (and instructors) was the trimester system that required faculty to teach two of the three semesters each year; the third semester was theirs for research and writing. Students could enrol in as many semesters as they wished. While this system gave great flexibility, Bawtree notes that the lack of continuity made it difficult to develop a cohesive culture when the participants were continually changing. But it did contribute to an environment that appealed to many older students, especially, who brought diverse skills and a rich life experience to SFU, whose mature student policy enabled adults over twenty-one to enter post-secondary education without standard credentials.

Growing Conflict and Controversy

As time went on, long-simmering artistic troubles at SFU mounted. Tom Mallinson's unpublished essay notes that the seeds of future problems had been evident from the start. "At that time, we overrode our differences, but as innovative ideas crystallized into action, the implications of our decisions became obvious... The result was a digging in of heels, and increasingly acrimonious debates at the Committee of Heads."[14]

While John Juliani's often spectacular theatre productions provided mind-bending entertainment and artistic delight to many at SFU, administrative pressure mounted for him to present drama that appealed to a broader community, and at a lower cost. Peter Hay was an aggressive supporter of Juliani and his experimental theatre. While he also initially supported CCA director Patrick Lyndon, they soon butted heads. Three issues of Hay's newsletter *Horse Sheet* illustrate the growing rift between them. In a long open letter to Lyndon in *Horse Sheet* no. 1 (March–April 1969), Hay expresses disappointment that Lyndon's initial support, in July 1968, had deteriorated by early 1969 to requests for cutbacks in productions, perhaps because of worries about expense and the type of avant-garde presentations being mounted. Hay objected vigorously: "The bureaucratic web inside the theatre building [is] strangling our work." In *Horse Sheet* no. 3 (June 1969) he called for Lyndon's dismissal.[15]

Lyndon approached the breaking point. In late June of 1969, he confronted Hay about writing about him in his broadside. Hay denied any wrongdoing, whereupon Lyndon "hit him in the stomach." The next day, in the faculty lounge, assistant professor Iris Garland approached Hay, who was standing at a table around which six or seven students were sitting, and "slapped him powerfully on the face." She walked away without an explanation.[16]

Fortunately, such incidents were rare and initially regarded as just a clash of creative personalities. Nini Baird felt that Lyndon was never comfortable with the Centre—that he just didn't understand the residents and the students. People were "very unpleasant" to him, and his time at SFU was not an experience he enjoyed.[17] Over time, however, it became clear that more fundamental differences were at play.

Changes in the CCA's Status and Structure

As early as 1967, the Senate Committee on General Education began to lose enthusiasm for the non-credit program. They planned an arts program for the university, but administrative churn and student unrest prevented it from getting off the ground.

Meanwhile Patrick McTaggart-Cowan was having his problems as the president of a fractious university. In Christine Hearn's recollection, "McTaggart-Cowan was perceived by many as a bit of a fuddy-duddy, someone out of touch with the times. He often seemed puzzled by the challenges of running a new university with no traditions and a fragile administrative structure. He was an easy target for all the frustrations roiling around under various student and faculty factions."[18] After his dismissal in May of 1968, in a comic opera of changing hats, John Ellis lasted one weekend in his place.

Archie McPherson then survived six weeks before being replaced by Ken Strand as president in 1968. The latter's appointment was one of the pivotal events leading to the eventual demise of the non-credit program, although this was accompanied by vigorous and sometimes acrimonious debate for the next few years, as many fought hard to preserve its best features. The non-credit courses had not always been a workable system. Many students had decided that the pressures of essays and exams for credit courses took priority. Some students complained that once the non-credit course was finished, there was seldom an opportunity to explore more deeply a particular area of interest.

In November 1968 many students occupied the administration building to protest the refusal of the senate to discuss various demands. Rehearsals for *Coriolanus* were taking place in the theatre. Jan Visscher set up large speakers outside and played a tape of a sound montage containing an excerpt from one of Hitler's hate speeches, with machine gun fire superimposed. Strand soon made it clear that he would take a tough stand. After sixty-five hours of their occupation, Strand called in the Burnaby RCMP, who arrested 114 demonstrators.

By early 1969, the face of the CCA was inexorably changing, with control becoming more centralized. After debate over the next two years, the senate decided to separate the CCA's service and academic functions. Brian Wilson was appointed vice president academic with a mandate to develop a credit program for the CCA, with Nini Baird as secretary to his committee. This would include formal communications courses, which would stay in one unit, remaining under the revamped Faculty of Education. Artistic activities would form a new independent unit, reporting to the vice president of university affairs, Stan Roberts. These would include workshops, noon shows and evening productions. In *Radical Campus: Making Simon Fraser University*, Hugh Johnston states that Nini Baird ran the operation. Both chairman Patrick Lyndon and theatre manager Nini Baird favoured the split. There were debates about the CCA being financed out of general university funds rather than the Faculty of Education. The only permanent faculty would be residents with research privileges and pay and professorial rank. Lyndon felt that some residents had not been doing a good job or were featherbedding, and their roles would need to be redefined. This would reduce the number of permanent faculty and, consequently, save money. There would be no more associates.

Seeing the writing on the wall, Murray Schafer chose to become a professor. Michael Bawtree, steeped in the gentlemanly culture of Oxford, was not in favour of that move for himself. "I was rather proud not to be a professor. I was rather proud not to have tenure, but all these things slowly became important to everybody else. As artists we were not interested in any kind of the university apparatus, but it slowly dominated us and in the end it became just another theatre studies program, another musical program."[19]

Eventually it was time to move on. Michael Bawtree, Jan Visscher, John Juliani and Peter Hay all left SFU in 1969 to follow their artistic interests in other venues.

Perry Long, intensely involved with theatre during his years as a student, from 1966 to his graduation in 1969, called for a renewed direction in theatre. He believed that "students are now ready (and willing) to become the focal point of theatrical activities at Simon Fraser... The general climate in Theatre, with few exceptions, has not been conducive to student initiative... In Theatre the Residents have not generally been willing to assume the background role of encouraging students to take on more and more responsibilities for their own activities. I think the Theatre Company is ready for a change—a change from a focus on the residents to a focus on the students."[20] Long's commendably idealistic vision echoes the early days of the theatre, but bureaucracy and financial accountability hampered developments in this direction.

Amid the instability, many people in the background were working hard to establish what they considered a structure that would satisfy both administrative and educational demands. In a paper presented for the University Services Retreat at Harrison Hot Springs, December 1–2, 1972, Baird mounted a spirited defence of the CCA, noting its valuable contributions in public relations and as a fundraiser. Dr. Evan Alderson, who was appointed manager of the new Centre for the Arts, concentrated on the formation of credit programs. Baird sought out artists and artistic ensembles that would complement this focus. The Centre thus became more of a service than an independent exploration of the arts.

The artists tried to keep the earlier vibrancy alive. The Purcell String Quartet, which had started as quartet in residence in 1972, frequently collaborated with other artists in fine productions, such as *Dido and Aeneas*. Numerous noon shows and theatre, music and dance events combined with film series, lecture series and readings. But the excitement of some of the earlier productions was gone.

Theatre resident Jim Garrard attributes the decline of theatrical activity in part to the facility. He feels that the play *How Our Love is Like a Dwarf* was his best work but notes that generally the main theatre had fallen into disuse, with most of the activity taking place in the much smaller concrete theatre. Garrard found the main stage too big for raw beginners to practise on. In his *Peak* article, "Theatre of Total Limbo," Gerry Warner attributes a perception of theatre as trivial to the decline. Warner notes the comments of Bruce Davis, an instructional specialist in the theatre: "in the Orient, theatre is regarded as a form of enlightenment while in the West it is simply regarded as entertainment. A member of one of the workshops said simply that at Simon Fraser, theatre was regarded [by some] as frivolous play activity—nothing more."[21]

Was the theatre program perhaps too close to the epicentre of the CCA? It was near the centre when the CCA began and near the centre when the CCA imploded. In contrast, artists in other arts programs like film continued to produce quality work well into the seventies and beyond. Students of Vincent Vaitiekunas's film workshops (1972 to 1974) won many awards, and some went on to productive careers in film. And the young poets kept on writing, apparently unhindered (and perhaps even energized) by the turmoil.

Throughout, Nini Baird retained her buoyant optimism. While she recognized that low energy levels affected activity, especially in the theatre, she pointed out that dance and music workshops were up. The Madrigal Singers were a success, Karen Rimmer was with the Alwin Nikolais Dance Theatre, and the Theatre Company had put on productions downtown in the past year.

Baird left SFU in July 1977 to develop the provincial outreach program for Emily Carr College of Art and Design. She was not replaced and remains active in BC cultural affairs.

The End of an Era?

Despite its precipitous demise, the CCA's brief efflorescence left brilliant memories. Michael Bawtree recalls these times nostalgically: "Institutions involve hierarchies and basic principles, which you can't diverge from so easily. Everything from one extreme to the other had to be invented. And so people who were quite used to inventing, like artists, felt quite comfortable in a place where they could be spontaneous and make things up on the spur of the moment."[22]

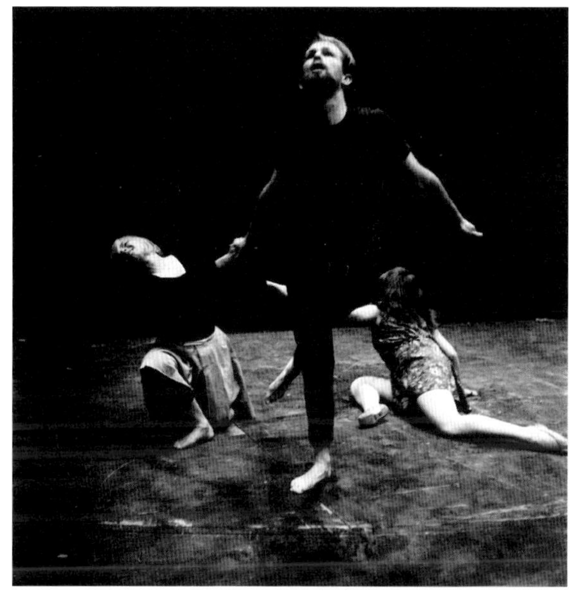

Members of the SFU Dance Workshop in a 1967 performance of *No Exit*, choreographed by Iris Garland.
The Peak, *SFU Archives*

Could anything have been done to sustain the great experiment? John Juliani's wife, Donna Wong-Juliani, for one, thinks not. She states: "So the whole philosophy of what the Centre was about and in a sense, by extension, what the university was about, closed down. You know, when you think about it, that was kind of the end of the era... nothing could have been done because somebody like John wouldn't want to be there. He was never interested in becoming an academic."[23]

On the other hand, Bawtree notes that the eventual changes benefited "people who felt they needed to have a structure through which to work."[24] And certainly structure became more unavoidable as universities expanded their scope and assumed the trappings of the corporate world.

The SFU of the sixties may have been a naïve dream, but it was a seductive one—a dream that survives in the minds and hearts of many who played roles in that glorious experiment. And perhaps more than a dream. Now, more than ever, our society needs practical visionaries if we are to take steps toward the world we envision: a world that is conducive to the expression of the best of human nature. These times still have much to teach us.

CHAPTER 2

Experiments and Explorations

BURNABY MOUNTAIN AS A CREATIVE WELLSPRING

by Christine Hearn

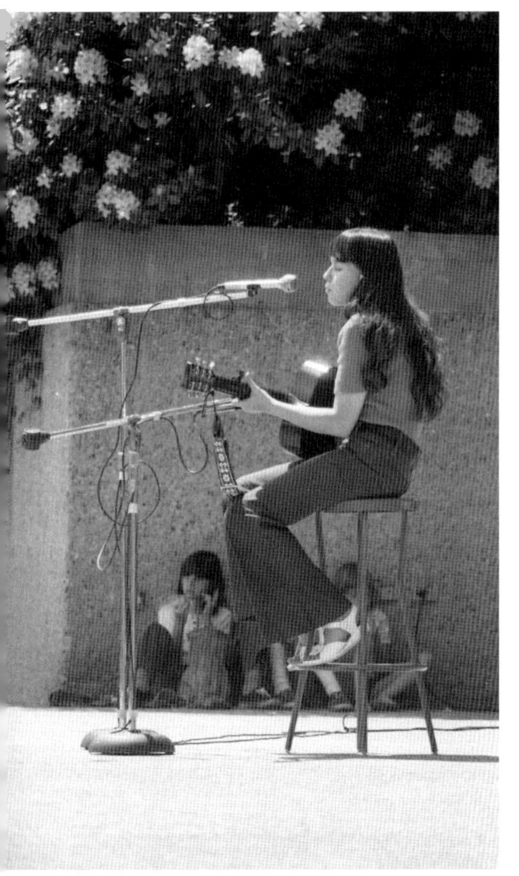

Folk singer playing to an attentive audience in 1973.
IMC, SFU Archives

THE EXPLOSIONS OF CREATIVITY AT SIMON FRASER University from 1965 to 1975 left an enduring legacy. Actors, dancers, writers, filmmakers and musicians all contributed to and benefited from the profusion of artistic activities on campus over the decade. Many went on to successful careers in the arts. But what of the general student body? What impact did it all have on those not directly involved in the creative processes?

To get a taste of what was offered, let us look at the month of February 1967 as an example. There were nearly thirty listed events, most in the theatre, that students could attend. They included classical, jazz and folk music performances; a film series on World War II; lectures on filmmaking by filmmaker in residence Stan Fox; readings by Canadian poets John Newlove, Fred Candelaria, Seymour Mayne and Patrick Lane; and a speech by René Lévesque, who was about to become the separatist leader of the Parti Québécois.

Or jump ahead to November 1969, another month with nearly thirty events. This time there were plays, including John Juliani's production of *Coriolanus*; a modern film series with accompanying lectures; a broad spectrum of music performances; and lectures by Greenpeace co-founder Bob Hunter and author Mordecai Richler, who spoke on "Paris in the '50s."

Most months were equally full of entertainment. Who had time to go to classes? Or to review presentations, even? A *Peak* reviewer wrote on April 5, 1967: "The Communications Centre by itself and in cooperation with a number of other various departments of the University kept the Theatre almost constantly busy, and I should have had to be twins to cover everything."[1]

The Centre for Communications and the Arts (CCA) was involved in almost everything presented during those years. In a memo to staff in November 1972, CCA director Nini Baird outlined the Centre's role: "The Centre is an impresario presenting an average of 300 events each year to more than 50,000 people. This program of concerts, plays, exhibits, film screenings, dance, concerts, and theatre productions is unique in North American universities because the program's close ties to a workshop program in the arts emphasizes short-term visiting residencies for maximum contact between artists and Centre students, the university, and the outside community."[2] Everyone in the SFU community and broader environs benefited.

The Noon Shows

The noon shows were a staple of the Centre's activities. Students were exposed to a wide range of events, some traditional, others—in keeping with the times—experimental. The performers included the famous, the not-yet-famous and the never-to-be-heard-of-again. On October 25, 1967, undergraduate Wilfrid Mennell wrote in *The Peak*: "The regular capacity crowds at each weekly Noon Show must be a direct reflection of the regular maintenance of a consistent high level of performance. Whatever shortcomings each particular show may have had, one never fails to be entertained."[3]

Unexpected exposure to great artists was also a common occurrence, as recounted by then-student Douglas Patterson: "When I enrolled in SFU in 1969 quiet study space around the campus was at a premium so I discovered the lobby areas of the theatre as not only quiet but a place to enjoy the sun during the dreary winter days on the mountain. One day after I walked into the theatre lobby I heard some piano music coming from inside and decided to check it out. I entered and sat down at the back and enjoyed some amazing jazz music... It wasn't until later that I realized the source of the music was none other than Oscar Peterson, who was practising for upcoming concerts at SFU and other Vancouver venues."[4]

1969
Elmer Gill, jazz ('S)
Tom Hawken, folk singer
Oscar Peterson Trio (S·)
Papa Bear's Medicine Show (S)
Mother Tucker's Yellow Duck (S)
Henry Young Trio featuring 8.J. Cooke (S)
Patricia's Victorian Jules (S)
The Poppy Family (S)
Tom Hawken, folk singer (S)
Rhythm and Blues Concert (S)
Jamie Brockett, folk singer
New Vaudeville Band
Seeds of Time, The Addled Cromish Light Show!!!
Papa Bear's Medicine Show (S)
High Flying Bird (S)
Al Grierson, country and western (S)
Buell Kazee, folk music (S)
Roger Lee and Kathy Payne, folk singers
Jim Rutter and Mike Otter, folk singers
Seeds of Time, Trees, Addled Chromish Light Show
Patrick O'Neill, folk music
Bruce Singer, folk music (S)
Walter Zuber Armstrong Ensemble (S)
Mock Duck (S)
Preservation Hall Jazz Band (S)
The Spring (S)

A list of each of the musicians who performed at SFU Student Society Shows in 1969, including the Oscar Peterson Trio. *SFU Archives*

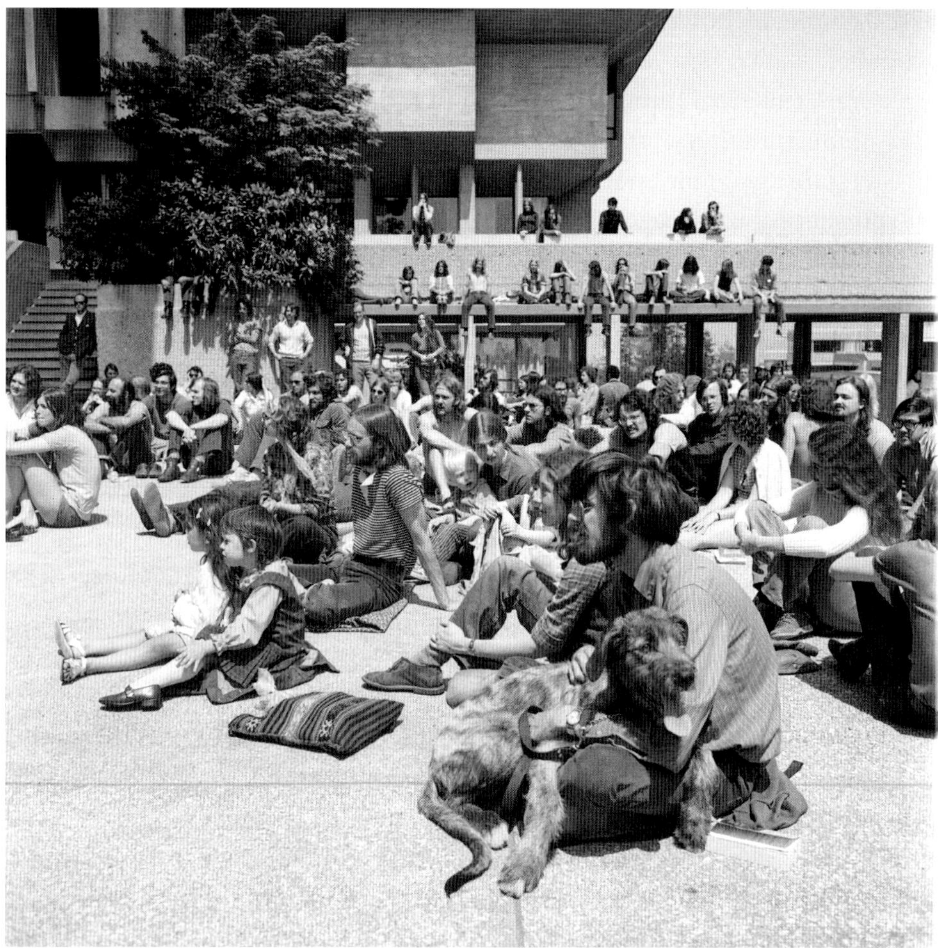

Countless lunchtime programs took place over the years. Summer was the time for lunch performances in the mall, including this one in 1972. It was a nice change from the regular mall protests of earlier years. *IMC, SFU Archives*

The reach of the noon shows extended beyond the student body and the faculty. Mature student, poet and single mother Heidi Greco recalls the importance of the shows to her two small sons, Jeremy and Jevon: "The shows really enriched their lives; all the daycare kids would sit on the floor at the front of the theatre with their little legs crossed—eighty or so kids—and just enjoy whatever was going on."[5] She recalls that her two really loved Muddy Waters and the Swiss mime troupe Mummenschanz. The SFU Mime Troupe also did specific workshops and shows for the daycare kids.

Simon Fraser Student Society Shows

Jazz legend Oscar Peterson's concert was just one of many activities sponsored by the Simon Fraser Student Society (SFSS). The first event sponsored by the

SFSS was Erick Hawkins and the Dance Company, November 3, 1965. *The Peak* promoted it in its October 27, 1965, edition: "Hawkins, one of the most widely acclaimed modern dancers of our time, is flying up from the U.S.A. with his own orchestra to present his program. Cultural director Art Tomlinson said: 'This is probably going to be the biggest cultural event of the semester. I urge everyone to get out to see him.'"[6]

The number of noon-hour shows put on by the SFSS varied. Some semesters, including the fall of 1966, listed no SFSS-sponsored noon shows. Spring 1968 featured a record fourteen shows—in an average semester the SFSS put on between three and ten shows. Included in that magical semester were local groups Mother Tucker's Yellow Duck (who toured with Deep Purple, Alice Cooper and the Yardbirds), Bobby Hales and His Big Band, Three's a Crowd (which included well-known singers Bruce Cockburn and Colleen Peterson), the Night Train Revue, Tom Northcott, and Papa Bear's Medicine Show. The last, a regular crowd pleaser, enchanted audiences on several occasions, including again in the summer of 1968. According to R. Serge Denisoff, in a rave review in *The Peak*: "Papa Bear's compositions by and large are original and professionally done... Papa Bear in a word is undefinable, therefore, unique and interesting... The Medicine Show is highly entertaining visually and audiowise, although several attempts at humour kinda bombed."[7]

The SFSS also brought in other local big names, including the Poppy Family, with several international hits, including "Which Way You Goin' Billy?" and "Where Evil Grows," who appeared at least twice; the Seeds of Time, with

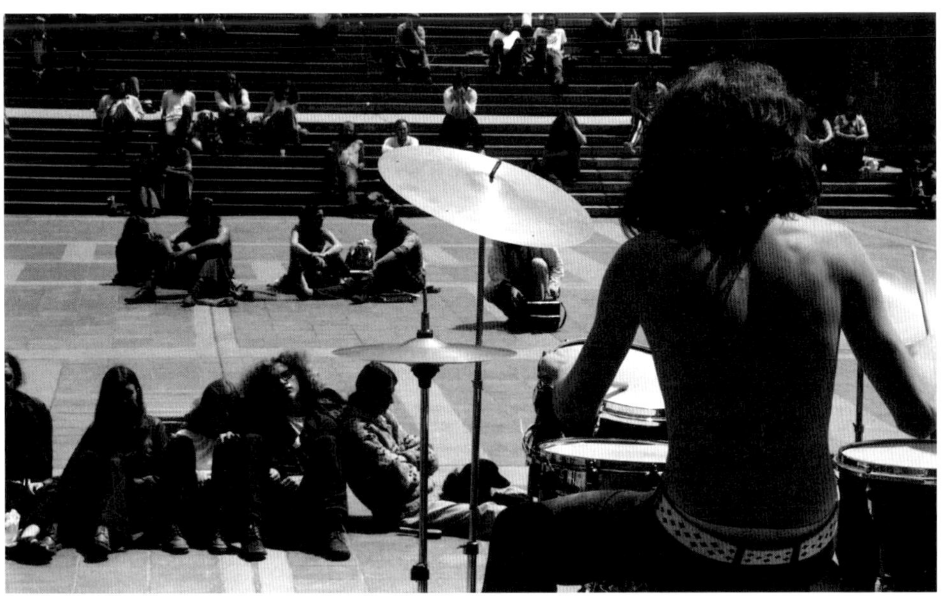

Local rock group High Flying Bird (1969-1973) was one of many that played at noon-hour and other concerts. *The Peak* described their music as a mix of "hard rock" and "soft psychedelic." *IMC, SFU Archives*

Jerry Doucette; Bim (Roy Forbes); the Collectors (later Chilliwack); Cement City Cowboys; Joe Mock and Friends; and High Flying Bird, who opened for Jethro Tull, Fleetwood Mac and Steve Miller, among others. A *Peak* review of High Flying Bird by "Peak Freak" in June 1969 touched on the music: "And the lead singer is worth hearing; he has a voice which gets around a blues lyric well, and also suits the more lyrical songs which the group does."[8] But "Peak Freak" was more interested in the group's appearance than in the music: "This group has joined the trend toward casual clothes on stage: jeans, sloppy hats, messy shirts, and flying hair. And the drummer went halfway towards onstage nudity by taking off his shirt. Too bad there was no hair on his chest. But still, the music was pretty hairy."

On September 17, 1969, the Seeds of Time got accolades from *Peak* reviewer Peter Magnani: "If Vancouver has anything better to offer I'd certainly like to see it because Seeds of Time impressed me as the best thing I've listened to live in a long time... there's something about the Seeds of Time that never stops sparkling and flashing when they are up on stage."[9]

Some rock acts, including the Raible Brothers, Hudson Carr Poole and the Small Town Band, joined together in concert. And there were many folk singers, including mature student Al Horne, who went on to a regular gig at the SFU pub. Jazz artists included Mr. Wood, Popcorn and Gavin Walker Jazz, among others.

The SFSS also brought in big national and international acts. In addition to Oscar Peterson from Montreal, New Orleans's Preservation Hall Jazz Band appeared, as did blues singers Sonny Terry and Brownie McGhee. Rock legends Country Joe and the Fish appeared in 1967, well before their breakout performance at Woodstock in August 1969. Bo Diddley appeared in January 1975, and Lightning John Hopkins in October 1975.

Grammy-winner Paul Horn, fresh from meditating in India with the Beatles, played several noon-hour concerts. By then a Victoria resident, Horn was transitioning from jazz to world and new age music. Horn was also famous for playing his flute in 1972 to captive orca whale Haida, resulting in a National Film Board short movie by Tom Shandel, who also had an SFU presence as an artist in residence.

CCA Dance Shows

Dance was an integral part of the CCA offerings. Artists ranged from big names in the international dance world to dancers specializing in ethnic dance, to dance troupes from other universities and cities. Some were presented as noon shows, some were in the evening. The big names ranged from the classical performers to the most modern and experimental dancers, and included the Merce Cunningham Dance Company with John Cage, Vancouver's own Paula Ross Dancers, the Paul Taylor Dance Company, the Martha Graham Dance Company, and James Cunningham and his Acme Dancers.

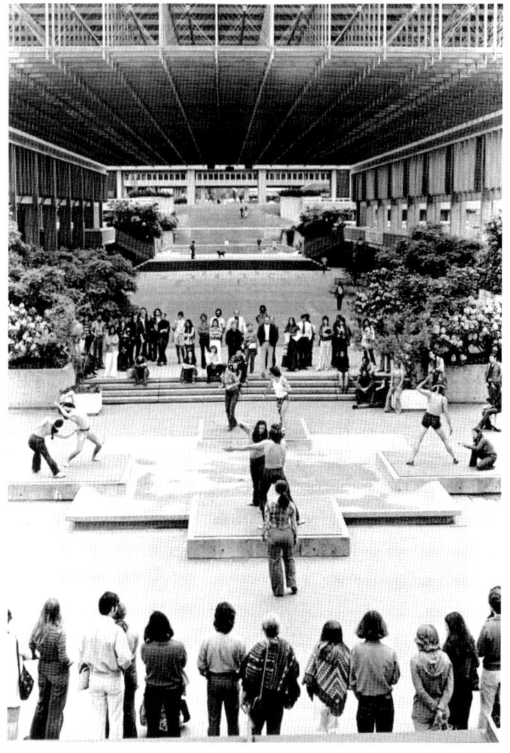

Dance workshops took place all over campus, not just in the theatre. For example, this 1972 workshop by the Progressive Dance Program brought people to the mall. *Peter Higdon, SFU Archives*

Many visiting artists combined workshops, lecture-demonstrations, intensive dance residencies, and master classes for SFU dancers, with public performances in the theatre, so their expertise was available for all to view. This cross-fertilization from those teaching non-credit courses to the general student population was key to the SFU arts legacy. As Nini Baird explained in *Remembering SFU*, "The more than 1200 public events provided a showcase for works created by university artists in residence and students, and introduced audiences to numerous Canadian and international artists, with a particular emphasis on engaging artists whose work complemented what was being experienced by students in the non-credit workshops. Students were inspired by choreographers and dance companies, musicians and composers, playwrights and theatre companies, filmmakers and visual artists."[10]

SFU's own dancers started to make a splash as early as March 22, 1966, with the first listed Simon Fraser Dance Workshop with Iris Garland as artist in residence. From then on, nearly every semester included at least one dance workshop performance. On May 30, 1969, they presented *Mediums*, described as a "mixed media production of dance, film and sound conceived by Edith Feinstein and Karen Rimmer, with music by Phillip Werren and film by David Rimmer."[11] Sometimes the workshop productions were teased with an abbreviated noon show, followed by a full evening show. Students could view a selected program for twenty-five cents at noon or really blow the budget with the full concert for seventy-five cents that evening.

CCA Music Concerts

The CCA was quick off the mark with music when the university opened in the fall of 1965. The first CCA-sponsored musical event was Maria Varro on piano

In the early years, the theatre was termed "the nerve centre of the university" by *The Peak* because there were so many activities. By 1972, they were calling it "the first victim" of "inward rot," i.e., budget cuts. *IMC, SFU Archives*

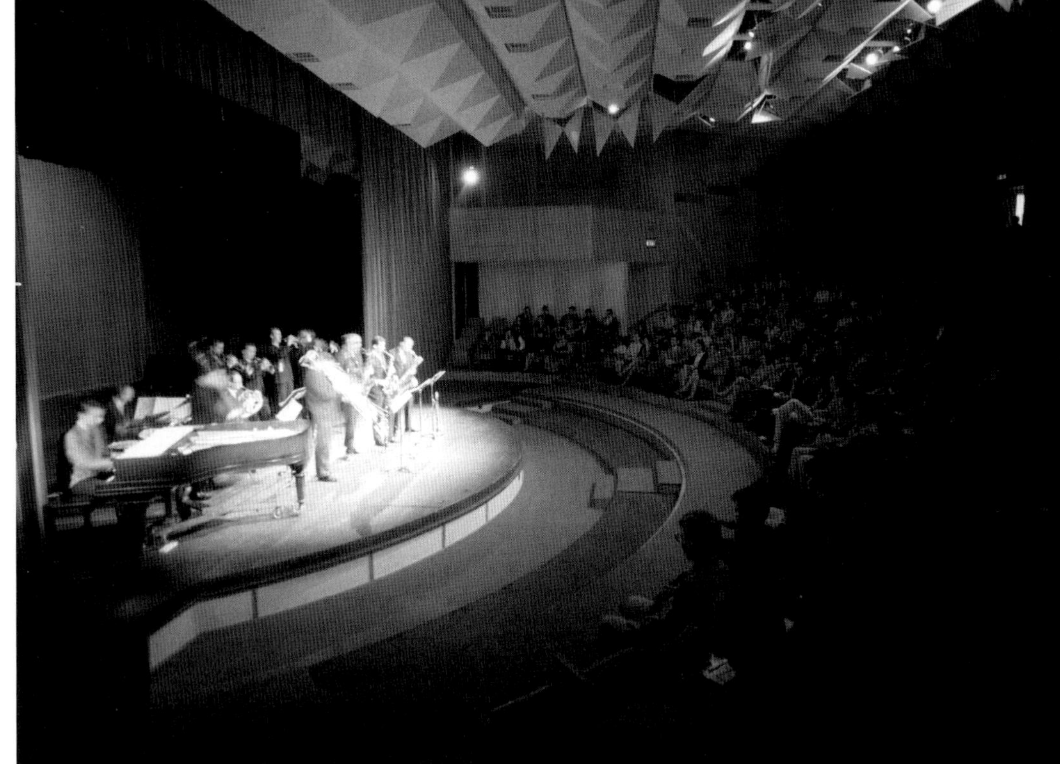

with the CBC Chamber Orchestra on October 30. There were four other CCA concerts that first fall: the Orroz Chamber Ensemble, Jeunesses Musicale with Christian Larde on flute and Marie-Claire Jamet on harp, the Vancouver Brass Ensemble, and Robert Rogers on piano. That set the pace going forward. Most semesters, there were between ten and fifteen concerts; the spring of 1966 had a record twenty-one. That semester's offerings ranged from the Beethoven String Trio to the Burnaby Civic Opera, to Les Petites Chanteurs du Mont-Royal, to the Mennonite Bible Choir from Winnipeg. Something for everyone. SFU artists in residence were front and centre every semester. Regulars included mezzo-soprano Phyllis Mailing; composers R. Murray Schafer, Jack Behrens and Phillip Werren; early music and French horn player David Skulski; and the Purcell String Quartet. There were student performances by the SFU Choir, the SFU Brass Consort, the flute duo of the SFU Chamber Ensemble, the SFU Jazz Group with Byron Pope, and the SFU Madrigal Singers.

Local classical offerings included the UBC Piano Trio, the UBC String Quartet, the Vancouver Symphony Orchestra, Simon Streatfield on viola with Elizabeth Winship on piano, and North Vancouver's Carson Graham Secondary School with the SFU Pipes and Drums, among others. Local pianist Antoinette Fraase made her Canadian debut after four years of study in Austria. According to *Peak* reviewer Jody Berland, "The concert began with Schubert's Sonata in A Major which was played with great insight and skill. The third movement in particular was handled brilliantly through several variations on a central theme.

There were quick changes in mood through which Miss Fraase managed to maintain an excellent balance of tone."[12]

There were several collaborations with off-campus entities. One of the first was Burnaby bass-baritone Donald Bell in a concert jointly sponsored by the CBC and the CCA. "The voice is rich, dark, and well-focused although he possesses the very German trait of making pianissimo attacks slightly flat, especially in lieder. The quality of the voice is almost constant from top to bottom, with a slight change of timbre in the lowest notes," wrote Van Ishkanian for *The Peak*.[13]

Not everything was so well received. Arthur McDougall was scathing about UBC cellist Eugene Wilson and pianist Kathryn Bailey: "Both players seemed to be playing more against than with each other, and served a very lovely work very badly."[14]

International stars included New York's John Handy Quintet, Quebec chanteuse Monique Leyrac, Alvina Thakore on sitar, singing rabbi Shlomo Carlebach, the Festival Singers of Canada, and mezzo-soprano Judith Forst.

Some performances were part of wider campus themes. In January 1967, battle music of the sixteenth, seventeenth and eighteenth centuries was played by Hugh McLean on harpsichord and piano, Jack Kessler on violin and James Hunter on cello. November of the same year gave us "Fanfares" and "Dance of Life" for the opening of Fourteenth Century Week. In September 1968 four concerts celebrated the Guitar Festival. The late 1960s and early 1970s produced much experimental and electronic music, and the CCA noon shows provided a showcase. Fall 1968 marked the beginning of the electronic experience at SFU. Rick Kiataeff and Richard Anstey, Phillip Werren and Peter Huse, Al Neil, Gregg Sampson, and the Bobby Hales Quintet all played electronic music; J.K. Randall played computer music.

And then there was the California Time Machine: "Perhaps the time has come for us to differentiate music, even the most contemporary works, from the new hybrid of intermedia or mixed media. Electronic music 'happenings' often degenerate into trite, deplorable stunts, into utterly boring, tediously meandering compositions which seem purposeless or must beg a purpose," Paul Tang wrote in *The Peak*.[15] Tang was not against all electronic music. He wrote in the same issue that "Our own SFU composer, Murray Schafer, has written several electronic works of some merit and his recent *Son of Helden leben*, which I heard performed over CBC last year, or his *From the Tibetan Book of the Dead...* seem to me to be examples of 'where good electronic music is at.'"[16]

Schafer's *Okeanos*, a ninety-minute quadraphonic tape production commissioned by the CBC, premiered at a noon show on March 25, 1972. In

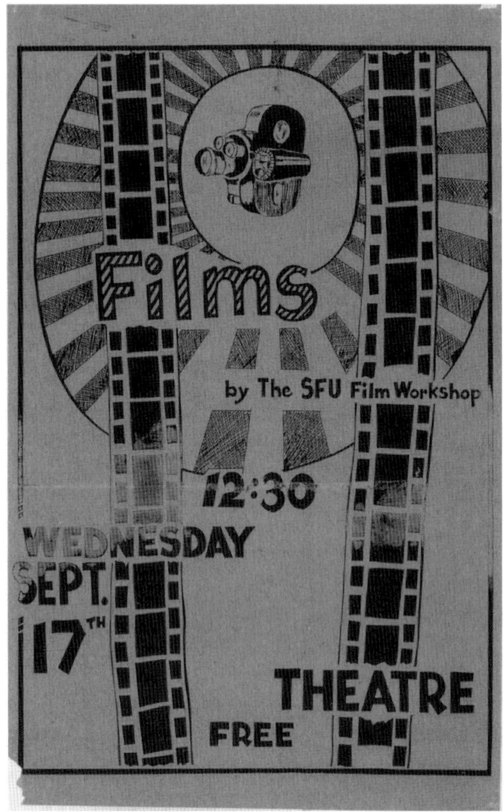

Poster for films by members of the SFU Film Workshop, 17 September, 1969. Starting in 1968, the SFU Film Workshop hosted regular screenings of its members' work. *SFU Archives*

addition to Schafer, *Okeanos* was written by artist in residence Bruce Davis, and poet and student Brian Fawcett, and formed an early part of SFU's World Soundscape Project. There was other electronic music coming out of SFU as well. The three-part *Phases* project (produced in April and June 1969, and April 1971) was described as "a sound-space experiment" and featured excerpts of poems by W.B. Yeats read over disjointed synth and sequencer tones. Written by artist in residence Phillip Werren and student Wilf Mennell, and narrated by English professor Phillippa Polson, it is considered a masterpiece of early electronic composition.

There were assorted lectures around music as well. Some, like Murray Schafer's "The Two Frontiers of Music" and Terrance Bailey's "Dance of Life," were connected to performances, in these cases music for Fourteenth Century Week. Others, including an Alan Hovhaness discussion, were stand-alones. Again, starting in 1968, there was much talk about electronic music: Peter Huse gave "An Historical Look at Electronic Music" and Schafer lectured on electronic music produced in SFU's Sonic Research Laboratory and participated in a panel on computer music, while David Rosenbloom lectured on "Problems and Prospects for Computers in Electronic Music."

CCA Film Shows

Film was a big part of the arts experience, open to aspiring filmmakers and the general student population. The SFU Film Society, in conjunction with the CCA, opened its first season with Norman McLaren's Oscar-winning National Film Board short, *Neighbours*, on November 10, 1965.

The first SFU student filmmakers' show was on April 3, 1967. This was followed by a joint production by the SFU Film Workshop and the SFU Theatre Company called *Hurrah!*, directed by John Juliani, in February 1968. Film workshop productions were shown nearly every semester after that. Next up were Peter Bryant's *Felix*, J. Andrew de Lilio Rymsza's *The Dream*, Bryan Small's *Apres Demain* and Sandy Wilson's *Oh Gosh*, all in November 1968. In 1969, with six artists in residence—Stan Fox, Shelah Reljic, Tom Shandel, David

Rimmer, Fritz Hunrath and William Squibb—there were twenty-one student films, including Sandy Wilson's *Penticton Profile* and *Garbage*.

Felix, while still under production, received a snarky review from Tony Westman: "The film is about a kind of groovy hippy named Felix, who does all sorts of groovy things. The plot thickens (or becomes thickening) when Felix's friend Louie, played by Vancouver filmmaker Arnold Saba, tells him of a stash of Acapulco Gold… Other Simon Fraser stars acting in the film include Anita King as Spuz's chick, Tandi Johnson as the teeny bopper, Jackie Crossland as the nice lady, Sharon Riis as Felix's chick, and hundreds of other assorted people."[17]

There were other negative reviews. Mike Rust wrote, "The showing of the films made last semester by the SFU Film Workshop, which took place Tues., Jan. 28th, was exciting even if most of the films were not."[18] Rust did give praise to Bill Squibb's *Bust at SFU*, about the fall occupation of the administration building. "The achievement of this film was in its evocation of the almost mystical fraternal emotions of the 114 and their supporters and the drama of the confrontation. The 'you are there' feeling of the camera work is exciting and the shots of the University at night in silence set the action scenes off well."[19]

In addition to student and film society showings, there were many viewings put on by other groups. Some were themed: "Art and Architecture" in the spring of 1966, the history department's "Propaganda and Violence" in the spring of 1967, Canadian filmmakers in the summer 1967, and both an underground film series and a "Friday Film Study" series in the fall of 1968. The following year brought newsreels, a World University Service "Challenge" series, "Dancers on Film," "Art in Canada," "Anti-War" movies and "Kinetic Art." Subsequent semesters brought many, many more films, ranging from classic Ingmar Bergman and Marlene Dietrich movies to French-Canadian, Canadian and experimental Latin American shows. And of course, there was a computer-themed film festival.

Stand-alone films were shown at noon as well. One that particularly stands out is the National Film Board's *Ladies and Gentlemen… Mr. Leonard Cohen*, shown on May 29, 1969. Cohen was not yet the star he was to become, but he had released his first album and was well known in literary circles for several books of poetry and his novels *The Favourite Game* and *Beautiful Losers*. I was so struck by his references to the *I Ching*, the Chinese book of divination, that I immediately hitchhiked to downtown Vancouver to buy a copy for $10, one quarter of my month's rent. I still have it and consult it occasionally.

The many lectures on film included a discussion on September 15, 1966, called "Should There Be a Film School at SFU?" by Vancouver Film Festival judges Patrick Watson, Arthur Knight, Nauki Togawa and Fulton Fisher.

There were ongoing film study series, film workshops for high school students and faculty, a lecture series on Ingmar Bergman's films by various academics, including economics professor Larry Boland on *The Virgin Spring*, and a fall 1973 symposium on "The Future of the Independent West Coast Film-maker."

Some events were presented live and filmed to be shown on CBC. These included Patrick Watson interviewing zen guru Alan Watts in the spring of 1968, and two sessions of *Dr. Bundolo's Pandemonium Medicine Show* in 1975. *Dr. Bundolo*, described as "a weekly half-hour of comic mayhem and post-Freudian ersatz,"[20] was a CBC radio and TV success from 1971 to 1981. It was the brainchild of SFU English students Jeffrey Groberman and Colin Yardley, and legend has it that Groberman went to Yardley and said, "You realize that with MAs in English Lit there are two things we can do in life. Teach or eventually wind up slogging logs in a pulp mill." They wrote some jokes and Groberman pestered the CBC. Then located in the bottom of the Hotel Vancouver, they got a regular five-minute gig on the radio followed by a full program on CBC TV. Groberman went on to form his own film production company, Prime Time Creative Services.

Acclaimed director and screenwriter Dalton Trumbo, a victim of McCarthy-era blacklisting as part of the "Hollywood Ten" in the United States, spoke to a sold-out crowd on September 18, 1971. He talked about his then-current film

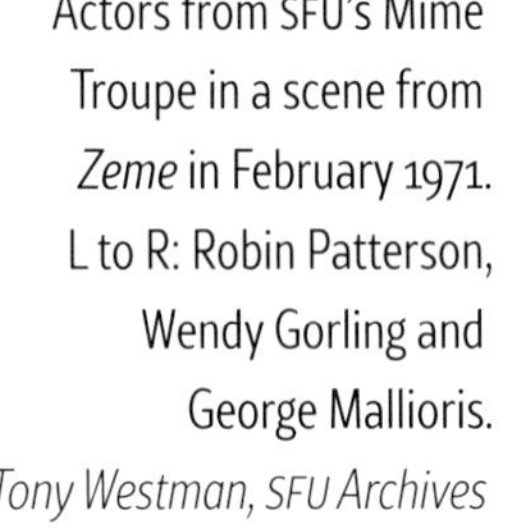

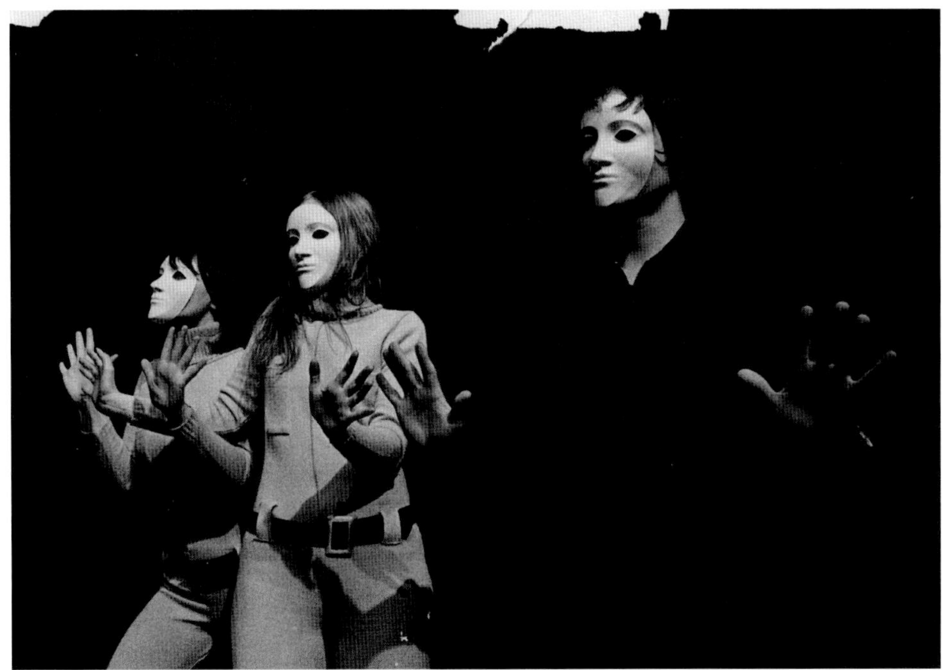

Actors from SFU's Mime Troupe in a scene from *Zeme* in February 1971. L to R: Robin Patterson, Wendy Gorling and George Mallioris. *Tony Westman, SFU Archives*

Johnny Got His Gun, based on his eponymous book, which had been published in 1938. The lecture was a favourite with the anti-war, draft dodger and activist crowd, which included most of SFU at that time.

CCA Theatre Productions

Theatre productions galore—twenty in an average year—ranged from large-scale productions by the theatre company to dramatic readings, mime productions, and experimental shows. Again, some were put on as noon shows, while others were evening performances. The first major production opened in the fall of 1965. "The first student production at Simon Fraser Theatre, Robert Bolt's *A Man for All Seasons*, exceeded all expectations... [Dan] Singer played his part with considerable humour... the performance was impressive and was rewarded by a standing ovation."[21] Actress Rita Tushingham (*A Taste of Honey*) appeared as guest of honour at the opening.

Most theatrical events were directed by artists in residence John Juliani (Arthur Kopit's *Chamber Music* and *The Conquest of Everest*, John Whiting's *The Devils*, and Tennessee Williams's *The Glass Menagerie*), Michael Bawtree (Gogol's *The Government Inspector*, the SFU-created *Centralia*, and Edward Albee's *The Sandbox*), Tom Kerr (Robert Bolt's *A Man for All Seasons* and Harold Pinter's *The Caretaker*), Richard Ouzounian (Peter Weiss's *Marat Sade* and Harold Pinter's *The Homecoming*), Paul Bettis (John Mortimer's *The Dock Brief*) and Peter Hay (Julius Hay's *The Horse* and John Barton and Jay Law's *The Hollow Crown*), among others.

Some were directed by students, including Norm Browning (Beverly Simons's *Greenlawn Rest Home*), Wilfrid Mennell (Sam Shepard's *Chicago* and Jean Anouilh's *Humulus the Mite*), Perry Long (Chekhov's *Samaritan* and *Harmfulness of Tobacco*), Arthur McDougall (student Sharon Riis's *Jelly Beans and the Bastard*) and Mark Vulliamy (an abridged version of Christopher Marlowe's *Dr. Faustus*).

Nini Baird recounted an outstanding five-day residency in 1967 by members of the Royal Shakespeare Company: "SFU worked with the University of California at Santa Barbara to secure the only Canadian engagement for Juliet Aykroyd, Sheila Allen, Richard Pasco, Patrick Stewart and Ben Kingsley. Kingsley, who in 1982 won an Academy Award for *Gandhi*, was only 37 when he gave us a free lunch-hour lecture demonstration called *The Play's the Thing*. Stewart was then only 34, long before his Star Trek fame."[22]

Student actor Norm Browning was featured in 1967: "The Noon Show of Friday, July 7—by William Butler Yeats—was a dark play in a dark mood about a dark subject on a dark stage. Celtic twilight and not much chance of a moon... Norm Browning tackled the whole bag of tricks heroically and brought a lot off."[23] Student playwright Frank Powley got accolades from Thaddeus Cadaver in *The Peak* for his *Zarathustra Has Bronchitis*, performed in October 1967: "This collective title is absurdly irrelevant, of course. But I suppose that in a way it characterizes the author, Frank Powley's light self cynicism—his refusal to take either himself or his work too seriously... Zarathustra may have bronchitis, but Powley has talent."[24]

Van Ishkanian, a student actor and director, also got praise that fall for Molière's *The Doctor in Spite of Himself*: "A group of untried young actors was led with a strong sense of style by Van Ishkanian as Sganerelle. Ishkanian also directed the piece, and it is greatly to his credit that the humour of the situations and the essence of the characters, stereotypes of the period that they are, came across with a freshness that is often not achieved by a smooth professional group."[25]

Mime played a big part in the SFU theatre scene, starting with a visit from the San Francisco Mime Troupe in November 1966. Artist in residence Jan Visscher and student Ian MacKay put on a mime performance in the spring of 1967, while Fritz Hunrath presented *Complexion*, *Know-Won* and *Rack* in 1968. The SFU Mime Troupe also appeared that year with *Mime Blowing* and *Under-Mime*. In subsequent years they put on *Alice*, *Variations on a Seem* and *Black and White*. Mime troupe members Perry Long (*Splaces*), Jackie Crossland (*Duelsday*) and Richard Bolivar (*Zeme*) put on individual shows, and there was even a rehearsal show for the Mime Caravan, a touring show sponsored by Opportunities for Youth and led by SFU's Doug Vernon.

Reviewer Philip Henry could hardly contain his enthusiasm about *Under-Mime*: "Should a critic enthuse (ugh, what a word)? Why not if an experiment in theatre pleases and enchants? What two young men and a girl achieved at the Noon Theatre was remarkable. They held us in thrall with their sincere, tense imagery, with silent presentation of five sketches, each of which pointed to a moral, underlined a facet of human behaviour."[26]

Complexion was also lauded: "My first impression was to say 'Charming' and let it go at that. But on thinking about it I don't think it was as slight as it seemed... As an experiment in form the play was successful; as an experiment in communicative style, the Mime Troupe is a welcome addition to the Theatre Company's roster."[27]

Some dramatic productions melded with the music and dance elements of the theatre. Case in point: "Stravinsky's *The Soldier's Tale*, a work not often presented in its original form, was given a delightful performance by a group of actors from the Theatre Company assisted by a group of musicians."[28] August 2, 1968, saw a presentation of Sophocles's *Antigone*, directed by Peter Hay with music by Phyllis Mailing and choreography by Iris Garland. In November there was Samuel Beckett's *Cascando*, a "sound-space" experiment by Wilfrid Mennell and Phillip Werren.

Community connection was also part of the Centre's mandate. University of Victoria students presented several workshops in the fall of 1966. In February 1967 the drama group of the Haney Correctional Institute brought the play *Naked Island* to campus. Directed by Anthony Holland of Vancouver City College (VCC), it was the first time the group had performed outside the prison. In March that year University of Victoria students appeared in *The Potter's Field*, while in February 1968 VCC students brought *Oh What a Lovely War* to campus. In March 1970 students from various junior secondary schools in Burnaby presented a mime workshop directed by SFU student Ted Hicks. There was also a mime workshop for children in 1972.

Cross-connections between the theatre and academic departments were relatively common, and the English department was involved in many drama productions. Professor Ralph Maud presented a Chaucer workshop production. Students in English 103, a first-year drama course, took part in many dramatic readings and productions over the years. These included Kenneth H. Brown's *The Brig* and Bertolt Brecht's *Measures Taken*. Various faculty, including Jerry Zaslove, Andrea Lebowitz and Clark Cook, gave lectures that tied in with both CCA productions and English department classes.

CCA Lectures and Readings

Perhaps the biggest name to speak was American futurist, architect, author and inventor Buckminster Fuller, who addressed an overflow crowd in the gymnasium on January 27, 1967. Fuller, who taught at Black Mountain College, was most famous for popularizing and refining the geodesic dome. John Cage, who performed at SFU, was at Black Mountain at the same time. *The Peak* devoted two pages to promoting the memorable event and then covered it fully. "Nearly 2,000 rain-soaked students and faculty members filed into the Gymnasium to hear Buckminster Fuller 'think out loud' on campus last Friday... A fourth of the audience did not stay to hear Fuller's full discourse, but those who remained gave the 71-year-old pioneer in world livingry [*sic*] a rousing, standing ovation when he finished."[29]

Marshall McLuhan's visit to SFU is noted in the 1966 yearbook: "McLuhan's ideas in many ways coincide with the philosophy of this university. McLuhan is a prophet of instant communications, and Simon Fraser is an instant university, trying to achieve excellence overnight."[30] Like McLuhan, the staff of Simon Fraser were obsessed with the communications problem, and with attempting the total integration of campus activities that McLuhan claimed was being achieved in the new "global village." The people of SFU were also involved in the world in a manner that McLuhan said was the inevitable outcome of the electronic age.

British writers Colin Wilson, Malcolm Muggeridge and Anthony Burgess gave lectures. Wilson, a pioneer in true crime writing who wrote more than 100 books, spoke on "Existentialism and Modern Literature" in the fall of 1967. *The Peak* enthused, "His visits to universities and schools are events. Highline College, Seattle, stated that 'Students are talking more and investigating more than they have ever done before'... Wilson is sometimes called 'The Elder Statesman of the Angry Young Men.'"[31] In the spring of 1968, Wilson became artist in residence for a semester.

Streams of Canadian poets and authors, including Margaret Atwood, Milton Acorn, Lionel Kearns, Robin Skelton, Stanley Cooperman, Fred Candelaria, Seymour Mayne and Patrick Lane, along with SFU students Brian Fawcett and Colin Stuart, gave readings. Mennonite novelist Rudy Wiebe read as well, and playwrights George Ryga and James Reaney discussed their works.

Russian poet Andrei Voznesensky, with American poets Robert Duncan, Robert Bly and Lawrence Ferlinghetti, read on February 9, 1971. Everyone and his dog were there. Literally. Voznesensky was so impressed by all the dogs in the audience that he delivered a reading in San Francisco in its memory that he called "Dogalypse," which was later published by City Lights Books as *Dogalypse: Selected San Francisco Poetry Reading*. Translator William Jay Smith says,

> Andrei Voznesensky tells of reading his poems once at Vancouver, British Columbia, in an unusually informal atmosphere. Students came—hundreds of them—and sat about on the floor of the hall, and with them came a number of pets, chiefly dogs, but there were other animals as well, even a raccoon among them... He said he had been happy to have the animals in his audience; they made no distinction

> between Russian and English, and seemed delighted with the performance of—as Voznesensky terms himself at the reading as—a 'Moscow Mutt'." *The Peak* headlined the review of the SFU reading with "Were you there?" and gave it an unusual full-page review with four pictures. Reviewer Ron Verzuh summed it up "...we have witnessed a historical moment, which if missed can never be recaptured."[32]

But all was not momentous and serious at the noon shows. Mandrake the Magician appeared numerous times, Vancouver's town fool Joachim Foikis was there once, and who can forget the Happy Hooker, Dutch author Xaviera Hollander? *The Peak* decided not to review her talk or her book but published a front-page picture with the cutline: "You can't write a non-sexist caption about the Happy Hooker at SFU."[33]

A Glorious Ten Years

It was a glorious ten years of shows, concerts, films, workshops, lectures and readings. It was a time to remember, not just because we were young, but because we were exposed to so many performances that elevated our consciousness and introduced us to so much that was out there in the arts world.

The View from *The Peak*: Conscience and Megaphone

In SFU's first ten years, the Centre for Communications and the Arts was the heart of the university. By the same token, *The Peak* was both the conscience and the megaphone. From the start, the Centre and *The Peak* shared a symbiotic relationship: each relied on the other for success, support and, yes, frequent criticism. *The Peak* profiled everything going on in the Centre, while the Centre, with its regular stream of ads, contributed heavily to *The Peak*'s always shaky bottom line.

A close look also reveals considerable crossover between students involved in the Centre and those writing for *The Peak*. Those involved in theatre, film and music contributed articles and reviews to *The Peak*. Many Peakies also went on to become noted journalists, nonfiction and fiction writers, poets and, in one case, an internationally renowned cartoonist.

The first campus newspaper appeared October 13, 1965. It didn't yet have a name. In fact, one of the headlines called out to students to "Name Your

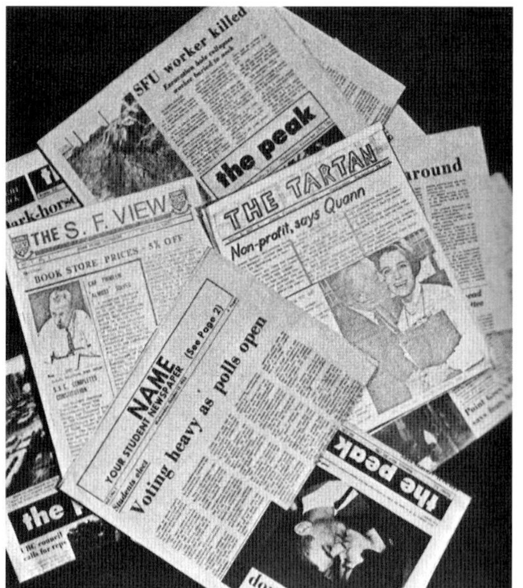

The first issue of *The Peak* appeared October 22, 1965. It replaced the short-lived *S.F. View* and was named as the result of a student poll. The first headline captured both the times and years going forward: "No fee increase, says McFog." *Fred Wong*

Student Newspaper." Editor Sam Steinhuus set out the mandate for the paper that was to replace the competing and short-lived *S.F. View* and *The Tartan*: "A student newspaper must arrive at its policies in a truly democratic fashion... It is encouraging to see that so many students were wholeheartedly in favour of establishing one single newspaper to be a vehicle for the student body as a whole."[34]

On October 27, *The Peak* first took notice of the Centre with an article entitled, "Famed dancer to open centre." New York's Erick Hawkins and the Dance Company, plus an orchestra, would be presenting a program of modern dance. "This is probably going to be the biggest cultural event of the semester. I urge everybody to get out to see him," said cultural director Art Tomlinson.[35]

A large picture of student actors Norm Browning, Dan Singer and Blain Fairman appeared in a promo for the theatre's upcoming production of Robert Bolt's *A Man for All Seasons* in November 1965, followed by a front-page promo the following week and a rave review the week after that. "Play Packs Campus Theatre" read the headline, and the review noted that the play "exceeded all expectations."[36]

The next week's issue featured the first criticism of the theatre, by director Tom Kerr: "Canada is famous for putting up auditoriums without consulting theatre people. Technical difficulties are sometimes almost insurmountable." Of the SFU Theatre he said, "...the sound and lighting are terrible. There are technical errors built into that theatre that should never have happened. They created a great many problems for the producing of 'A Man for All Seasons.'"[37]

In that first semester there were also two mentions of poet Milton Acorn's reading, with an introduction by English professor John Mills, in the theatre, as well as an "Olson Orgy," featuring tape-recorded discussions with and readings by poet Charles Olson when he was in Vancouver. It was not the only performance noted by *The Peak*. The first print show, the Annual Burnaby Art Show, was held in the foyer of the theatre in early November 1965 and was so popular that it was held over. All in all, it was a good beginning for both the CCA and *The Peak*.

The spring and summer of 1966 brought a renewed commitment to the arts. Newly elected editor Allen Garr said: "A campus newspaper should provide intellectual guidance and stimulation to the readers as well as being an outlet for literary creativity."[38]

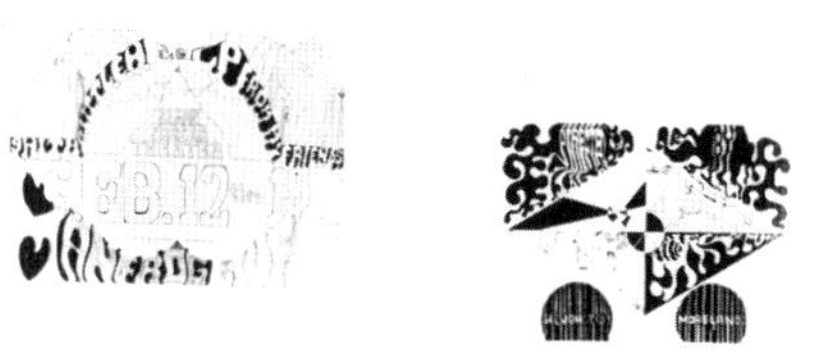

In that same issue, actor Perry Long recapped the aims of the SFU Theatre Company, with its challenges and successes: "When the theatre company was formed in December 1965, two goals were established: First, to provide a focus for theatrical activity on campus; Second, to establish and integrate the technical operation of the theatre. In reviewing the activities of the theatre company during the past semester, we think that a solid foundation has been laid from which the company can build in the future."[39]

Long was not the only CCA stalwart involved with *The Peak*. Actor Norman Browning was on *The Peak*'s board; filmmaker J. Andrew de Lilio Rymsza ran for the board in September 1967; filmmaker and writer Jaan Pill was a reporter and then editor for the summer of 1968. Filmmaker Peter Bryant and actor and playwright Mark Vulliamy were also *Peak* writers. On the visual side, filmmaker Sandy Wilson was a *Peak* cartoonist, and filmmaker Tony Westman was a *Peak* photographer.

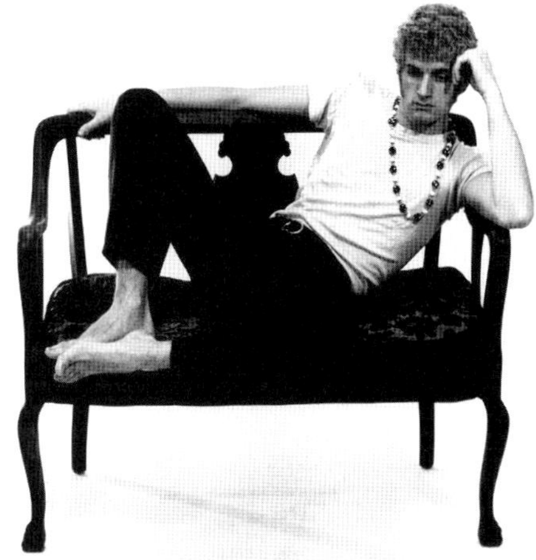

Norman Browning, actor in *The Easter Egg* in 1969, went on to a highly successful acting career. *Tony Westman, SFU Archives*

Throughout the first ten years, *The Peak* provided frequent reviews as well as news about the Centre. A two-page spread in the summer of 1966 sought to capture the essence of the Centre for Communications at SFU. The five men in charge—Tom Mallinson, R. Murray Schafer, Bruce Attridge, Michael Bawtree and Iain Baxter—discussed innovation and the creative process. "Their purpose is not fine arts or the performing arts (as such), but electronic media of communication coupled with artistic means of communication... Communication encourages creativity... Thus there can be no stability in the policies or courses of the Communications Centre."[40]

The hiring of John Juliani in June 1966 was greeted with enthusiasm, as was the hiring of Jack Behrens in September of that year. Juliani himself contributed a lengthy statement of belief, mixed in with a review of the San Francisco Mime Troupe, in November 1966. The theatre troubles were later covered in detail, starting in October 1968 with a large, ominous, anonymous ad: "Should Theatre at SFU Be Abolished?" A follow-up article appeared in early November 1968, then an ad in February 1969 stated, "Theatre to be shaken up." Many more details emerged in the ensuing months. Through it all, the reviews and promotional pieces continued unabated.

Despite the ebb and flow of criticism appearing in the paper's pages, the Centre consistently provided ad support for *The Peak*. The first ad was a small one in July 1966 for *Savage God*, quickly followed by full-page ads for the Centre's open house in September 1966 and each semester thereafter. There were ads for programming, activities and individual performances. All in all, the Centre and *The Peak* were fairly co-dependent.

Meanwhile *The Peak* was covering political news, administration wrongdoings and student council antics, plus running national and international stories from various wire services, including Canadian University Press.

The Peak as a Career Launching Pad

The first SFU student journalists to join the mainstream media were Lorne Mallin, founding editor of *The Tartan*, and Dave Watters. Mallin had a lengthy career with the *Vancouver Sun*, *The Province* and the *Toronto Star*, among other publications. Watters become a long-time sports reporter for the *Vancouver Sun*.

Student newspapers are a traditional route to a reporting career, but Kerry Waghorn followed a different path. He first appeared as a *Peak* cartoonist in September 1967, then moved on to designing rock posters with the legendary Bob Masse. His first poster advertised singer Laura Nyro, then there were posters for the Beach Boys, Chicago, Taj Mahal and many others.

Waghorn captured the attention of the *Georgia Straight*, which syndicated his work to several alternative newspapers, and then moved on to the *Vancouver Sun*. During a trip to San Francisco, he visited the *San Francisco Chronicle* and was brought on to Chronicle Features, one of the world's largest syndication services. There he worked with a team that included Gary Trudeau (*Doonesbury*), Gary Larson (*The Far Side*) and Cathy Guisewite (*Cathy*). His talent as a caricaturist was recognized, and in 1977 the *Chronicle* launched "Faces in the News" by Kerry Waghorn. He still creates about three caricatures a week for syndication; his drawings have appeared in more than 700 newspapers and magazines in more than sixty countries.

Bob Mercer was another *Peak* cartoonist. His iconic *Little Man* cartoons, based on Karl Marx, were a *Peak* staple during the most raucous political times. Buttons saying "Follow the Little Man" were everywhere. Mercer was also a musician, writer, editor and layout artist. His eerie 1978 song "Wilson, Lucas, and Bruce," about the death of SFU grad Mary Steinhauser at the hands of three inmates of the BC Penitentiary, still sends chills.

After writing for and editing *The Peak*, Mercer decamped to found and edit *The Yellow Journal*, then on to the *Georgia Straight*, radical paper *The Grape*, *Calgary Magazine*, *Vancouver Magazine*, VLM and finally *The Province*.

While Waghorn climbed the visual ladder and Mercer moved from radical to mainstream, others, including John Sawatsky, took a more traditional route. Sawatsky left his *Peak* "Merry-Go-Round" column and joined the *Vancouver Sun*. There he became an investigative reporter in the Ottawa bureau and received a Michener Award in 1976 for his articles about the misdeeds of the Royal Canadian Mounted Police (RCMP). Those articles eventually led to the Macdonald Commission and the establishment of CSIS. He followed this investigative work with several books: *Men in the Shadows: The RCMP Security Service*; *For Services Rendered: Leslie James Bennett and the RCMP Security Service*; *Gouzenko: The Untold Story*; *The Insiders: Power, Money, and Secrets in Ottawa*; and *Mulroney: The Politics of Ambition*.

A bit later, Marc Edge joined *The Province* and then the *Calgary Herald*. Twenty years later he took early retirement, did a PhD at Ohio University, and started writing books on journalism. *Pacific Press: The Unauthorized Story of Vancouver's Newspaper Monopoly*, based on his doctoral thesis, won the annual dissertation award of the American Historians Association. He followed with other books about journalism: *Asper Nation*; *Greatly Exaggerated*; *The News We Deserve*; and *The Postmedia Effect*.

Rick McGrath joined the *Georgia Straight* as rock critic and wrote for CREEM, the *Terminal City Express* and *The Grape*. He is owner of Terminal City Express and has donated his extensive files to the SFU Archives.

Ron Verzuh embraced a non-journalistic path and became the national communications director of the Canadian Union of Public Employees. He wrote two books during that time: *Underground Times: Canada's Flower-Child Revolutionaries* and *Radical Rag: The Pioneer Labour Press in Canada*. After retirement he returned to SFU to complete a PhD in history and then wrote numerous books, including *Remembering Salt: A Brief History of How a Banned Hollywood Movie Brought the Spectre of McCarthyism to Rural British Columbia*; *Codename Project 9: How a Small British Columbia City Helped Create the Atomic Bomb*; *Smelter Wars: A Rebellious Red Trade Union Fights For Its Life in Wartime Western Canada*; and *Printer's Devils: How a Feisty Pioneer Newspaper Shaped the History of British Columbia's Smelter City, 1985–1925*. He is also a documentary filmmaker.

Kate Braid also took a different path. She became one of the first journeywoman carpenters in BC, building everything from homes to high-rises and bridges. Her first book, *Covering Rough Ground*, won the Pat Lowther Award for best book of poetry by a Canadian woman. She is the winner of numerous awards for both poetry and prose, including the Pandora's Collective BC Writers Mentor Award and the Vancouver Mayor's Arts Award for the Literary

Arts. She has written more than seventeen books, including *Journeywoman: Swinging a Hammer in a Man's World*; *Emily Carr: Rebel Artist*; and *Turning Left to the Ladies*.

Several more journalists from *The Peak*'s first ten years went on to publish books. Allen Garr (*The Province*, CBC TV, *Vancouver Courier*), who won a 2014 Jack Webster award, published *Tough Guy: Bill Bennett and the Taking of British Columbia*; Neal Hall (*Vancouver Sun*), who won a 2005 Jack Webster award and a 2007 National Magazine Award, has published four books, including *The Deaths of Cindy James* and *Hell to Pay: Hell's Angels vs. the Million-Dollar Rat*; Rod Drown (*Golden Times*), with *No Dog Barked: Who Killed the MacLauchlans?*; and playwright and actor Mark Vulliamy published *Through Thorns*, a novel.

Other Peakies who went on to careers in journalism include Gerry Warner (*Kamloops Daily News*, *Edmonton Journal*, *Cranbrook Daily Townsman*), Glenn Bohn (*Vancouver Sun*), Terry O'Neil (positions at many print publications, including as editor of *B.C. Report*), Keith McQuiggan (*Trail Times*), Michael Bernard (Canadian Press), Ray Tomlin (*Vancouver Magazine* and *Festival*) and Christine Hearn (*Vancouver Sun*, BCTV and *aq*).

The same spirit of creativity, optimism and enterprise that propelled the CCA forward and led many of its student participants to careers in the arts also infused *The Peak*. It was truly a special time, and *The Peak* captured many of those magic moments.

Chapter 3: Theatre and Mime

The Play's the Thing

Acting on the Mountain

by Francis Mansbridge

The years from 1965 to 1970 were golden for theatre at Simon Fraser University. A group of talented students combined with resident artists to strike a tenuous balance between artistic control and artistic anarchy. They believed in and practised a theatre that was more than entertainment, which fearlessly probed our preconceptions about drama and our lives. The theatre itself became the physical, social and cultural hub of the university.

Until the 1960s, professional Canadian theatre had been largely conservative, although a lively amateur context provided some excellent productions.

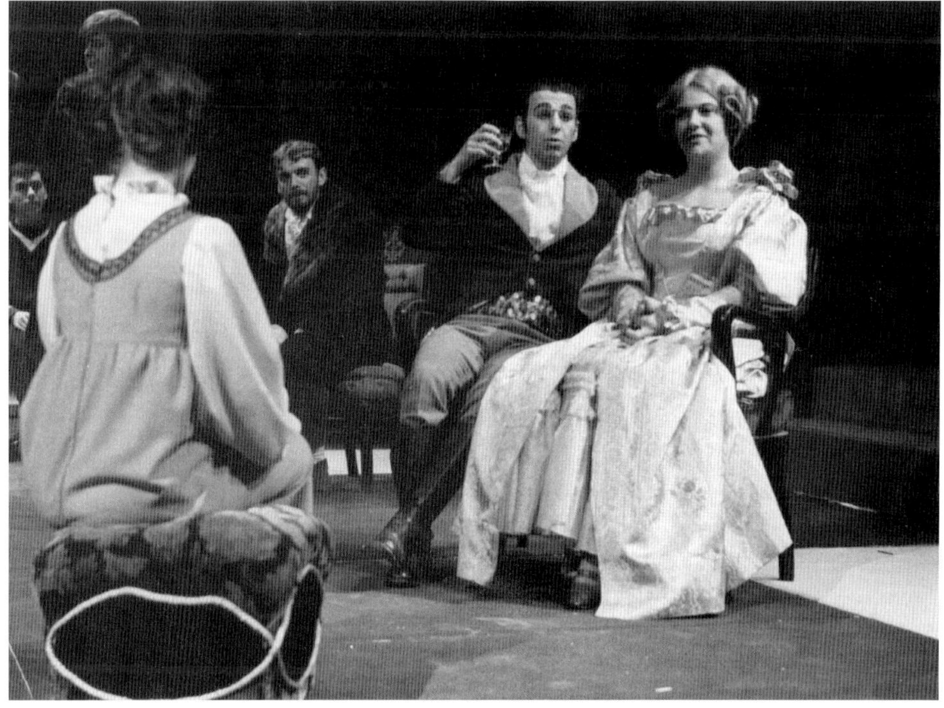

Rehearsal for Nikolai Gogol's *The Government Inspector*, directed by Michael Bawtree in 1966. *P. Knowlden*, The Peak

Much of the action took place in the festivals. The Dominion Drama Festival, which began in 1933, was well established and fostered dramatic productions across Canada. The Stratford Festival, founded in 1953, limited its offerings at this time to Shakespeare. While they did not provide venues for Canadian plays, the festivals did nurture the development of theatrical skills and creativity. Some unique people who had benefited from these experiences brought their talents to SFU. The bulk of this chapter tells the story of the two main figures who actively shaped SFU theatre during this period and some of the many they influenced. The different personae of Michael Bawtree and John Juliani gave early SFU theatre a scope and variety that enriched the university experience of many.

Michael Bawtree Gets It Going

Australian-born and Oxford-educated Michael Bawtree, the first theatre resident, was hired by Bawtree's friend and former Toronto colleague Bruce Attridge, the new but short-lived chair of SFU's Centre for Communications and the Arts. Murray Schafer was hired at the same time, as a resident music specialist. While they were still in Toronto, Schafer had discussed with Bawtree his vision of the Bauhaus movement and the way it and Marshall McLuhan's philosophies could help create a new artistic world at Simon Fraser. Bawtree recollects, "Murray Schafer was a real iconoclast who really wanted everything to be new, different. I caught the fever of Simon Fraser, and I also wanted to do things new. And I think that was very good for me. If I had always stayed in Toronto, I think I would have become a bit of an old fuddy-duddy. Schafer was very much a philosophical influence, the closest thing we had to a guru of communications."[1]

The theatre opened with Erick Hawkins and the Dance Company on October 27, 1965. Film star Rita Tushingham was the guest of honour at its official opening on November 24. SFU's first theatre production, Robert Bolt's *A Man for All Seasons*, was directed by mature student Tom Kerr, enabled by the focus on encouraging students to take responsibility and control. Kerr had taught at North Kamloops Secondary School, beginning in 1959, where he formed the Theatre Wing, featuring his students and fellow teachers. In 1964, he had taken his production of Arnold Wesker's *Chips with Everything* to the Dominion Drama Festival, where he was awarded the Louis Jouvet Trophy for Best Director.

Bawtree, meanwhile, was relieved not to have to direct the production himself. He wrote, "I believe that my relief at being able to pass the job on

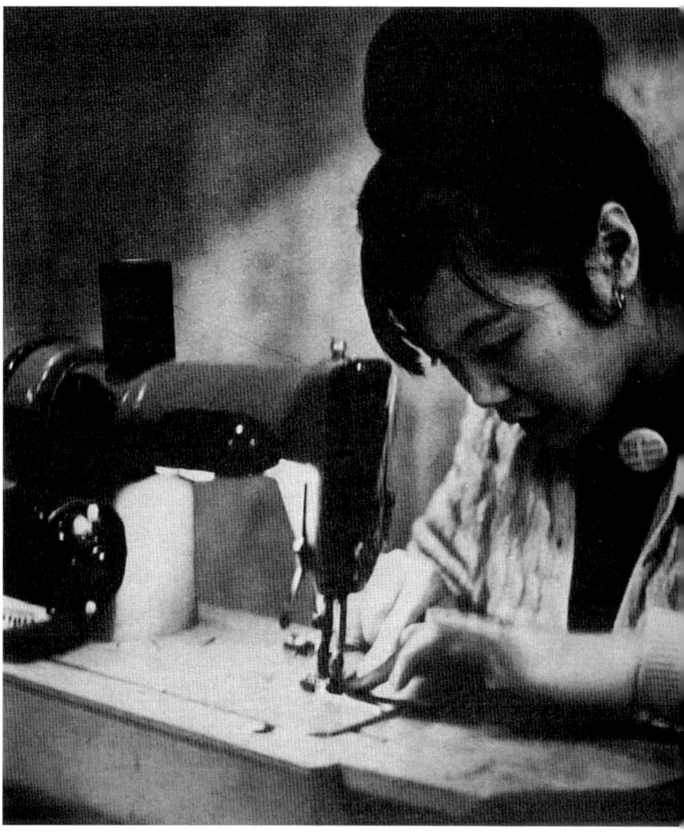

Student Shirley Chan, seen sewing costumes for theatrical productions, was one of many behind-the-scenes volunteers contributing to the theatre's success. *Fred Wong*

to Tom came partly from my lack of self-confidence as a director in my own right."[2] He says it took him a long time to become comfortable directing, as he was strongly influenced by the anarchic principles of SFU English department colleague Jerry Zaslove, who objected to any top-down leadership. Eventually Bawtree realized that someone had to take charge.

When *A Man for All Seasons* opened on November 25, 1965, it received a standing ovation. Blain Fairman as Sir Thomas More, Owen Foran as Wolsey, and Norman Browning as Cromwell gave impressive performances.

Kerr was less enamoured with his academic experiences at SFU, as Tessa Perkins Deneault describes in her article on early theatre at SFU: "I did three terms and got the hell out… I sometimes barely got to class," he admitted. "But I could write an essay, so I got through. I just wanted to get out and get on with my career."[3] Kerr returned to teach and direct in Kamloops. His highly successful theatrical career in subsequent years included founding the Western Canada Youth Theatre in 1969, which in 1973 won an Edinburgh Festival Fringe First Award for his production of George Ryga's *The Ecstasy of Rita Joe*. He later directed for Halifax's Neptune Theatre.

The next term, Bawtree took on his first full-length directing enterprise with Nikolai Gogol's *The Government Inspector*. "I soon came to relish the comedy of it, finding in fact that I had some skill in making things both pointed and funny."[4] When actor Norman Browning fell ill, Bawtree stepped in from his director's position to act his role. The resulting undirected play was very much in line with Bawtree's collaborative approach at the time. The set was designed by Peter Howie and built by John Jeffrey with a crew of student carpenters. Major set construction was needed to raise the level of the stage and project it into the audience.

In 1966, Bawtree used the summer term to write a commissioned play, *The Last of the Tsars*, for performance at the Stratford Festival in Ontario. In his introduction to the published version of the work, University of Toronto drama professor Clifford Leech stated that he had been "moved and exhilarated" by the production at Stratford and praised Bawtree as "a Canadian dramatist with a strong sense of the modern theatre and the theatre in the past."[5]

While most of the major plays produced in the SFU Theatre were from the international repertoire, the creative ferment at SFU fostered several budding playwrights. In October 1967 two original plays were part of the noon-hour offerings. Student Van Ishkanian, who had attended the National Theatre School, directed *Expiation* by Robin Shiakis and *David's Apple* by Gorson Thorson. Ishkanian also ventured down the hill to Burnaby South High School and Centennial School, where he presented Molière's *The Doctor in Spite of Himself*.

During its first decade, SFU's most active playwright was Betty Lambert, a charter professor in the English department. Whether satirical or serious, her work expressed her feminist approach toward social concerns. Many of her plays, including some for younger audiences, aired on CBC Radio or CBC Television, or were performed on stage in Vancouver and elsewhere. One play, *The Good of the Sun*, enjoyed a public reading in the SFU Theatre in March 1972 and was published in 1975 in SFU's *West Coast Review*. Her 1979 play *Clouds of Glory*, set on the SFU campus during the October Crisis in 1970, mocks the posturing and rhetoric of administrators and radicals alike.

Fostering Interdisciplinarity

Interdisciplinarity was a founding principle of the Centre for Communications and the Arts and most resident artists took it seriously. Bawtree commented,

> [W]e continued to discuss how our different arts could work together, and had been exploring models like the Bauhaus school. Murray Schafer introduced us to Wagner's *Gesamtkunstwerk*, the artwork that combines music, drama and visual art. The original group of our artists (Schafer, Iain Baxter, and Bawtree) had grown considerably, as a direct result of the trimester system. Iain Baxter had been joined by miniaturist painter Joel Smith, and Murray Schafer by composer Jack Behrens. In fact we had gathered together infinite riches in the little room of the Centre."[6]

However, competition and a lack of leadership soon asserted themselves. Bawtree again: "We were grievously lacking a master spirit, a Walter Gropius [founder of the Bauhaus] who could harness and direct our energies...

in the absence of visionary leadership, individual ambitions and competitiveness began to assert themselves for all our attempts at accommodation and compromise."[7]

Still the resident artists persevered. Bawtree continues,

> We even came to an agreement that fall to test out one way of exercising our interdisciplinary inclinations: this was to decide on a theme for each term, with one of our number selected to mastermind and program the term's thematic activities. I offered to co-ordinate the second term, and chose my theme: BRIDGES. The bridge was an ancient and very physical communication device, but also heavy with metaphorical symbolism. We were all searching (with varying degrees of enthusiasm) for ways to link up our disparate activities, and for this we needed bridges to ease the passage between our very different artistic territories. The "bridge" theme also brought together the two somewhat intractable parts of our title, "communications" and "the arts."[8]

For *Bridges*, Bawtree invited a bridge engineer to give a talk on the value of bridge-building, including the collapse of the Tacoma Bridge in Washington State.

In the summer of 1967, Bawtree attended the Canadian Conference of the Arts in Kingston, Ontario, where he met Colombian playwright and director Enrique Buenaventura, who was devoting his energies to confronting the violence in Colombia. The concept of a dangerous political theatre dealing with violence and foreign influence intrigued Bawtree, ensconced as he was in a relatively placid Canada. This was Bawtree's first exposure to magic realism, where daily events outpaced any events a playwright could compose. Buenaventura handed him a manuscript of his latest play, which became *Documents from Hell*, performed at SFU in May 1968.

As described by Bawtree:

> The performances of *Documents from Hell*, scheduled for May 1968, were of course part of the Bridges program, and provided a springboard to introduce the campus to Colombia and its almost twenty years of violence and unofficial civil war. I invited young Director Tim Bond from Toronto to co-direct the piece with me, with each of us directing four of the eight episodes. Susan Benson designed the clothes. The central and longest episode, directed by Tim, was called "The

Orgy" and took place in a brothel, with beggars, a mute and a dwarf; strongly influenced, it seemed, by the poems...

During the play's production week, we arranged a "Colombia Workshop" with talks and discussions on the situation in Latin America, and of course including the role played by the United States through the CIA. Somehow I even managed to find the funds to fly Enrique up from Colombia to see his play, and to talk about his *Teatro Experimental de Cali*. He felt that [the play] was generally over-designed and over-produced. He particularly disliked the judges' magnificent red robes, and emphasized for us the true shabbiness and banality of evil. But he was generous in his criticisms, and spent time with the company sharing his thoughts about the play and its characters, and telling them about his work in Colombia. For the students it was an eye-opener.[9]

Early student Christine Hearn was deeply affected by the tumult of the times, especially the development and production of the play *Centralia*.

The Centralia Incident was an innovative experiment in collaboratively putting on a play. As they neared the opening, students and faculty held a weekend gathering at the theatre in which they worked around the clock, sleeping when they could in the theatre foyer. *L. Popoff, SFU Archives*

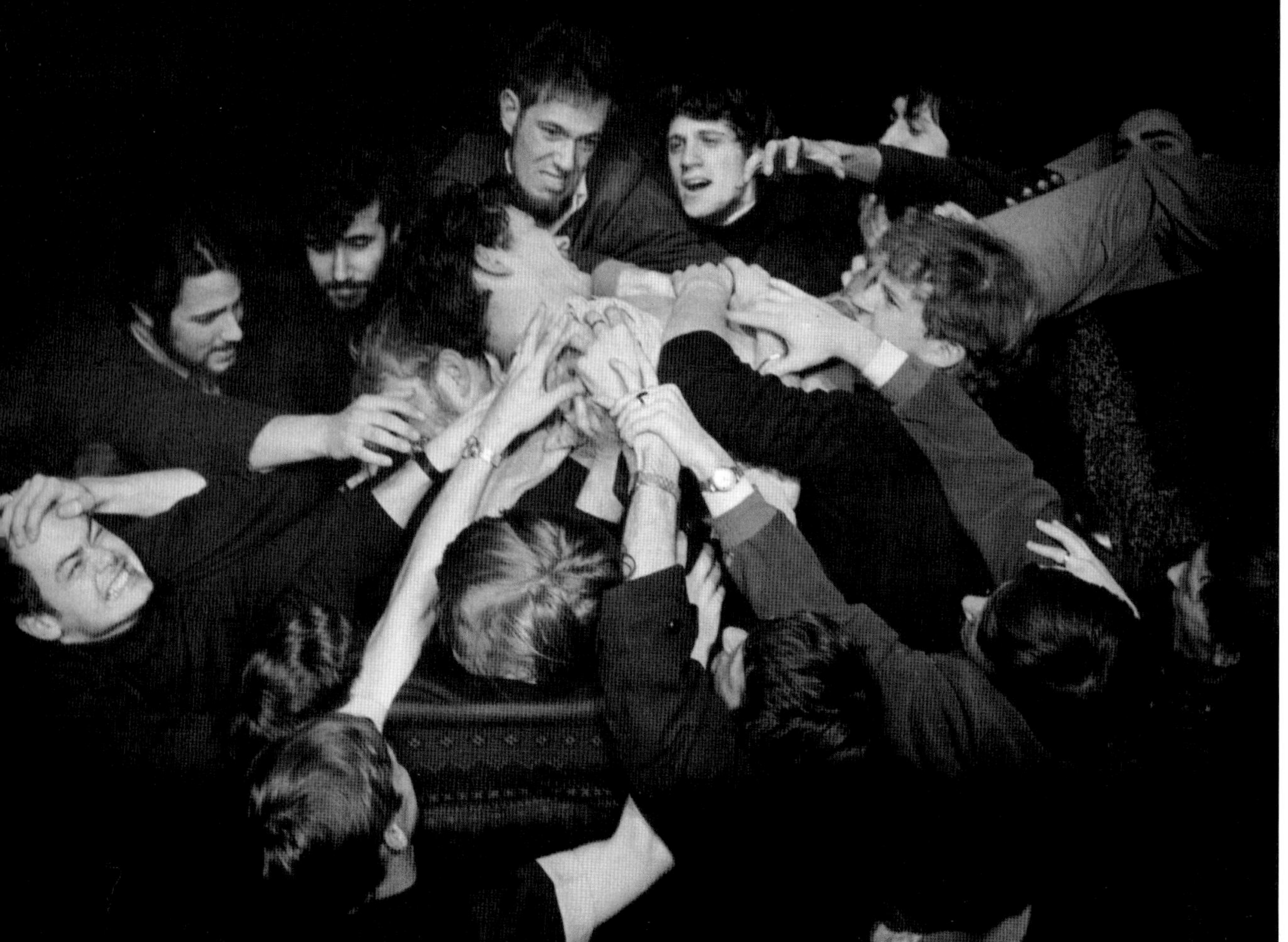

The Story of Centralia

by Christine Hearn

Spring 1967: The Beatles were posing for the cover of their iconic *Sgt. Pepper's Lonely Hearts Club Band* album, the Doors were lighting everyone's fire, and Jimi Hendrix was burning his guitar on stage.

The Vietnam War was in full flight and so were the anti-war protests in both Canada and the US. "Hey, hey, LBJ, how many kids did you kill today?" was a rallying cry.

The first Human Be-In at San Francisco's Golden Gate Park was a huge success, setting the stage for the Summer of Love. Vancouver had its own Easter Be-In. Everyone was there.

Far away in Montreal, Expo 67 was about to open, showcasing Canada to the world.

On Burnaby Mountain, eighteen-month-old Simon Fraser University was poised on the verge of a student strike. Five teaching assistants, including student leader Martin Loney, had led a protest at Vancouver's Templeton High School in support of student free speech.

The university's board of governors met, threatening to fire them. Students, including me, lined the hallways outside the meeting room on the top floor of the library.

We sat on the floor, most of us experiencing our first, but not our last, student protest. The board backed down, but not without some nasty exchanges.

Board member George Wong said to student leader Stan Wong (no relation), "Well, you are free, white and twenty-one, so you can do what you want." To which Stan fired back, "Well, one out of three isn't bad."[10]

Across the mall in the SFU Theatre, another radical event was going on: Michael Bawtree's Centralia Theatre Workshop had just finished its run. Bawtree, with an Oxford education and a background acting at Stratford, was the first resident in theatre in the Centre for Communications and the Arts. In his autobiography *The Best Fooling*, Bawtree called the Centre "a strange creature" in which "everything was to be invented fresh." He wanted to do something different and dramatic, something that would engage both participants and audiences and bring them into the theatre-making process.

Bawtree's friend John Mills, an English professor, suggested looking at the 1919 Centralia Massacre as a subject. The labour protest turned deadly during an Armistice Day Parade in 1919 in Centralia, Washington, pitting members of the Industrial Workers of the World (Wobblies) against members of the American Legion.

Six people were killed: four Legionnaires, one deputy sheriff who failed to give the right password, and one Wobbly, who was sprung out of jail by Legionnaires and hung in the town centre. Many more people were injured, but the event was largely forgotten, even though it led to the first Red Scare in the US. John dos Passos briefly fictionalized it in his novel *1919*, but that's about it. Later, in 1985, Chaim Potok used it as a key element in *Davita's Harp*.

Mills thought the Centralia Massacre was the perfect subject for a theatre project that embraced social conflict, workers seeking fair treatment, the little guy against the big corporations, and many other ideas roiling around at student and faculty levels. Another friend, English professor Jerry Zaslove, who was immersing Bawtree in political and philosophical anarchy, agreed. And besides, Centralia was almost in our backyard—just a couple of hours south of Seattle.

They set up a workshop, hoping to develop the play together and mount it during the fall of 1966. Zaslove said their task was "to set the limits of non-leadership," while Mills called it "a happy socialist enterprise."[11] Bawtree went out of his way to involve a cross-section of people, not just students interested in theatre. He wanted "a model for creation, a model communal activity in general." He wanted to explore the idea of an "un-led theatre."

Although they had developed some improvised scenes, it became clear that they would not make their fall deadline. The workshop development was time-consuming, and Bawtree said during the process that he had repudiated the whole idea of leadership in the theatre and was "watching himself closely for covert manipulation or failed democracy."

Realizing they needed more information about the actual event, students went to Centralia during the Christmas break to research the history. They discovered that the story had effectively been erased. Local newspapers were missing issues that would cover the span of the events, and people still alive from the time refused to talk about it.

Ann Gerson, who was barely eighteen years old when she participated in the Centralia Project, still recalls the experience vividly when she drives to Vancouver from her current home in Portland: "We took a trip to Centralia—John Juliani and a small group of people who were involved with the play. It was the 60s: draft evaders and student protests. We were afraid to say anything

SFU Theatre Workshop

Scenario and Script devised and written by
Michael Bawtree, Paul Bettis, Roger Cooter, Brian Freeman, Wilfrid Mennell, Frank Powley

Actors
Barbara Barron, Michael Bawtree, Colin Bernhardt, Steven Block, Milton Bogoch, Bob Brophy, Roger Clarke, Joe Cooper, Roger Cooter, Tony Craig, Mark Dolgoy, Pete Frederickson, Les Gallagher, Tom Galu, Aileen Gee, Ann Gerson, Len George*, Janis Hanen, Judy Henrichsen, Ted Hicks, Bob Irving, John Juliani, Daryl Kaufman, Gwen Laidlaw, Jeff Lilly, Perry Long, Ian McKay, George Malliaris, Ken Martin, Brian Mather, Jon Moreland, Wendy Newman, Sharon Ozol, Steve Pearce, David Rimmer, Doug Scott, Jocelyn Smith, Drew Tait, Ron Ulmer, Henry Vandenberghe, Jan Visscher, Brian Freeman.*

**Members of the theatre program at Vancouver City College.*

Production
Michael Bawtree *(Executive Producer)*
Paul Bettis *(Stage Director)*
Linda Findlay *(Production Assistant)*
Brian Freeman *(Lobby Display)*
Aileen Gee *(Workshop Secretary)*
John Juliani *(Movement)*
Jill Karaim *(Lobby Display)*
Wilfrid Mennell *(Assistant Director)*
Douglas Rempel *(Production Manager)*
Jan Visscher *(Movement)*
Donna Wong *(Stage Manager)*

Sound and Music
Milton Brodey *(Sound Effects)*
Mark Dolgoy *(Music Research)*
Brian Freeman *(Editor)*
John Juliani *(Editor)*

Lights
Joe Cooper
Melanie Roy
Jan Visscher *(Design)*

Costume Design
Susan Benson

Costume and Properties
Shirley Chan
Janis Hanen
Judy Henrichsen
Jane Latter
Louisa Spencely
Winnifred Tovey

Set Design and Execution
Pete Frederickson
Russell Henrichsen
Art McDougall
Brien Priest
Douglas Rempel

Publicity
Nini Baird
Greg Hill *(Research)*
Brian Mather
Wilfrid Mennell
Winnifred Tovey

Voice Training
Shelora Fitzgerald

Photography
Lloyd Popoff
Tony Westman

Acknowledgements to
John Mills, for contributing the Centralia story; Tom Hood, U.B.C. Record Library, Canadian Broadcasting Corporation, S.F.U. Library, University Interlibrary Loan, University of Washington Library, Charles Dunn, Vancouver Representative of the American Legion and to several individuals associated with the original incident.

CENTRE FOR COMMUNICATIONS AND THE ARTS
Chairman: Dr. T. J. Mallinson. Nini Baird, Michael Bawtree, Iain Baxter, Jack Behrens, Christine Chester, Ann Fisher, Adrienne Hunter, John Juliani, Phyllis Mailing, Jacquie Murphy, Brien Priest, Murray Schafer, Jan Visscher, Douglas Rempel. Associates: Paul Bettis, Brian Carpendale, Iris Garland, Al Sens.

"THE CENTRALIA INCIDENT"

a play in three acts

by the

SFU THEATRE WORKSHOP

There will be two 15-minute intermissions.

The Workshop wants it to be clear that no accusations are being made, or even implied, against individuals involved in any phase of the Centralia Incident. The names spring at us out of history and we attach to them our own honest ideas of how the persons thought and felt. To help us do this, we have used all the factual evidence we have found: where the evidence stopped, we carried on. Where named individuals appear in violent action, it is the violence not in them but in ourselves that we portray. We confess ourselves part of all that men do and have done.

Michael Bawtree

The Development of "Centralia"

The Workshop began with improvisations. As we freely acted out what happened in Centralia in 1919, we found ourselves to be quite unrestrained by the usual self-controls. The violent historical events actually invited over-acting; not only that, but we felt a disturbing sense of release in over-action.

At first we thought that this might work against a dramatic presentation of "the truth" about Centralia. But then it struck us that this tendency to over-act might illuminate the incident itself: there might be some link beween the way the Centralians dramatized their feelings in the events of 1919 and our attempt to act out those events meaningfully on the stage.

If we were to understand how what happened to us related to what happened in Centralia, then we had to find some point at which action becomes over-action and drama becomes melodrama. To find this point might be to say something about the human potential for violence; about the urge to find in action a "resolution" of strain; and about the brutalizing need to seek out an enemy and a victim. All these aspects of man's efforts to exert his will upon the world as a god or Fury are contained in the act of making theatre itself. The on-stage actor is a metaphor for man in action.

—Paul Bettis

WORKSHOP DIARY

SEPTEMBER
Chose the Centralia incident because close to us in time and place and seemed dramatic.

SEPTEMBER-NOVEMBER
Researched the story, discussed it, improvised scenes from it. Taped the discussions and scenes. So developed a shared "memory" of the incident.

NOVEMBER
Split into groups to design set, write scenario and script, research further, develop publicity, design costumes.

DECEMBER
Scenario completed. Rehearsal draft begun.

JANUARY
Rehearsal draft completed. Open auditions held. Play cast. Rehearsals begun.

FEBRUARY 17-19
48-hour rehearsal ACT-IN — eating, sleeping and working in theatre.

Program for *The Centralia Incident.* SFU Archives

that could be viewed as subversive. Our perception was that the United States was a dangerous place where you could be arrested on a whim. Seeing the statues was surreal: those fictional characters became real."[12]

Also, using information gleaned from national news accounts of the time, Bawtree said that he would write the play, but because he had contracted mononucleosis, he didn't want to direct it; theatre co-director John Juliani, who had established a strong base during Bawtree's summer semester off, was too busy directing his *Savage God* series of Arthur Kopit's plays to direct. Besides, by this time Bawtree and Juliani each felt uncomfortable about the other's methods. Paul Battis stepped in as director, and Bawtree set about to write the script.

He said he envisioned a scenario in which development of the play mirrored the process of a theatrical workshop. The central conflict would be

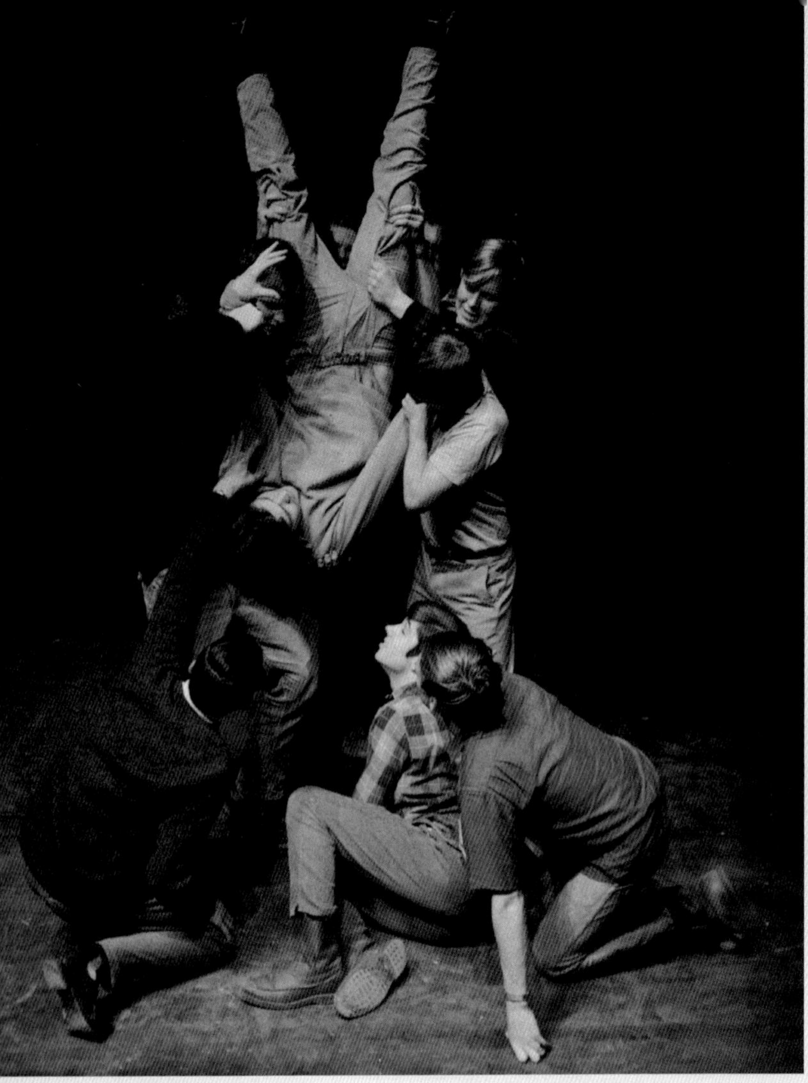

Centralia was a big success, bringing together the differing visions of theatre residents Michael Bawtree and John Juliani. The result was unforgettable, both for the actors and the audience. *Peak Publications Photo Services, SFU Archives*

between the Director (played by Bawtree), who wanted to stay true to the authenticity of the portrayal of events, and the Stage Manager (played by Juliani), who insisted on maximum drama. "I created the humanist 'Director' overwhelmed by the insistence of violent melodrama; John was the charismatic leader impatient with the niceties of human behaviour and ready to embrace violence," said Bawtree in his memoir.[13]

He called this conflict a "dramatic version of a parallel real-life situation" taking place in the SFU Theatre at the time, and that tension was a key element in the play and in reality.

As they rushed closer to opening night in March, Bawtree's script was still short, so he gathered all the participants for a weekend "act-in" to finish things. Everyone brought sleeping bags or blankets so they could stay all weekend and work around the clock. They hunkered down on the floors throughout the theatre and slept in between sessions of script development. Bawtree said this act-in "created community and bound the community into a single group."[14]

On opening night, the audience was let into the theatre at the same time the actors arrived on stage for warm-up and improvisation exercises, led by Juliani. The script called for Juliani to "be in autocratic control of them, able to change their pace and direction with gesture and handclap… There should be no acknowledgement of the audience."[15]

Actors, in tightly structured movements, mimed the events that would eventually take place in the play—but the audience, of course, was not aware of the foreshadowing or why the actors were doing what they were ordered to do. It was a little confusing, but totally in keeping with the spirit of things at SFU in those days.

Bawtree rushed onstage, apparently late, and the entire tone changed. He explained what would happen going forward with the play and set up the dynamic that would play out between Director and Stage Manager. The play, disguised as a workshop, proceeded with frequent tension between Bawtree and Juliani over the history of the incident, the play's portrayal of it and the two men's visions of theatre.

A short excerpt from the end of the play sums up the clash:

> Michael: What the blazes do you think you're doing John?
>
> John: I'm doing my job, and doing it a damned sight better than you.
>
> Michael: What job, what job? Do you think it is your business to turn this thing into a bullfight? Just twist—and bend the lives of people?
>
> John: What are you talking about, twisting whose lives?
>
> Michael: You don't even know, do you. Look John, fifty years ago something happened. We call it the Centralia Incident. We're on the trail here of what did happen...
>
> John: We have a responsibility to our profession. This is theatre, right?[16]

The tension played out for three acts, ending with the lynching of one of the Wobblies. In the finale, Michael entered the stage at the climax of the lynching, actors frozen until Michael woke them with a tap on the shoulder and they were ready for the curtain call.

Bawtree was pleased with the production, and says he felt it achieved its aims, but was disappointed there was little reaction from the wider arts public in Vancouver. There was a brief mention in one of the Vancouver newspapers, but the only review came in *The Peak*, from his friend Jerry Zaslove. Zaslove said the play was "groping towards audience," but that the theatre remembered what the town forgot and that is "to treat human beings as though they were real and to make them life-size."[17] Bawtree called the review "incomprehensible." SFU English professor Malcolm Page recalls being very impressed by the production: "What we saw appeared to be the innovative creation of a fact-based piece of theatre, engaging with what can and cannot be shown on stage. I was fascinated; I have never seen anything like Centralia."[18]

Other SFU students played significant roles in the making of *Centralia.* The production needed photographs for background projections. SFU photographer and cinematographer Tony Westman and fellow photographer Lloyd Popoff were tasked with the job, which required a quick trip across the border to Centralia. For Tony this was a risky adventure, as he was still classified as a draft dodger and subject to a $10,000 fine and five years in jail if caught. Fortunately for him, the US border guard waved them through without issue. Tony's Centralia roots were deep. His family was closely involved with social activism in the past century: as a longshoreman and lumberjack, his uncle was on the front line of protesting labour conditions in the 1920s and 1930s in Washington State; his father and uncle, Swedish immigrants and therefore perhaps suspected of socialism, were targeted for their activism; and people on his mother's side of the family were active during the Great Depression, supporting the rights of farm workers in California. Due to the turmoil of the Vietnam years, his mother encouraged him to go to Canada and attend SFU.

Leonard George, son of Chief Dan George and Chief of the Tsleil-Waututh Nation, acted in *Centralia.* Subsequently he had roles in numerous films and TV productions, including *Little Big Man* (1970), *Spirit Lodge* (1986) and *MacGyver* (1985).

Discouraged by Broader Conflict

Despite significant successes, Bawtree was deeply, perhaps painfully, disappointed with his SFU experience; he appeared out of synch with the aggressive radical politics that drove most of the theatrical and other endeavours at SFU at the time and found the internecine struggles "absurdly childish."[19]

In *The Best Fooling*, Bawtree described being affected by the atmosphere of conflict at SFU as a whole:

> The drama of Simon Fraser University's escalating conflicts continued as soon as term [fall of 1967] began… Opposing forces were hardening: The Students' Union, led by Martin Loney, was becoming increasingly vocal, and had joined forces with the revolutionary elements of the faculty, located primarily in the Political Science, Sociology and Anthropology Department. One struggle took place over whether chairmen (they were all men) of departments should be appointed by the University or elected by their department. No fewer

> than six chairmen, some of them distinguished scholars who had been tempted from places like Cambridge to head a new department at an exciting new university, were peremptorily voted out of office by their junior colleagues. The Student Union also called for the University's name to be changed to Louis Riel University on the grounds that Louis Riel was a true hero and that the explorer Simon Fraser was one of the group of "pirates, thieves and carpet-baggers" who had come west to exploit the land and dispossess the aboriginal inhabitants.[20]

After a few years he realized that it was going to be like every other human endeavour: very aspirational but not really going to change the world. By becoming an institution, he recalls, SFU had already given up a certain amount of spontaneity; institutions involve hierarchies and repetition and basic principles which you can't diverge from easily.[21]

In the middle of June 1969, Bawtree handed in his resignation. The idealism of the school's beginnings as a beacon of the independent arts in academia had died. That summer, Bawtree directed his last play at SFU, *Faces of Summer*, a Peruvian play starring Perry Long and Manuel Busquets.

When he left SFU, Bawtree went on to direct at various locations in Ontario, including at the National Arts Centre, and the Stratford and Shaw festivals. His productions at Stratford included *Requiem for a Party Girl* by Murray Schafer.

Decades later, Bawtree summarized his philosophy while in the SFU theatrical limelight:

> My belief was that a theatre workshop, formed to create a production through the collaboration of all participants, was in fact ideally suited to the situation of an inclusive university theatre. What it demanded of its members was not merely acting skill but the experiences and ideas of different backgrounds, lives and studies. The voluntary and extra-curricular nature of the theatre program meant that the students would come from all departments and faculties of the university. They would not be "drama students", but a cross-section of people interested in making theatre, and bringing to it the experiences and interests of their own work—political science, chemistry, philosophy, biology, history, literature. Acting during this process thus became a secondary or complementary activity. This, I felt, was at least a part of what acting should be—a response to life rather than a substitute for it.[22]

Bawtree's cultivated presence was not always appreciated at SFU. He combined serving on the university senate with writing, directing, teaching and acting, but he was often out of step with some of his more aggressive colleagues. While he was disappointed to find that the changes he wanted to make often fell by the wayside, he produced some fine theatre, and several of his students went on to have distinguished careers in theatre. He remembers *Centralia* as his greatest accomplishment.

John Juliani Introduces Avant-Garde Drama

Savage God: "the expression of that which is buried deepest in human nature."

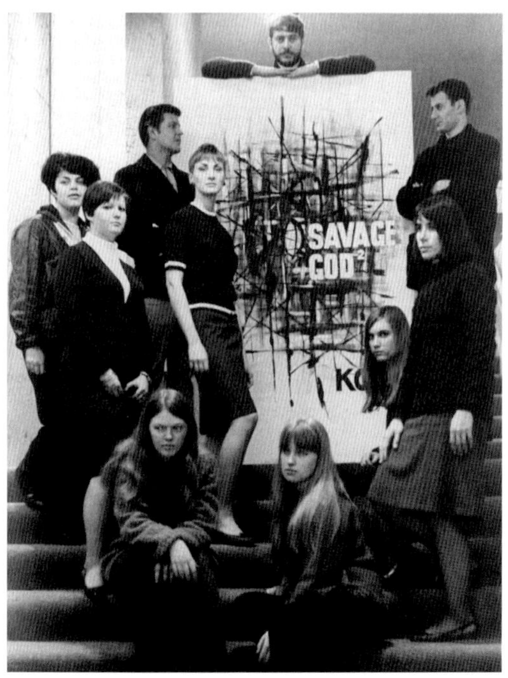

The cast for Arthur Kopit's plays *Chamber Music* and *The Conquest of Everest*, directed by John Juliani. *Tony Westman, SFU Archives*

Michael Bawtree and John Juliani were the two main figures in the theatre at SFU in the early years. Their contrasting styles intrigued people. According to English professor Malcolm Page, "Juliani's charisma drew many students, but Bawtree's subdued English approach to understanding scripts also attracted students." Page also states: "The Juliani-Bawtree rivalry [was] central to the period from Fall 1966 to Summer 1969."[23] On the other hand, Juliani's wife, Donna, comments, "There was no kind of rivalry. But those students who liked the more dynamic version would tend to get involved in plays that John would be in charge of directing."[24]

Bawtree had hired John Juliani in the summer of 1966 to replace him while he was writing *The Last of the Tsars* for presentation at the Stratford Festival. It's a curious fact in the strange world of the 1960s that the two most radical SFU theatre people—Juliani and Peter Hay—were hired by Michael Bawtree, who was closer to the liberal mainstream and a cultured Oxfordian.

Juliani was energized by the openness of SFU and the abundant resources in the early years of the university. The short plays he chose for his first presentations were by the avant-garde dramatists Fernando Arrabal and Michel de Ghelderode—two each.

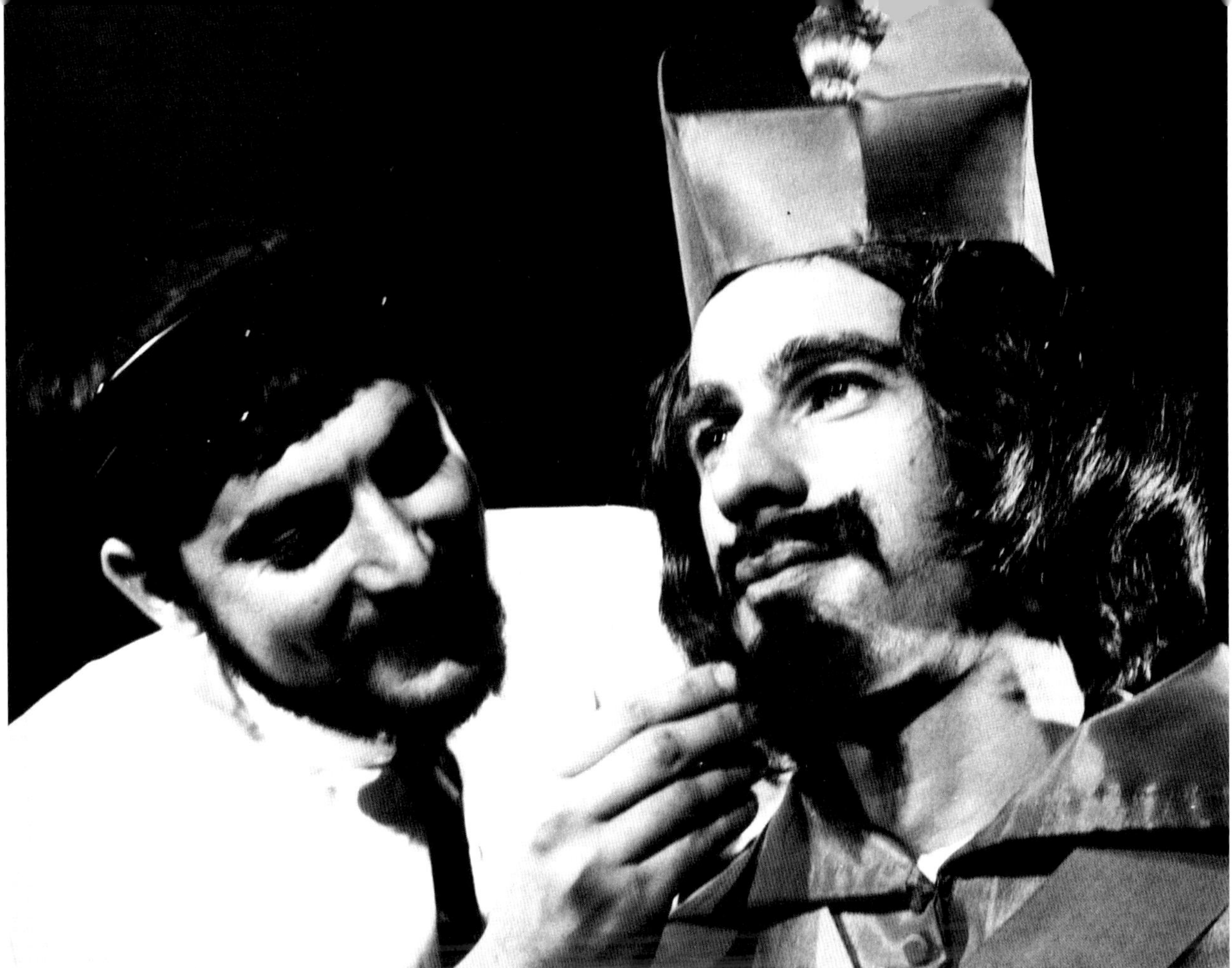

Director John Juliani with Jace Vander Veen as Cardinal Richelieu in John Whiting's *The Devils*. *Tony Westman,* The Peak

Donna Wong-Juliani recalls being present at a meeting between Nini Baird and John as they discussed publicity for upcoming plays:

Nini: Nobody understands or knows who these people are. We can't, you know... nobody knows these plays. Can you just come up with some kind of title for the whole evening?
John: Well, call it Savage God.
Nini: What? What is that?
John: Well, actually, that's a quotation from Yeats.
Nini: Oh, okay, okay. That sounds like probably a good marketing name, right?

Christine Hearn evokes the other main figure in the powerful theatrical presence of Juliani.

The Story of Savage God

by Christine Hearn

To the casual SFU theatre observer in the late 1960s, John Juliani was more than the producer of *Savage God*—he was a Savage God. He was larger than life, charismatic, creative, challenging and difficult. He was pushing the limits—to where we weren't sure, but we had to follow.

Juliani's short tenure at SFU, from 1966 to 1969, transformed our hidebound ideas of theatre from something pretty and entertaining into something to feel uncomfortable about, something to think about. No one left a Juliani production feeling neutral—you either loved it or hated it, but you *felt* it.

But where did *Savage God* come from? Originally, the term stems from a statement by William Butler Yeats after seeing Alfred Jarry's play *Ubi Roi* in Paris in 1896. According to K.K. Ruthven in his 1968 article "The Savage God: Conrad and Lawrence," Yeats took this term to be the ultimate *fin de siècle* sentiment, the "rough beast, its hour come round at last" of his poem "The Second Coming." As Yeats wrote, "After Stéphane Mallarmé, after Paul Verlaine, after Gustave Moreau, after Purvis de Chavannes, after our own verse, after all our subtle colour and nervous rhythm, after the faint mixed tints of Conder, what more is possible? After us the Savage God."[25]

In the turmoil of the late 1960s, the Savage God was symbolic of the new age of iconoclasm and irreverence in art. It also mirrored the upheaval and uncertainty of the times. The Vietnam War was in full flight, civic leaders in the United States were being assassinated, race riots crippled major American cities. We were on the cusp of something wonderful or something cataclysmic.

Juliani took this energy and transformed it into theatre art. He said Yeats was "very right about what happened to the arts: Cubism, Dada, Futurism, etc. All we're really doing now is redoing or rediscovering things that were discovered during a relatively brief period at the turn of the century. We are not doing any really new experimental work—simply following up its use by earlier iconoclasts."[26]

And who was John Juliani? He was born in 1940 in Montreal, where he attended both Loyola College and the National Theatre School of Canada. He acted at Stratford and spent one season with Vancouver's Playhouse Theatre Company. I remember him as Mercutio in red velvet in the Playhouse's 1965 travelling production of *Romeo and Juliet* that I saw in Nelson, BC, as part of a high school English class.

In 1966 he was hired by SFU to teach theatre. And theatre in Vancouver was forever changed.

According to theatre academic Renate Usmiani in her book *Second Stage: The Alternative Theatre Movement in Canada*, Juliani took "Savage God" to mean "imagination in a Blakean sense."[27] Juliani wanted to take the essence of a production and change it, mould it and make it unique. He wanted to do so with each play he produced, highlighting them all with the overall title *Savage God* and using a small troupe of SFU actors who were with him all the way.

Juliani told *The Peak*, "For the first time in the history of the theatre we have the power and ability to significantly alter the very nature of a work by means other than the adjusting of its verbal contents."[28] That became one of his mantras.

One of my clearest memories of a Savage God play puzzled me for years—until I started researching this piece. Tennessee Williams's *The Glass Menagerie* was staged by Juliani in 1968. For more than fifty years I have held this vision: a disco ball is slowly spinning in the centre of the stage, casting its spangled light on audience and cast alike. But off in one corner are flickering black-and-white images that I could never reconcile with the main play. Until now.

The Glass Menagerie (Savage God 4) was one of the earliest multimedia productions presented in the Vancouver area. The black-and-white images I was seeing in my mind were film clips and still photographs of other Williams productions. As Juliani explained it to *The Peak*, "This is our boldest attempt to date in the interpretation of visual and verbal information of the stage. There are some 40 minutes of film ranging from black and white to colour and over 100 slides also ranging from literal and photographic to abstract."

According to SFU English professor Malcolm Page, "Savage God was creating and defining the actual concept of alternative theatre."[29] The contents varied from little-known or neglected avant-garde plays from Europe to untraditional approaches to classic texts to new Canadian work.

First up at SFU were works by Michel de Ghelderode, followed by Arthur Kopit, John Whiting, Peter Foster, Tennessee Williams and Julius Hay. In the same *Peak* interview from October 2, 1968, Juliani said, "From the onset Savage God has been defined quite simply as 'The Imagination, insatiable, unrelenting, fiercely energetic, wary of categorization, and inveterately iconoclastic.'"[30]

His aim was to challenge and challenge he did.

In *The Peak* interview, Juliani explained:

> The plays in the Savage God series have all provided a robust emotional fabric that could be "torn to tatters" without making unique

> demands on dexterity of speech. There has been an attempt to provide a progression thematically from the "todayness" of *Fando and Lis* to the Elizabethan proportions of *The Devils* where we have an example of a work Shakespearean in scope and contemporary in content and execution, with none of the demands made by the difficulties of blank verse.

By the summer of 1969, Juliani was gone from SFU. As a result of a dispute with the university administration, Savage God, with actors including Anne Hungerford and Peter Hay, came down from the mountain to hold performances at the Vancouver Art Gallery. In a sense it was a new beginning, taking the Savage God ethos to another audience.

Juliani told the *Vancouver Sun*'s Christopher Dafoe, "The occasion for Savage God to leave the mountain has been advantageous from some points of view. More importantly, it has enabled us to reach a wider audience, both quantitatively and qualitatively, than was possible at SFU."[31]

Juliani went on to establish a graduate theatre program at York University, produced *Savage God* productions in both Toronto and Edmonton, and became the executive producer of special projects for CBC Radio drama. In 2000, Savage God initiated the Shakespeare Project, with the aim of reading the entire Shakespeare canon in staged readings at two Vancouver churches.

Subsequent productions of different plays were numbered *Savage God 2*, *Savage God 3* and so on. In the turmoil of the late 1960s, this approach was symbolic of the new age of iconoclasm and irreverence in art. It also mirrored the upheaval and uncertainty of the times.

In an interview in *The Peak* shortly after he was hired, Juliani discussed what was for him the essence of the theatrical experience: "This total experience, or effect, must be an overtly physical one, blending every element in a production so that the sounds, colors and movements make a coherent whole that elicits SOME reaction from the audience that in itself should have a physical component. Theatre should not be dead from the neck down."[32]

In the summer of 1967, assisted by Jan Visscher, Juliani turned to the production of John Whiting's *The Devils (Savage God 3)*. He imported Kenneth McBane from Montreal for the complex task of producing the costumes for the fifty actors. Set in seventeenth-century France, the plot concerned a priest and the Mother Superior of a convent. Loud sound and electronic and cinematic techniques, with two scenes being played at the same time, enlivened the production of nearly four hours.

Reviews were mixed. For Jack Richards, in the *Vancouver Sun*, "Stunning is perhaps the only word to adequately describe the Simon Fraser University production of John Whiting's *The Devils*. The audience was stunned by the length of the play, which ran 4 1/2 hours from an 8 p.m. start. It was stunned by a production that outdid Cecil B. de Mille in an effort to be an epic. It was stunned by the volume of sound which poured through the loud-speakers at times. It was stunned by some of the deliberate shock effects of stage... There was much on the debit side."[33]

James Barber, in *The Province*, took the opposite view: "The Devils may frighten you, even revolt you, but the only way it can affect you is by not being seen."[34] SFU reviewer Arthur McDougall, in "Post Mortem on the Savage God," gave a perceptive, detailed analysis: "There are two films used in the play. These are films of scenes (one written, one invented) between King Louis XIII, Cardinal Richelieu, and de Laubardemont... These people represent the immense distant powers (equals God) that have ultimate control over the lives of men... The implication is that the distant powers have won."[35]

When Wendy Newman entered SFU in 1966 she immediately gravitated to the theatre, where she became involved in dance and drama. She recalls that rehearsals with John Juliani began with memorable warm-up exercises: "Half an hour before rehearsal would start, John would have all of us lying on the floor, doing breathing exercises, teaching us how to control the voice, how to control the breath." She participated in several noon shows and well remembers her experience in Juliani's version of *The Devils*, in which she was a member of the chorus of "nuns who were all having this kind of an erotic orgy on stage in these black costumes and crosses going everywhere. I think John Juliani, as a Catholic, was getting revenge." She particularly recalls a note from Juliani: "'Wendy, do not wear those bright green underpants that have daisies all over them. It ruined...'—cuz, you know, like you're rolling around on the floor? Then he suggested that we wear nothing. My searing memory of *The Devils* is being told not to wear the underpants I had on." After assorted experiences at SFU and elsewhere in many different artistic domains, Newman found her niche as an arts administrator and is probably best known for her management of the Vancouver East Cultural Centre (The Cultch). She began there as associate director in 1973 and later returned as director. She later founded the ArtStarts in Schools Society, which "toured over 100 different arts groups through the 2,000 schools in BC" and worked as a consultant specializing in crisis management in the arts before retiring to her garden in the Okanagan.[36]

In February 1968 John Juliani directed two productions: *Hurrah for the Bridge*, a play by Paul Foster starring Norman Browning and Iris Garland; and the film *Hurrah!*, with cinematography by Danny Singer, which was a joint project of the SFU Theatre Company and the SFU Film Workshop. The film was based on an idea in the play, and the two were presented together as *Savage God 3 1/2*. As an article in *The Peak* on January 31, 1968, stated, this "'evening of theatre' represents a fusion of acting, actor-audience relationship, 'text' and direction as they operate in two different media with the same material."[37] It was a creative application of Michael Bawtree's theme of "Bridges."

Norman Browning became Juliani's lead male actor in 1969 and followed Juliani downtown to continue his dramatic career when he was ousted from SFU. He refused to join the American-run Actors' Equity Association and was blacklisted until control returned to Canadian hands. Later he performed in nearly a hundred productions for the Arts Club Theatre, Vancouver Playhouse and the Shaw Festival. He was particularly drawn to classic roles with, as Vancouver reviewer Mark Leiren-Young wrote in the *Vancouver Sun*, "the type of looks Jane Austen heroines swoon over."[38] Browning also did substantial work in film and television and won Vancouver's Jessie Richardson Theatre Award for best actor three times.

One of Juliani's innovations was to undercut traditional relations between the performers and the audience. In his Vancouver Playhouse production of José Triana's *The Criminals (Savage God 8D)* in 1970, the audience of only twenty-five was "split into two distinct halves, each part of which corresponded to one act of Triana's play. To see the entire piece it was necessary to attend twice and to

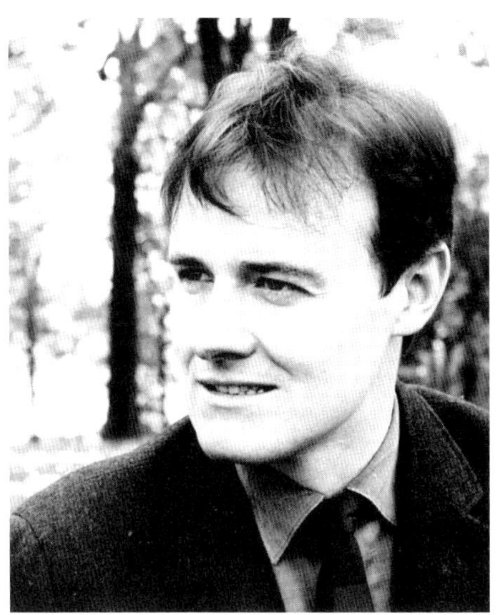

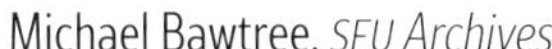
Michael Bawtree. *SFU Archives*

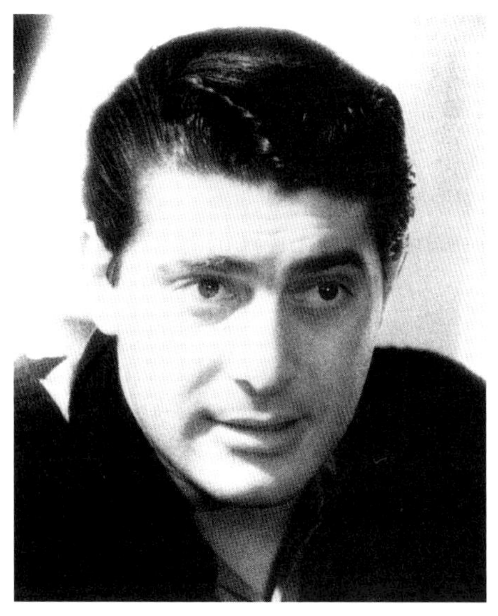
John Juliani. *SFU Archives*

Each of Bawtree and Juliani's approaches to presenting drama resulted in some rich theatrical experiences. Bawtree drew on his Oxford experience, while Juliani ground a more iconoclastic axe in his dramatic creations.

choose one's seating according to the degree of vulnerability (not involvement) one wished to expose or be exposed to."[39] Because the play is about alienation, "we are attempting to create the experience for the audience by fragmenting their perception of the piece... The audience will, in a way, be eavesdropping on the performance in much the same way they might were they to peep through a keyhole in their own closets."[40] Embracing multiple points of view to incorporate a more truthful vision echoes the approach taken by many of those writing in English professor and poet Robin Blaser's poetry courses.

While Bawtree was strongly opposed to the ills of our society, as shown in his work on plays such as *Centralia* and *Documents from Hell*, Juliani's truth was more artistic. He described *Ready or Not You Must Be Caught* as "less interested in the trappings and the extravagances of the theatre. It deals with the core of existence, with the ability to feel and to share that feeling. It is on this concern for sharing one's emotions that the theatre and the pursuit of life must coincide."[41]

According to Juliani,

> The modern theatre is still waiting for a form that will harmonize with the moral, intellectual and emotional viewpoint of our age, an age that has been accused of wearing its complacency like a laurel wreath. The history of the theatre arts in our century has been an attempt to shatter that complacency by means of a bombardment of our senses. In every case, it has been a matter of shocking man until

> he momentarily loses control of his reasoning mind and a destructive 'second state' springs forth from the discursive intelligence.[42]

While Bawtree appeared comfortable switching hats between being an administrator (he had been elected to the university senate) and a creator, Juliani was more committed to a radical theatre. He was a genuine Dionysian Canadian, a rare presence in Canadian universities, or anywhere, who fearlessly probed taboo subjects. He resembled no one more than the Montreal poet Irving Layton, who around this time was delighting in loosening the poetic knickers of Eastern Canada. Both were energized by their conflicts with those who opposed them. Layton had even applied (unsuccessfully) for a teaching position at UBC in the early 1960s. The prospect of Layton and Juliani in sister universities hurling invective at the parallel institutions—how that might have changed Canadian literary history.

Savannah Walling, whose career as a performer is recounted in this book's chapter on dance, was one of the many talented young people who were energized by her experience with John Juliani. She found the atmosphere in his workshops welcoming and inclusive, his theatre workshops "interesting and scary." "What I really remembered from that time period was seeing the work of the Savage God ensemble and the kind of passion and rigour with which they were working... And that whole value of committing yourself to exploring that was expressed by the work of Savage God theatre... bringing your whole self, your body, your mind, your soul to the work that you were doing, and engaging with your audience."[43] SFU's collaborative approach, which emphasized the integration of the arts, proved the ideal learning experience for someone who was herself multi-talented in dance, music, mime and performance art. Walling went on to establish a connection with Juliani's work that continued until his death. In later years, she and her life partner, Terry Hunter, participated in the Downtown Eastside-centred Savage God project *I Love the Downtown Eastside* (their young son was one of the creator/performers in the multigenerational cast) and were involved in some of Juliani's projects at Christ Church Cathedral, including his final celebration of life.

Student Shelora Fitzgerald recalls how Juliani's strong sense of social justice and depth of commitment inspired a loyal following among his students. "During the SFU student uprising, when there [were] uniformed guards policing the students in the theatre, Juliani staged an irreverent piece of guerrilla theatre on the mall, a statement which triggered the administration into locking him out of his theatre (with chains on the door!). His students held a sit-in to protest, but both sides remained entrenched in their positions."[44]

Juliani met his wife among the students he worked with during this decade. Donna Wong was in the dance program at SFU but was involved with the theatre, as her boyfriend of the time, actor and filmmaker Danny Singer, was playing the lead role in the Bawtree-directed play *The Government Inspector*. In an interview, Wong describes responding to a poster requesting auditions for the next play, which John Juliani was directing. She nervously decided to audition and hesitantly asked Juliani, "Are there any parts for Chinese girls?" She wasn't cast, but she did become his theatrical assistant and the relationship blossomed into a lifelong marriage.

Juliani's Resignation and Post-SFU Career

John Juliani's last months at SFU—between November 28, 1968, and May 15, 1969—were acrimonious. As discussed in detail in the CCA chapter, a back-and-forth dispute with the university administration took hold, including Juliani submitting his notice of resignation, his pay ceasing, Juliani withdrawing his resignation, and then being offered full retroactive back pay but only a non-permanent faculty position. Then, the first weekend of May 1969, the theatre was locked. The theatre people, including Juliani and Visscher, were not allowed into the building to rehearse their play *Arrabelesques*. Juliani finally accepted a compromise solution on May 3 that reinstated him as theatre resident with full pay but required him to leave campus permanently by May 15. A court injunction that barred him from appearing on campus was later modified to allow him to visit the university, but only as a private citizen and as a guest.

Juliani had been rehearsing Beverly Simons's play *Greenlawn Rest Home* (starring Jackie Crossland) prior to being ousted from campus. Norman Browning took over the direction of the play, only to be told by Centre director Patrick Lyndon that Juliani was barred from attending. In response, Browning resigned from the Theatre Company Co-ordinating Committee but continued directing the play. It went ahead and was received enthusiastically.

Jackie Crossland acted in many of John Juliani's *Savage God* plays and went on to a long and successful career in theatre, playing Nurse Bea Cross in *The Beachcombers* and having a role in Robert Altman's film *McCabe & Mrs. Miller*. She started a company, Random Acts, that created stories about lesbian and other working women, and presented at festivals in Canada and the US. In later life painting became her major form of artistic expression.

In the summer of 1971, Juliani used Stanley Park's Hollow Tree as the setting for his production of Samuel Beckett's *Happy Days*, starring Jackie Crossland as the main character, Winnie. The loneliness of the character was emphasized by the visual images and metaphors available in the environment. "To observe Winnie against the backdrop of setting sun and shimmering trees when she became a mere silhouette became impossibly diverting as a play watching experience."[45]

Juliani found more appreciative environments in downtown Vancouver, where he continued directing plays from the summer of 1969. In 1983, he earned a Genie nomination for the best original screenplay for the film *Latitude 55*, co-written with novelist/screenwriter and SFU graduate Sharon Riis. In his later years, he was an active member of several artists' unions and organizations. He died in 2003 after a tumultuous career in which he helped dragoon Canadian drama into the modern age. After his death, the throng of 1,000 people who gathered to say their farewells were "greeted on the steps [of] Christ Church Cathedral by a whimsical troop of actors wearing commedia dell'arte masks and Shakespearean doublets, each holding a colourful bouquet of balloons, a fitting escort for his final performance."[46]

A Student's Take on the Heady Early Days

Reviewing the early theatre scene in an article in *The Tartan*, Tessa Perkins Denault presented the memories of student Penn Lewis. He recalled one "scandalous" incident during a production of John Juliani's *The Devils* when a harpist from the Vancouver Symphony came up the hill to be part of the show:

> "She almost stole the show. She had to sing, and she was a streetwalker wearing a tight bodice, and she was well-endowed," laughed Lewis. "She came out and sang her tune, and there was a gasp in the audience because she had made little rosettes as if her bosom had popped out a little bit from her corset. This caused a scandal. It was controversial... We sold out every night." Through the common goal of creating meaningful theatre, Lewis said, he developed lasting relationships and trust with his classmates, describing the way the theatre helped create the strong sense of community that SFU became known for. "You learnt about joint efforts and working together... They were phenomenal times... People were looking forward to it... I was getting

messages from Europe and from friends and relatives in the East, and I know other people were [too]. You were getting these phone calls, and they would say 'what is your new play; what are you going to do?' ... I had friends and relatives who went to other universities and they didn't come away with the same type of intellectual fervour at all... And, of course, they were looking at us saying—oh, that's too radical. But if you don't have it in university, when is there time to express it?"[47]

Pushing Electronic Boundaries

Regardless of controversies around the star figures, students often took the creative reins and pursued their own interests, with or without direction from the theatre residents. Charter student Wilfrid Mennell and resident musician Phillip Werren brought an eclectic creativity to their projects, discovering forms that pushed their art into new areas. Mennell arrived at SFU when they were still "trying to find doors that had knobs on them."[48] Werren (primarily as composer) and Mennell (primarily as director) collaborated on two significant electronic music/theatre projects. *Cascando* was first produced on November 27 and 29, 1968, with voices read by Jan Visscher and Perry Long. Praise from the *Province*'s James Barber was effusive: "Something new and exciting, something original and unique, something spontaneous emerging from our culture."[49]

Mennell recalls he and Werren collaborated on *Cascando* soon after the latter arrived on campus. They used a Beckett play and a radio play, with music composed by Werren playing throughout. The difficulty was how to present the music: "So what we did was put everything on tape, and played it in a completely darkened theatre, using surround speakers."[50] They were using quadraphonic sound on a half-inch Ampex tape with three synthesizers. As well, Mennell was part of the original research and writing team that created *Centralia*, and he coordinated the audiovisuals for Enrique Buenaventura's *Documents from Hell*, directed Sam Shepard's *Chicago* and completed a one-act play titled *Complex*.[51] He directed *A Star Shines But Once*, one of two one-act plays by fellow student Frank J. Powley, for a noon show in October 1967.

Work on their next project, *Phases*, began in mid-February 1969. Mennell suggested using some of the poems of W.B. Yeats, particularly "The Second Coming." While they originally considered a highly structured composition based on the twenty-eight phases of the moon, they found the technical complexities limited this aspect of the production. "*Phases* used only one voice, Philippa Polson, who was a lecturer in English. She had a voice that was almost androgynous," Mennell recalled.[52]

Wilfrid Mennell is a good example of a student who benefited from the interdisciplinary environment that SFU made possible. While he had no connection with theatre before coming to SFU, it soon became his driving passion, along with music. However, his life took a different direction when a rogue sapling growing in his orchard in Cawston, BC, just outside of Keremeos, was discovered to bear apples with a crisp, delicious taste. He patented them as Ambrosia apples, and the variety is now grown worldwide.

Creative Explorations with Mime

Mime was a popular art form at SFU during the 1960s. While its public appeal is less now than when artists such as Marcel Marceau were household names, mime's use of communication through movement and gesture effectively bypasses words that can often obscure meaning rather than reveal it. Mime allows and often encourages improvisation and audience participation.

In 1966, the San Francisco Mime Troupe performed *Civil Rights in a Cracker Barrel* at SFU, a burlesque of the minstrel show, which satirized the absurdities of US racial issues. Reviewing the presentation in *The Peak*, Arthur McDougall wrote, "No punches were pulled, and the problems and injustices of race relations were unflinchingly exposed... within the framework of a theatrical milieu so total as to beggar description."[53] Juliani wrote in *The Peak* the next week that this mime troupe had grasped "the very essence... of the theatrical medium."[54] A few years later the visiting Swiss group Mummenschanz was, in reviewer Rod Drown's words, "the most incisive and paradoxical display of symbolism and many-levelled meaning I've ever seen."[55] These visiting groups created a high bar against which the local groups could measure themselves.

Mime played an important part in several SFU theatrical productions. In the September 27, 1967, issue of *The Peak*, Art McDougall noted the success of two presentations, *Hole* and *Blow-Up*, at a noon show: "They were neat and well-paced and had just the right length for maximum effect."[56] Philip Henry praised several sketches presented in September 1968 by SFU students Perry Long, Fritz Unrath and Robin Patterson in his review for *The Peak*. "As long as youth has the imagination, drive and creative spirit to stimulate thought and feeling as it has done in *Under-Mime*, then I for one refuse to grow old."[57]

In September 1967 Jan Visscher initiated plans for the formation of a mime troupe at SFU, partly inspired by the San Francisco Mime Troupe. Thanks to an Opportunities for Youth grant, Terry Hunter, who was hired to do a "Summer in the Parks" program, formed the Simon Fraser Mime Troupe, which toured BC and performed at the Okanagan Festival of the Arts in Kelowna as well. He was soon joined by his life partner, Elaine (later Savannah) Walling. Among the many arts groups with which they collaborated was the Mime Caravan (1973–1974), which performed at SFU in July 1973. Doug Vernon, a fellow member of the SFU Mime Troupe, later performed with Ratatouille Clown Theatre, Cirque du Soleil and Theatre Beyond Words. In his later years, Vernon has helped in many roles with Vancouver Moving Theatre productions and festivals—as props maker, crew, stage manager and administrative assistant.

Terry Hunter believes much of the early creativity was driven by the backdrop of the Vietnam war. People,

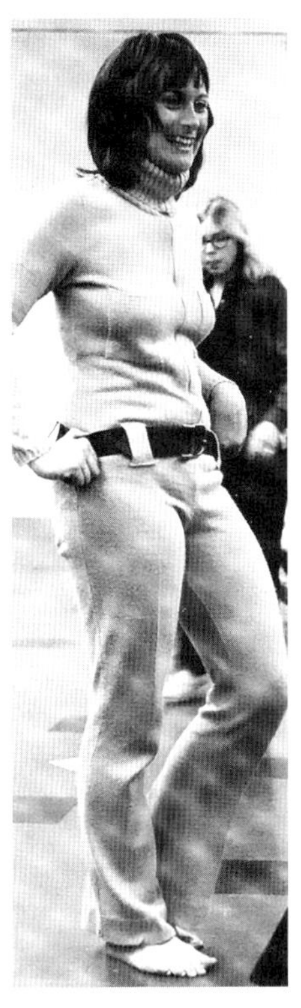

Robin Patterson attended the École internationale de théâtre Jacques Lecoq in Paris, where she was especially interested in the writing of mime. She has subsequently produced and performed in numerous mime productions. *Tod Greenaway, SFU Archives*

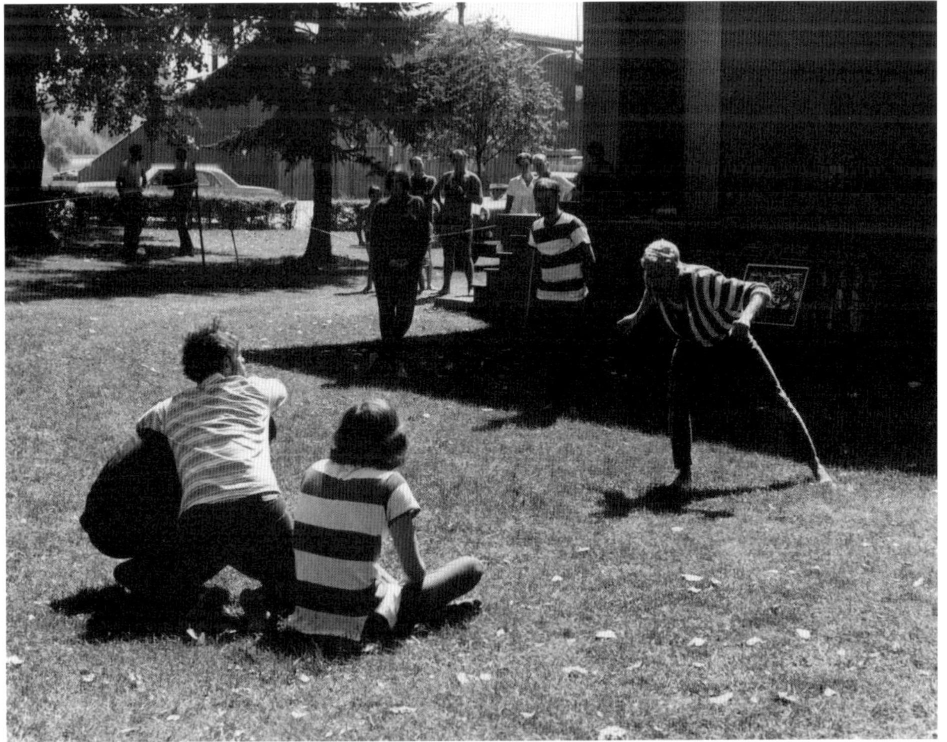

As part of their outreach through the province, the SFU Mime Troupe took their show on the road to Kelowna and elsewhere. *SFU Archives*

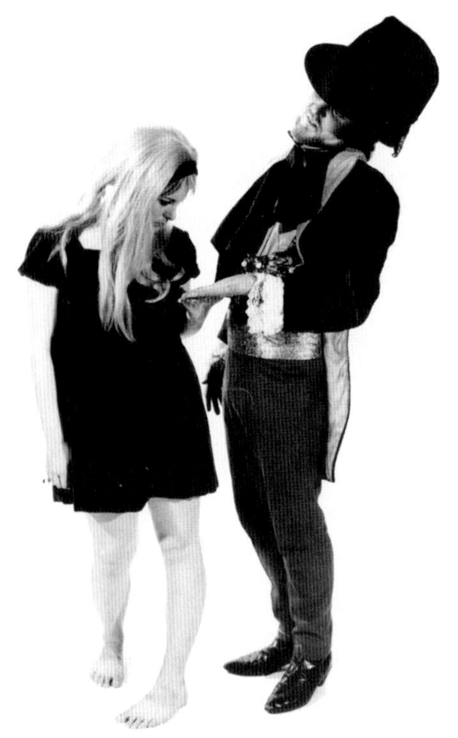

Robin Patterson and Perry Long demonstrate improvisation in their mime *Aliice* based on Lewis Carroll's *Alice in Wonderland*. *SFU Archives*

he says, were wanting to create work and have a voice in a context where they sensed their leaders were "sending people to die on behalf of the top. This is the way of us having a voice and saying, 'We're following our own path. We're not following a voice that's telling us this is the way we should be doing things.' Part of that voice was protesting against the war, but part of that voice was also doing personal creativity and really expressing yourself."[58]

Robin Patterson entered university with the intention of becoming an English professor, but the draw of SFU theatre proved more compelling and ultimately led to her later work as a Canadian artistic director and a founding member of Theatre Beyond Words, which specialized in the creation of original works using mask, puppetry, music and mime. Through mime she worked on noon shows and a production of *Aliice*, a mime-dance version of *Alice in Wonderland* adapted for deaf children, showing a "genuine understanding of and apparent compassion for the human race."[59]

For Patterson, the question of how to write for mime was central to her creative exploration. "How do you write a mime play so that people other than the author know what it's all about? Do you fill the page with lengthy description of movement, mood and expression? Do you plot the action with dotted lines and arrows? Do you use line drawings or photographs to get your point across?"[60]

Visiting artists, including those with the nonverbal National Theatre of the Deaf, invigorated the creativity of the SFU Mime Troupe. Patterson's was one of two BC groups invited to perform at the National Showcase of Theatre at the National Arts Centre in Ottawa. They presented their original drama *Meme*, written by troupe member Richard Bolivar, which explored "dream responses working with time and man's behaviour in the past."[61] Patterson stated, "With the aid of special lighting and sound, the effect will be a dream—beyond reality, beyond a basic one-celled organism into another dimension."[62]

Besides Patterson and Bolivar, members of the SFU Mime Troupe included Rod Drown, Wendy Gorling, Bob Ableson, Doug Vernon, Pat Hildebrand, Stuart McKea, George Mallioris and Sonja Lafferty. They were thankful to Centre director and "fairy godmother" Nini Baird, who secured $4,000 for expenses related to their Ottawa trip.

Actor, choreographer and teacher Wendy Gorling started at SFU as an English student but switched her focus when one of the Canadian Mime

Theatre members, Harro Maskow, performed on campus and then taught a neutral mask class. "This experience was the impetus to change my career pathway. Good-bye English department; hello France!"[63] With Lin Bennett, Elizabeth Murray-Byers and Wayne Specht, she founded Axis Theatre in 1975, for which she was artistic director for thirty-eight years. With Morris Panych she co-created five nonverbal theatre pieces, the best known of which is *The Number 14*, an exuberant celebration of late-night bus travel in downtown Vancouver. A six-time Jessie Award winner, she taught physical theatre at Studio 58 at Langara College for many years, passionately devoted to encouraging the success of her students.

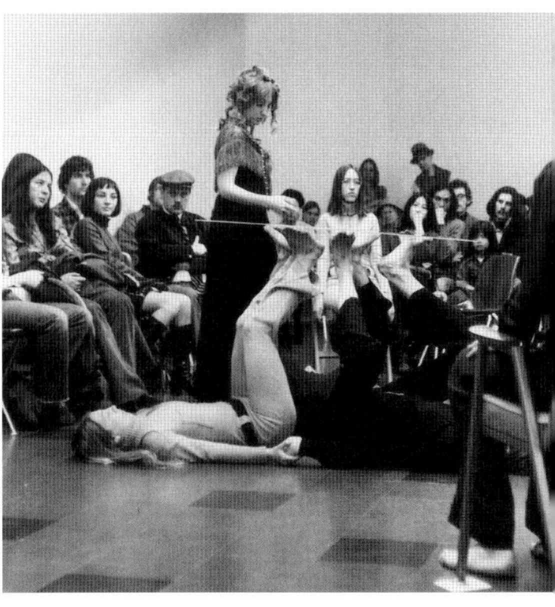

SFU Mime Troupe in a Vancouver Art Gallery Performance. Wendy Gorling stands. Among the seated are Sonja Lafferty and Stuart McKea. On the floor are Karen Birch, Rod Drown and Bob Ableson. *Tod Greenaway, SFU Archives*

Aided by Canada Council and Koerner Foundation grants, Robin Patterson left Canada in 1971 to study in Paris, joining some eighty other students from fifteen different countries to learn more of the magic of mime from Jacques Lecoq. After graduating from L'École International de Théâtre, she took her BA in English at SFU. She has continued as a practising artist throughout her life, including touring internationally for four years with the Canadian Mime Theatre as its first female soloist, writer and director. She conceived the well-known *Potato People* series of nonverbal mask plays for intergenerational audiences, and wrote, directed and performed in many of its fourteen pieces. In May 2007, she received the Women of Distinction Award in the field of arts and culture from the Niagara Region YWCA.

SFU Theatre After 1969: More Conventional Expectations

In "Theatre at SFU: The First Ten Years," English professor Malcolm Page narrates the smaller sphere forced on theatre when most of the resident artists had left: "Very little happened in theatre between Summer 1969 and Summer 1974. The university no longer wanted to emphasize experiment, preferring neat organization charts."[64] Page notes that after the departure of Bawtree and Juliani, several theatre residents, each staying only eight months, failed to sustain much continuing interest in plays, although they did present some intriguing work. Mostly, if the reviews in *The Peak* are any indication, the main interest was in mainstream movies.

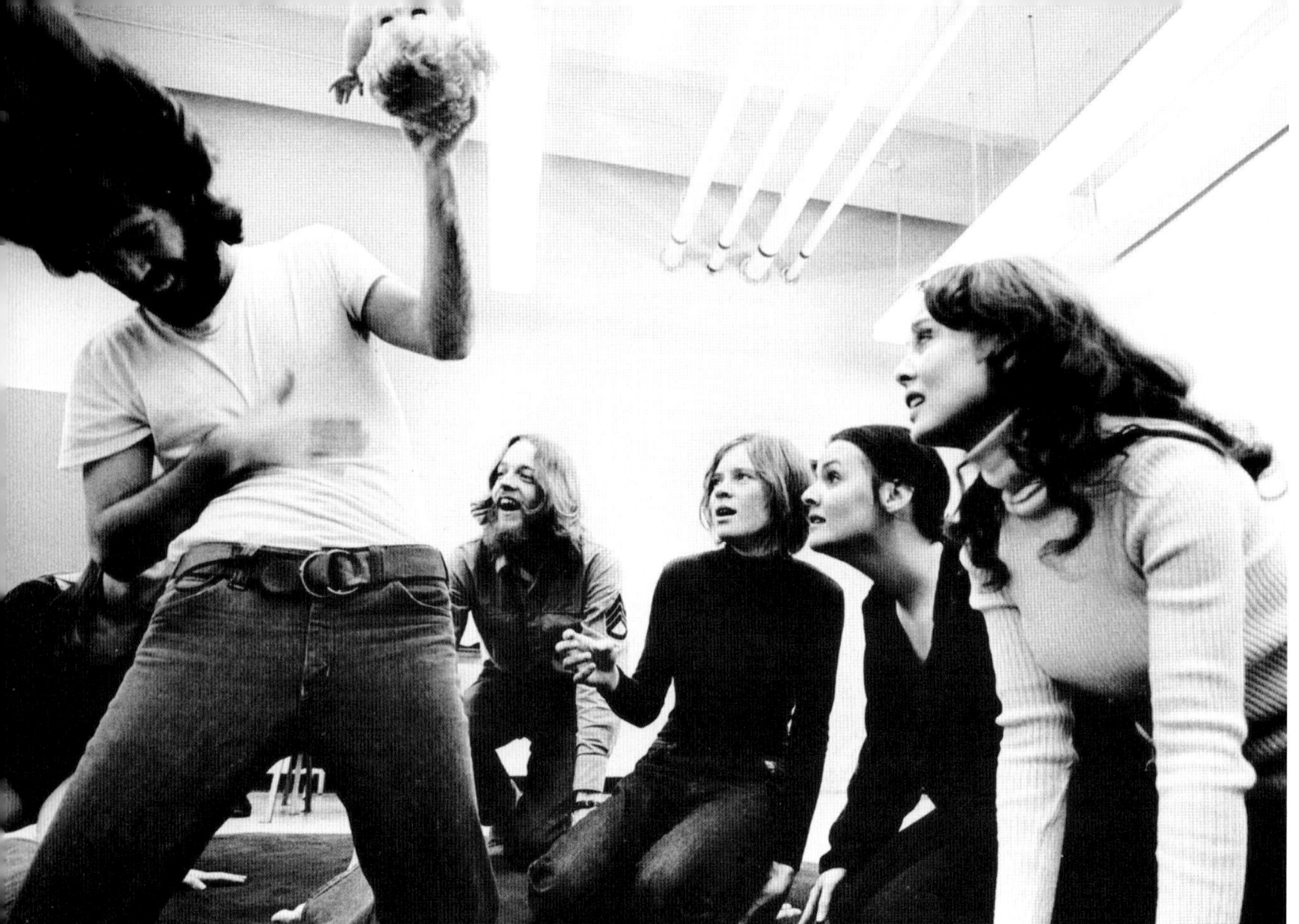

Rehearsal of *How Our Love Is Like a Dwarf*, directed by Jim Garrard. From left to right: Guy Robinson, (Polly Wilson hidden), John Oldfield, Megan Arundel, Marie Fontaine and Gwen Franks. *SFU Archives*

Page notes that instead of the SFU Theatre, "which was too big to fill and inflexible, the theatre used either a bare room, the Concrete Theatre, in the basement, or the portables which had emerged between the theatre and the Academic Quad."[65]

Theatre resident Jim Garrard helped revive the idea of theatre as a serious art form at SFU in the early 1970s, often annoying and disturbing those who had more conventional dramatic expectations. His presentations included Brecht's *Mother Courage* and *How Our Love Is Like a Dwarf*, the latter inspired by William Blake's poems. Michael Fletcher directed another Brecht play, *A Man's a Man*, in 1973. Unfortunately, the Concrete Theatre, where many of the plays were held, seated only forty-five to fifty people—great for an intimate theatrical experience but not large enough for many of the potential audience, who were often turned away.

Page states that when he arrived in 1972, two of his students gave three performances of Edward Albee's *The Zoo Story*, which filled the main theatre. A *Peak* reviewer described this as "a learning experience of the best sort, for it is a totally active involvement in every respect."[66] These developments encouraged English student Allan Safarik to write in *The Peak* that "This semester of theatre at Simon Fraser with 'The Magician' and 'The Mother' and now 'The Collection' and 'The Lover' has achieved excellence reminiscent of Juliani a long time ago."[67]

Resident artists made concerted efforts to re-create some of the past glories. In September 1973, Keith Pepper and Hagen Beggs, both with a long list of theatre credits, were hired to be theatre co-residents. Their initial presentations of three plays that month were prepared in just one week: *There* by Thomas Cone, *Edward and Agrippina* by René de Obaldia and *Preparing* by Beverly Simons. Don Clark, reviewing these plays in the September 19 *Peak*, was enthusiastic. He was especially moved by Anna Hagan's creation of a woman as she aged in *Preparing*.

In the spring of 1974, the co-residents organized their instruction into two workshops: one for the development of acting skills, the other concentrating on design. In February 1974, John Arden's *Serjeant Musgrave's Dance*, directed and with sets designed by Hagen Beggs, was presented in conjunction with Malcom Page's English 103 course. *Peak* reviewer Terry O'Neill singled out Alan Davis as the best of an excellent production.[68]

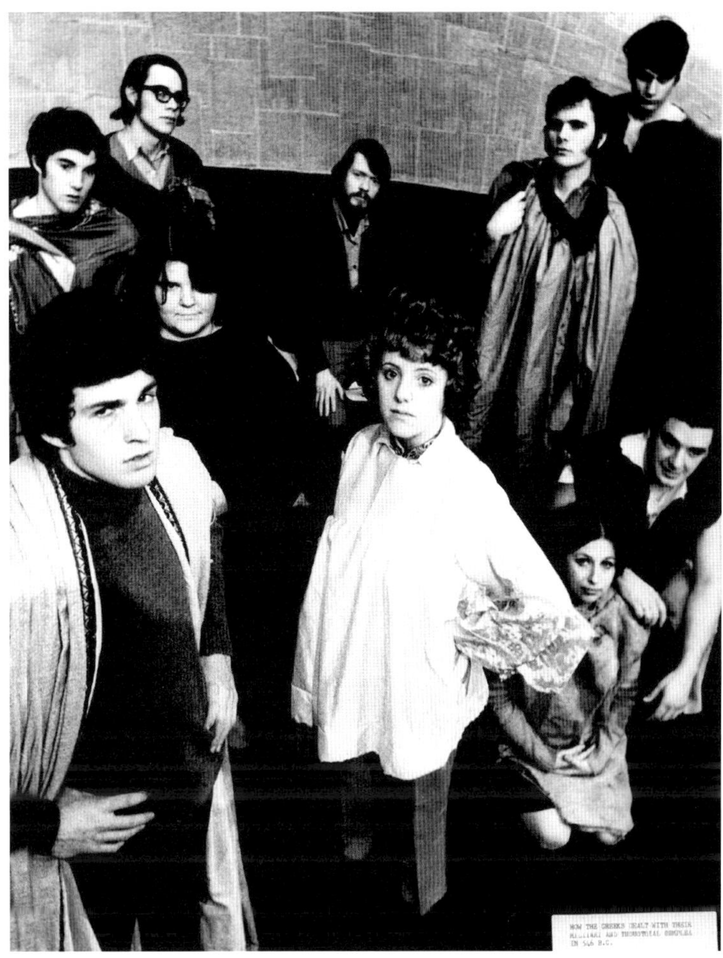

Cast of the play *How the Greeks Dealt with Their Military and Industrial Complex in 546 B.C.* written by Leonard Angel. Actors include John Barker (in glasses, back left) and John Donald to his left. Wendy Newman in white, Jackie Crossland behind her to the left in black. *Tony Westman, SFU Archives*

In 1976, credit courses began, and the programs changed. Student Perry Long outlined some reservations on the direction of SFU's theatre program in *The Peak*, noting that drama at SFU from 1965 to 1969 had mainly been driven by the resident stars and their concerns. While he felt that those concerns were valid, they had often taken priority over responding to student experience. Long believed that Juliani viewed it as his job as director to unleash the dark imagination that lay within the lines of any good play. To do so, he used film, sound, visual images, or anything else that would shock the viewer into new imaginative truths. It was not a power that he could surrender to students, no matter how talented.[69]

Keeping the Spirit of Theatre Alive

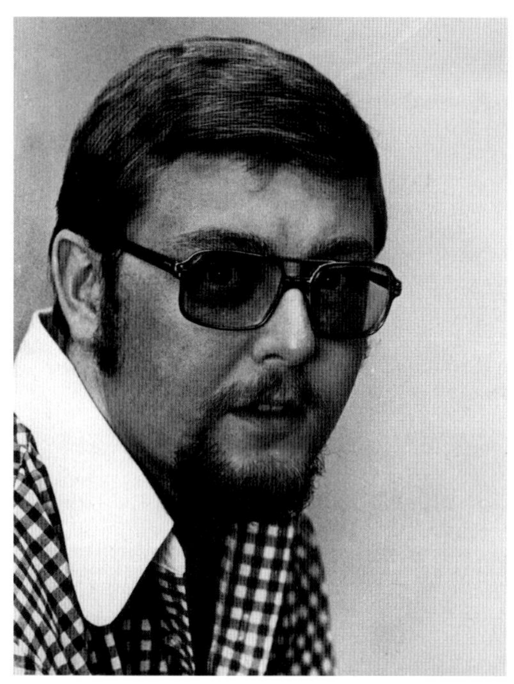

Richard Ouzounian arrived at SFU in September 1974, where he directed several plays. *SFU Archives*

Within a few months in 1969, most of the resident artists in theatre left SFU. John Juliani's noisy departure is often discussed, but residents Peter Hay, Jan Visscher and Michael Bawtree also departed, either voluntarily or with a firm nudge. Students Perry Long and Tom Kerr left upon completion of their studies.

People wondering why the theatre program faltered thought that the initial excitement had faded as the university became more of an institution and bureaucracy affected the spontaneity and engagement that had driven so much of the action. Some blamed the Centre for Communications and the Arts and expressed disappointment over its apparent lack of direction. *Peak* reporter Gerry Warner was more scathing, lamenting what he saw as "apathy… throughout the theatre and the workshops."[70] Warner quoted an administrative assistant in the Centre as saying, "The theatre is drifting… lacks proper direction… and could die from lack of nourishment," and attributed the deterioration to the transformation of the original CCA structure.[71] It was likely that the Centre was under considerable financial pressure as the university shifted its resources to fund credit programs. This pressure likely also came from the provincial government, which found that non-credit courses did not harmonize with the FTE (full-time equivalent) system of funding that was being implemented.

Richard Ouzounian arrived at SFU in September 1974 and formed a repertory ensemble of about twenty-five from both within and outside the university. His major shows were *Joan*, a collage of text from Shaw and other authors, and *The Chekhov Kids*, which was also written by Ouzounian. Set in Nelson in winter, the latter is a condensation of Chekhov's *Uncle Vanya*. During his long career as a writer, actor and director, Ouzounian would go on to serve as artistic director for five Canadian theatres and as theatre critic for the *Toronto Star*.

While the battles raged, many students found continuing pleasure in their theatrical experiences. Susan Baxter, for one, epitomizes the theatrical spirit of the early years that was far from dead:

> In the fall of 1974, I joined up again. That year the Artist in Residence was Richard Ouzounian. With Richard we didn't use the main stage in

the theatre; instead, we were in a large warehouse-y room behind the trailers (next to the theatre) where the Centre for Arts "offices" were. The first production was *Joan*, a mashup that I think Richard created using several plays about Joan of Arc. Kayla was Joan. She looked rather splendid in her armour. I didn't have much of a role; I was a witch—not sure why there were witches in France à la *Macbeth*—and I had to writhe about on the floor, which I did not like at all. Richard kept telling me to loosen up. (Linda Lawson was also a witch and she seemed to enjoy the writhing on the floor thing, but I did not.)

Then Richard decided on a play, *Lenny*, about Lenny Bruce. Wayne played Lenny and Richard somehow convinced SFU to procure a liquor license so we could turn the space into a nightclub and serve real drinks. (I was a waitress.) There was also a bit of fuss about Geri something, who played a stripper. She was gorgeous and I think had worked as a model; she had that tall, skinny frame. When she was on stage she wore a skimpy bikini costume and danced around a pole, kicking up her long, long legs. Some years later I saw her in a bit part in some police drama on TV, so I guess she subsequently tried her luck in Hollywood.

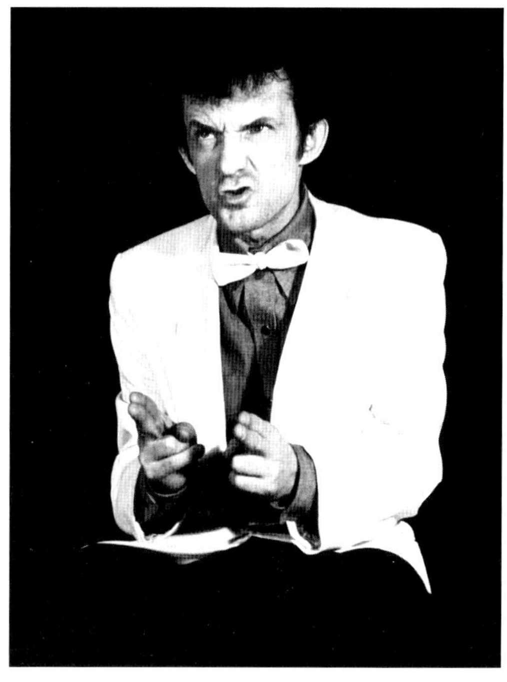

Wayne Robinson as Lenny in Julian Barry's play on the social satirist Lenny Bruce, directed by Richard Ouzounian. *SFU Archives*

Richard Ouzounian was definitely a force to be reckoned with. I liked him a lot. He was so smart and creative. He was younger than his manner suggested, late twenties as I recall, but he was so self assured he came across as older. We got along really well and he would ask me to drive him here and there and we'd chat about all sorts of things.[72]

Theatre is the most democratic of the arts: at SFU even the directorship was often shared, and a broad cross-section of students and faculty shared in the success of many productions. Actors are needed, and assistants contribute their energies to publicity, set design and construction, costumes, lighting. Audiences are also nice to have. Many SFU students gained imaginative memories that nourished them for many years. Some pursued successful theatrical careers, but more often they carried with them their personal experiences and lasting friendships wherever life took them.

CHAPTER 4: DANCE

Dancing on the Mountain

THE HISTORY AND LEGACY OF SFU'S DANCE PROGRAM

by Tessa Perkins Deneault

GRADUATES AND ASSOCIATES OF THE SIMON FRASER UNIVERSITY DANCE PROGRAM have been shaping the Vancouver dance scene since the university opened. Artists such as Karen Jamieson, Savannah Walling and Terry Hunter were influenced by their time at SFU and went on to form their own companies. Other dancers and choreographers would go on to join national or international companies, freelance with local artists, or form their own independent practice. In 1988, Raewyn White wrote in *VanDance* that SFU's dance students "have coloured the Vancouver dance scene with bold, brash, bizarre and beautiful multimedia works. They've enlarged the possibilities of dance through their use of text and film; they've shattered expectations through the places they've chosen to perform and their choices of themes and movement vocabularies; and they've brought a new excitement to dance viewing through their disregard of the conventions."[1] By this time, dance had become a four-year degree, but the first decade of dance at the university were less structured, with few for-credit offerings and no formal program.

Dance at SFU had its beginnings in the Faculty of Education's Physical Development Centre, where Iris Garland was hired in 1965 to teach dance courses that were often theoretical and served as elective courses for student athletes and others interested in learning a bit about dance. Originally hailing from Chicago, Garland came to SFU from the University of Washington and was determined to create a proper academic dance program at the university. That would come years later, after a period of intensely experimental and inclusive work as part of the Centre for Communications and the Arts, the interdisciplinary creative hub. In the meantime, Garland set to work creating as many opportunities as she could for SFU students to be exposed to

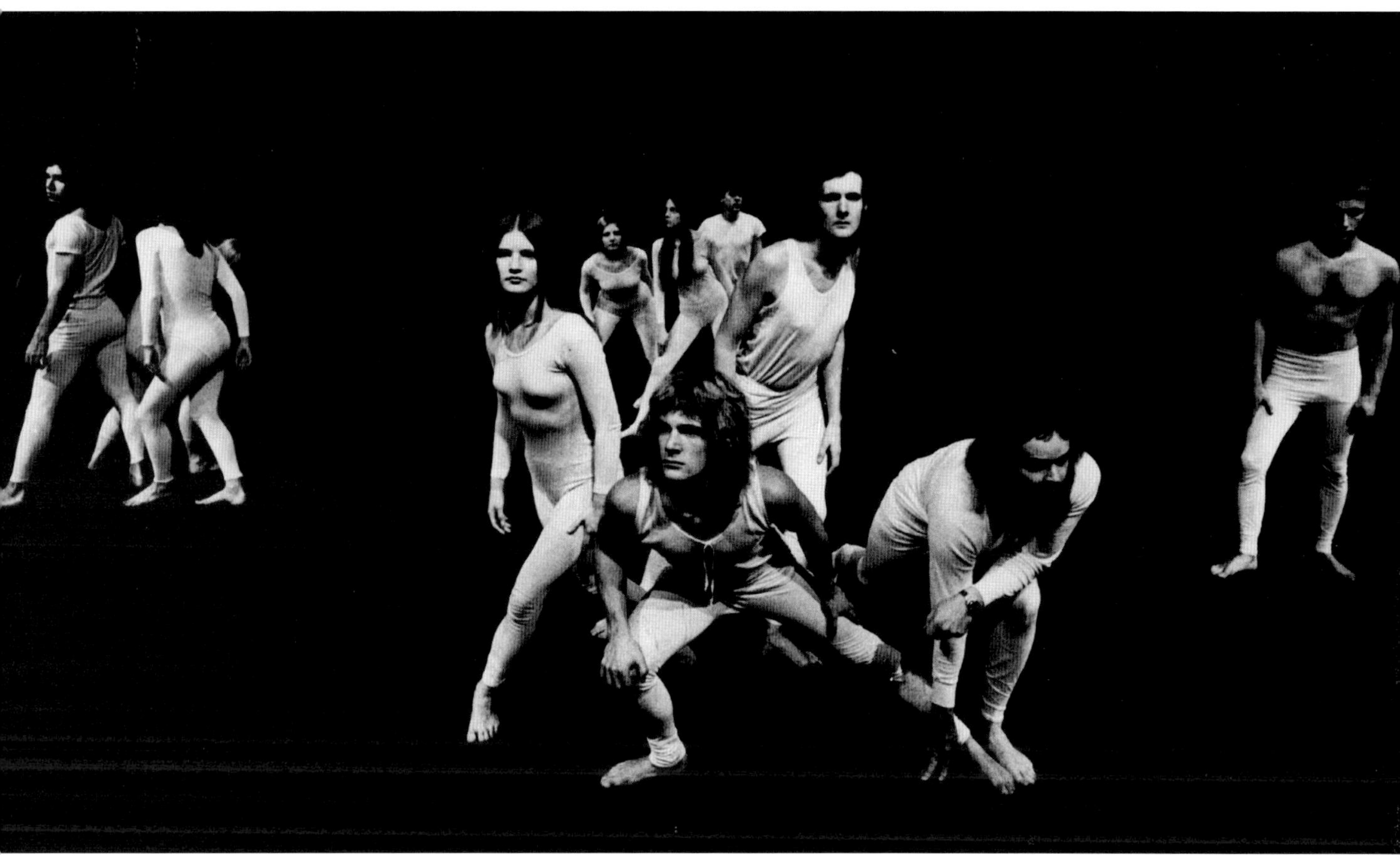

Members of the SFU Dance Workshop performing in 1970. *Tony Westman, SFU Archives*

dance—most famously, her informal dance workshop that welcomed anyone who wanted to dance, regardless of experience or training. "Dancers met a few times a week, mostly in the basement studio of the SFU Theatre on Burnaby Mountain and were led by the driving force behind dance at SFU: the late Iris Garland," explains dance scholar Alana Gerecke, a graduate of SFU's dance and English programs.[2]

Alongside the exciting work happening on the hill, the late sixties were a formative time for dance in Vancouver. In 1964, Norbert Vesak, who had trained with many pioneers of modern dance, including Ted Shawn, Merce Cunningham and Ruth St. Denis, founded Pacific Dance Theatre. The next year, Paula Ross founded the Paula Ross Dance Company, whose members included many dance artists—such as Barbara Bourget and Jay Hirabayashi, who founded Kokoro Dance and the Vancouver International Dance Festival—who went on to form their own companies and shape the dance landscape of the city over the next few decades. The arts collaborative Intermedia was formed in 1967 by a group of artists including Glenn Lewis and Jack Shadbolt, and offered

One day, one of the draftsmen headed down to the theatre basement to take some measurements for a dance-floor extension, but before long he rushed back to his office, flustered, to tell his colleagues about three quite nude dancers he had found on the dance floor. Not one but three draftsmen dashed downstairs but then there was a change of pace. They commenced to take the most careful and accurate measurement of a dance floor ever taken, for their flustered colleague had told them the truth.[3]

—Marilyn Cairns

dance classes that were frequented by the next generation of modern dancers, including Karen Jamieson, who studied there before joining Garland's workshop at SFU. Max and Anna Wyman moved to Vancouver from London, UK, in 1967; Anna formed the Anna Wyman Dance Theatre and served as a visiting instructor at SFU, while Max became a highly regarded dance, music and drama critic who spent a lot of time on the mountain. Within the span of a few years, Vancouver went from having very few opportunities for modern dance training or performance to having a strong foundation for a thriving modern dance scene.

Every spring, the students from Garland's dance workshop would present a performance of their original work in the SFU Theatre. Max Wyman describes one of the performances in 1969: "Freshness, vitality and a good deal of tongue-in-cheek charm are the outstanding qualities of the concert of modern dance currently presented by the Simon Fraser University dance workshop. Permanent workshop director Iris Garland has gathered around her 26 young people with an evident enthusiasm for movement—and she has very properly allowed them to shoulder the burden of choreographic creativity."[4]

Karen Jamieson (then Rimmer) participated in the CCA's dance program, and she remembers it being a formative time for her. She originally came to SFU to become a teacher, but soon found her way to Iris's dance workshop. Jamieson's husband at the time (filmmaker Dave Rimmer), who was an SFU student, mentioned to Garland that his wife loved to dance, and Garland, always inclusive, said Jamieson would be welcome to join the group. "I was going to be a teacher, but I took that dance workshop and abandoned all notions of being a teacher," says Jamieson. "I just wanted to dance."[5]

Soon after joining the workshop, Jamieson premiered her first piece in July 1969. For its experimental, interdisciplinary aims, *Mediums* is a notable production that came out of the Centre and the dance workshop. Under the direction of Garland, the piece was choreographed by Jamieson along with Edith Feinstein. Other dancers included Maureen McGinness, Debbie Bowes and Cecalee Coffey.[6] An original score was composed by Phillip Werren (then Feinstein's husband), and an abstract film was created by Dave Rimmer. With its abstract film backdrop, modern dance movement and electronic score, *Mediums* was innovative for its time. "Multimedia" was a new fad, and critics like Max Wyman loved it:

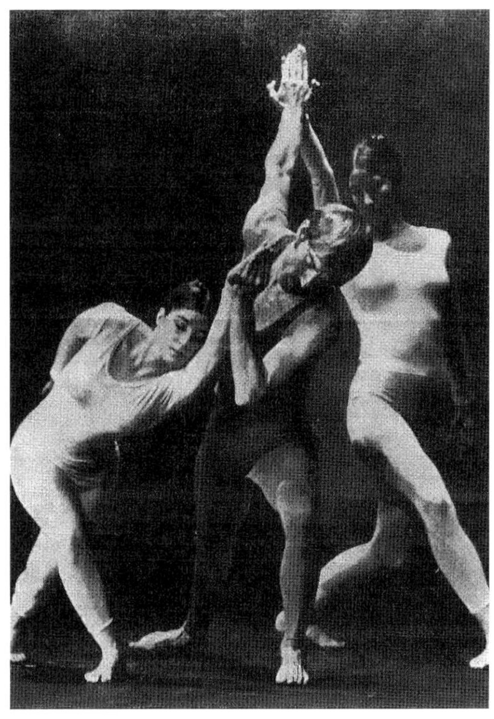

Edith Feinstein (left) and Karen Rimmer (right) in *Mediums*, their first piece of choreography as part of the SFU Dance Workshop. *Tony Westman, SFU Archives*

> Film, dance and electronic sound were blended for a Simon Fraser University presentation Friday noon that proved to be one of the most intriguing theatre events I have seen on that campus. The production, titled Mediums, was an attempt to express visually and aurally some of the implications of W.B. Yeats' theories about life—and it showed how effective mixed or parallel media can be when they're handled in a circumspect manner... Within the range of their performance abilities, the dancers did considerable justice to the work's dance ideas. And these ideas—despite what seemed to be an abrupt slackening of tension and invention around the middle of the work—were at times gratifyingly fresh and arresting: writhing diagonals, squirming circles and whirling starburst shapes created moments of bewilderment and desperation, and moments of great sadness."[7]

In the days when critics still reviewed student productions (before faculty members decided student productions should not be scrutinized in the same way as professional productions), Wyman was a prolific arts critic for the *Vancouver Sun*. "The student performances on the hill were open to the public and the paper had a much more generous and inclusive vision of what we should cover in terms of the arts than today," says Wyman. "I'd be up there two or three times a week looking at dance and listening to music."[8] James Barber added his approval in *The Province* when *Mediums* was staged for a second time as part of a mixed program of works from the dance workshop. He described it as "the most exciting local multi-media production I have seen...

an outstanding trip, which in its subtlety, its complete integration, its rich and exciting sensory blendings, comes close to mysticism."[9]

Moving Off the Mountain: Founding New Dance Companies

Aside from being a seminal production for the Centre, *Mediums* was also a pivotal moment for Jamieson's career, as it was her first dance performance and first piece of choreography presented publicly. "It was absolutely terrifying, but also exhilarating when it seemed to work," says Jamieson. "*Mediums* got me on my way, and I thought 'I can actually do this.'"[10] Soon after, Jamieson and eight of her classmates from the dance workshop, including Savannah Walling, Sharon MacDonald, (Carol) Dickie Uhte, Edith Feinstein and Betsy O'Neill, were invited to join Garland for intensive dance training and exploration during her sabbatical. With Garland's instruction, support and direction, they rehearsed at Alexandra Neighbourhood House in Kitsilano.[11] The Centre's director, Patrick Lyndon, was also supportive of their endeavour: "Look at Iris Garland's dance section. Her students have reached the point where they want to set up their own company, independent of the university. I'm thrilled. That's what we want."[12]

Savannah (then Elaine) Walling and Terry Hunter are notable alumni of the non-credit dance workshop who met in SFU's mime troupe and soon teamed up with Jamieson. The three developed their love of dance, forged a lifelong friendship and went on to co-found, along with others, Terminal City Dance (later known as Terminal City Dance Research) in 1976.[13] It was an influential collective that also served to provide a space for other artists to rehearse and create. Their studio in Chinatown became a hub of creative activity, and Hunter and Walling went on to found Vancouver Moving Theatre in 1983. Their artistic influence in East Vancouver endures today: their Downtown Eastside Heart of the City Festival and their community-engaged collaborative arts practice bring together artists from all walks of life and cultural traditions. Hunter and Walling have also gained national recognition for this work, including being appointed Members of the Order of Canada.

Walling found her way to SFU because she was looking for a job; she didn't expect to be drawn into the arts scene on campus and for it to radically change the direction of her life. "Although I was never a registered student at Simon Fraser University," says Walling, "my life has been interwoven with it."[14] She had moved to Canada with her first husband, resisting the war in Vietnam, with a degree in anthropology from Stanford University and no intentions to get involved in the arts, aside from continuing folk dancing.[15] "After I got a job as a library clerk at Simon Fraser University on Burnaby Mountain, I enrolled in the non-credit dance workshop that I discovered," says Walling. "My first teacher was Anna Wyman, who replaced Iris Garland who was on sabbatical, and I continued with Iris Garland after she returned. These free workshops attracted dancers of all skill levels from across the city. Such an exciting opportunity and life-gift when I think back to those days."[16] Walling went on to study dance in New York and teach dance as a sessional instructor at SFU.

Hunter came to SFU in 1969 to study geography and political science but was soon drawn into the arts scene:

> I was walking by the theatre; there was a sign outside that said, "audition at two o'clock," and I thought, "Well, I've always wanted to do that, and I'm looking for a job, so I'll come back at two o'clock." I came back and did the audition, and I got a part. They told us to come back next week or whenever rehearsal was, and I remember during a break I was sitting there with one of the other actors, and I said to him, "So when do we get paid?" He looked at me and laughed. He said, "Paid, man? This is a workshop. We don't get paid for this!"[17]

Although Hunter had his first taste of on-stage performance in a theatre production—*Chronicles of Hell* directed by Owen Foran—he easily found his way into mime. He then turned to dance after he met Walling in 1971 and began appearing in her works, before collaborating with her on choreography. He recalls the first time he encountered dance on campus:

> I remember walking into the theatre, I think it was a Phyllis Lamhut summer intensive workshop. Savannah Walling was one of the participants, and Karen Jamieson was another. I remember being fascinated by what the dancers were doing and thinking, wow, people actually make a living doing this, something that I love doing in the pub. People are actually making a living doing this and studying it and creating actual choreography. That really fascinated me, because I was not aware of modern dance at all before that. Seeing that for the first time at SFU was really fascinating, very inspiring.[18]

He soon left his academic pursuits behind to focus on the arts. "Simon Fraser provided the opportunity for me to become involved in the arts, and it

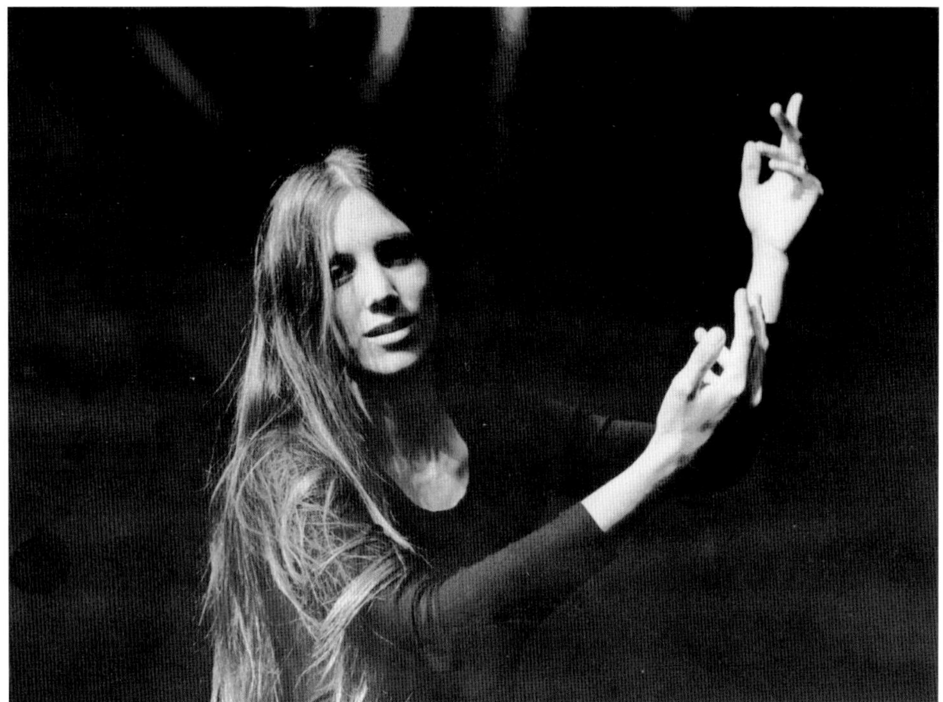
Savannah Walling performing with the SFU Dance Workshop. *SFU Archives*

became, for me, a lot more interesting than academics. It was something that I really enjoyed, and I got a lot of meaning and pleasure out of doing it."[19]

In 1974, after spending a few years studying dance in New York, Karen Jamieson came back to teach dance at SFU alongside Iris Garland, and she remembers teaching athletes in the kinesiology department. "The athletes were urged to take dance so they could get a little more flexible because they were subject to groin injuries. It was fun, but, ultimately, I didn't really want to teach at university. I wanted to go to the big bad world and be a professional."[20] Jamieson established her company, Karen Jamieson Dance, in 1983. Since then, she has gained national recognition for her work, including being inducted into the Canadian Dance Hall of Fame. Her work *Sisyphus* (1983) is acknowledged as a top ten "Canadian Choreographic Masterwork" of the twentieth century by Dance Collection Danse.[21]

Jamieson remembers her time at SFU fondly: "There was a spirit of inquiry and of experimentation; a spirit of you can do anything you want, as opposed to the more rigid sense of what was possible in the professional dance world. It was a wild and woolly time."[22] Jamieson and Walling collaborated on many works while at SFU, including a concert featuring *Two Ladies*, choreographed by Jamieson and danced by Walling and Mauryne Allan, in 1975. The piece

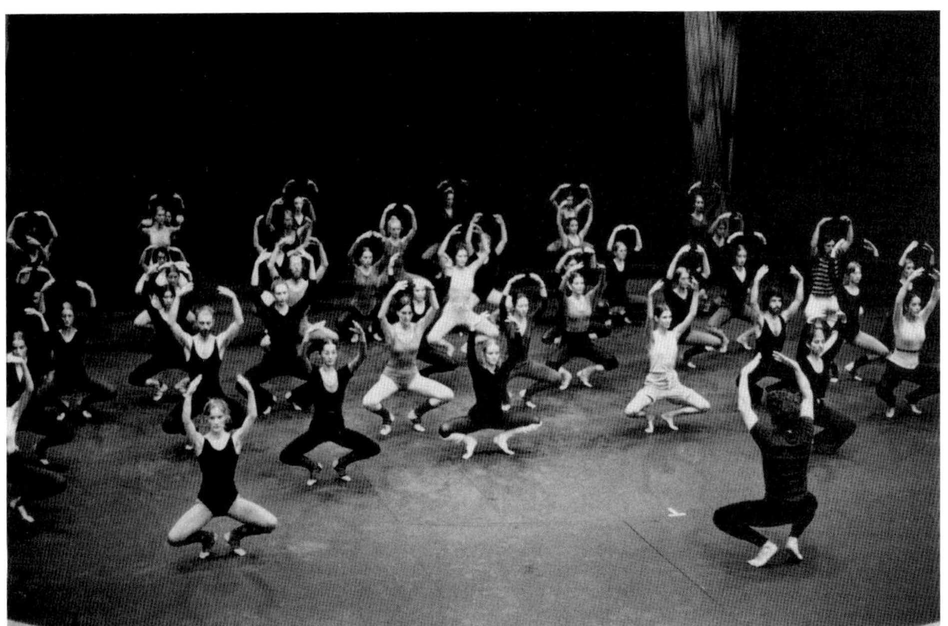

Dan Wagoner leading a masterclass in the SFU Theatre in 1975. *SFU Archives*

was accompanied by Stravinsky's "Elegie," which was played by guest artist Philippe Etter, violinist with the Purcell String Quartet.[23]

A Catalyst for Collaboration

The SFU Theatre was home to countless dance performances during the university's first ten years; it served as classroom, rehearsal space and performance venue for experimental, interdisciplinary work. It didn't matter if you had any prior dance training; all students needed was a desire to learn and a passion for movement. "I do remember that the atmosphere in those early years in the theatre and around the theatre was welcoming and hugely inclusive," says Walling. "The non-credit program was free for everybody in the city. So that meant it was drawing dancers, theatre artists, and others from all areas. They were coming from a whole lot of different movement backgrounds, and they were hungry for the accessible programs and the high-quality instruction of guest artists that were being brought in and the dance intensives that were happening. We were always being exposed to these multi-art influences and cross-disciplinary exploration."[24] Because the theatre was shared with all the arts disciplines, the space served as a catalyst for collaboration with students spending their free time there and watching many free performances.

And there was always something happening. As James Barber writes, "I cannot remember ever seeing the theatre without an almost packed house, evenings, lunchtimes and weekends, and there are more variations of theatre performed than anywhere else. People go to look, and they leave as they should leave, in some way affected by what they have seen. And nobody in the theatre appears really to care whether the audiences like them or not, so long as they do not ignore them. Which is what a theatre is for."[25]

An example of cross-disciplinary work is *Tubule* by Mary Staton, a visiting artist from New York, which was performed in 1968. The "three-dimensional film-dance" had dancers creating sculptures out of polyurethane tubes, and Staton's solo was accompanied by a film of SFU's architecture created by the SFU Film Workshop. Sometimes, the performances also made use of the interesting architectural spaces outdoors. In 1972, a press release described a spring performance of the dance workshop choreographed by Iris Garland, Zella Wolofsky, John Lunam and Douglas Super as "an outdoor, progressive dance programme" that "will begin under the Rotunda in the Transportation Centre and progress across the campus utilizing the architecture and outdoor space as settings for their dances. From the Rotunda, the dancers will move to the fountain, the steps of the academic quadrangle, the reflecting pond, and the mound. The audience is invited to travel with the dancers."[26]

In *Choros*, choreographed by Garland and Mary Staton, dance was mixed with poetry, lights, and vocal and instrumental sound, as Wyman explained in his review: "Choristers bearing globular glowing-red bowls lit from inside by candles spoke the words, as Ron Wattier and Donna Wong danced the meaning… As the moods of the poetry changed, so did the colors on the screen and the tempo of the shadows' dance… and the effect these changes achieved was sometimes lightly lyrical and sometimes gently sad."[27]

International Choreographers at SFU

While SFU students were busy creating new dance works, renowned choreographers from New York were visiting to share their unique style in feature performances and inspire the next generation in workshops and masterclasses. Invited by Iris Garland and administrator Nini Baird, American modern dance heavyweights such as Martha Graham, Yvonne Rainer, Alwin Nikolais, Paul Taylor and Merce Cunningham all presented their work at SFU. The lasting influence of these visits is reflected in the current dance program, where many faculty teach modern dance styles pioneered by these artists. "Iris's influence

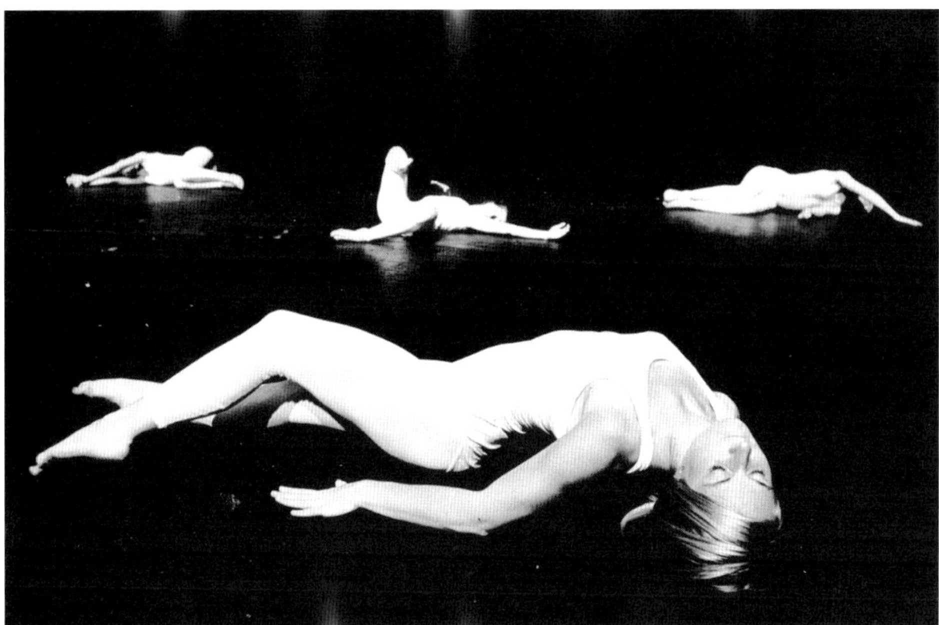

Judy Newbergher (foreground) performs in a piece with other members of the SFU Dance Workshop in 1969. *Tony Westman, SFU Archives*

was, I think, fundamental," explains Max Wyman. "She brought in all kinds of people from New York who showed our local people, our local students and people who were interested in the arts, that there were new ideas to be looked at. Nikolais worked a lot with improvisation and that was a big influence... There was a sense of people able to make a contribution to what was going on themselves as artists."[28]

Hunter also remembers the strong influence of New York-based modern dance at SFU:

> So here I am, heavily involved in the dance program as opposed to university, before it was a credited program. They were called workshops, and they were later in the day at four or five o'clock. It was a very active, thrilling place to be, very much driven and influenced by the Alwin Nikolais and Murray Louis school from New York, which was based a lot on composition and people creating their own work, choreographing. It was a very accessible form for people who, like myself, and Karen and Savannah, did not have training as children, to be able to enter the form and to quite quickly be able to be dancing and creating.[29]

Phyllis Lamhut, a disciple of Nikolais, brought her company from New York to perform at SFU. "I loved it up there," says Lamhut. "I just loved the university, everybody was really very nice, I love the area." She adds with a laugh, "I was going to buy a house. I just thought the university was refreshing."[30] In 1973, Lamhut returned to teach a four-week workshop that was intended to, according to a press release, "awaken the senses in relation to motion and to stimulate through creative effort."[31] Alongside visiting artists from out of town were impressive local guest instructors, including Anna Wyman, Norbert Vesak and Karen Uretsky Hering.

Judy Newbergher remembers her time as a student in the dance program: "My first encounter with a professional 'visionary arts dancer' was in the Aesthetic Forms of Human Movement course with Iris Garland," she says. "She showed her students how she interpreted a world of possibility and of the probable. She helped develop pathways of personal energy for things I did not understand and could not describe." The class was also unique in that it was not required that students have dance training. "For those of us who did not have classical ballet backgrounds," says Newbergher, "improvisational dance had become a quest for enlightenment and self-realization using personal visionary and interpretive disciplines." In 1969, Newbergher met Yvonne Rainer and began to look at modern dance in a new way. "I experienced a time, a place and a space where I was becoming more expressive, more interpretive," she says. "Dance was becoming therapeutic, empowering, enabling and opened up information so different from my usual frame of reference."[32]

In 1966, Merce Cunningham and John Cage visited SFU for a public performance and lecture. In 1969, Garland planned to bring Cunningham back to campus for a four-week summer residency including classes, lecture-demonstrations, performances and choreographic development, but the plan fell through due to lack of funding. As Wyman explained in a *Vancouver Sun* article, the Canada Council turned it down because their priority was funding Canadian companies.[33] Cunningham's residency would have been a welcome taste of current modern dance to infuse the local dance scene with new influences.

Local dance companies and those from across Canada also presented their works at SFU, including Vancouver's Paula Ross Dance Company, Toronto Dance Theatre and Entre Six (Montreal). Folk and classical dance were also represented, with visits from the Cosmopolitan Folk Dance Ensemble, Chetna and Usha Thakore (classical Indian dance), and Teo and Isabel Morca (flamenco).[34] In 1970, the Don Redlich Dance Company brought *Slouching Towards Bethlehem* to the SFU Theatre. As Wyman described the performance, "It follows the contemporary trend toward deliberate audience bewilderment and hyper-stimulation through the frantic juxtaposition of multiple images in multiple media." Such companies continued to bring avant-garde work not only to SFU but to the broader dance community in the city. "Wednesday night's performance by the Don Redlich company was an important event in local dance circles," said Wyman, "—and Iris Garland and the SFU dance department should be congratulated for arranging his visit."[35]

Credit Programs: A Serious Academic Pursuit

Up on the mountain, in the late sixties, the open, experimental, come-one, come-all spirit of the non-credit Centre for Communications and the Arts was a pioneering force that produced exciting works, inspired a generation of dancers, and made a lasting mark on the city's arts ecology. The magic of those early years, however, would soon come to an end. The Centre suffered from unstable support from the university administration, and, by 1971, the senate had decided that the Faculty of Interdisciplinary Studies would have a new department of fine and performing arts that would offer credit programs—although it took a few more years before it was up and running. As Alana Gerecke explains: "From the beginning, SFU had a complicated relationship with its fine and performing arts program: on one hand, the university was accommodating, encouraging and respectful, and yet, as Alderson puts it, 'the arts were subject to academic scorn—as they always are.'"[36]

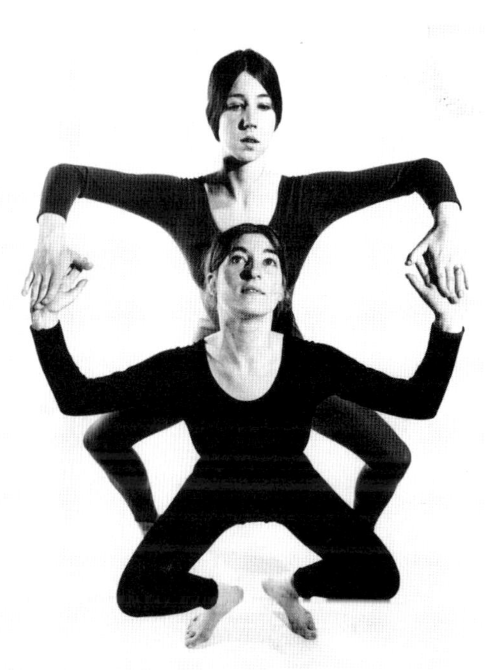

Karen Rimmer (above) and Edith Feinstein (below) in *Experiment at Noon* in 1970, a multi-media improvisational event created by the SFU Dance Workshop, SFU Electronic Music Workshop and other members of the university Arts Centre community. *Tony Westman, SFU Archives*

The early seventies were a time of tension at the university as artists and administrators debated what should be included in credit programming, with some resisting the changes in form and content. Gerecke notes that the art coming out of the Centre eventually merged with the work produced in credit programs, resulting in some of the original energy being lost, along with some of the artists who craved a less institutional environment.[37]

A modernist debate about technique versus pure creativity was playing out in the early seventies as the department struggled to settle on what type of courses would be counted for credit. Its first director, Evan Alderson, said that the department was founded during a passing "modernist moment": what began as a grand interdisciplinary vision became, in practicality, a department offering separate programs in each artistic discipline.[38] Canada's first university dance program was established at York University in 1970, and in 1975 SFU became the first university in Western Canada to offer credit courses in dance, in the new Centre for the Arts. Finally, in 1980, students could pursue a BA with a major in dance at SFU. As Iris Garland wrote in 1979:

> Attaining the stature of an independent area of study within the university is an important recent milestone in the growth of dance in the Canadian cultural scene. At this writing there are only three other such programs: York University, University of Waterloo, and Concordia University, although several other universities are in the process of planning major programs in dance. The trend augers well for the art as it broadens the scope of study for the prospective artist that is not readily available in an isolated studio or even conservatory situation.[39]

Dance, no longer considered a frivolous pastime, had finally become a serious academic program amidst an interdisciplinary school that offered dance students the opportunity to study a broad range of electives.

When Iris Garland hired Santa Aloi in 1976 as a member of the faculty of Dance, the momentum to create a credit program was growing. Aloi was eager to leave New York and move to Vancouver, where she would be instrumental, alongside Garland, in establishing the credit program. As Gerecke explains, "Whereas the Centre's non-credit offerings were sometimes perceived as frivolous and a financial drain, credit-based arts courses would bring in tuition for each registered student and would validate the fine and performing arts programs by producing an annual cohort of graduates, a barometer of success within the structure of the university."[40]

In 1975, a program development committee was appointed, says Gerecke, that, according to its chair, Evan Alderson, was meant to "draw on the strengths that are already in place [with the non-credit program] and do something interesting academically."[41] The process was long and not without its obstacles, such as Alderson questioning Aloi on the need to teach dance technique. She explained that it was foundational to improvisation and composition, which were fundamental cornerstones to a dance curriculum—to create new art in a given form you must learn about its antecedents.[42] Garland and Aloi co-designed SFU's credit program in dance and lobbied for its existence at a time when the government of BC was careful not to allow duplication of programs in the province. They had to show that SFU's program was unique in its interdisciplinary approach and focus on choreography, unlike any other dance program.

SFU's enduring commitment to interdisciplinarity and community engagement set the stage for renowned modern dance artists to visit SFU and for students interested in both a university education and a career in dance to join the program.

As Max Wyman says in his introduction to this book, "Every time an SFU dance class graduated, we used to joke, three new dance companies sprang up." This still rings true. To date, half of the ten recipients of the Iris Garland Emerging Choreographer Award, established in 2002 and administered by the Dance Centre to recognize exceptional choreographic ability, are alumni of the SFU dance program, including Sara Coffin, Vanessa Goodman, Deanna Peters, Shion Skye Carter and Anya Saugstad. The broad reach and impact of SFU's dance program is demonstrated by the sheer number of alumni, students and faculty populating local dance productions. Today you would be hard pressed to attend a contemporary dance performance in Vancouver that did not involve at least one artist with a connection to SFU. This enduring legacy continues to grow as each new class of dance students graduates and joins their predecessors to make their own mark in the dance world.

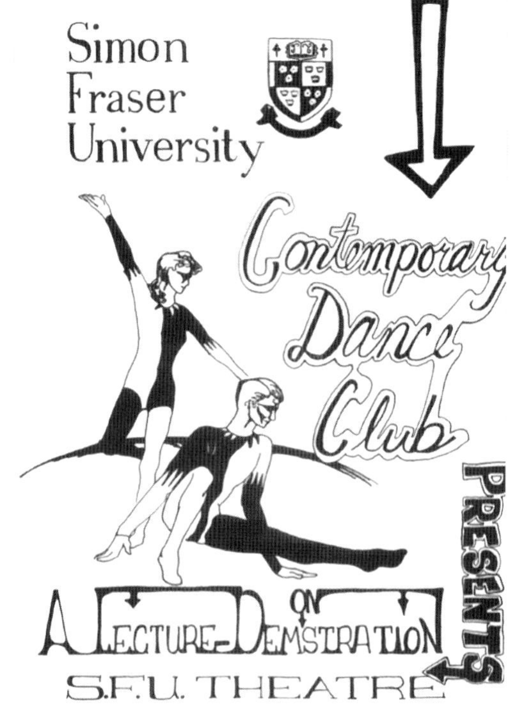

A hand-drawn poster advertises one of the first public events held by the SFU Contemporary Dance Club (later known as the SFU Dance Workshop). *SFU Archives*

Chapter 5: Sound and Music

Listening on the Mountain

SOUNDSCAPES TO OPERA

compiled by Carole Gerson

DURING ITS FIRST DECADE, THE SFU CAMPUS RESOUNDED WITH MUSIC. Everyone enjoyed frequent concerts by touring popular and classical musicians, as well as productions featuring students, some of whom performed outdoors. In the SFU Theatre, there were usually two or three musical events each week, ranging from folk soloists to significant classical groups, from expected pieces by artists in residence to utterly unexpected performers such as the Mennonite Bible Choir from Winnipeg (February 4, 1966), Quebec chanteuse Monique Leyrac (September 30, 1967) and the popular local band Mother Tucker's Yellow Duck (February 13, 1968). Many of these events were sponsored by organizations other than the Centre for Communications and the Arts.

On the one hand, the campus's thriving new age electronic composers, such as Phillip Werren, alongside the development of sound studies, pioneered by Murray Schafer, contributed to SFU's avant-garde identity. On the other, abiding interest in early music fostered the Madrigal Singers, workshops with ancient instruments, multidisciplinary events such as Fourteenth Century Week, and a memorable production of Henry Purcell's seventeenth-century opera *Dido and Aeneas*. As well, the SFU Student Society frequently brought mainstream rock, jazz and folk musicians to campus, as detailed by Christine Hearn in chapter two. This rich aural environment contributed significantly to the vitality and social ambiance of campus life. Although Schafer left SFU in 1975, his approach to sound and music established an ongoing climate of innovation that flourished under the leadership of composer Barry Truax, who had joined SFU in 1973 and would become a much-honoured professor in what are now known as the School of Communication and the School for the Contemporary Arts.

R. Murray Schafer and the World Soundscape Project

by Barry Truax

The Sonic Environment: Archiving Soundscapes

The development of the basic concept of the World Soundscape Project (WSP) and its establishment by R. Murray Schafer occurred at Simon Fraser University during the late 1960s and early 1970s. It grew out of Schafer's initial attempt to draw attention to the sonic environment through a course at SFU in noise pollution, as well as from his personal distaste for the more raucous aspects of Vancouver's rapidly changing soundscape. This work resulted in two small educational booklets, *The New Soundscape* (1969) and *The Book of Noise* (1970), plus a compendium of Canadian noise bylaws (1972). However, the negative approach that noise pollution inevitably fosters—always being against something—pointed to a lack of knowledge about what one might achieve as a positive example. It also proved not to engender enthusiasm in students, but rather cynicism and a fatalistic attitude that nothing much could be done. A more positive approach had to be found, with the first attempt being Schafer's extended 1973 essay "The Music of the Environment," which describes examples of acoustic design, good and bad, drawing largely on examples from literature.

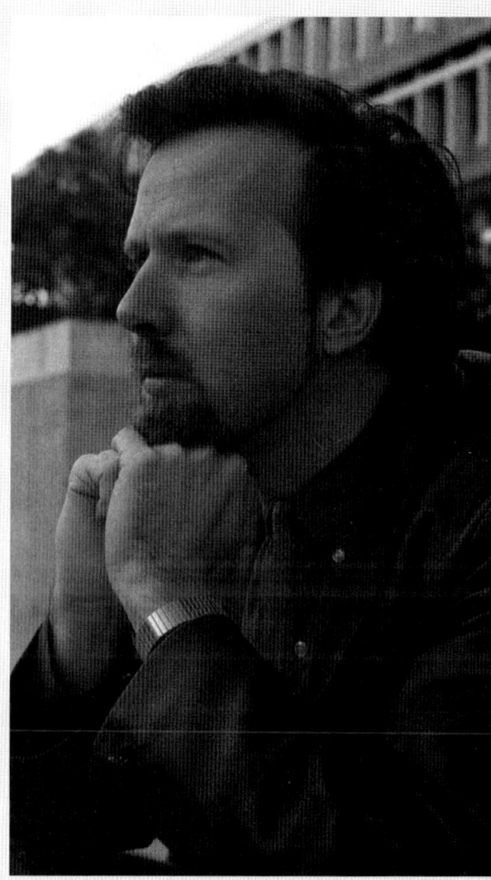

Murray Schafer.
SFU Archives

Schafer, the charter faculty member at SFU who established the Electronic Music Studio in the basement of the SFU Theatre, moved the studio to the newly formed Department of Communication Studies in 1971 and renamed it the Sonic Research Studio. His call for the establishment of the WSP was answered by a group of highly motivated young composers and students. Supported by the Donner Canadian Foundation, the group embarked first on a detailed study of the immediate locale, published as *The Vancouver Soundscape* in 1973, followed by a cross-Canada recording tour by Bruce Davis and Peter Huse. In 1975, supported by another research grant, Schafer led a larger group on a European tour that included lectures and workshops in several major cities and a research project that made detailed investigations of the soundscape of five villages (one in each of Sweden,

Germany, Italy, France and Scotland). The tour completed the WSP's analogue tape library, which included more than 300 tapes recorded in Canada and Europe with a stereo Nagra. All the tapes have been catalogued by Bruce Davis and Hildegard Westerkamp (who went on to her own career as a composer and author), with their subject matter classified and converted into an online digital database, along with numerous additions and more recent material.

The work also produced two publications, a narrative account of the trip called *European Sound Diary* and a detailed soundscape analysis called *Five Village Soundscapes* (1977). Schafer's definitive soundscape text, *The Tuning of the World* (1977), and my reference work for acoustic and soundscape terminology, the *Handbook for Acoustic Ecology* (1978), completed the publication phase of the original project.

Soundscape Composition

Although the principal work of the WSP was to document and archive soundscapes, to describe and analyze them, and to promote increased public awareness of environmental sound through listening and critical thinking, a parallel stream of compositional activity also emerged that created, perhaps less intentionally, what I have called the genre of the "soundscape composition." What also characterizes it most definitively is the presence of recognizable environmental sounds and contexts, the purpose being to invoke the listener's associations, memories and imagination related to the soundscape.

The mandate to involve the listener in an essential part of the composition, namely to complete its network of meanings, grew naturally out of the pedagogical intent of the project to foster soundscape awareness. At first, the simple exercise of "framing" environmental sound by taking it out of context (where often it is ignored) and directing the listener's attention to it in a publication or public presentation, meant that the compositional technique involved was minimal, involving only selection, transparent editing and unobtrusive crossfading. In retrospect this "neutral" use of the material established one end of the continuum occupied by soundscape compositions, namely those that are the closest to the original environment, or what might be called "phonography" or "found compositions." The aesthetic proposed by John Cage of treating any such material as music can be justified in that it emphasizes that the listening process is musical, not necessarily the inherent content. However, the WSP avoided proclaiming any such distinctions by, firstly, not attributing these "compositions" to a single individual (instead, they were collectively authored by the group) and, secondly, by emphasizing the educational rather than the possible aesthetic intent of the exercise.

A subtle but important extension of this practice occurred with the "Entry to the Harbour" sequence from the recordings of *The Vancouver Soundscape*: here, in order to simulate the experience of entering Vancouver Harbour on a boat, past the various foghorns and buoys, it was necessary not only to compress the event in time, but also to mix together all of the separately recorded components, with appropriately engineered illusions of their approaching and receding. A recording of an actual boat trip would have been dominated by motor noise that would mask the desired sound signals and natural sounds. Of course, this abandoning of the ear as a navigational aid in favour of modern electronic instrumentation and visual orientation is indeed symptomatic of the modern experience, which leads away from soundscape awareness, and historical examples drawn from aural history accounts with boat captains were reported in the written document. But the purpose of the composition was to stimulate soundscape awareness by presenting a possible, if simulated, aural experience. By being potentially familiar but strangely imaginary at the same time, the composition invoked various levels of listening activity, ranging from identification to symbolic communication. The piece begins with a resonant, low-pitched diaphone, suggesting solitude, darkness and primal nature, and ends with an unloading sequence and people retrieving baggage in a small, confined room with bright high-frequency scrapes and a squeaky door. This form suggests a larger metaphorical transition for both the city and the individual that is symbolized by the simulated voyage. Every sound can be heard as it was originally recorded, but the discourse of the resulting work is not merely documentary because of its various levels of possible meaning.

Soundscapes of Canada

Between the Canadian and European recording tours in 1974, the WSP members assembled a series of ten one-hour radio programs for the CBC called *Soundscapes of Canada*. These included, and for the first time essentially defined, the entire range of soundscape compositions, from naturalistic documentaries that were collectively authored through to "abstracted" compositions attributed to individual composers. In the former category were documentaries that were narrated in a fairly traditional way, such as "Signals, Keynotes and Soundmarks," as well as a set of listening exercises conducted by Schafer, through to "Six Themes of the Soundscape," which substitutes three independent voices for narration, each presenting either a factual, subjective or literary historical perspective on the theme in question.

From the point of view of soundscape composition, the most remarkable documentary was the collectively authored "Summer Solstice," in which two minutes representing each hour of a midsummer day and night, as recorded beside a pond near a rural monastery outside Vancouver, were combined into a fifty-minute composition. Although it was introduced with narration and examples in the broadcast version, the piece itself includes only minimal narration in the form of a verbal identification of each hour (done during the original recording). Edits are transparent, with no mixing, so the effect is a compressed span of time that an individual would seldom, if ever, experience directly. An expanded version of the morning section, called "Dawn Chorus," was also made. The choice of time and location was designed to present to the listener what might be called the natural acoustic ecology, disturbed only minimally by the monastery bell on the one hand, and aircraft and distant train horns on the other. The most striking example of the intricacy of that ecology was observed at dawn when the aural "collision" of high-pitched frogs with the dawn chorus of birds in the same frequency range was avoided by the cessation of the former. This is a small example of what Bernard Krause terms the "niche hypothesis" of natural species and their acoustic communication patterns, where each species occupies a specific frequency band or, as in the solstice example, a different time frame. The composition of the "Summer Solstice" documentary, then, was largely realized by natural forces, with the studio manipulation intended to evoke an appreciation of that ecology.

Two interesting, and more humanly composed, documentaries by poet and composer Peter Huse made effective use of field-recorded language material. These are both organized from the east to west, the first being "Soundmarks of Canada," which features the unique sound signals of the country, identified by locals or the recordists themselves, and the second being "Directions," which is entirely composed of fragments of conversation that the recordists had with locals while asking for directions. The close juxtaposition of sound signals and local dialects provides an aural map of the country that is experienced within a short space of time.

Howard Broomfield assembled an even denser collage of found radio material in his "Radio Program About Radio Programs." In this sometimes-bizarre piece, the composer plays on the simultaneity on the airwaves of unrelated material, using both historical and current examples, as well as the habit of radio to jump cut between items in a surreal fashion. The piece treats the disembodied soundscape of the broadcast medium as an environment with its own conventions and syntax, which the composer gently satirizes. Another experiment in sudden juxtapositions is my "Maritime Sound Diary," in which three "stories" taken from three original recordings are interleaved by an automated signal switching process that, instead of crossfading the material, jumps into the next sequence in a series of short, then increasing, durations. The points of transition throw both soundscapes into high relief, and the narrative line is maintained when the listener picks up each story later, despite the gaps that have intervened.

Several pieces within the set went further than those described already by using transformations of the chosen environmental sounds. Here the full range of analogue studio techniques came into play, with an inevitable increase in the level of abstraction. However, the intent was always to reveal a deeper level of signification inherent within the sound and to invoke the listener's semantic associations without obliterating the sound's recognizability. These pieces include Bruce Davis's poetic documentary "Bells of Percé," where clouds of filtered bells and voice fragments symbolize the memories surrounding the historic bells in the Gaspé region of Quebec as colourfully described by the parish priest. Davis's pair of works, "Play" and "Work," include more elaborate rhythmic and timbral alterations of the material that highlight the character of the sounds accompanying these two classes of human activity. And finally, my "Soundscape Study" takes a set of sounds with archetypal imagery—for instance, footsteps, a clock ticking and chiming, water gurgling, a tree being chopped and church bells ringing the Angelus—and subjects them to a series of transformations in speed, pitch and textural density (usually independently). The piece invites the listener to follow the resulting changes in morphology and imagery that the transformations produce, and hence to become more aware of how these variables condition our habitual responses to environmental sound.

Schafer himself did not produce any soundscape compositions with environmental sound directly, the exception being the collaboratively produced (with Bruce Davis and Brian Fawcett) quadraphonic tape *Okeanos* (1971), which predates the WSP and is based on literary imagery of the sea. However, soundscape concepts influence many of his later instrumental and vocal works. Perhaps most strikingly, he has created site-specific works, such as *Music for Wilderness Lake*, which takes place at dawn and dusk, and several musical theatre works for outdoor or unconventional performance environments.

Schafer left SFU in 1975 to pursue his compositional career independently, but the legacy of the WSP has continued and broadened ever since, first in the teaching program in the School of Communication, now expanded with international webinar courses that I have designed, and secondly with the formation of the World Forum for Acoustic Ecology, an international federation of soundscape practitioners, among many other projects. In fact, in various circles, SFU during this initial 1965–1975 period is recognized for its pioneering role in acoustic ecology and soundscape composition.

Carole Gerson

Music New and Old

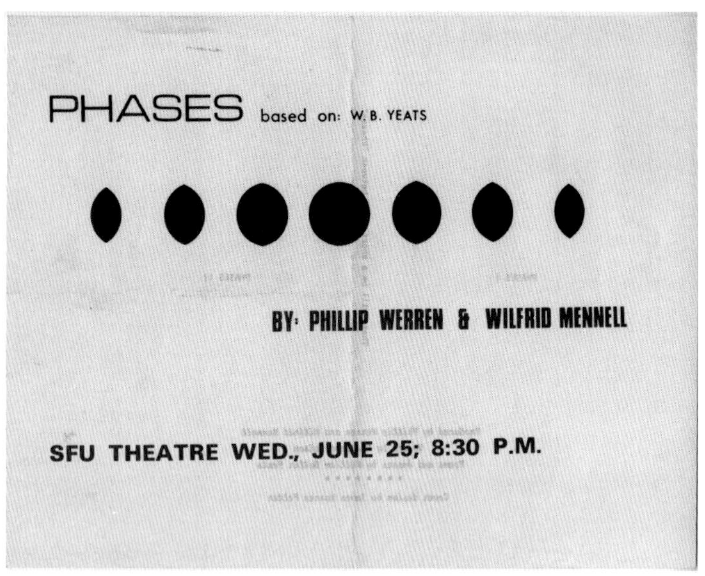

Phillip Werren and Wilfrid Mennell's *Phases* was produced in 1969. *SFU Archives*

Across the creative spectrum, music at SFU was distinguished by fascination with the very new and the very old. During the 1960s, most Canadian campuses enjoyed the flourishing musical scene of the times, reflected in the folk music, protest songs and rock bands that characterized the revolutionary spirit of a vocal and rebellious generation. Whereas such activity was often regarded as student entertainment, at SFU artists in residence and some members of faculty seriously engaged with the frontiers of new music, which were facilitated by quickening advances in technology. Others sought new connections with the arts of the pre-modern era. Some of this activity is described in chapter three, such as the creative collaborations of charter student Wilfrid Mennell and resident artist Phillip Werren, in their creation of pieces that also involved theatre participants, such as *Cascando* (1968) and *Phases* (1969).

Contemporary Music: Phillip Werren

Composer Phillip Werren, in residence from 1968 to 1971, was known for his extensive collaboration with artists in other media, namely dance, music, theatre, film and visual arts. He produced a long list of integrated projects with filmmakers, dancers, mimes and actors. Results included the creation of music for three films (*Leanings* with Mark Dolgoy and the SFU Mime Troupe; *Migrations* with David Rimmer; and *Vortex*, incorporated into *Aaeron*, with Al Razutis). They also include music for three theatre productions: *The Horse* with John Juliani and Peter Hay; "Heroica Overture" for *How the Company Went to an Island, What They Saw and How They Came Back* with Michael Bawtree and Brian Freeman; and *Zeme* with Robin Patterson, Richard Bolivar and the SFU Mime Troupe. Werren was also involved in numerous dance productions, including *Mediums* with dancers Edith Feinstein and Karen Rimmer and filmmaker David Rimmer; *To Phyllis*, commissioned by New York visitor Phyllis Lamhut (in residence at SFU during the summer of 1970); and "Polish Wedding

Music," a score for *Revelations*, choreographed by Iris Garland for the SFU Dance Workshop.

In a more literary vein, Werren worked with student Wilfrid Mennell on *Cascando*, a sound-space experiment based on a radio play by Samuel Beckett (1968). The following year, English professor Philippa Polson collaborated with Werren on the three-part *Phases* project, which involved the poetry of W.B. Yeats. Many of Werren's compositions, including *Phases*, were compiled and issued as a four-LP set in 1971 with input from other SFU practitioners: a cover from James Warren Felter's painting *HUAN* and a photograph of the composer by Tony Westman. When this set was digitized and reissued in 2014, the album was described as "a nugget of Canadian psychedelic avant-garde history, up there with the early works of Bill Bissett, The Nihilist Spasm Band, and Intersystems. Also in line with early American works by Robert Ashley, Ted Dockstader, and Gordon Mumma."[1]

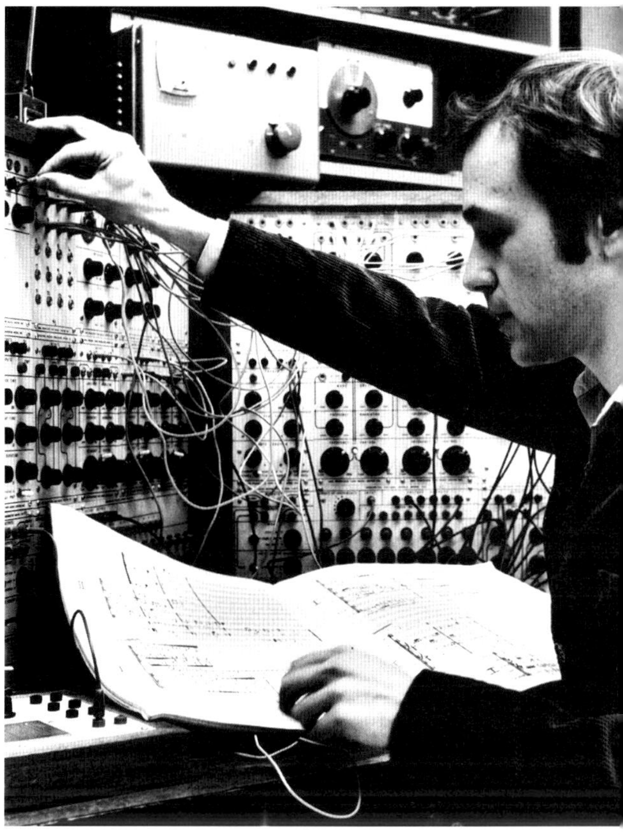

Composer Phillip Werren, in residence from 1968 to 1971, is known for his extensive collaboration with artists in other media. *Tony Westman, SFU Archives*

The Purcell String Quartet

In the CCA, Nini Baird expertly facilitated a sequence of resident musicians. The impacts of this program ranged from teaching students to play an instrument (the recorder) to housing the Purcell String Quartet. Founded in 1969, the quartet's wide repertoire included classical and contemporary works. It was active until 1991 and enjoyed a ten-year residency at SFU from 1972 to 1982, funded by the Canada Council, the Leon and Thea Koerner Foundation, the university and individual donors. The ensemble's presence enhanced both the campus on the hill and the wider community in BC and beyond, and not only with their performances. For instance, the PSQ commissioned Bruce Davis, a student in the communications department, to compose a piece that won a grand prize of $3,000 in the first national CBC–Canada Council Awards for Young Composers competition, announced in January 1974.[2] The records of the Purcell String Quartet are now housed in the SFU Library. In 1974, CCA publicist Mary Trainer summarized the quartet's range of community impact, from remote communities to elite cultural contexts:

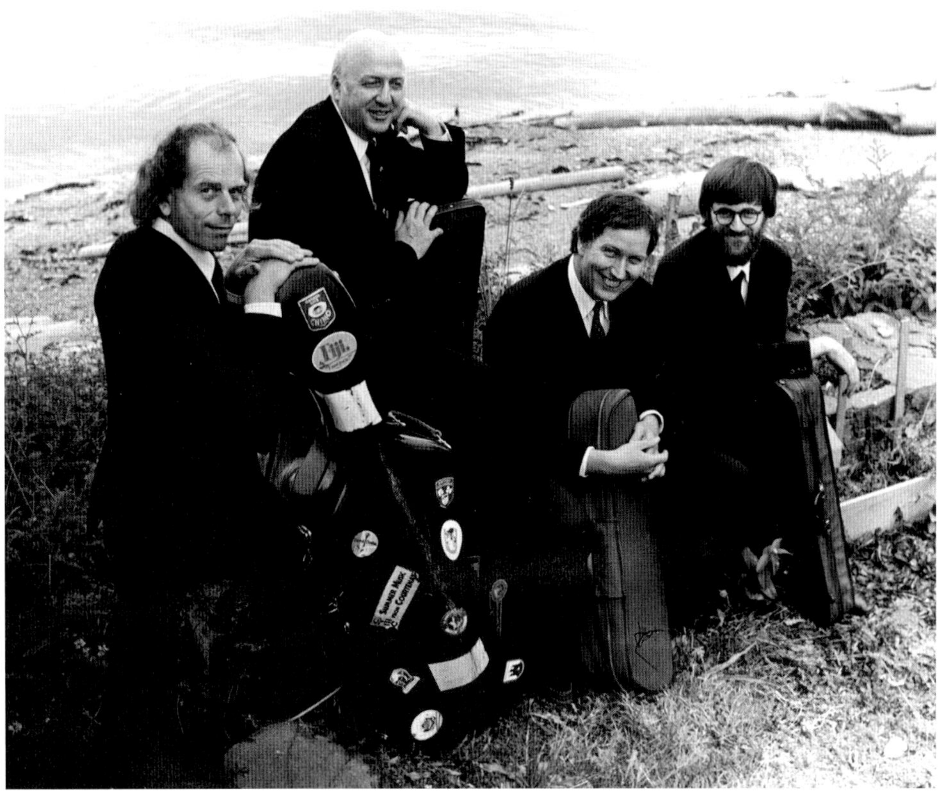

The Purcell String Quartet enjoyed a long association with SFU, from 1972 to 1982. *SFU Archives*

They've performed at weddings, in living rooms and open-air plazas. Their school concerts and workshops have taken them into band rooms, libraries, cafeterias and gymnasiums. The sounds of their music have filled the Simon Fraser pub. The Purcell String Quartet, based at Simon Fraser under the title "quartet in residence," is a breath of fresh air on the music scene of British Columbia. Standing up to take their bow are Ian Hampton (cello), Philippe Etter (viola), Norman Nelson (violin) and Fred Nelson (violin). The Nelsons are not related. Before moving to Simon Fraser the four were leading members of the Vancouver Symphony Orchestra. Aside from their international tours and local engagements, their residency at the University since September 1972 has made it possible for them to participate in "community outreach" programs in British Columbia. As a result, many small towns and isolated communities throughout the province, some as far as 1,500 miles [*sic*] from Vancouver, are now enjoying "live" classical and contemporary music...

The Quartet has had several pieces commissioned by the CBC and the Canada Council. Two of the works by contemporary Canadian composers, Graphic II (Harry Freedman) and Quartet No. 1 (R. Murray Schafer) have met with the most immediate audience appeal…

How have their performances been accepted outside Canada? Five of their commissioned works were performed to great acclaim at a special Canada Day concert in Canada House, London, last summer during the Quartet's second English tour (both were sponsored by the Department of External Affairs). R. Murray Schafer's Quartet No. 1 has become so popular with the BBC that it has been repeated six times.[3]

David Skulski

At SFU, interest in early music was bolstered by the presence of David Skulski. After occasional performances that began in 1969, he was an artist in residence from 1973 to 1976, working with the Madrigal Singers, giving workshops in the performance of early music and music history, and contributing lectures on music to the course on the Renaissance taught by professor Robin Blaser of the English department. Much as he enjoyed participating in various activities at SFU, Skulski recalls that his effort to teach the singing of madrigals to students in the tutorial for Blaser's course was "something of a disaster."[4]

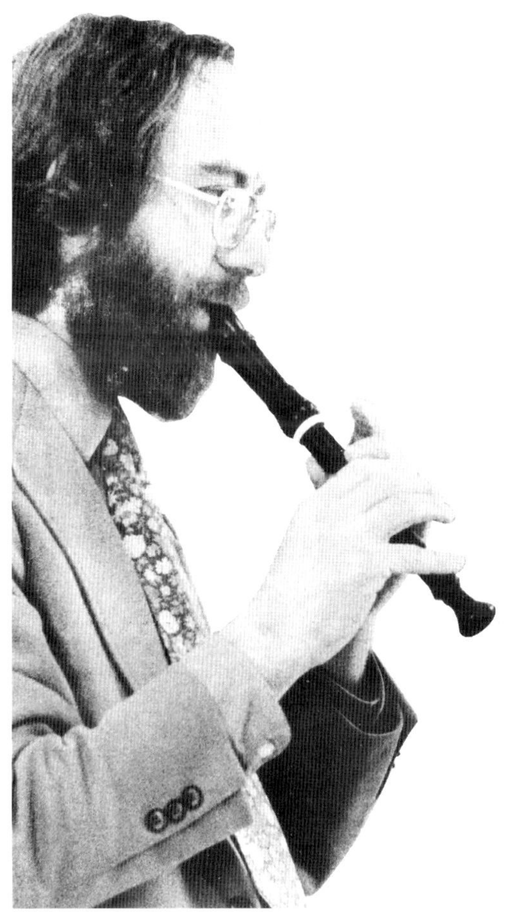

David Skulski contributed to the interest in early music at SFU. *SFU Archives*

Phyllis Mailing

During SFU's first decade, an interest in early music abounded, which was particularly intriguing on a campus known for radical creativity. Much of this interest was owed to mezzo-soprano Phyllis Mailing, who held the position of artist in residence from 1965 to 1967, and again from 1970 to 1975. Her interests ranged across the historical spectrum, and she achieved renown as an interpreter of new music, including works by Murray Schafer (to whom she was then married). Mary Trainer described Mailing's contributions preceding the landmark production of *Dido and Aeneas*:

She founded a choir which managed bravely to sing about peace and goodwill on earth while the University itself was going through that period known as "campus unrest." She taught music sightreading and helped launch the now highly successful Tuesday Lunch-Hour Concerts. The Madrigal Singers were created from the University Choir in 1970 to prepare for the World Shakespeare Congress at Simon Fraser a year later. The group met with outstanding success at the Congress and went on to receive acclaim throughout the Lower Mainland.[5]

Dido and Aeneas

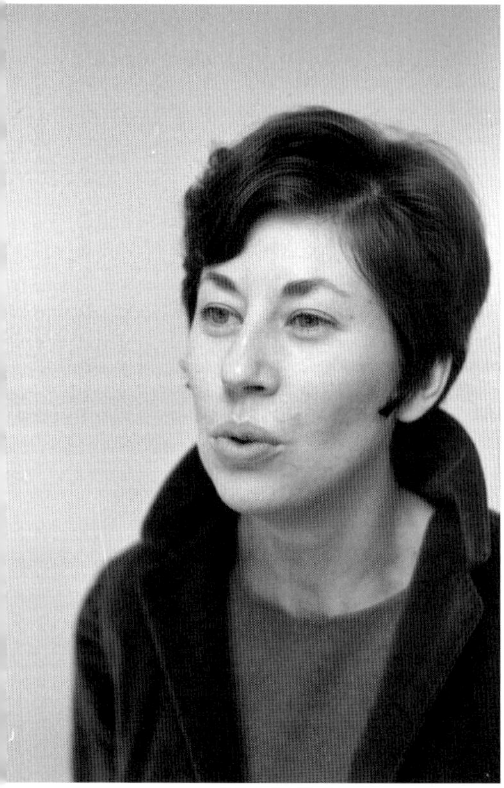

Phyllis Mailing.
SFU Archives

One of Mailing's most remarkable contributions to SFU's cultural impact was her musical direction of Henry Purcell's seventeenth-century opera *Dido and Aeneas*, performed in June 1973, in which she excelled in the starring role of Dido.

The following production notes have been excerpted and edited from the report on *Dido and Aeneas* in the SFU archives:

Early in 1973, Workshop Co-ordinator Tony Besant was approached by Phyllis Mailing and Michael Fletcher with the proposal to perform the opera *Dido and Aeneas*. It was decided that it could be done if financial limitations were imposed... On March 7 a meeting between Phyllis Mailing, Michael Fletcher, Cy Appleby and Tony Besant was held to discuss further the feasibility of actually producing the opera. An attempt at a first cost estimate turned out a figure of $10,625. It was decided that this cost was too high and should be cut to 3/4 that amount. The problems of booking rehearsal times in the theatre were discussed... An initial casting plan was put forward: 10 soloists, 10 dancers, 15 orchestra and 30 chorus. Iris Garland agreed to choreograph the dances; Michael Fletcher agreed to direct, in addition to playing the male lead Aeneas; Phyllis Mailing agreed to be the music coach as well as play the lead Dido, and Simon Streatfield agreed to conduct. Ticket prices were decided upon at one and two dollars, non-reserved seats. Michael Irwin agreed to be the stage manager for this show because of his abilities in reading music.

At the meeting of April 4, chaired by Tony Besant, who was acting as the producer, budget controller, referee and PR man, Martin Johnson presented his design and costume sketches, which all met with unanimous approval. It was questioned whether or not the size of the orchestra should be cut down, as an examination of the size of the orchestra pit determined that the pit could not hold 15 musicians and their instruments. It was suggested that a check be made with the Musicians Union and with Actors Equity regarding hiring procedures. On April 29 Tony Besant built a final budget estimate, which came to $7,500.

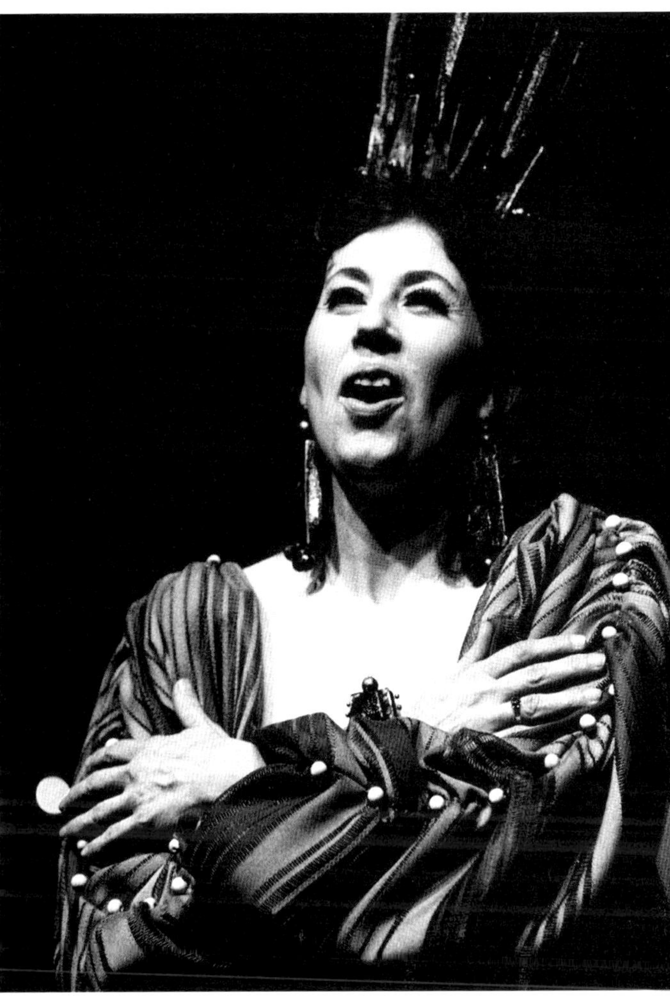

Phyllis Mailing starred as Dido in the well-reviewed production of Henry Purcell's *Dido and Aeneas* in June 1973. *Peter Higdon, SFU Archives*

Concerning the budget there were certain problems regarding hidden costs and charges. For example, the general lighting area was destroyed by the new lighting for *Dido and Aeneas*. The question arose, after the opera was over and the Dance show was being rehearsed, as to which show the costs of redoing the lights should be charged. Another question of charges arose concerning Martin Vicksten, the set constructor. It was undecided whether or not his services should be charged to the opera or to the theatre because he was the resident set constructor.

All in all, it was agreed that Simon Fraser's first attempt at such a production as *Dido and Aeneas* was a success not only in regard to the show itself but also in regard to the production end of the opera. Relatively few problems were encountered and most aspects of the production were handled efficiently and smoothly, with patience and professional concern from all.[6]

Former student Susan Baxter (then known as Susan Azima) describes her extensive involvement in this production:

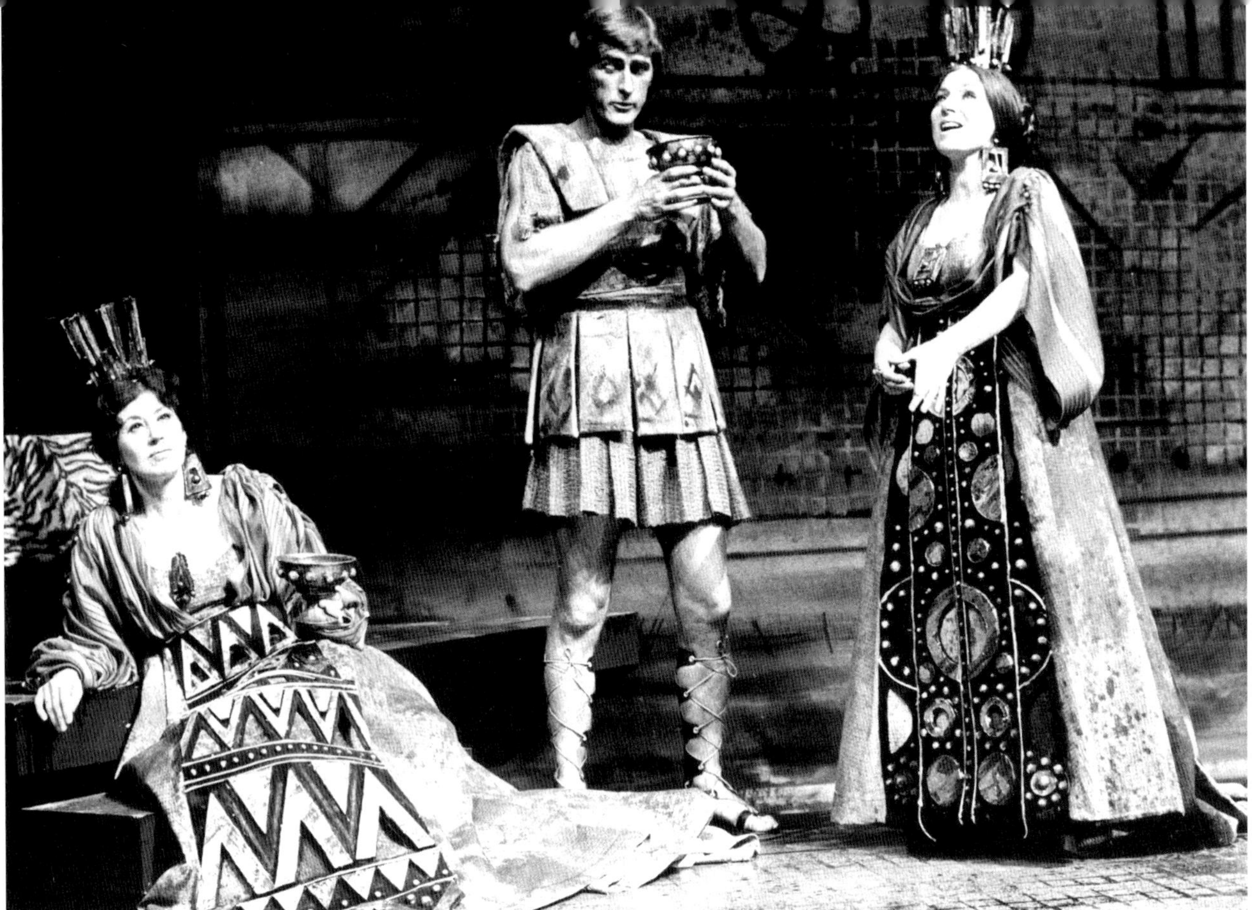

Phyllis Mailing as Dido, with a goblet in hand, Michael Fletcher as Aeneas and Margarita Noye as Belinda.
Peter Higdon, SFU Archives

In 1973, à la Benjamin Britten, Michael Fletcher decided we should end the year on a bang and put on an opera. As I recall there was some resistance from SFU, but Tony Besant was on board and it went ahead. *Dido and Aeneas*. Phyllis Mailing was Dido and Michael Fletcher, Aeneas. She was great; him, well, he was all right. Max Wyman wrote something about him being like a stiff GI Joe but otherwise raved about the production.

Every artistic part of SFU's Centre for the Arts was involved. There was a choir (who knew SFU had a choir?!) and Iris Garland's dance company; the orchestra was the Purcell String Quartet, and the conductor and keyboard player came from the VSO. They were expensive, so they pretty much showed up just for the tech rehearsal and the performances.

I was the production manager, so the budget was my domain. I was paid the princely sum of $500, which seemed like a fortune to me at the time. I had a tiny office in the bowels of the theatre; I suspect it had been a broom closet prior to this. I also had a huge bunch of keys hanging at my waist, and I felt very important striding about in my platform shoes.

Dido and Aeneas

CAST

Dido	Phyllis Mailing
Aeneas	Michael Fletcher
Belinda	Margarita Noye
2nd Woman	Lynda Boothby
Sorceress	Judith Chertkow
Singing Witches	Jill Karaim June Davis Rosalind Bell
Dancing Witches	Brenda Broughton Helga Johnson Sharman Smith
Attendant Women	Freddie Long Betsy O'Neill Sharon Verrall
Sailor (Singer)	David Karecki
Soldiers/Sailors (Dancers)	Bill Roberts Paul Vodak Dale Woodland

Chorus:

Keith Slessor	Elaine Dunn
Lawrence Boland	• Rosalind Bell
Al van Winckel	Kathleen Swink
Gordon Ambrose	Gigi Huxley
Andrew Yim	Liisa Fagerlind
• David Karecki	Cynde Grubis
Marilyn Cairns	• Jill Karaim
Gail Nash	• June Davis
Karen Jones	Susanne Lloyd
Ainslie Mills	

• See principles above (sailor, witches)

Torchbearers	Alan Davis Peter Murphy Roger Welch Dale Woodland

PRODUCTION

Director	Michael Fletcher
Musical Director	Phyllis Mailing
Conductor	Simon Streatfeild
Choreographer	Iris Garland
Stage Manager	Michael Irwin
Assistant Stage Manager	Susan Azima
Set Design	Martin Johnson
Costume Design	Martin Johnson
Lighting Design	Michael Irwin
Lighting Operator	Ken Didrich
Lighting Crew	Doug Alder Ann Roberts Susan Sherwood
Sound Operator	Doug Alder
Rehearsal Pianists	Arlie Thompson (staging) Alliece Graham (chorus)
Costume Construction	Margaret Ryan Patricia Smith
Set Construction	Martin Viksten
Production Assistant	Susan Azima
Program and Publicity	Mary Trainer
Make-up & Hair Styling	Diana LaMonte

Special thanks to Jon Washburn and Sharon Verrall for advice and assistance. Additional assistance provided from Centre for Communications and the Arts staff. The designer wishes to acknowledge the guidance of Mr. Harold Laxton.

ORCHESTRA

Norman Nelson	First Violin
Susan Colonval	First Violin
Kathy Stewart	First Violin
Frederick Nelson	Second Violin
David Stewart	Second Violin
Philippe Etter	Viola
Ian Hampton	Cello and Continuo
David Brown	Double Bass
Patrick Wedd	Harpsichord and Continuo

The signed program for *Dido and Aeneas*. *SFU Archives*

I can't speak for the actual opera, as I'm no judge, but the set design for *Dido* was brilliant. To design the show Michael brought in Martin Johnson from Toronto. Martin and I worked closely together and we got along famously. I drove him all over town to find all the bits and pieces he needed. We borrowed Michael's green military-style Jeep and got lost a lot, as neither of us knew the city. Martin could just "see" the set in his mind, and I thought that was amazing. Still do.

Given our budget constraints (because I managed the money, I was always the one saying no to people) Martin had to be… creative. He decided that the set would consist of people all dressed in the right colours as they did whatever they did, whether it was sing or dance or just stand about being spear carrier number two. We drove down to a fabric store somewhere near Chinatown, I think, where Martin bought bolts and bolts of an off-white coarse cotton. Curtain material I think. He then had the crew, consisting of myself, the stage manager and a few people we managed to shanghai, lay these long bolts of cloth

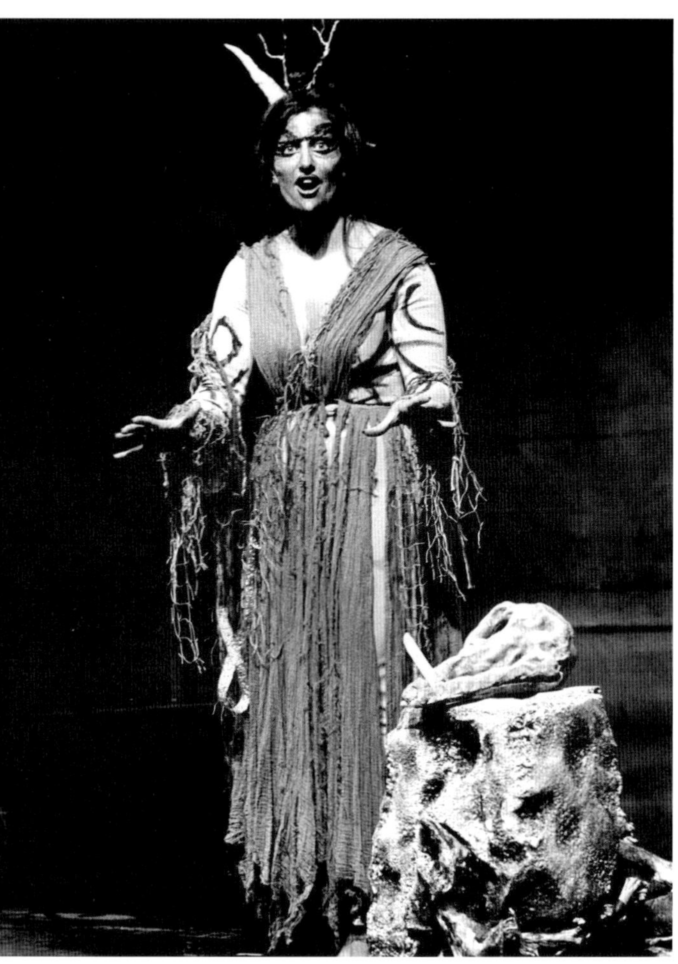

Judith Chertkow as the Sorceress in *Dido and Aeneas*. *Peter Higdon, SFU Archives*

on the floor of the stage. He'd also bought some kind of paint that worked on fabric, and we spent the long weekend (Easter probably) painting them. Stripes and blobs and splashes of paint à la Jackson Pollock. The colours were somewhat muted—greys and light browns and light pinks—but then there'd be a large round splash of black or red or orange. I couldn't see the point, but then I realized he was having these pieces cut into squares, with a hole cut out for the head and two for the arms, and the choir would wear them. At the back of the stage in the right light they "became" the set. There was also a scrim, which I thought was just magical, as I'd never seen one before.

Some members of the choir balked at their shapeless costumes, not to mention the fact that they were essentially part of the woodwork. I had to soothe a few bruised egos and managed to convince Martin to give them a piece of fabric to use as a belt so they didn't all look like potato sacks. I think the dancers also had bits of the fabric on their costumes, but in their case it was just bits sewn onto their leotards.

I suspect one of the reasons Martin had come to Vancouver to work on a university production was that he loved opera and nurtured dreams of one day designing sets for a major opera company. La Scala maybe. Naturally, being this great opera buff, he also knew that the weekend we were painting that cloth (which was bloody hard work I might add) CBC Radio had come up with the diabolical plan to broadcast Wagner's entire *Der Ring des Nibelungen*. Martin brought in a radio and insisted we listen. I have loathed Wagner, and opera, in general, ever since. (Well, I don't mind *Carmen*, and Anna Russell's version of *The Ring*, but that's about it.)

The set, however, was simply amazing. The blend of colours with the costumes and lighting, as well as whatever else Martin did, made the whole thing look like a Dutch painting. I hope there are pictures. Phyllis Mailing stood out, wearing a bright colour, red I think, and of course she was a bit of a celebrity; she had a lot of presence. Nonetheless she was perhaps the most pleasant, uncomplaining, professional person in the cast. Everyone adored her, for good reason.

There was an orchestra, with the VSO's Simon Streatfield conducting, and Patrick Wedd played the harpsichord. I remember that harpsichord rather balefully—the dratted thing had to be tuned every time it was used, and hiring a tuner put a large hole in my budget.

Apparently, the choir was SFU's Madrigal Singers and the Purcell String Quartet was part of the orchestra. Other than making sure the pit was safe for humans I didn't have much to do with the musicians—they were pros, and other than managing some scheduling conflicts for them they didn't need me: they came, they played, they packed up their instruments and left.

Even the front-line staff at the theatre were rather dazzled by the whole opera motif. The theatre manager, Ray, even ordered red velvet curtains special for the occasion and did what he could to make the lobby look festive. He even insisted the ushers wear suits, I think.

I think the opera went well but, again, I'm no judge. Max Wyman liked it.[7]

Acoustic Ecology: Opening Ears, Opening Minds

From Renaissance to rock, from traditional folk songs to the brave new world of electronic innovation, music at SFU embraced an abundance of styles, genres and eras. These would soon be joined by Indonesian gamelan, brought to SFU by Martin Bartlett in the 1980s and still flourishing as an area of teaching and research. Also destined to flourish was the SFU Pipe Band. It began in 1965 as a small-scale "Pipes and Drums" club—former students from the 1960s recall querying those intriguing words painted onto a closet door that opened directly onto the mall—composed mostly of students and fostered to provide Scottish colour for ceremonial occasions. Freshly re-conceived in the 1980s, the University Pipe Band went on to win multiple international prizes and to become SFU's musical signature. In 1969, when Murray Schafer wrote, "The universe is your orchestra,"[8] he might well have had the campus in mind.

My "Aha" Moment with Murray Schafer

by Hildegard Westercamp

Breaking Conventions: Ear Cleaning and Inspiration

In 1970 or 1971, my habitual patterns of listening were shaken up profoundly when I heard a guest lecture by Murray Schafer at the University of British Columbia (UBC), where I was studying music. It was an "aha" moment whose significance was revealed gradually over years to come. The immediate impact was that my ears opened up freely and suddenly to the sounds of my surroundings, and I was inspired and excited to notice them. Later, I recognized that I had experienced a first kind of ear cleaning.[9]

Murray Schafer in his studio. *SFU Archives*

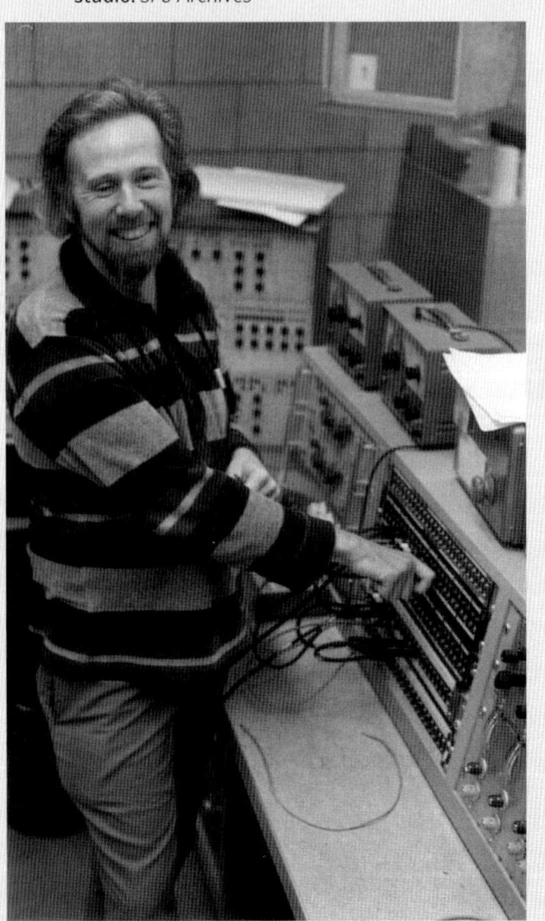

Schafer had surprised us by structuring his lecture against our expectations of what a lecture should be. He had placed three or four music stands in different areas of the stage and each one of them was dedicated to a certain topic of music or sound: one to his journey and sound experiences in Persia; the second one to music composition; the third one to soundscape and noise issues. A fourth one may have been dedicated to silence, to not speaking. Throughout the lecture, he moved freely between these topics, connecting them with the sound of his footsteps moving from music stand to music stand.[10]

As if this was not enough, someone in the audience stood up in seemingly random intervals, interrupting whatever was going on in the lecture, and asked questions like how many airplanes have you heard today or what was the first sound you heard today or how many birds have you heard today and more. Of course, these individuals—some of them my later colleagues in the World Soundscape Project—had been placed in the audience intentionally and were instructed to speak at certain points in the presentation. We were in fact listening to a highly composed talk, something I had never experienced before. The unusual format alone, breaking all conventions of standard university lectures at that time, heightened our listening attention and created alertness and utter delight in many of us. And for me personally, my listening woke up from the conventional music studies with which I had grown up and in which I was immersed at that time at UBC.

The moment of leaving the music building after the lecture is imprinted in my memory like a physical sensation: whatever had blocked my listening perception up to that point had been removed completely, as if pulverized. Suddenly and literally, I heard all sounds around me without any mental constructs obstructing my full and welcoming aural attention. I experienced this process as inspiration. In fact, it was as if my ears would never close again, and indeed, this very moment—so I realized later—was the beginning of my life's work.[11]

Schafer's lecture, an invitation to open our ears to the whole world, created a sense of liberation and delight. It gave me permission and therefore a sense of security that it was quite okay to apply my listening to more than the tasks of my musical studies. In fact, it placed my musical education into a larger cultural, environmental context and gave it relevance beyond the walls of the music school and its practice rooms. Ultimately it gave me hope that my love of listening, my ways of listening, could also find a place of action, work and creation in the world.

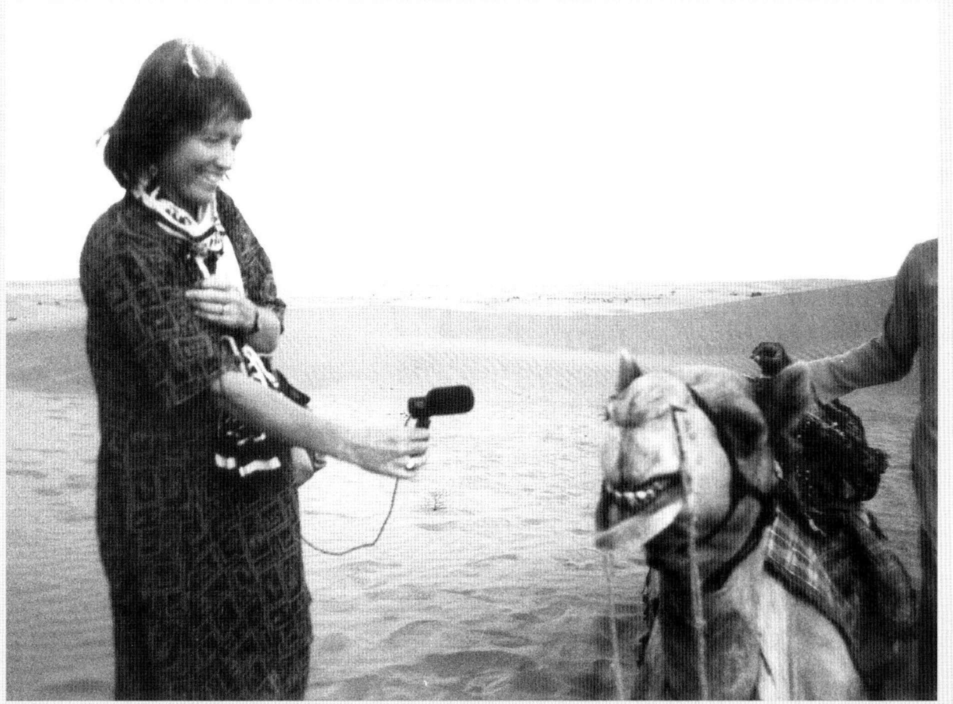

Hildegard Westerkamp recording a camel in Jaisalmer, Rajasthan, India, in 1992. The recording of this camel resulted in a short sound piece entitled *Camelvoice*, as part of a performance piece from the *India Sound Journal*. *Peter Grant*

New Ways of Thinking about Music, Listening and Soundmaking

The lecture made a deep enough impression that I remembered it and phoned Schafer a few years later in the hope that I could work with him and the World Soundscape Project. I was hired within a few weeks of this phone call and for almost a year I was the main researcher on his seminal book, *The Tuning of the World* (1977). This experience basically set the stage for the rest of my life. My involvement with this project not only activated deep concerns about noise and the general state of the acoustic environment in me, but it also changed my ways of thinking about music, listening and soundmaking. Vancouver Co-operative Radio, founded during the same time, provided an invaluable opportunity to learn much about broadcasting, and ultimately enabled me to introduce and host my weekly program *Soundwalking* in 1978–1979.

One could say that my career in soundscape composition and acoustic ecology emerged from these two pivotal experiences and found support in the cultural and political vibrancy of Vancouver at that time. While completing my master's thesis at SFU in the 1980s, entitled "Listening and Soundmaking—A Study of Music-as-Environment," I also taught acoustic communication courses until 1990 in the School of Communication at SFU, together with colleague Barry Truax. Since then, I have written numerous articles and texts addressing issues of the soundscape, acoustic ecology and listening, and I have travelled widely, giving lectures and conducting soundscape workshops internationally.

The World Forum for Acoustic Ecology

In 1993, I helped found the World Forum for Acoustic Ecology, an international network of affiliated organizations and individuals who share a common concern for the state of the world's soundscapes. I was chief editor of its journal *Soundscape* between 2000 and 2012. In 2003, Vancouver New Music (VNM) invited me to coordinate and lead public soundwalks as part of its yearly concert season. This in turn inspired the creation of the Vancouver Soundwalk Collective, whose members are continuing the work on a regular basis. My compositions have been performed and broadcast in many parts of the world. The majority deal with aspects of the acoustic environment: with urban, rural or wilderness soundscapes, with the voices of children, men and women, with noise or silence, music and media sounds, or with the sounds of different cultures, and so on. In 2017, CBC *Ideas* with host Paul Kennedy dedicated a program to my work and "how opening our ears can open our minds."[12]

CHAPTER 6: FILM

Cameras on the Mountain

"GO OUT AND SHOOT STUFF"

by Francis Mansbridge

VANCOUVER EMERGED AS A HOTBED OF EXPERIMENTAL FILMMAKING through the late fifties and sixties. The energy flowed naturally up the mountain when the film program began at SFU, with many CBC film personnel and others establishing strong personal and artistic connections with the young student talents. The regionalization of the National Film Board in 1966 and the establishment of the Canadian Film Corporation in 1967 provided supportive structures. Filmmaking is an expensive enterprise, and most filmmakers rely on grants and community support for their films to see the light of day (or perhaps the dark of night). The filmmakers at SFU benefited greatly from this environment.

At many universities in Canada and elsewhere, "taking film" meant an academic initiation in which preparatory courses inculcated background information often of marginal use when it came to making film. Film production often did not happen until the final year of the program. SFU was different. As film student Peter Bryant emphasized in a *Cinema Canada* article in 1975, "There are no courses, degrees, academic structures or requirements. As a group they are older than students in traditional film departments, since many of them have degrees, have been working for a few years, and return only to take advantage of the film activity... The ones that are allowed in must have something to offer... They must offer either energy, ambition, talent, technical skills, desire, hustle or a willingness to work... Each year, with only about fifteen or less students actively involved, the workshop produces 90 minutes of films."[1] Along with the usual student self-indulgence, an unusual amount of genuine talent found its expression.

CCA Residents and Enlarged Possibilities

Many students also explored the possibility of other venues outside SFU. This fluidity makes it difficult to define filmmakers as from SFU or some other school or university.

A case in point is David Rimmer, who wasn't formally enrolled in a film program at SFU. He briefly attended graduate school in English at SFU but was dissatisfied with the program. In 1967, he took a non-credit filmmaking course from CBC's Stan Fox, who was then a film resident at SFU. Fox invited him—along with Tom Shandel, Gary Lee Nova and Sylvia Spring—to contribute films to an experimental series on CBC. Rimmer became immersed in film and shifted his focus to downtown and to Intermedia, a collaborative artists' association that had been founded in 1967. Intermedia was founded by Jack Shadbolt and Glenn Lewis and located at 575 Beatty Street. It represented many of the ideals of SFU's Centre for Communications and the Arts. The NFB gave them two boxes of old film, which Rimmer found to be useful raw material to produce his own work.

Since the late 1960s, Rimmer's films *Square Inch Field* and *Migrations* (music by Phillip Werren), celebrating "the interconnectedness of all things," have remained iconic landmarks in the history of Canadian experimental film. With Michael Snow, he is generally considered Canada's most important avant-garde filmmaker. In the 1980s he returned to SFU to teach for four years in the film program. He later won the Governor General's Award in Visual and Media Arts in 2011.

Another filmmaker with strong ties to SFU is Al Sens. After he graduated from the Vancouver School of Art in 1957, he began his artistic career as a cartoonist, founding his studio in 1958. A self-taught animated filmmaker, he also worked for SFU's audiovisual department making short animated films that drew on the legacy of Norman McLaren and his work for the NFB. His 1966 film *Henry* was featured in a television miniseries, *New Filmmakers*. Author and media studies professor Zoë Druick states that Sens's films "combine a critique of US media culture with bemused observations about the human condition, often expressed by domestic pets."[2] He was widely acknowledged as the leader of the West Coast animation scene.

The SFU Film Workshop: An Experimental Showcase for Young Filmmakers

The SFU Film Workshop began in May 1967 when the university first obtained 16 mm production facilities, which allowed students to focus all their time and creative energy on making film. A total of sixteen residents in film between 1966 and 1976 brought diverse perspectives that enriched the educational experience and filmmaking abilities of students. Most of the individual workshops were short-term, sometimes lasting only a week. Longer-term residents included Stan Fox and Shelah Reljic. The latter took some of the workshop's films to the first University Conference on Film and Related Media, sponsored by the National Film Board, in April 1969. Fox was particularly important for his connections to the CBC, which provided many students with a gateway to other projects.

In May 1969, Fox and Peter Bryant represented the SFU Film Workshop at the first meeting of the Canadian Association of Media Studies in Montreal. These ventures greatly elevated the exposure of SFU film. Fox compiled a series of programs to support the nascent filmmakers. CBC Television precursor CBUT's shows *Enterprise* (1967–1968) and *New World* (1969) provided an experimental showcase for young filmmakers to share their work with local audiences. Stan Fox stayed on as film resident until the summer of 1971 then went on to head the film program at York University, while Reljic became a producer at the NFB's Vancouver office.

Many workshop participants wandered up the mountain from downtown, no doubt drawn by SFU's reputation for being a good place to develop one's creative talent, with the opportunity of learning the craft without time and creative energy being devoured by academic courses. People benefited from the stimulation of joint (unintended pun) activity. Bryant became a fellow of the American Film Institute in 1970 and went on to teach at UBC; he found that, while his students at UBC were as capable as any, production had to share time with the four or five other courses that the students were required to take. As Tony Westman told me in a conversation, "The workshop promoted an attitude of working together toward common goals." He continued, "When you're getting both your feet into it as you do at SFU, you make a lot of mistakes, but hopefully you won't repeat them."[3] It was a community within a community.

Danny Singer was one of the most talented to emerge from the SFU film milieu; his art has grown in diverse directions throughout his artistic career of

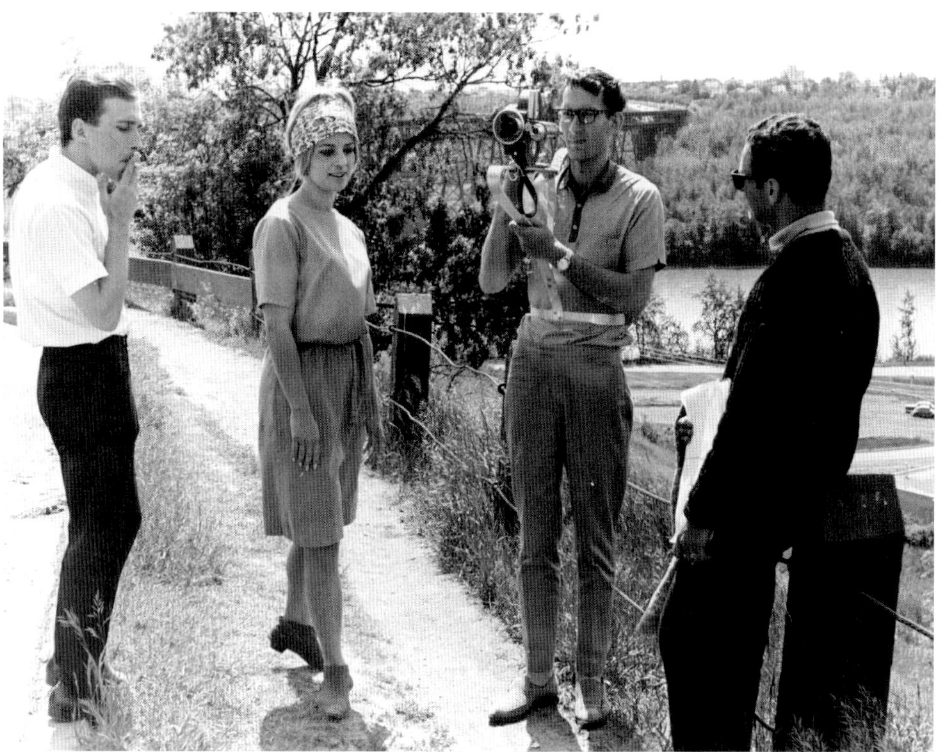

Danny Singer, on the right, made a career in filmmaking and later photography. Jim Salt holds the camera. *Tony Westman, SFU Archives*

almost sixty years, combining technical proficiency with an emotional intelligence. He came to SFU in 1965 with no background in film. While he later attended film workshops, his first film, *The Beginning*, the first student film at SFU, was made before the workshops were initiated. Singer described its genesis to me in a telephone interview:

> After my first semester at SFU, when I went back home to Edmonton, my father gave me a Bolex camera. I had been doing theatre at SFU and the participants were asked if anybody had any ideas. I said I would like to make a film. I got in touch with the SFU Film Society, who gave me $200, and received another bursary for $200. Starring Aileen Gee and Jan Visscher, it was written by Ed Turner, with the music supervised by Murray Schafer and composed by Music 001 [Schafer's electronic music class]. Nora Clemons, Wayne Elwood, Joanne Rabinovitch and Peter Horn helped with the sets."[4]

The Beginning took about a month to make and was shot over a period of about a week. A review in *The Peak* describes it appropriately as "the fanciful and frantic hopes of representatives of the two sexes to break through a barrier that they have accepted as terminal," with Visscher "displaying considerable talent at mime" as a main actor.[5]

Singer continues: "When I went home in the summer of sixty-six I made a short feature film, *d'Evita*, about fifty-five minutes. I wrote the script, which was about somebody who spent his entire life making a film. There was no SFU financing, although there was a screening at SFU. I didn't have enough money to properly finish the film, so it never was. I left SFU when I was offered a job at CBC by Stan Fox. I did a variety of work—sound, acting."[6] Singer was also active in SFU theatre, playing "The Common Man" in Michael Bawtree's production of his initial play, *A Man for All Seasons*. He moved to Montreal in 1970 to work for the CBC, where he became active in still photography and other visual arts forms, often exhibiting his photographs in galleries. Later he became the main photographer for the 1976 Olympics in Montreal.

While at SFU, Singer was good friends with John Juliani. He filmed Juliani's *Hurrah!*, based on an idea from Paul Foster's play *Hurrah for the Bridge*. The film is a sometimes confusing romp as a homeless man and his dog attempt to evade pursuers, eventually unsuccessfully, until finally an ethereal Iris Garland welcomes him, possibly to the afterlife. Made mostly by theatre people, it starred Norman Browning, Manuel Busquets, Jan Visscher, Perry Long, Iris Garland and Henry Vandenberghe.

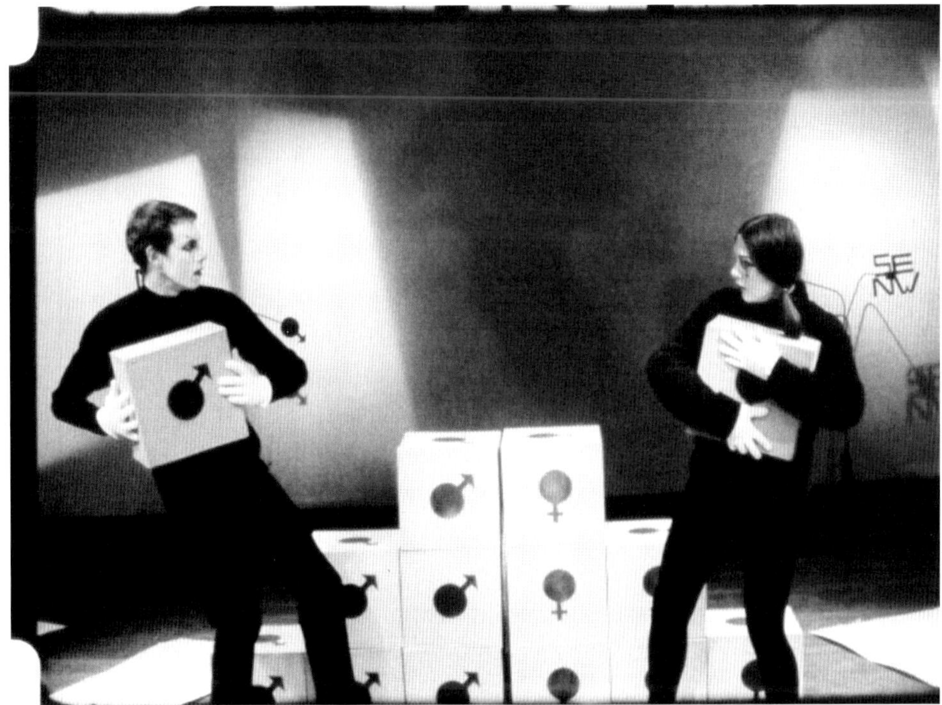

A scene from Danny Singer's film *The Beginning*, the first film made at SFU. *Danny Singer, SFU Archives*

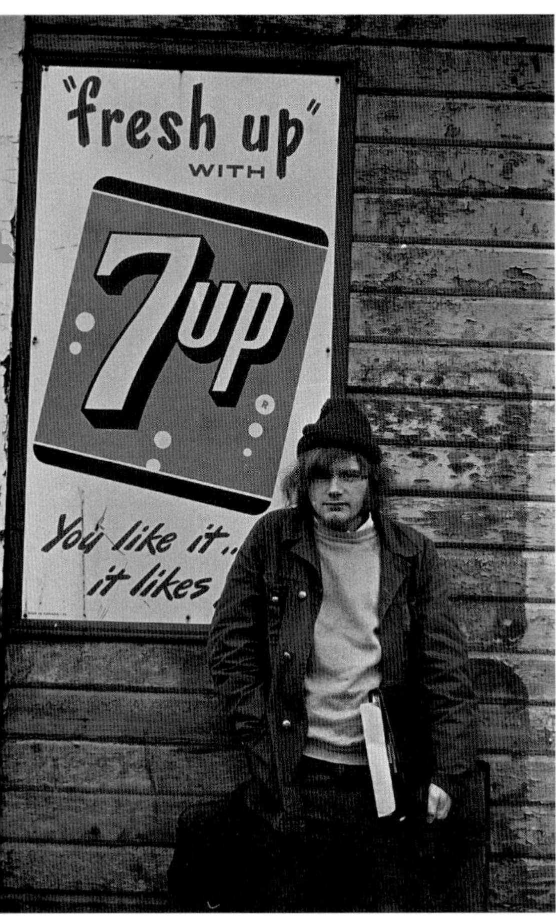

Peter Bryant, SFU student filmmaker. *Tony Westman, SFU Archives*

Singer became particularly known for his meticulous composite photographs of the main streets of small prairie towns. These are composed of up to 140 sequential images digitally joined into seamless panoramas. Each is filmed straight on, creating an unusual perspective. He made five prints of the composite photographs, which now sell for about $25,000 each. Singer reminisces, "What did I take away from my early days? My learning of motion control was important in my later photography. I have never regretted moving from film to photography. Perhaps the title *The Beginning* was prescient."[7]

Peter Bryant made nine short films while at SFU. He co-starred with Arnold Saba in the popular *Felix*, which he also wrote and directed. Like several of his films, it's a rollicking adventure by two denizens of the streets in Vancouver's East Side who devise inventive if often politically incorrect ways of earning money. It played well to the SFU crowd and won the Famous Players Award for best student film in 1969. In *The Rocco Brothers* (1973), made on a $7,500 grant from CFDC, two bad-ass greasers "steal hubcaps, have chain fights, steal old ladies' purses, or just cruise around and pick up some 'tomatoes.'" *Cinema Canada* reviewer George Koller describes Bryant's direction as "smooth, sensitive, and polished," and adds "we get to know these three guys on a lot deeper level than this hastily written synopsis suggests."[8] A few years later *The Supreme Kid* (1976) came out, a feature Bryant made for $115,000 after he became a lecturer in UBC's Department of Theatre. The film narrates the adventures of a "couple of modern-day hoboes," played by Frank Moore and Jim Henshaw, who engage in picaresque adventures as they roam the country. The film became Canada's official entry in Czechoslovakia's prestigious Karlovy Vary International Film Festival.

In addition to filmmaking, the CCA offered students the chance to gain experience in the relatively new realm of video production. In "Memories of SFU Centre for Communication [*sic*] and the Arts 1969–70," instructor David Rousseau recalls arriving at SFU in January 1969 after working with a company that built video and audio systems. High-quality video was just emerging, and Nini Baird wanted to see something happening with that form. Rousseau instructed a video workshop for a couple of terms, while also introducing students to the Electronic Music Studio. He loved the workshop atmosphere,

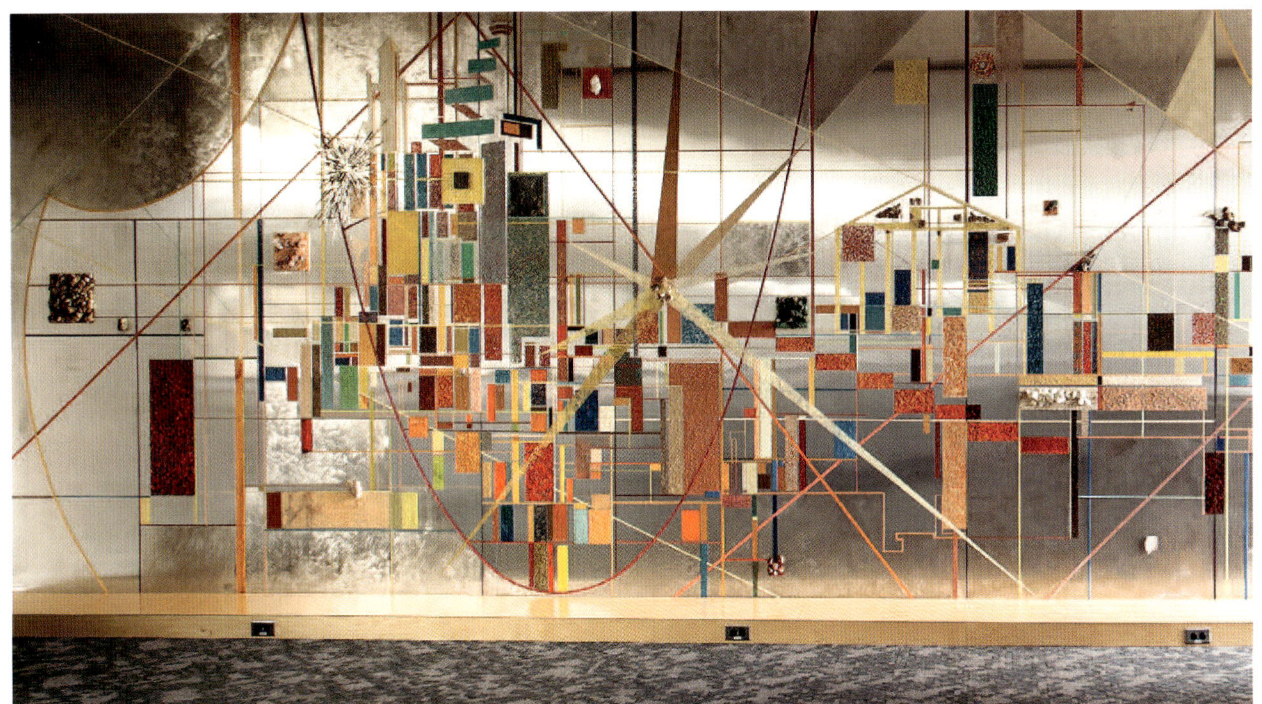

Theatres of the World, 1964-65, stainless steel, nickel, gem stones, paint. This mural, by Chicago artist Buell Mullen, was permanently installed during construction of the SFU Theatre in 1964 as a gift from the International Nickel Company of Canada Ltd. The mural is part of SFU's public art collection and still resides in its original location, now known as the Leslie & Gordon Diamond Family Auditorium. *SFU Galleries*

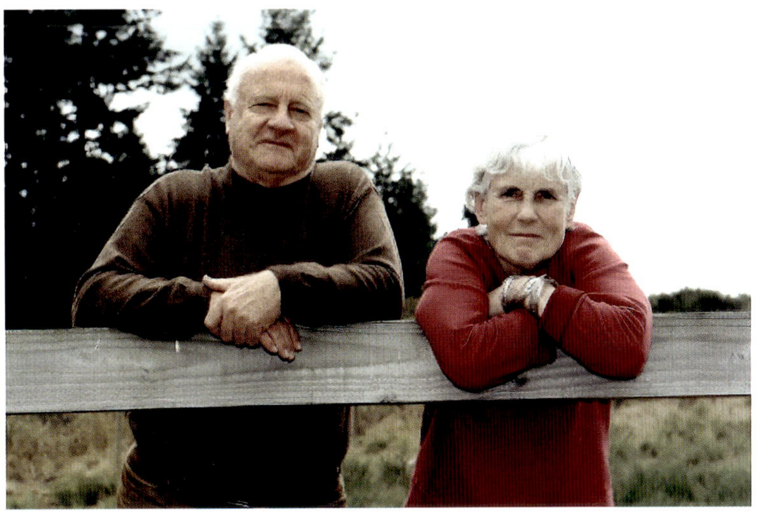

Marianne and Edward Gibson on Cloudcroft Farm in Cowichan Valley where they raised highland cattle from 1990 to 2000. It was during these years that they discussed with President Stevenson their vision of a teaching gallery on the Burnaby campus. *Marianne Gibson*

Centre for Communications and the Arts

Presents

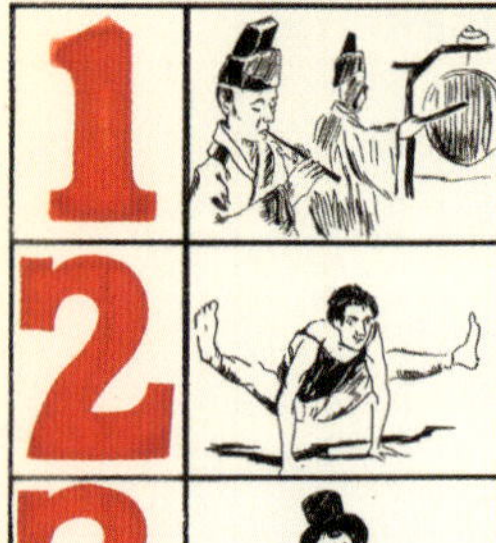

1		AH AHK: Performing Arts of Korea **SATURDAY, SEPTEMBER 30** **8:00 P.M.**
2		James Cummingham and the Acme Dance Company **Friday, October 27** **8:00 P.M.**
3	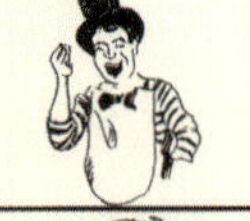	Claude Kipnis Mime Troupe **Thursday, November 2** **8:00 P.M.**
4	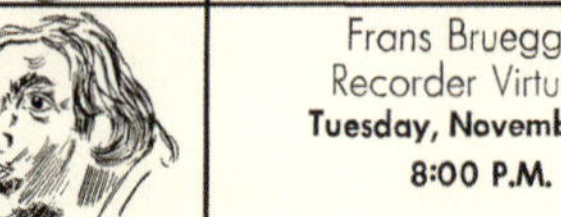	Frans Brueggen, Recorder Virtuoso **Tuesday, November 21** **8:00 P.M.**

RESERVED SEATS: **$2.50 General Admission**
$1.50 Students

SIMON FRASER UNIVERSITY THEATRE

FOR INFORMATION ON TICKETS AND SPECIAL BUSES CALL 291-3514

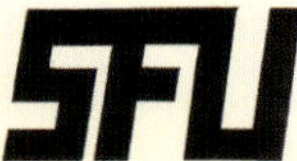

The CCA hosted a wide variety of guest artists, including AH AHK: Performing Arts of Korea, James Cunningham and the Acme Dance Company, Claude Kipnis Mime Troupe and Frans Brueggen, Recorder Virtuoso, who all performed in 1972. *SFU Archives*

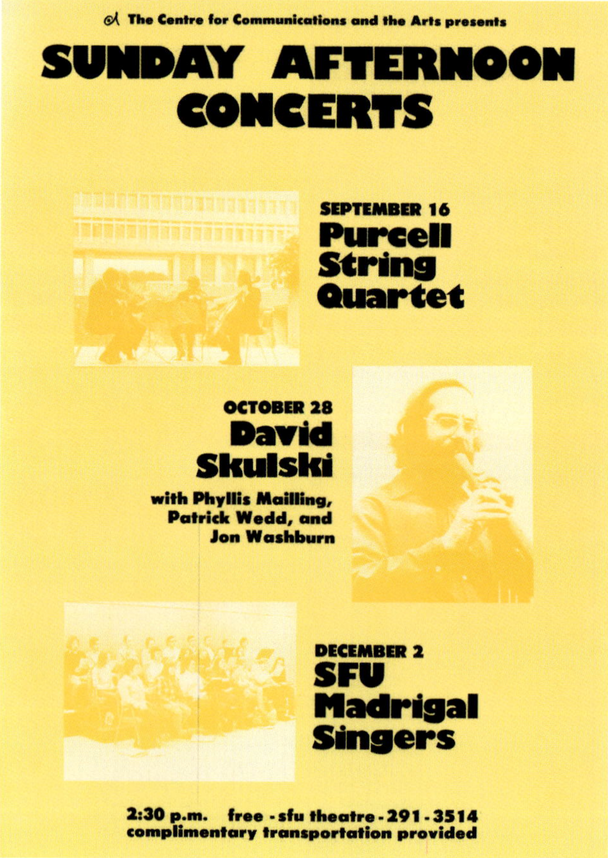

As shown by this poster from 1973, the Sunday Afternoon Concerts featured many local artists. One of Canada's most important musical ensembles, the Purcell String Quartet was the quartet-in-residence at Simon Fraser University from 1972 to 1982. *SFU Archives*

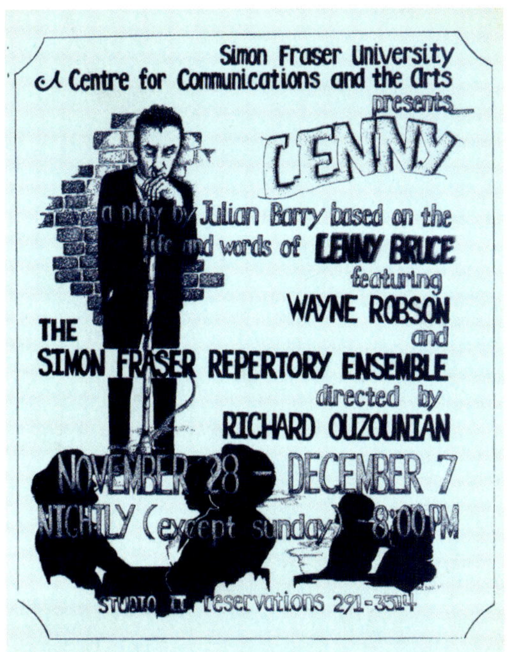

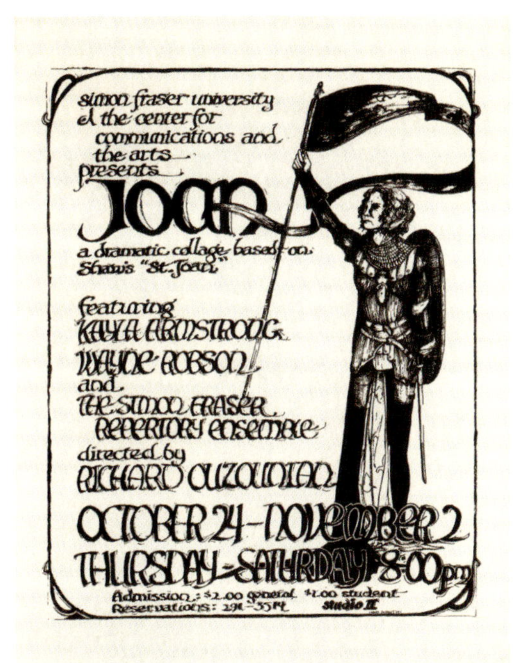

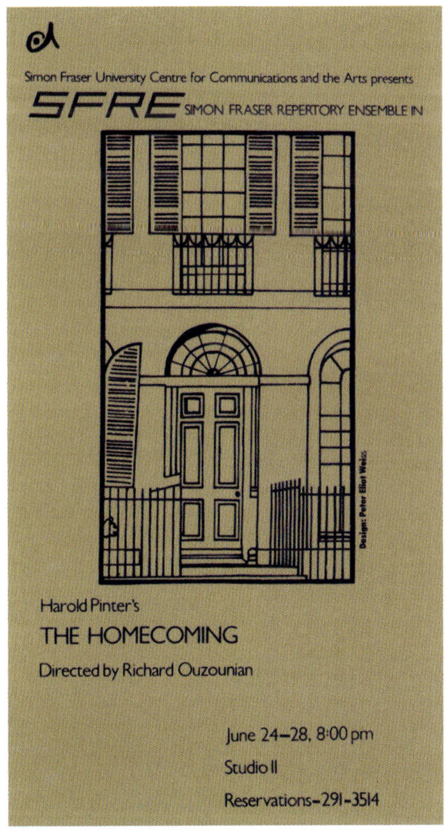

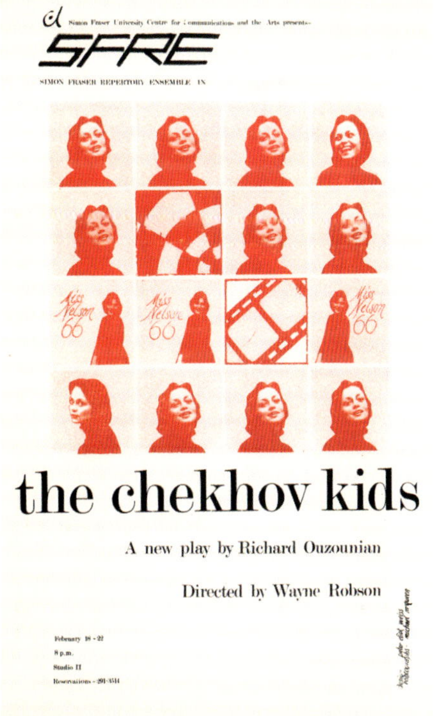

Posters for some of the productions directed or written by Richard Ouzounian during his time at SFU in 1974 and 1975. He went on to serve as artistic director for five Canadian theatres and as theatre critic for the *Toronto Star*. *SFU Archives*

A poster for a performance by the SFU Dance Workshop in 1970. *SFU Archives*

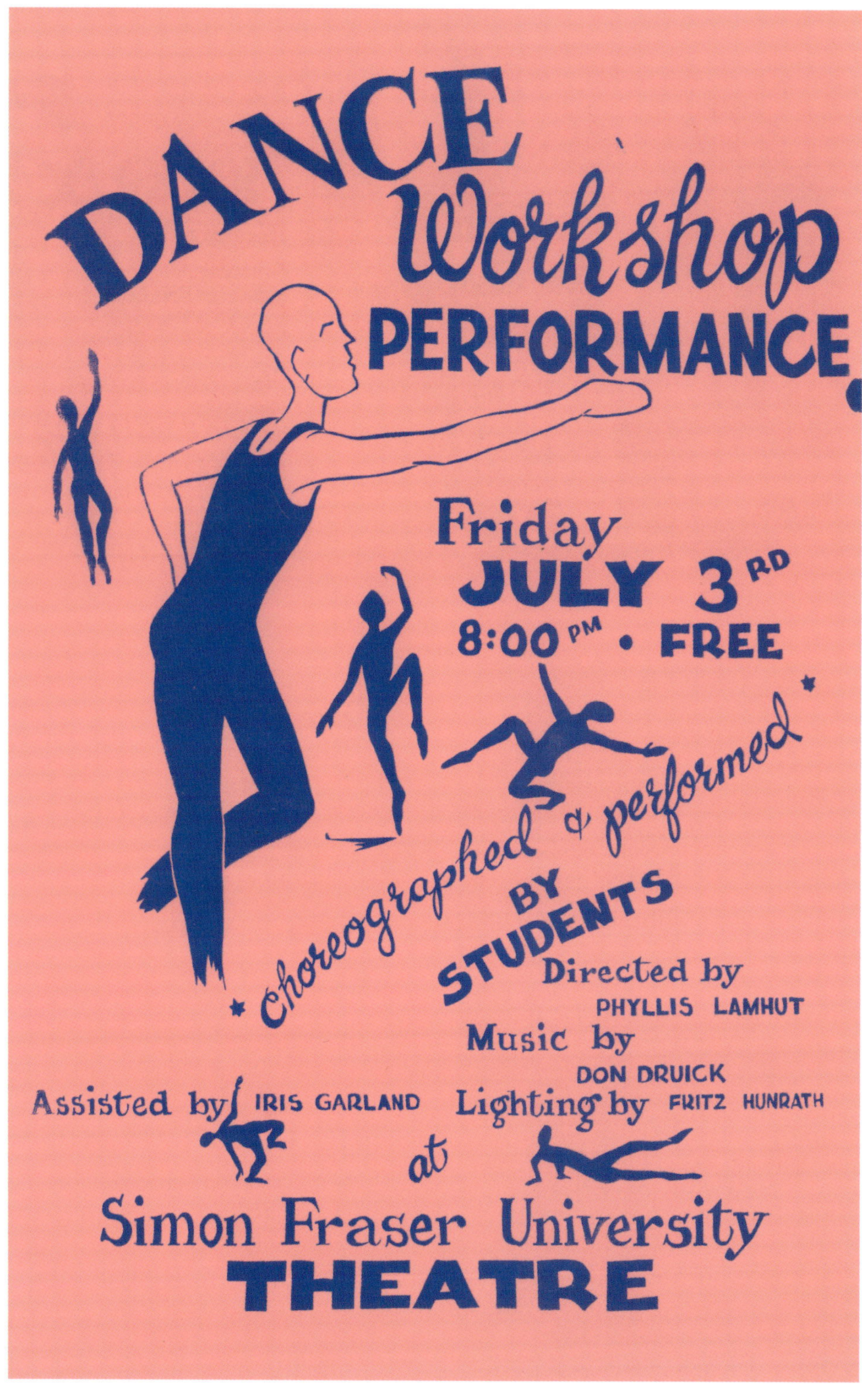

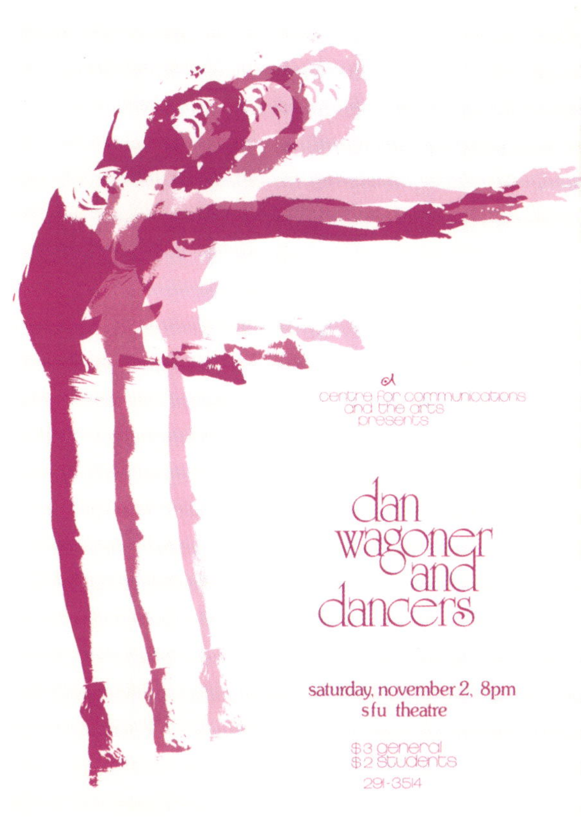

Choreographer Dan Wagoner, who danced with Martha Graham, Merce Cunningham and Paul Taylor, visited SFU as a guest artist in 1974-75 to teach a masterclass and choreograph this piece with the SFU Dance Workshop. *SFU Archives*

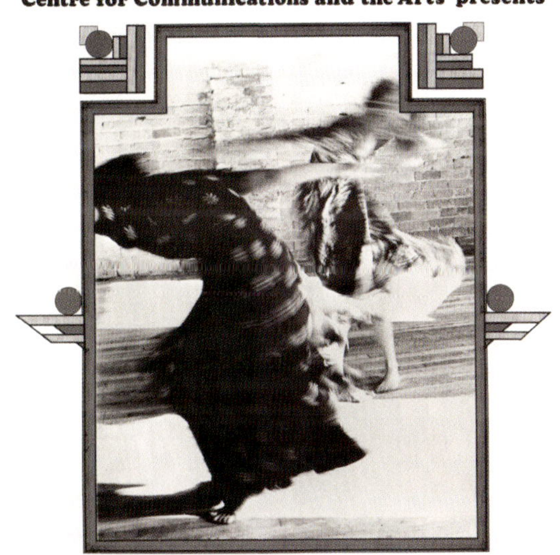

An early collaboration between Karen Rimmer (later Jamieson) and Savannah Walling in 1974. They would go on, along with Terry Hunter, to form Terminal City Dance. *SFU Archives*

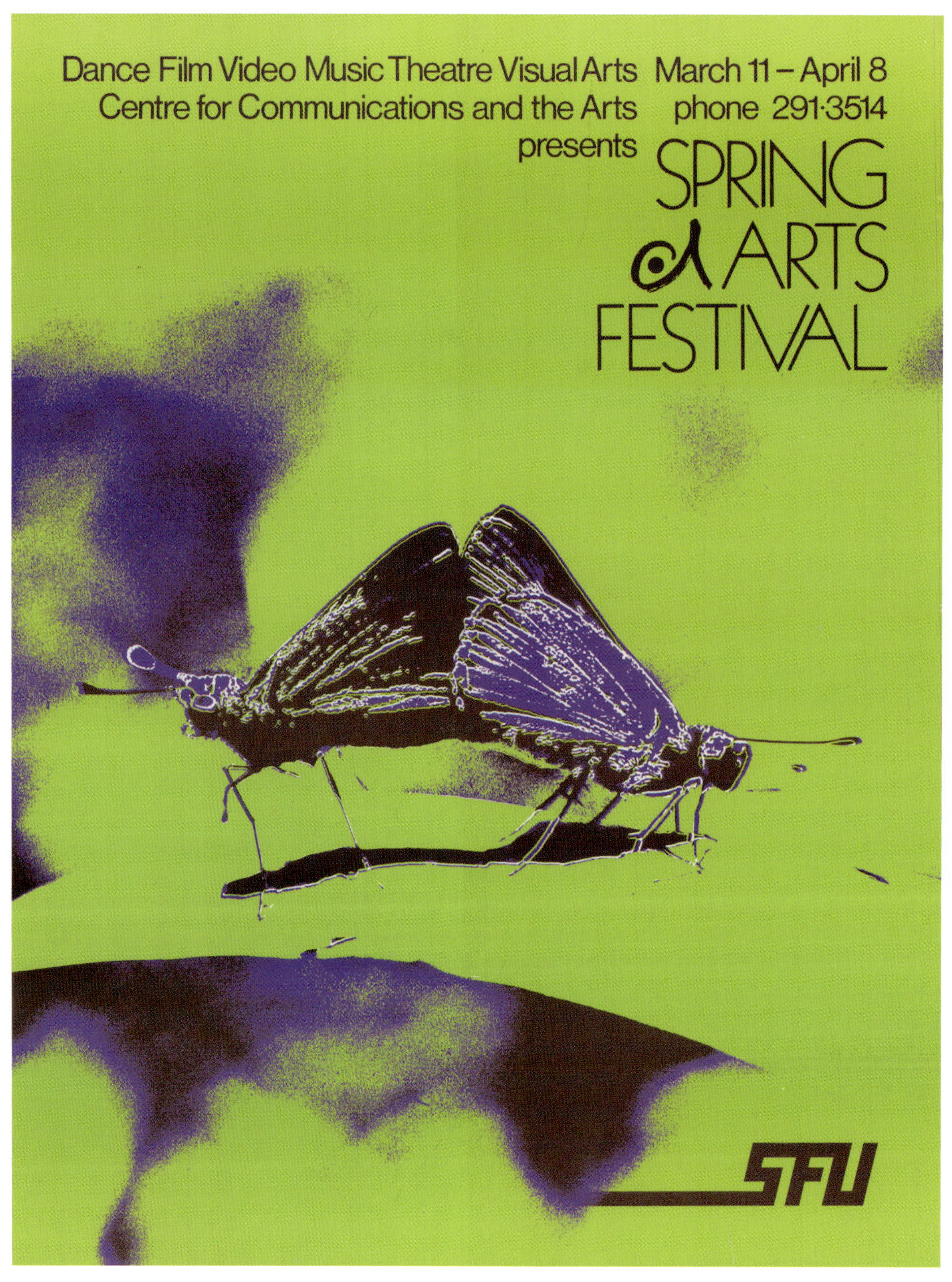

A poster for the Spring Arts Festival in 1973. *SFU Archives*

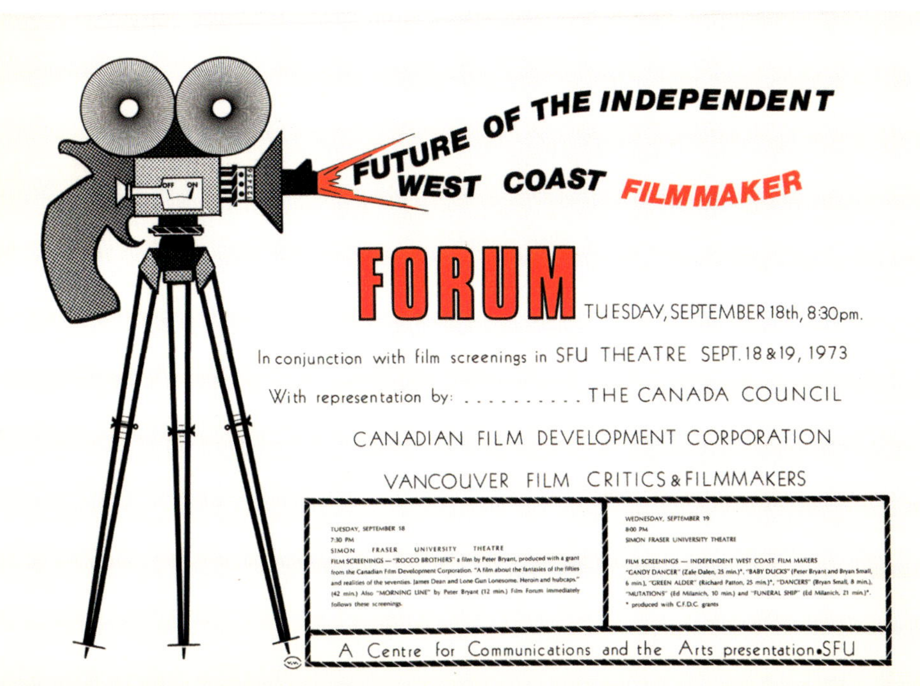

A poster for the *Future of the Independent West Coast Filmmaker Forum* in 1973, which also featured a screening of Peter Bryant's film Rocco Brothers. *SFU Archives*

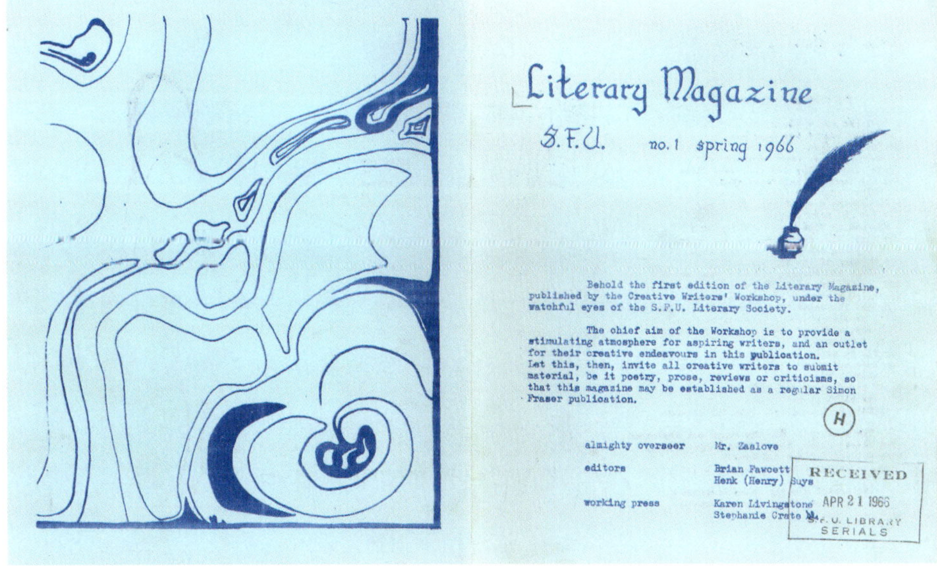

Literary Magazine

S.F.U. no. 1 spring 1966

Behold the first edition of the Literary Magazine, published by the Creative Writers' Workshop, under the watchful eyes of the S.F.U. Literary Society.

The chief aim of the Workshop is to provide a stimulating atmosphere for aspiring writers, and an outlet for their creative endeavours in this publication. Let this, then, invite all creative writers to submit material, be it poetry, prose, reviews or criticisms, so that this magazine may be established as a regular Simon Fraser publication.

almighty overseer — Mr. Zaslove

editors — Brian Fawcett, Henk (Henry) Suys

working press — Karen Livingstone, Stephanie Crate

The short-lived *Literary Magazine*, issued in 1966 by the equally short-lived Creative Writers' Workshop, exemplified the spirit of collaboration between faculty and students that prevailed during the 1960s. *SFU Archives*

The Vancouver Symphony Orchestra was hosted for a concert in the SFU Gym in 1973. *SFU Archives*

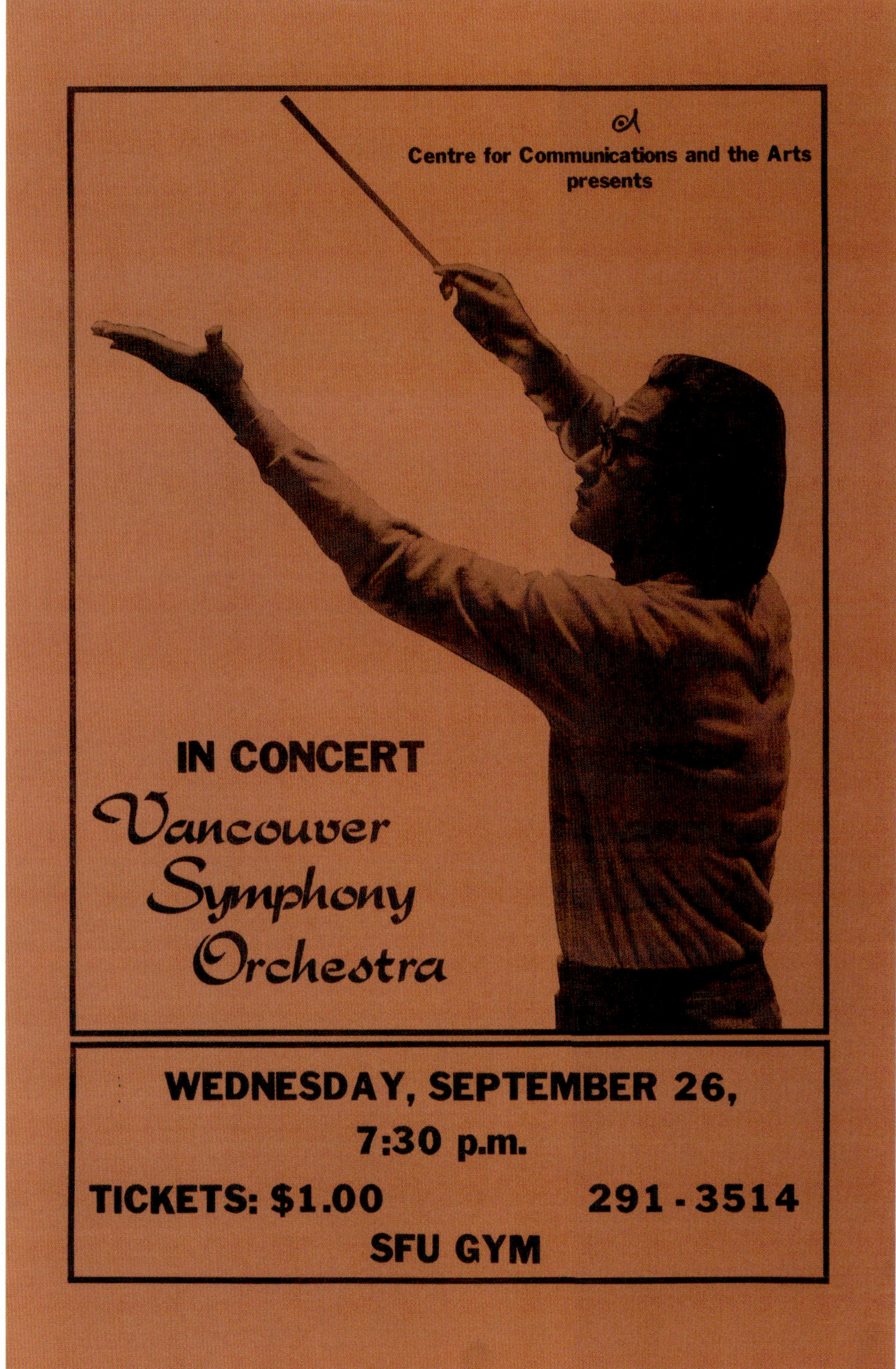

THE soundscape of the world is changing. Noise pollution is now a problem. It would seem that the world soundscape has reached an apex of vulgarity in our time.

R. Murray Schafer
(1977)

A quote by R. Murray Schafer on the changing soundscape of the world. *SFU Archives*

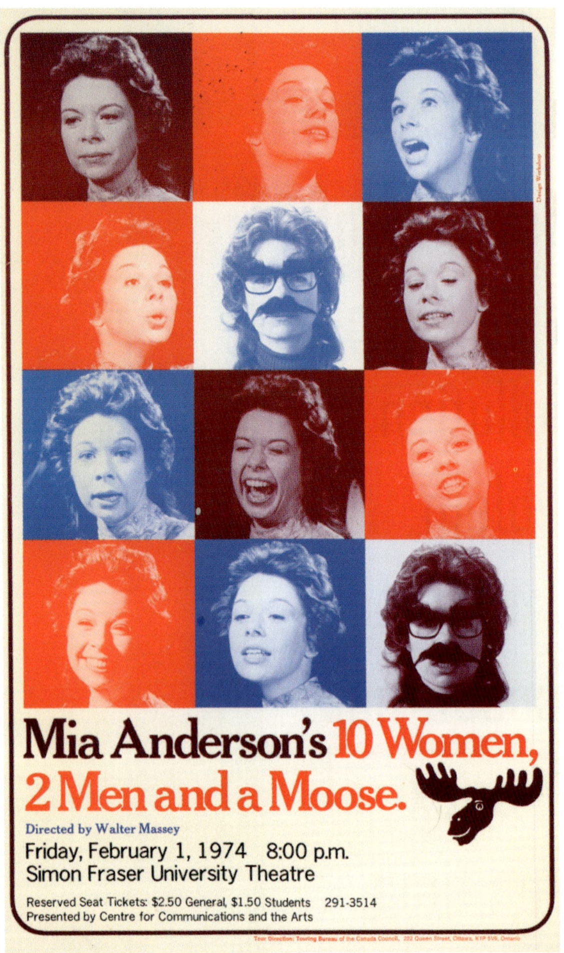

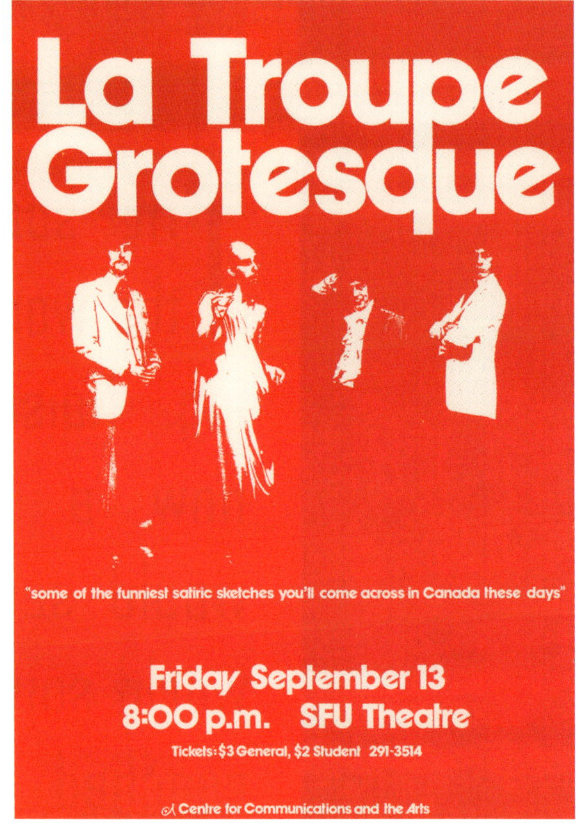

During the early 1970s, SFU was host to many acclaimed theatre groups, including Mia Anderson, the Manhattan Theatre Project, La Troupe Grotesque, the National Theatre of the Deaf and Redlight Theatre. *SFU Archives*

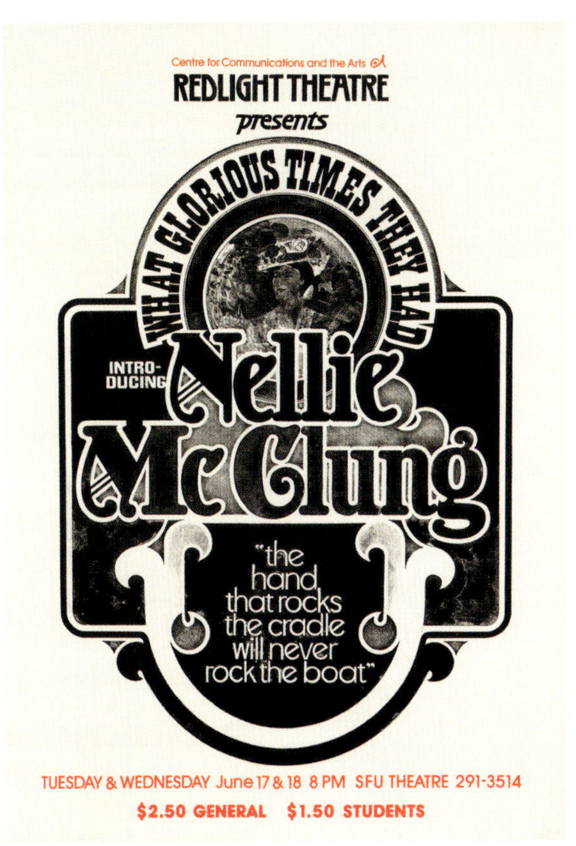
Centre for Communications and the Arts
REDLIGHT THEATRE
presents
WHAT GLORIOUS TIMES THEY HAD
INTRO-DUCING
Nellie McClung
"the hand that rocks the cradle will never rock the boat"
TUESDAY & WEDNESDAY June 17 & 18 8 PM SFU THEATRE 291-3514
$2.50 GENERAL $1.50 STUDENTS

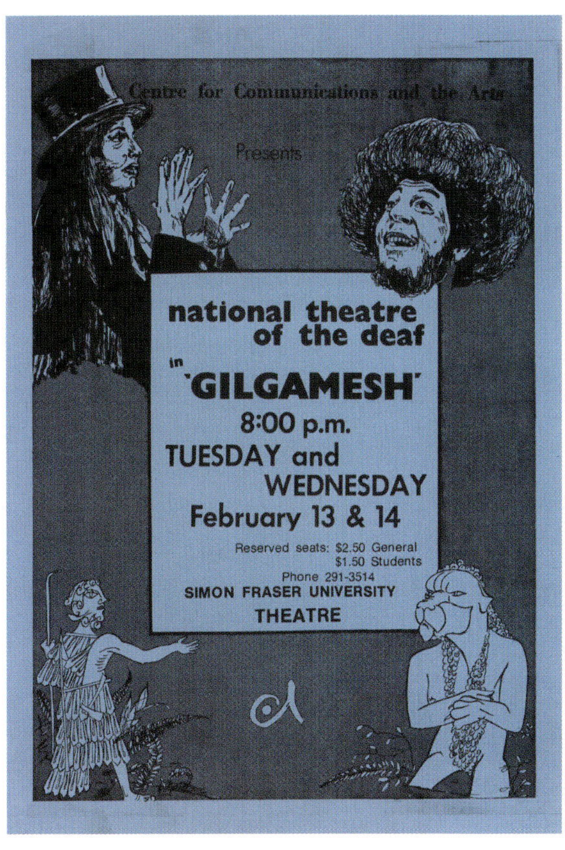
Centre for Communications and the Arts
Presents
national theatre of the deaf
in 'GILGAMESH'
8:00 p.m.
TUESDAY and WEDNESDAY
February 13 & 14
Reserved seats: $2.50 General
$1.50 Students
Phone 291-3514
SIMON FRASER UNIVERSITY
THEATRE

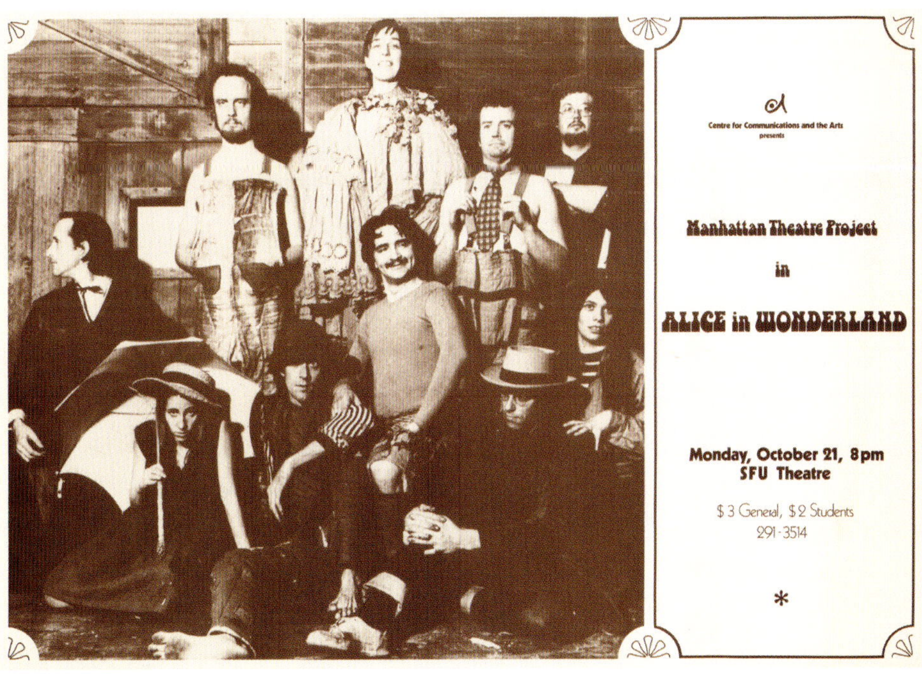
Centre for Communications and the Arts
presents
Manhattan Theatre Project
in
ALICE in WONDERLAND
Monday, October 21, 8pm
SFU Theatre
$3 General, $2 Students
291-3514
*

Henry Purcell's Opera

Dido and Aeneas

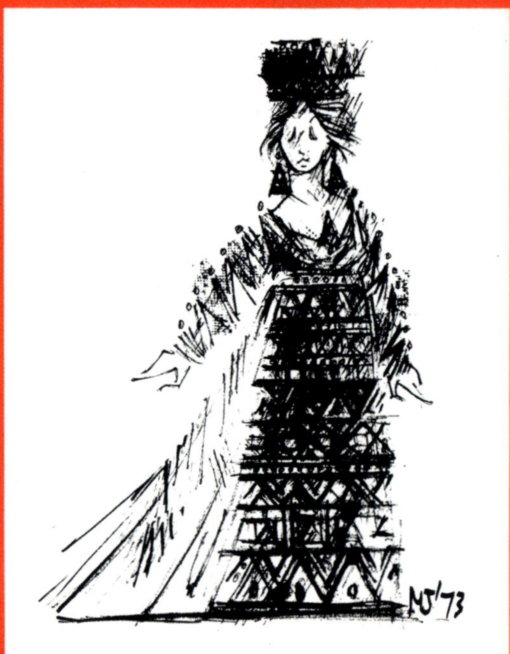

June 8 and 9 (8 pm)
June 10 (2:30 pm), 1973
SFU Theatre

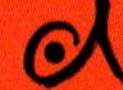 Presented by Centre for Communications and the Arts

The opera *Dido and Aeneas* was produced in June 1973. *SFU Archives*

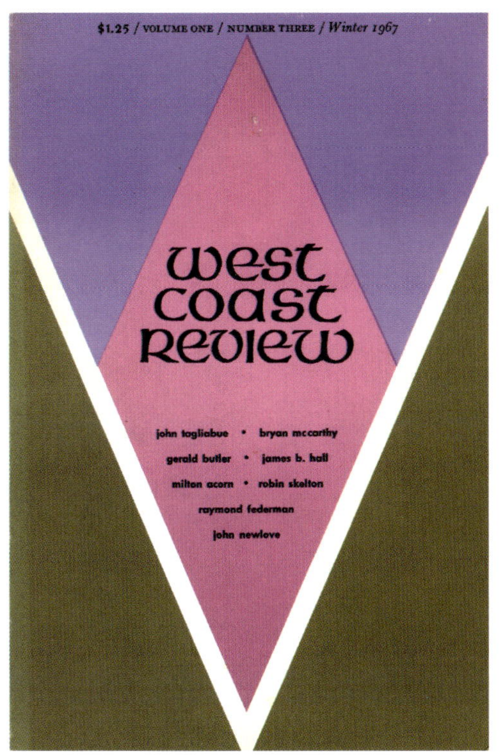

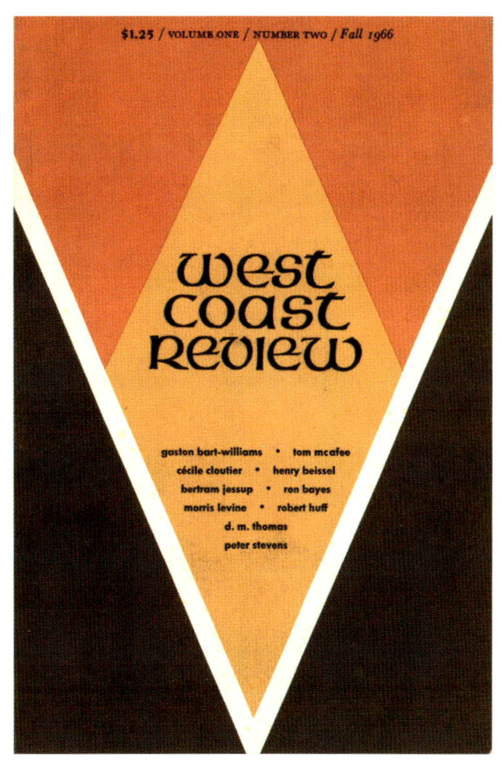

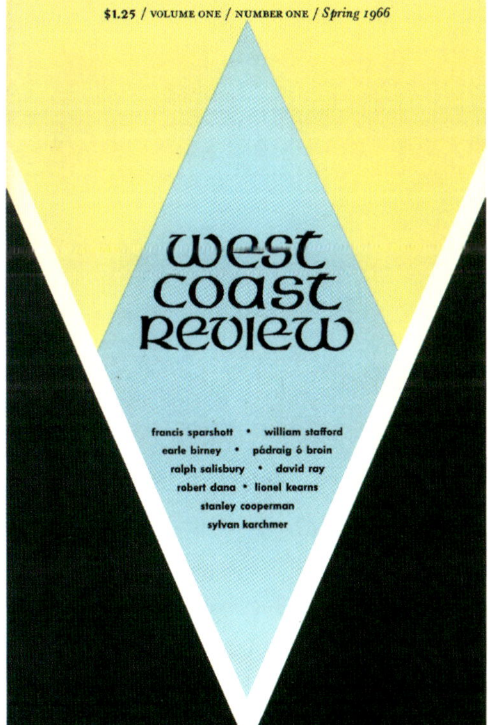

The *West Coast Review* was founded in 1966 by professor and poet Fred Candelaria. *SFU Archives*

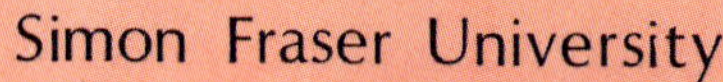

Religion and the Arts

January 19 – 30

An experimental project designed to bring together and explore a variety of artistic manifestations of the vitality of contemporary religious faith and to stimulate an awareness and appreciation of the spiritual dimension of life within the university.

Co-sponsored by the Simon Fraser University Chaplaincy, representing seven denominations, and the Centre for Communications and the Arts.

Monday January 19

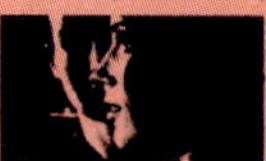

the silence

"Bergman at his most powerful!"
NEW YORK POST

12:30 P.M. BERGMAN FILM

The third film of Bergman's religious trilogy, THE SILENCE depicts a world in which God is silent, a world of despair. United since childhood in lesbian incest, two sisters struggle and part as the younger seeks her freedom in a heterosexual affair. Bergman's somber view of modern man's condition, wherein human relations are grotesquely ego-centric and perversely sexual, is shattering yet a plea for hope from man himself.

Followed by informal discussion in Green Room, led by reactor Mrs. Pearl Williams, President, Vancouver International Film Festival.

Tuesday January 20

12:30 P.M. CONCERT
SCHLOMO CARLEBACH, the "Singing Rabbi".

2:30 P.M. ART FILM
WE HAVE NO ART 26 minutes, color, featuring Sister Mary Corita. Described by one critic as "an ultimate view of the methods Sister Corita uses to help students re-learn how to use their senses, find joy, form and new content in diversity," the film shows how the artist takes his materials from the streets (man hole covers and fire engines), from Madison Avenue (collages and constructions), and from literature.

Wednesday January 21

12:30 P.M. MIME SPLACES
A new mime production conceived and directed by Perry Long, an original member of the SFU Mime Troupe who has appeared in many theatre productions on and off campus, including the full-length mime play MAN WHOLE and ALIICE.

"SPLACES" will be followed by a work specially choreographed and performed for the Festival by members of the SFU Dance Workshop.

wild strawberries

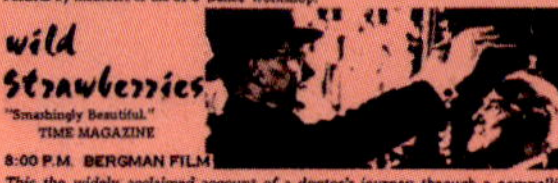

"Smashingly Beautiful."
TIME MAGAZINE

8:00 P.M. BERGMAN FILM

This the widely acclaimed account of a doctor's journey through a compelling landscape of dream and memory. Traveling to receive an honourary degree, he is confronted with a series of haunting flashbacks and events that in a day's time reveals his very depths. Richly visual and startlingly dramatic, WILD STRAWBERRIES is a cinematic landmark.

Followed by informal discussion in the Green Room, led by reactor Dr. Gunter Stroethotte, Luthern Pastor and Lecturer in Department of Religious Studies, UBC, and at Union College.

Thursday January 22

12:30 P.M. POETRY READING AND LECTURE
THE RELIGIOUS FOCUS IN ART: THE WRITER IN HIS TRADITION. A reading of poetry with commentary by Dr. Stanley Cooperman, Professor of English, SFU. He is the author of four volumes of poetry: *The Day of the Parrot and Other Poems, The Owl Behind the Door, Cappelbaum's Dance,* and *Cappelbaums' Lament* .

Friday January 23

12:30 P.M. MIME SPLACES
See Wednesday, January 23rd 12:30 P.M. program.

8:00 P.M. BERGMAN FILM

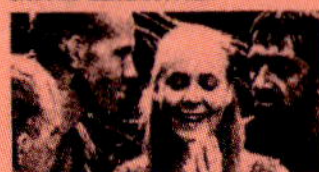

the virgin spring

"One of the Year's Ten Best"
N.Y. TIMES

THE VIRGIN SPRING grimly depicts a father's ruthless vengeance for the rape and murder of his virgin daughter. Bergman fills our eyes with highly contrasting black and white to evoke an imaginative medieval world, suggesting the battle of Christianity and paganism. For a man of Bergman's sophistication, the austere simplicity of this film is a rare achievement.

Followed by informal discussion in Green Room, led by reactor, Dr. Lawrence Boland, Assistant Professor of Economics, SFU

Religion and the Arts

RELIGION AND THE ARTS will centre on the Theology of Ingmar Bergman as expressed in his six films: The Silence, Wild Strawberries, The Virgin Spring, Through a Glass Darkly, Winter Light, The Seventh Seal.

Each of the screenings will be followed by an informal discussion in the Green Room of the Theatre, each led by a reactor who will bring a special point of view to bear on the film: theology, medieval history, psychiatry, film study and philosophy.

Theology of Bergman

"There is an old story of how the cathedral of Chartres was struck by lightening and burnt to the ground. Then thousands of people turned up from various places like a giant procession of ants from all points of the compass. All kinds of people came and together they began to build up the cathedral on its old site. They all stayed there until the building was completed – master builders, workers, artists, clowns, noblemen, priests, burghers. But they remained anonymous and no one knows to this day who built the cathedral of Chartres.

Regardless of my own beliefs and my own doubts, which are completely without importance in this connection, it is my opinion that art lost its creative urge the moment it was separated from worship. It severed the umbilical cord and lives its own sterile life, generating and degenerating itself. The individual has become the highest form and greatest bane of artistic creation. Creative unity and humble anonymity are forgotten and buried relics without significance or meaning. The smallest cuts and moral pains of the ego are examined under the microscope, as if they were of eternal importance.

Thus we finally gather in one large pen, where we stand and bleat about our loneliness without listening to each other and without realising that we are smothering each other to death. The individualists stare into each other, and cry out into the darkness without once receiving the healing power of communal happiness. We are so affected by our own walking in circles, so limited by our own anxiety that we can no longer distinguish between the true and the false, between the gangster's ideas and pure ideals.

If thus I am asked what I should like to be the general purpose for my films, I would reply that I want to be one of the artists in the cathedral on the great plain. I want to make a dragon's head, an angel or a devil – or perhaps a saint – out of stone. It does not matter which; it is the feeling of contentment that matters. Regardless whether I believe or not, regardless whether I am a Christian or not, I play my part at the collective building of the cathedral. For I am an artist and a craftsman; and I know how to chisel stone into faces and figures.

I never need to concern myself about present opinion or the judgment of posterity. I am a name which has not been recorded anywhere and which will disappear when I myself disappear; but a little part of me will live on in the triumphant masterwork of the anonymous craftsmen. A dragon, a devil, or perhaps a saint, it does not matter which."

—INGMAR BERGMAN

Material on Bergman reprinted by permission of the Janus Film Library.

JANUARY 19TH THROUGH 30TH

ART EXHIBIT
Recent serigraphs by Kent.

Saturday January 24

8:00 P.M. BAHA'I CONCERT AND FILM
IT'S A NEW DAY. Folk-singer and guitarist Phil Lucas.
and
CBS Film HIS NAME SHALL BE ONE. A 30 minute color program on the Baha'i Faith.

Monday January 26

through a glass darkly

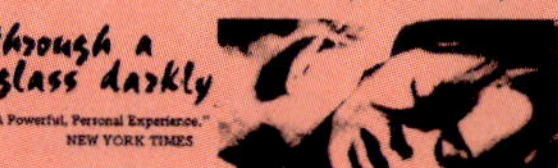

"A Powerful, Personal Experience."
NEW YORK TIMES

12:30 P.M. BERGMAN FILM

The first film in Bergman's religious trilogy, THROUGH A GLASS DARKLY chronicles the pathetic plunge of a young woman into madness. Karin, having read in her father's journal that she is an incurable schizophrenic, swoops through a series of compulsive acts and visions into a world of hallucination without God. Bergman has chartered with technical accuracy the moving psychological drama of a descent to insanity.

Followed by informal discussion in the Green Room, led by reactor Dr. Edwin Lipinski, SFU Psychiatrist.

Tuesday January 27

12:30 P.M. CONCERT
SFU CHOIR directed by David Keans.

Cantata .... Stravinsky
"Brich an, o schönes Morgenlicht" .... Bach
"Jauchet Erd und Himmel" .... Buxtehude

Wednesday January 28

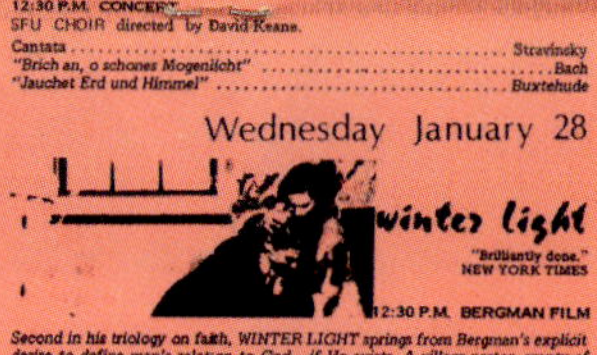

winter light

"Brilliantly done."
NEW YORK TIMES

12:30 P.M. BERGMAN FILM

Second in his trilogy on faith, WINTER LIGHT springs from Bergman's explicit desire to define man's relation to God – if He exists. A village pastor, empty of faith and desperately unloved, reveals his bitter failure to offer spiritual consolation to his flock. Somberly poignant, the film sketches a world of half empty churches but not entirely without a hope in God's universe.

Followed by informal discussion in the Green Room. Led by reactor Dr. Reginald A. Wilson, Professor of Systematic Theology and Christian Ethics, Union College, Vancouver.

Thursday January 29

12:30 P.M. PARTICIPATORY LECTURE
(STYLE), (CHANGE), (VIOLENCE) AS A CLICHE IN MODERN LIFE. A visual reaction to Bergman's Theology devised by a student workshop under the direction of Doug Eliuk of the National Film Board, who was co-director of the NFB Summer Institute of Film and Media Study in Vancouver and is now completing a book on film.

Friday January 30

12:30 P.M. FILM: MARY'S DAY
A celebration-happening at Immaculate Heart College in Los Angeles

8:00 P.M. BERGMAN FILM

the seventh seal

"Uncommon and Fascinating."
NEW YORK TIMES

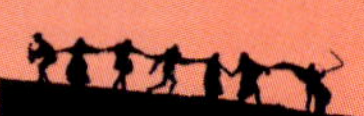

THE SEVENTH SEAL is Bergman's stunning allegory of man's search for meaning in life. A knight, after returning home from the Crusades, plays a game of chess with Death while The Plague ravages medieval Europe. An exceptionally powerful film, it is a work of awesome scope and remarkable visual pleasures.

Followed by informal discussion in Green Room, led by reactor Mrs. R.M. Clark, Elder of Ryerson United Church and Academic Planner for the new Regents College at UBC.

BERGMAN FILM TICKETS WILL BE SOLD ONLY AT THE DOOR
SFU STUDENTS, FACULTY AND STAFF - $.50 GENERAL PUBLIC - $1.00

The eight-page Spring 1970 event brochure created by The Centre for Communications and the Arts (CCA) illustrates the remarkable breadth of activities the CCA promoted. This excerpt describes an experimental project, *Religion and the Arts*, that the CCA co-sponsored with the SFU Chaplaincy. The project explored the theology of Ingmar Bergman as expressed in six films. The screenings were followed by discussions on theology, medieval history, psychiatry, film study and philosophy. *SFU Archives*

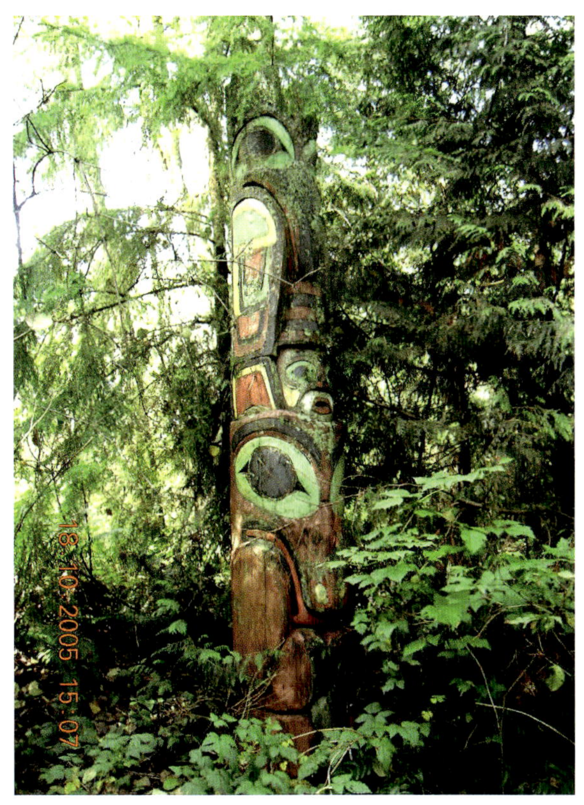

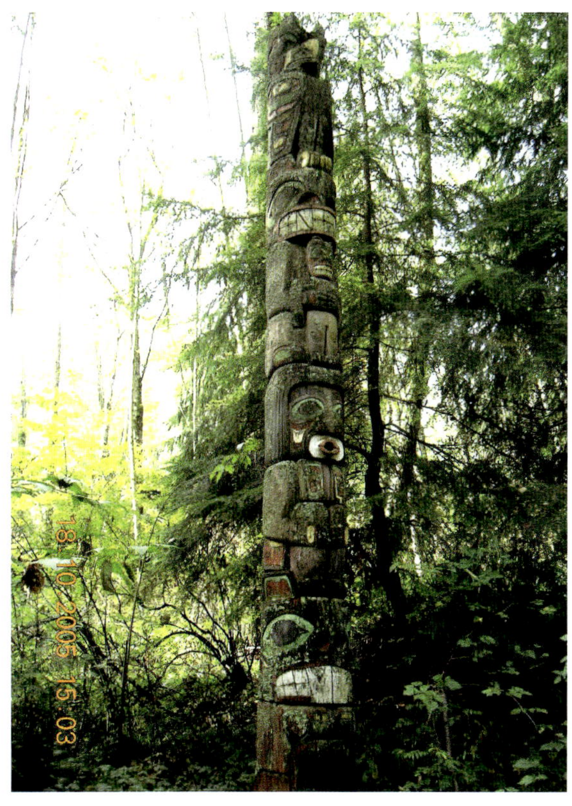

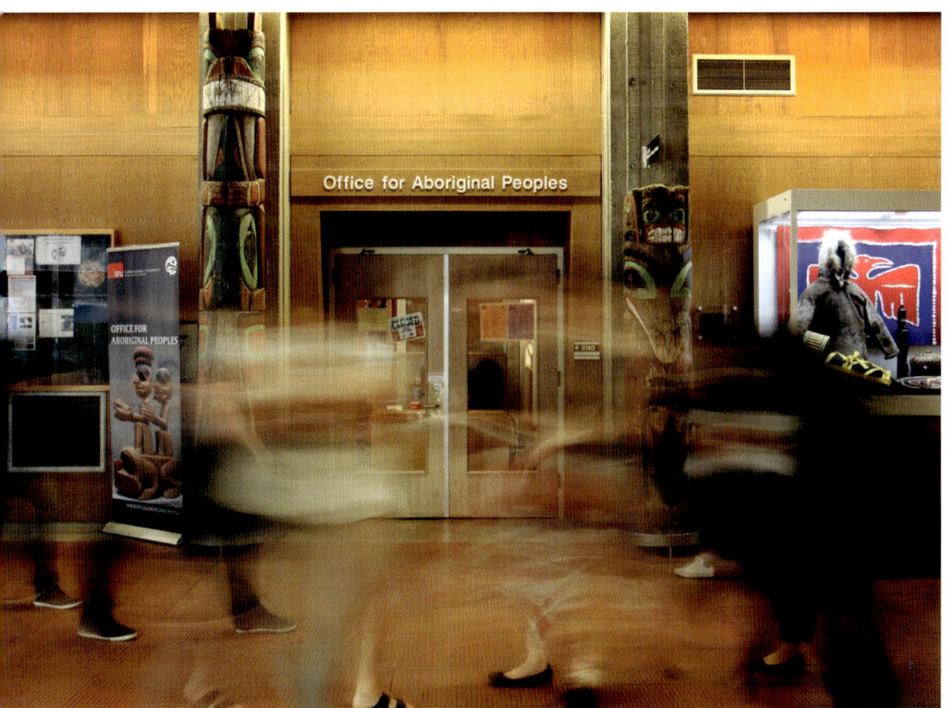

The two Ray Wesley poles, commissioned by the SFU Alumni Association in the early 1970s, were first placed in Naheeno Park. They were eventually restored and mounted in their current site at the entrance to the Office for Aboriginal Peoples in 2013. *Top: John Hebron; Left: Reese Muntean, Bill Reid Centre for Northwest Coast Studies*

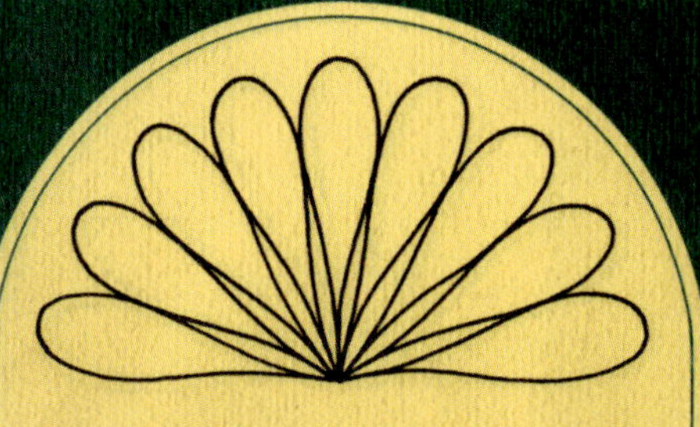

SIMON FRASER UNIVERSITY THEATRE

Spring Semester 1969

Evening or weekend events are listed in CAPS.

JANUARY

6-31 Exhibit—International Theatre Posters
13-31 Exhibit—Studies in Ambiguity
13-31 Photographs by Lynne Harrison
13 Concert—Tom Hawken (two shows)
14 Concert of SFU Electronic Music to University of Victoria
14 FILM—L'AVVENTURA
15 Centre Open House
16 Reading—Anton Vogt
20 Concert—Goethe Poems Set to Music
Cynthia Laurie-Hill, Soprano
William Babcock, piano
20 Exhibition Discussion—Lynne Harrison
21 Films—Animated Films from Vancouver School of Art Film Workshop
21 FILM—LA TERRA TREMA
22 Concert—University of Victoria Trio
23 Reading—Fred Candelaria
24 Noon Show—Modern Cemetery by Dennis Jasudowicz (tent)
25 SFU Mime Troupe to Victoria for CUDL regional competition
25 INTERNATIONAL NIGHT Program of Indian and Chinese dance, sitar, Chinese Defense Art, Chinese choir, Chinese violinist, Latin American guitar, and European dances by students at SFU with films from India and China.
27-15 Exhibit—Prints by Glen Alps
27 Reading—Earle Birney
28 Films—Selected 8mm and 16mm Films by SFU Film Workshop
28 FILM—RASHOMON
29 Concert—The Group for New Music
29 Theatre—The San Francisco Committee Workshop
30 Exhibit Discussion—Glen Alps (with two Alps films)
30 Reading—Mary Bruce and Lionel Kearns
31 Noon Show—Huit Clos (tentative)
31 THEATRE—HUIT CLOS (tentative)

FEBRUARY

3 Lecture—Walter Koch
4 Films—Three by Dave Rimmer of Vancouver
4 FILM—THE LOVERS
5 Concert of Indian dance and music—Arvind, Usha and Chetna Thakore
5 Concert of SFU Electronic Music to UBC
6 Lecture—Allan Solomon
6 Raeding—John Logan (3159)
7 Noon Show—to be announced
10 Concert—Oscar Peterson Trio (two shows)
11 Films—Prize winning films from Canadian Artists '68 John Chambers and Kee Dewdney
11 FILM—I VITELLONI (9200)
12 Concert—Christiane Van Acker, mezzo, and Michel Podolski, lute
12 THEATRE PRODUCTION—EASTER EGG by JAMES REANEY
13 Reading—Stanley Cooperman
13 THEATRE—EASTER EGG
14 Discussion with playwright James Reaney (tentative)
14 THEATRE—EASTER EGG
15 THEATRE—EASTER EGG
17 Lecture—Multiple-projection screening of slides by Fred Herzog and students in SFU Photography Workshop on topic of The City as an Environment
17 Reading—Robin Skelton (3005)
18—Film—MONIKA
18 Film Hurrah—by John Juliani
19 Concert—UBC String Quartet
20 Lecture—Robert Theobald
21 Noon Show—to be announced
21 THEATRE—SAN FRANCISCO MIME TROUPE in Gutter Puppets and The Farce of Patelin
24 Concert—French Art Song
Cynthia Laurie-Hill, soprano
William Babcock, piano
25 Films—Films by Al Razutis of Vancouver and Peter Svatek of Montreal (with Tony Westman of SFU)
25 FILM—THE 400 BLOWS
26 Concert—SFU Electronic Music by Schafer, Huse, Werren
27 Lecture—Geoffrey Aggeler on Anthony Burgess
28 Noon Show—to be announced

MARCH

3 Student Society Program—to be announced
4 Film—Premiere screening of Felix, a feature film by SFU Film Workshop
4 FILM—Three by GEORGE KUCHAR
5 Concert—to be announced
5 Lecture—Anthony Burgess (9201)
6 Lecture—Don Harvey
7 Noon Show—to be announced
10 Student Society program—to be announced (two shows)
11 Films—Animated films by Al Sens of SFU
11 FILM—THE SEVENTH SEAL (9200)
12 Concert—to be announced
14 Reading—Brian Fawcett
15 Dance Concert—SFU Dance Workshop
15 DANCE CONCERT—SFU DANCE WORKSHOP
17 Student Society program—to be announced (two shows)
18 Films—Arnold Saba/Gordon Fidler
18 FILM—YOUNG APHRODITES
19 Concert—Sound Experiments conducted by composer Phil Werren
20 Lecture Duayne Hatchett
21 Noon Show—To be announced
22 A VISUAL ENVIRONMENT with mime, visual arts and other media (day-long workshop especially for the deaf)
24 Student Society program—to be announced (two shows)
25 Concert—Dichterliebe
Cynthia Laurie-Hill, soprano
William Babcock, piano
25 FILM—BILLY LIAR
26 Concert—to be announced
27 Reading—John Mills
28 Noon Show—to be announced
31 Student Society program—to be announced (two shows)

APRIL

1 Films—Larry Kardish—Canadian Artists '68—Prize-winning film
1 FILM—HALLELUJAH THE HILLS
2 Composers Forum—John Rogers, Mark DeVoto, Peter Huse, Phil Werren
3 Concert—SFU Chamber Singers (tentative)
8 Film—Michael Snow—Canadian Artists '68 —Prize-winning film
9 Concert—to be announced
10 Concert—SFU Choir (tentative)
11 Noon Show—to be announced

No events will be scheduled April 14-May 11, 1969

INTERNATIONAL NIGHT

Saturday, January 25, 8:30 pm
Unreserved seats $1.00

INDIAN DANCE - - - - - - - - - - - - - Usha Thakore
GARABA (Indian folk dance) - - Fourteen dancers from UBC
SITAR - - - - - - - - - - - - - - - - Arvind Thakore
CHINESE DEFENSE ART - - - - - - - - - - Ken Yeun
VIOLIN - - - - - - - - - - - - - - - - - - Larry Lee
CHOIR - - - - - - Chinese graduate students in chemistry
plus two short films on India and China, a Latin American guitarist, Scottish bagpiper and other performers.

International Night, a project of the Simon Fraser University International Club, will introduce the community to many of the talented persons from overseas now studying at Simon Fraser University and elsewhere in the Vancouver area. The co-chairmen of the program, Arvind Thakore and John Anscomb, hope that this ethnic culture program will be "a projection into a new dimension of human understanding" and look forward to establishing International Night as an annual event.

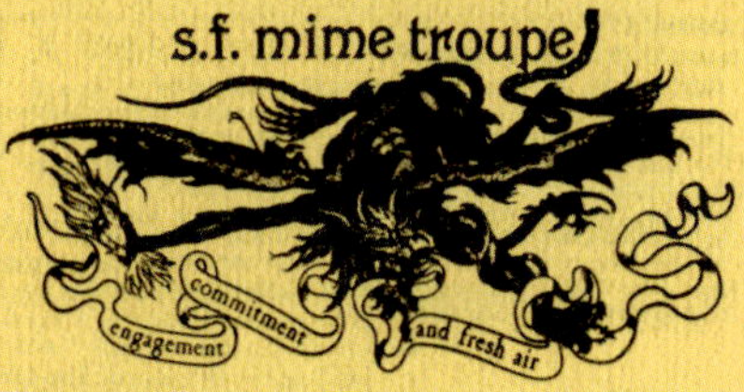

THE SIMON FRASER STUDENT SOCIETY
in co-operation with
THE CENTRE FOR COMMUNICATIONS AND THE ARTS
presents

SAN FRANCISCO MIME TROUPE

returning to Simon Fraser University for their first performance since October 1966 with

GUTTER PUPPETS and THE FARCE OF PATELIN
Friday, February 21, 8:30 pm
All Seats Reserved
Tickets $2.50 (students $1.50)

PATELIN, from a 15th century French farce, becomes a vehicle for protest and satire in this adaptation by R. G. Davis and Jael Weisman, directed by Sandra Archer. The San Francisco Chronicle called PATELIN "a triumph of free-wheeling commedia dell'arte—a thrashing, kicking, howling, posturing, mugging dissection of 'businessmen' and the law."

The puppet shows were built and written by members of the company to address subjects present to the minds of us all. "Disconnected from the powers at the top and answerable only to those on the bottom, the GUTTER PUPPETS, unlike their 'responsible' counterparts, are thoroughly irreverent, impeccably honest and brimful of information on how to succeed as a revolutionary in the midst of the labyrinth . . . They will agitate, feloniously incite, and generally blow your mind."

The San Francisco Mime Troupe was first started in 1959 doing silent mime. Mime has become a point of departure. These actor's intentions are best expressed by R. G. Davis: "We have tried to cut through the aristocratic and square notion of what theatre is by bringing movies into stage performances, presenting speakers who are sometimes far more dramatic than plays, applying broadly comic forms (the minstrel show, commedia) to serious issues. We have embarked upon a guerrilla scheme of living off the land and travelling, trying to provoke change . . . Mime is the point of departure for our style, in which words sharpen and refine, but the substance of meaning is in action."

Each semester from 1967 to 1975, the Centre for Communications and the Arts (CCA) created and distributed eye-catching event brochures. This excerpt from the seven-page Spring 1969 brochure lists a wide variety of scheduled events for that semester. It also promotes an international night, and showcases a visit from the San Francisco Mime Troupe organized by the SFU Student Society in co-operation with the CCA. *SFU Archives* which provided a place to view one another's progress and examples from the vaults. "There was very little formal 'instruction' and no assignments. Essentially it was like a free school for the arts."[9]

One of his most memorable collaborations was a thirty-minute video on hard drugs, done with film resident Tom Shandel for Cable 10, the community channel. The film included provocative and detailed information on drug use, but they managed to get it on the air by delivering the footage at the last minute. Immediately following the program, their time slot was cancelled, but they were told that there was more viewer response, both positive and negative, than had been received for any other program on the channel.

The Position of Film within the CCA

As early as 1966, a discussion started on whether there should be a film school at SFU. On March 9, 1966, *The Peak* reported on a panel on "The Experimental Film: An Illustrated Discussion." The impressive panel included three judges of a recent film festival: Naoki Togawa, co-director of the Japan Film Library Council and a lecturer at Nihon University; Arthur Knight, professor of cinema arts at UCLA and film critic for the *Saturday Review*; and Patrick Watson, one-time co-host of *This Hour Has Seven Days* and director of the Montreal Film Festival. All agreed that a good film school was desirable. A *Peak* reviewer concluded it "would offer the opportunity to blend the art and the industry, providing proficient technicians and creative directors and editors."[10]

Meanwhile, film activities were coordinated through the CCA and, as was common among the programs, many individuals from the other arts lent their talents to film projects. Murray Schafer played many important roles, and the names of theatre people such as John Juliani, Jan Visscher and Norman Browning often appear on the film credits. Besides his direction of the film *Hurrah!*, John Juliani acted in Sylvia Spring's *Madeleine Is...* (1971) as the boyfriend of the title character, played by Nicki Lippman. Sandy Wilson was assistant director on the film. It was a small world. The many interactions between theatre, dance and film fostered the cross-pollination among the arts that expressed the aspirations of the Centre for Communications and the Arts at this time, as well as providing a supportive environment.

For some, the ambience of the film community that existed under the umbrella of the CCA provided a comforting, almost home-like atmosphere. Zale Dalen "enjoyed the mechanics of filmmaking, as it was in those days. I found I loved being in an editing room. I found that writing in film came easy to me.

I could just imagine what I would see on the screen and what I would hear as the movie played, and then just describe that as simply and as clearly as I could. Forget the words. What do I see on the screen?"[11]

Dalen evokes the collaborative nature of the times:

> Everybody separated out according to their interests. Everybody did everything. Thus Tony Westman became our man to talk to if we needed help with camera or photography. George Johnson was the man heading for a career in editing. Ron Orieux was another cinematography resource. Peter Bryant was just an inspiration when it came to film content and appreciation, as were Doug White and Brian Small. Andrew de Lilio Rymsza provided enough pretentiousness to supply the entire group. For a person like me, with anti-authoritarian and anti-academic propensities, the film workshop became a second home and instant family.
>
> Corner the then current resident, Stan Fox or Tom Shandel, with a compelling idea and you could gain access to basic camera, sound, and editing equipment and possibly a few rolls of film. We all learned stuff and made short movies.
>
> Many of the bright young students went on to have long and satisfying careers in the film industry—Ron Orieux and Tony Westman as cinematographers, George Johnson as an editor and executive at the NFB. Sandra Wilson as a notable director making close to home personal movies.
>
> We enlisted each other in a variety of capacities on our projects. One day I might be providing a harmonica soundtrack for Peter Bryant's *One Man Went to Mow*. The next, Peter might be teaching me the basics of cutting for action as I edited my satirical short *Porn Maker to the World*. I tried to get any project I started to take me into an area of the technology that was foreign to me. So it was at the film workshop that I first used synchronized sound, matching sound recorded on 1/4 inch tape transferred to sprocketed 16mm magnetic. I don't remember where I found the money for that transfer, but money could usually be found. This is all so long ago, it's even possible that the film workshop had a transfer machine. The point is, we were all doing what we loved, enjoying the camaraderie, and having fun. It was the beginning.
>
> Probably the best thing the SFU film workshop gave me was access to the grapevine, the contacts that would keep me alive as I

> set out to sink or swim in the film industry. Thus when Peter Bryant, or Doug White, or Brian Small talked some schools into bringing us in to talk about film making, I got a piece of the action. When Tony Westman became a producer for Aldrich Pears, the architectural firm, to make the Saskatchewan film for Expo '86, I scored a directing gig that broadened my experience and kept me solvent for a year. This was the real value of the film workshop for me, and for others. It put us in the loop for opportunities in the future. You can't put a price or a numerical value on that.[12]

After he left the West Coast, Dalen found work editing Alan King's documentary *Come on Children* for the princely sum of $150 a week. When he returned to Vancouver, he continued his journey to become a well-known film director. Significant features he has since directed include *Skip Tracer, Hounds of Notre Dame* and *Expect No Mercy*.

Instead of lectures, film resident Shelah Reljic scheduled screenings of new SFU Film Workshop productions. Linda Johnston applauds the support of Reljic, noting that she "very much understood how the industry worked and agreed to be the external advisor for my master's thesis. Her example was inspiring, and her insight was invaluable. I got involved in the film workshop the second term of third year. We watched films and film clips, discussed approaches, looked at technical details and had lively discussions. Some equipment was available for students to use to make projects. At one point we arranged a weekly film screening in one of the lecture halls. It wasn't a large group and I think Sandy Wilson and I were the only women. Given the work that Stan and Shelah did, a lot of the focus was on documentaries."[13] Johnston was involved with the organization of the first Canadian Women and Film Festival in 1971.

Workshop director Vincent Vaitiekunas arrived in 1972 after extensive industry experience, which included the making of over 200 films. He welcomed the opportunity to teach students full-length dramatic filmmaking. In an article by CCA publicist Mary Trainer, he states: "Doing the feature film is the most complete training a young filmmaker can get because practically all different aspects of filmmaking are involved."[14] Quoted in a *Cinema Canada* article by Jaan Pill, NFB cameraman Eugene Boyko recalls the films of Vaitiekunas's first workshop. "It was the best I'd seen in college produced films. I had a reluctance against college produced films for a long time because I always found that the kind of people who were attracted to it were generally those who couldn't communicate. But here was a school that was here in Vancouver and it seemed to work."[15]

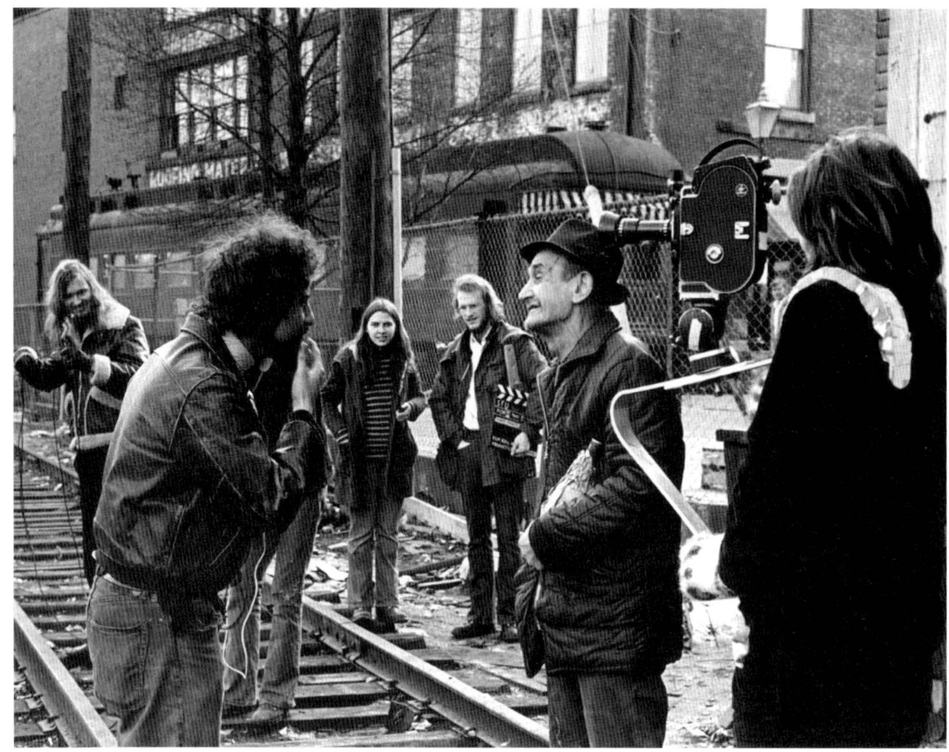

A scene from Chris Aikenhead's *Ivory Founts*, awarded Best Film at the Canadian Student Film Festival in 1973. *SFU Archives*

Vaitiekunas used a lot of tough love to pressure his students to bring out the best in themselves. "I had to push quite heavily and a lot of people complained. I don't know how many individual people complained, I don't know how many people do admit that they used to get these threatening phone calls. And I would put my foot down, because I knew that unless I did that, unless they take care of that particular stage of production now, that person will never have that film finished, and so it would be kind of a terrible loss because he will never have the opportunity of putting his work to test: Exposing it to the audience."[16]

Sometimes pushing pays off. In two consecutive years, films from Vaitiekunas's workshop won the McLaren Award for the Best Film at the Canadian Student Film Festival. For both filmmakers, Chris Aikenhead and Chris Windsor, it was their first 16 mm film, with Valerie Ambrose starring in both. Aikenhead put together the script for *Ivory Founts*, a postmodern film about making a film, in 1973. It evolved, he says, out of his own incapacity to come up with a *real* script. It's a lighthearted, exuberant film, which succeeds by not taking itself too seriously. Subsequently his artistic interests led him away from film to the study of English literature.

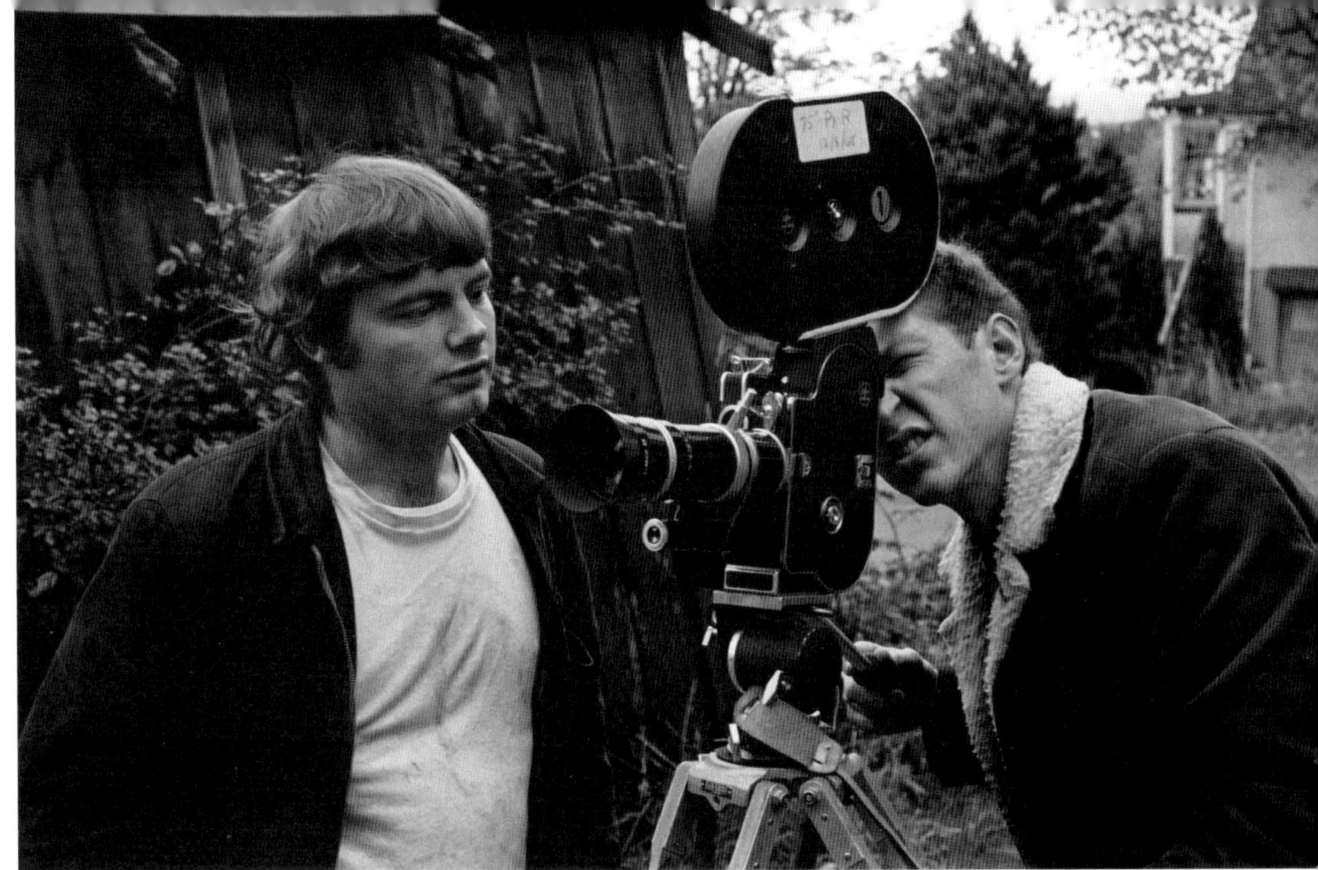

Peter Bryant with cameraman Tony Westman. *Tony Westman*

Chris Windsor had previously worked on *Ivory Founts*, acting the role of a student editor. He put together the script for his film *Trapper Dan* while he was working as a projectionist at a sleazy Vancouver theatre. Both award-winning films had solid scripts and were filmed in a short time. Chris Windsor went on to make the cult classic *Big Meat Eater* a few years later.

When Vaitiekunas left for a position in the film department at York University in 1974, French-Canadian filmmaker Guy Bergeron became the workshop resident. Bergeron dedicated himself to keeping the vibrancy of the film program alive: "My greatest concern is that future workshops retain the liveliness they have now. Students are brimming with energy. They demand a great deal from me, but at the same time find they must take on high pressure responsibilities of their own."[17] Bergeron left SFU in December 1975 to take a position at CBC Montreal as Chef de service de la réalisation.

Tony Westman, who has worked as a professional photographer and cinematographer for over half a century, welcomed the openness he found at SFU. "SFU created a philosophy of yes," he says. "I was lucky to hit the Golden Years of SFU and the National Film Board."[18] He arrived at SFU in the fall of 1966 as a student in the Department of Political Science, Sociology and Anthropology (PSA) after having spent a year at the University of Washington in Seattle.

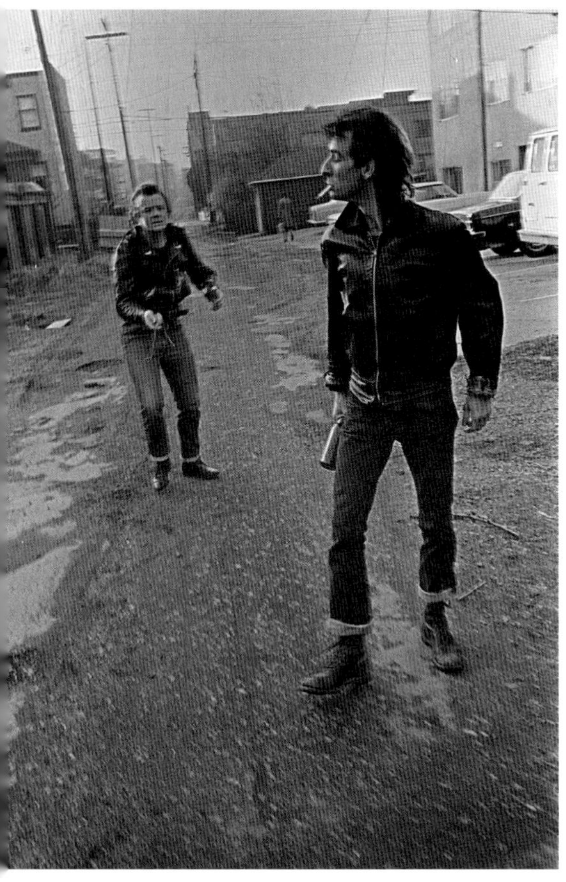

A scene from Peter Bryant's *The Rocco Brothers*. *Peter Bryant, SFU Archives*

A Canada Council grant for still photography in 1973 allowed Westman to spend three months in the high Arctic documenting the landscape and the people's lifestyle, both under threat of a proposed pipeline down the Mackenzie River. That project and his practice of street photography led to a photo exhibition entitled *Rites de Passage*. Some of the images were acquired by the National Gallery of Canada and the National Film Board stills division.

Westman spent many years in the US and Canada working as a cinematographer on major films. In the 1970s, he recalls, the Canadian film industry was a branch plant of US Local 659, but Canada was becoming more of a go-to place. He began work as a camera operator on films coming to Canada, such as *Rocky IV*. An all-Canadian Local 667 was created to deal with Canadian issues, and Tony became a union rep. It became clear that it was Toronto-centric—not a happy marriage between East and West. West Coast Local 669 was created, and Tony became president, a crucial step in the creation of Hollywood North.

Westman describes how his arrival at SFU allowed him to develop his work as a filmmaker and make his way into the industry:

I was a draft dodger, new to Canada, and trying to grow up and find my purpose. My interest then was still photography, so I gravitated to the student newspaper to photograph for *The Peak* from 1966 to 1968. In the summer of 1968 I had my first filming experience. I was asked to shoot a ten-minute B&W film *Harry the Hummer* on a local Okanagan character, directed by UBC film graduate Peter Svatek, in company with the young poets Seymour Mayne and Patrick Lane. I had never touched a film camera until this time, but I knew what "composition" meant in a photographic frame. I walked around Vernon to get supporting images for the film, which won an honourable mention at the Vancouver International Film Festival. Film was now my new passion.

In the fall of 1968 I stepped into the SFU Theatre basement and discovered a room full of enthusiasm, a set of rewinds, a viewer and a Bolex camera. Over the next several weeks I met George Johnson and Peter Bryant, Dave Scott (aka Zale Dalen), J. Andrew de Lilio Rymsza,

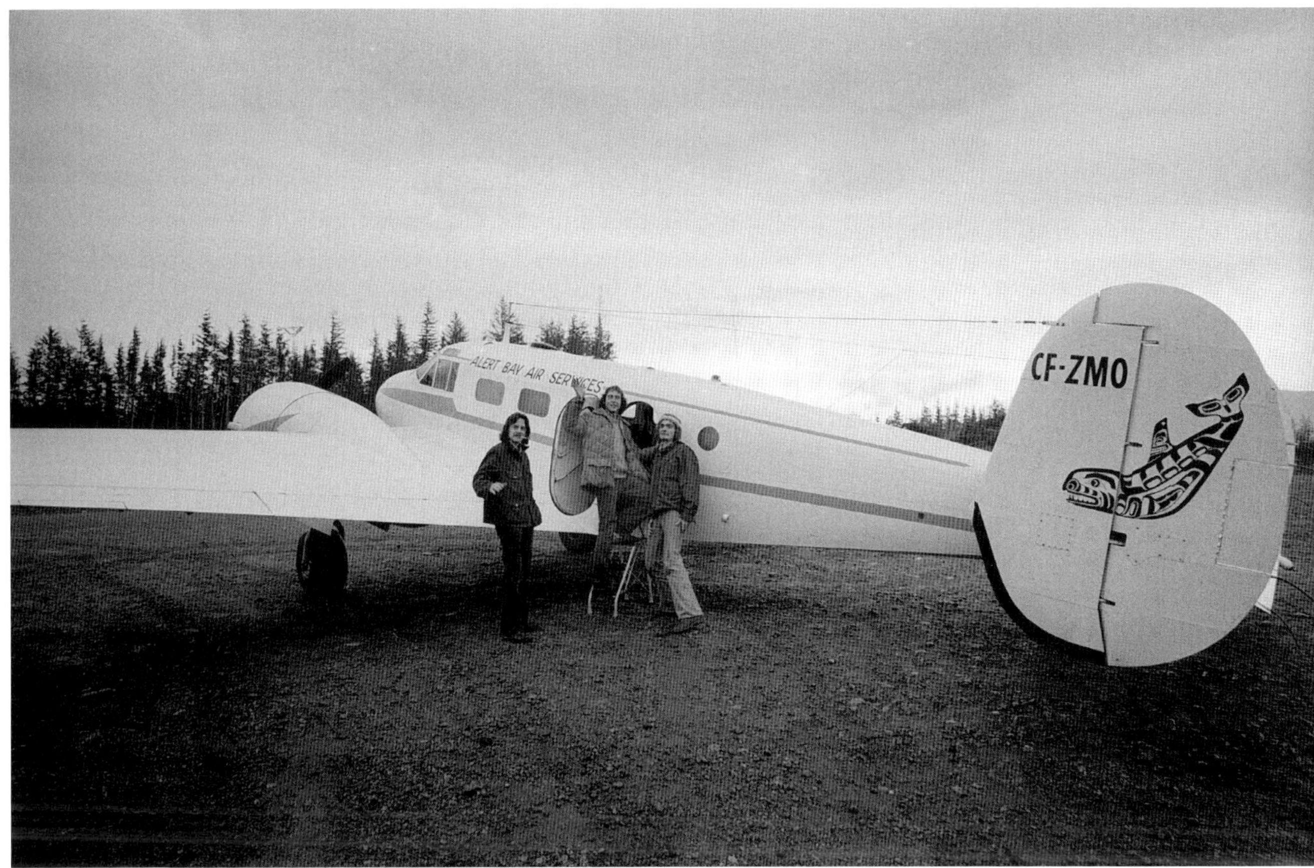

The SFU film crew in Alert Bay in preparation for filming what became *Noohalk*. *Tony Westman*

Don Shaw, Mark Dolgoy, Sandy Wilson, Doug White, Brian Small… all under the tutelage of former CBC editor Shelah Reljic, an all-around mother hen to this eclectic tribe. Peter Bryant and I became partners in some of his creative endeavours, first with his workshop dramatic production of *The Rocco Brothers*, then the documentary *Noohalk*.

After graduating in 1970 we were suddenly in the real world; eventually Peter managed to pull together the financing for his feature *The Supreme Kid*, which I photographed. By that time I had been shooting films for the National Film Board so my skill set had been refined, which was only possible with the support of Shelah Reljic, who had left SFU to become a producer for the NFB. As luck would have it, Peter Jones, the executive producer at NFB Vancouver, recommended me to the Montreal NFB office to work for a year as a camera assistant. I subsequently went on to direct and/or photograph several films for the NFB: *Salmon People*, *Beluga Baby*, *Man Who Chooses the Bush*, *Soccer* and *Family Down the Fraser*.[19]

The Bella Coola Project: SFU Filmmakers Creating Their Own Opportunities

The Bella Coola Project was a film venture into an Indigenous community up the BC coast, providing an opportunity for a group of SFU filmmakers to hone and develop their talents in a supportive but challenging environment. It began to take shape in the future participants' final undergrad year at SFU. Linda Johnston stated in an interview that the filmmakers discussed what would be next if they wanted to pursue working in film. Opportunities in Vancouver were next to nothing. "We decided if we wanted to work in film, we'd have to make it ourselves."[20]

Initial plans were ambitious, calling for delving into the rich anthropological history of the Seychelles, an island nation off the east coast of Africa. After discussion the group agreed that a smaller project closer to home might be more feasible. Professor Pat Hindley, who was supervising Linda Johnston's thesis, had been working with single sideband radio transmission to connect First Nations communities on the coast. One of these was a Nuxalk community in Bella Coola; the connection was made and plans for the project began. The resulting film, *Noohalk*, was a sensitive documentary in which the Indigenous people were able to voice their concerns over threats to their culture.

Johnston continued, "This sort of thing was very new in 1969 and few asks were out there. We were able to get flight passes, ferry passes and loans of camera and sound equipment. I only got to Bella Coola for ten days and it was everything I'd hoped. One of the band members, a very lovely young woman, stayed with me and my family during the editing. A screening was held in Bella Coola on completion."[21]

Tony Westman explained in another interview how the project got off the ground:

> The project already had a good start because we had a great crew: Peter Bryant director, me as DOP, Don Shaw sound, George Johnson editor, Peter Gaudi and Linda Johnston as liaisons... fuelled by the exciting possibility of actually making a documentary about real people in a real place... If nothing else, we had a big dose of blind enthusiasm... and the promise of a full semester's credit to boot. I am convinced that this kind of self-motivated learning could only happen in those early years at SFU that just happened to match the tumult of the '60's era.

> Getting film stock turned out to be fairly easy, as both CBC and NFB were now fully into colour, so we got several thousand feet of B&W stock. We needed a proper sync sound camera, as the workshop Bolex was too noisy. On a rumour I heard that BCIT had the perfect camera for the job in a BL Arriflex sitting unused in a closet. Somehow we got the use of a professional Nagra recording machine as well. On a cold call to the head of the department I managed to convince him of our purpose and integrity—having Shelah Reljic's magic wand probably helped. Somehow we managed to get free air transport to Bella Coola via BC Airlines. Accommodation was kindly provided by residents of the Bella Coola community. Filming lasted about six weeks. After many months of editing by George Johnson, the finished film was entered in the International Student Film Festival and won best documentary. This was the most amazing example of the elasticity of educational opportunities at SFU, that was unique to those formative years.[22]

Explorations into Indigenous cultures were rare in these early days of SFU (and elsewhere). Perhaps the filmmakers and the Indigenous community found affinities in the ways in which they were sometimes marginalized.

Linda Johnston feels that the relationships developed with the host community were central to the experience of making the film. "Our Bella Coola partners were pleased with the process at the time. Years later I had VCR copies made from my film copy and took them up to Bella Coola. The band council office was pleased to receive them, as many of the elders captured in the film had passed. Unfortunately, CBC TV turned down a request to show it on the network."

In the end, Johnston feels that the skills she and the others gained in making *Noohalk* were vital to their later success in filmmaking: "The Bella Coola Project gave us in one short year a set of skills that would normally take a decade. Not many worked in collaboration with First Nations in 1969. Learning how to communicate and build respectful working relationships cross-culturally is invaluable in today's world. Mass media does influence political and social decision making—always has—but social media has intensified it. Documentaries are key to its navigation. Fundraising, budgeting, administration and creative ways of approaching challenges are always useful skills. All of these have been invaluable to me and remain so."[23]

About the Bella Coola Photos

by Tony Westman

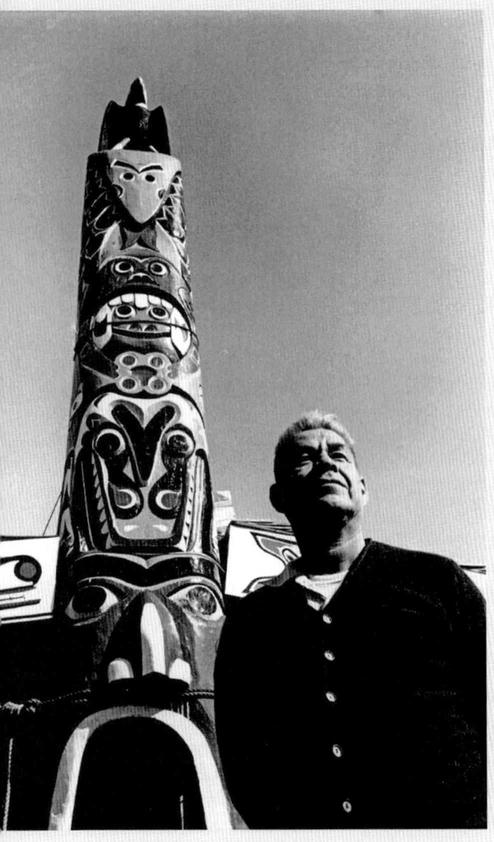

David Moody by the totem pole he carved. The pole stands at the entrance to a longhouse known as the House of Numst'. *"Soul of Bella Coola,"* *Tony Westman*

In the summer of 1969, I came to Bella Coola with Peter Bryant, Peter Gaudi and Gary Shaw. We were all part of the non-credit film workshop at Simon Fraser University, and this was our chance to make our first documentary film. It was also my first experience in a small and remote Indigenous community. Although a student of anthropology, I found myself sadly ignorant of the history and rich cultural heritage of the Nuxalk people, located in a remote area of the British Columbia coast. The community of Bella Coola was very kind and patient with us as we moved about, asking endless questions as we "learned on the job" about what was important and what should be in a film. Fortunately for us, tribal Elders like Margaret Siwallace, Agnes Edgar, Felicity Walkus, David Moody, Hank King, Andy Schooner and so many others gave us such great insight and direction. The film was finished in 1970 and won a best student film award. I subsequently made a trip to the Bella Coola community, where it was shown in the brand-new longhouse gathering place called the House of Numst'. Both screenings were packed. I asked Margaret Siwallace if she liked the film. She was silent for a moment then commented, "I didn't mind it."

These photographs are part of my own personal notebook of the time spent in Bella Coola. I had been working for the student newspaper, *The Peak*, for several years prior, and like everything else on campus, there was no rule book or tradition to follow. I had been practising the notion of "street photography" that captures fragments of everyday life, which is quite different from the narrative mindset of documentary filmmaking. During that time, I had developed the habit of what I called "visual curiosity," which synthesized people, places and things into a pictorial narrative as witness to wherever I happened to be.

Over several months living in Bella Coola for the filming, I had ample free time just to wander about the area with the camera, with my inner voice asking, "Why am I here, what is happening, who are these people, where are they going and how do I capture an image that does justice to the moment?" I hoped that over a period I would collect a reasonable sense of the place and its people, but

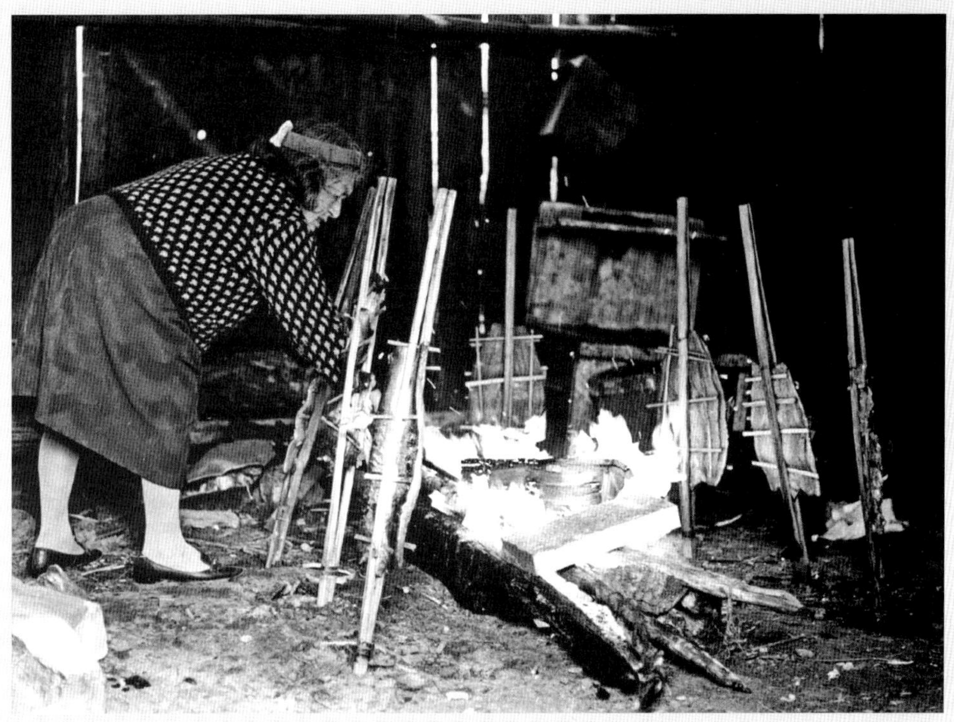

Agnes Edgar in a smokehouse. *"Soul of Bella Coola," Tony Westman*

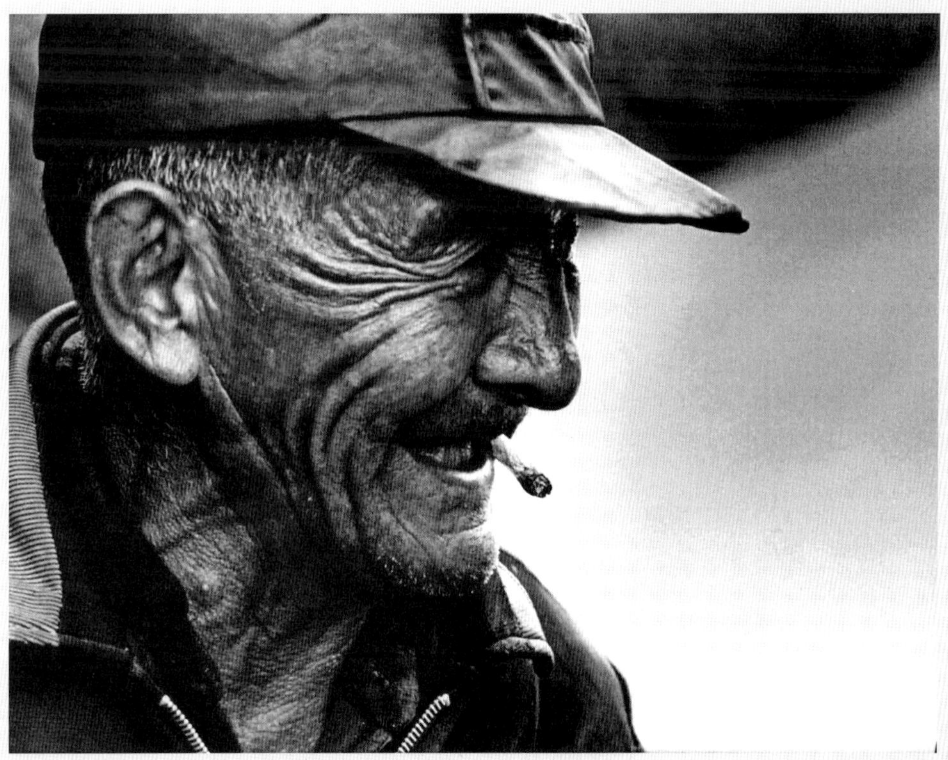

Sam Schooner. *"Soul of Bella Coola," Tony Westman*

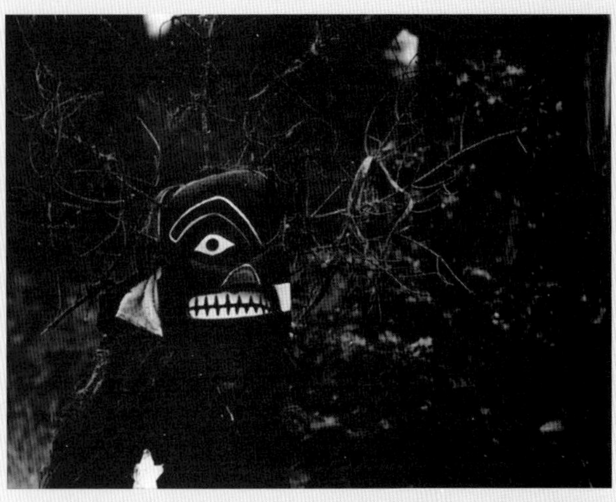

A rehearsal of the thunder mask scene in *Noohalk*. *"Soul of Bella Coola," Tony Westman*

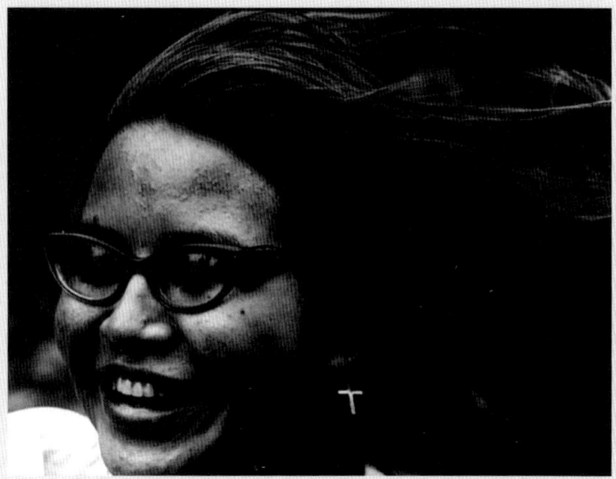

Darlene Tallio. *"Soul of Bella Coola," Tony Westman*

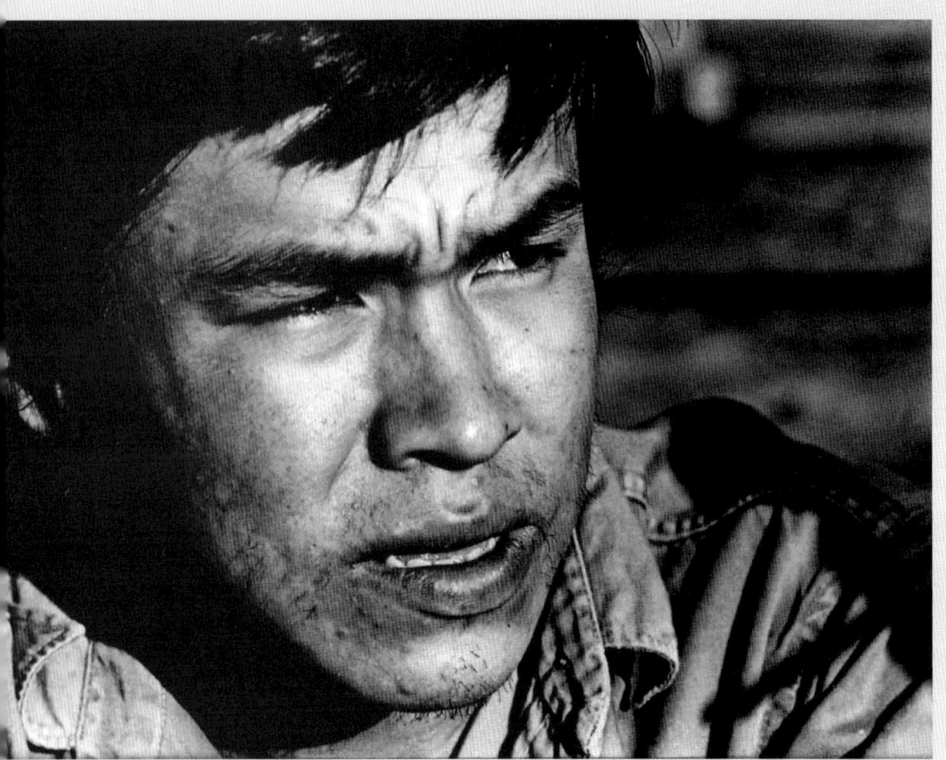

Harry Schooner. *"Soul of Bella Coola," Tony Westman*

such a judgement must be left to the subjects of the photographs and, if nothing else, attempts to anchor for them some memory of that time and place. Toward the end of our stay in Bella Coola, the tribal Elders held a little ceremony and conferred special traditional names on the film crew. My name was "Tall Man Who Walks in Peace." I hope the images do justice to the spirit of the warm-hearted Nuxalk people and embrace the memory of their place in history.[24]

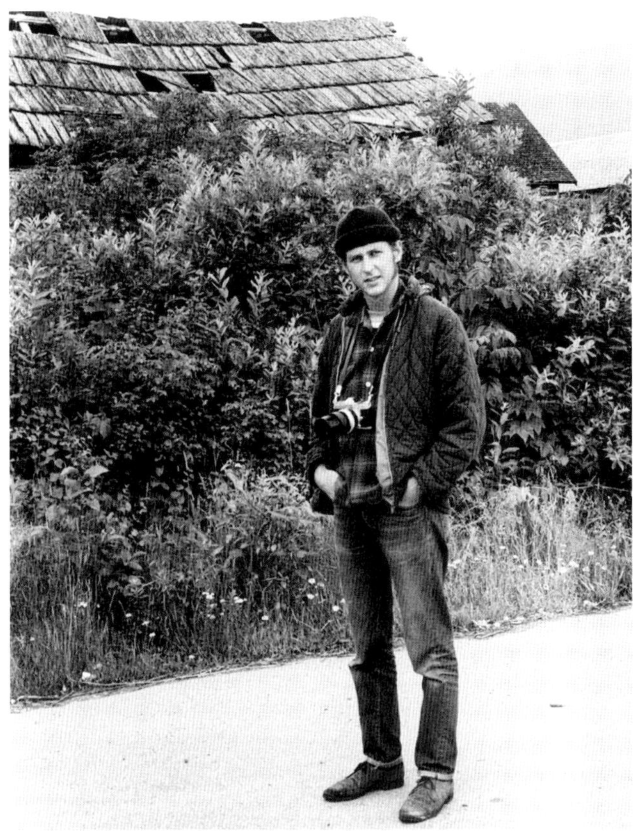

Tony Westman at Bella Coola. *Tony Westman*

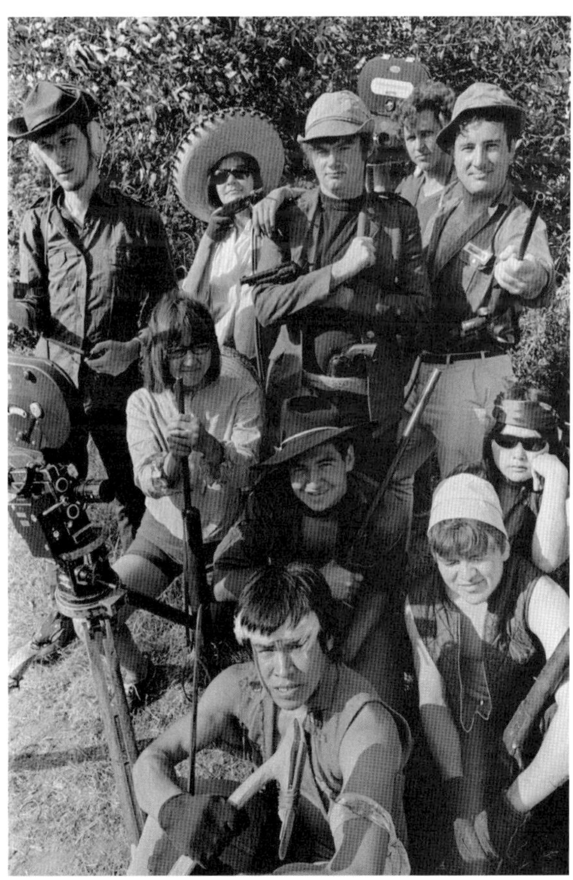

The Bella Coola Liberation Front with the SFU film crew. This group photo was film director Peter Bryant's idea to express the feelings of the young people who assisted in the filming of *Noohalk*. *Tony Westman*

The following is an excerpt of correspondence between Jennifer Kramer and Tony Westman from October 2012, when Jennifer visited Bella Coola and screened the film *Noohalk: The People of Bella Coola*.

Dear Tony,

I just got back from a wonderful trip to Bella Coola. I went for a memorial potlatch on Saturday for William Tallio. On Sunday people helped put up his memorial pole and afterward came to the house of his son Ernest Tallio for refreshments.

I decided to show the twenty-some people your film *Noohalk: The People of Bella Coola* (1970) since I was bringing the film to give back to the community and it was a rainy day so it seemed like a good activity. People were really entranced. Chief Rhonda Schooner Sandoval, Chief Jeffrey Snow, his mother Pearl Snow plus many others got to see it. Jeff recalled performing one of the masked dances in the film and his father Charles Snow is depicted as well in the film carving jewelry.

Rhonda immediately said they should schedule a film screening the very next day at the local Nuxalk school, Acwsalcta, and invite those who were in the film to the screening. As a result I stayed in the valley an extra day and we screened the film to about 40 people—Harry Schooner, Herbie Edgar, Emily Moody (now Anderson), Jeff Snow were all in attendance from the film as well as elders Karen Edgar Anderson, Eleanor Schooner, the Acwsalcta school culture and language teachers and 8th and 9th graders.

People really enjoyed it and loved recognizing either themselves or their relatives. Afterwards various elders got up to speak to impress upon the Acwsalcta students what it was like to be growing up in the 1960s when they were not sure whether the Nuxalk songs and dances would continue or whether they should assimilate to white people's ways. They explained to the kids that they had a much stronger Nuxalk culture now but they should be appreciative of those elders and artists who kept or keep the culture going such as Agnes Edgar, Felicity Walkus, Margaret Siwallace and Harry Schooner.

The student filmmakers from SFU did not in general become household names—at least not in most households. Apart from Sandy Wilson's *My American Cousin*, few mainstream films were made on the West Coast, and those mostly by Hollywood visitors. Vancouver provides a rich variety of locations, however. Scenes for the sorority house in *Carnal Knowledge*, for example, were filmed at the old Rogers residence (now an apartment complex) at Granville and 57th Street.

Yet this absence of distractions—like the Hollywood machine and its aggressive evangelists—allowed local filmmakers to grow their art independently. Danny Singer, Tony Westman, Sandy Wilson and others had the freedom to develop their own deepening vision as they penetrated the mysteries of how their art and the world interconnected.

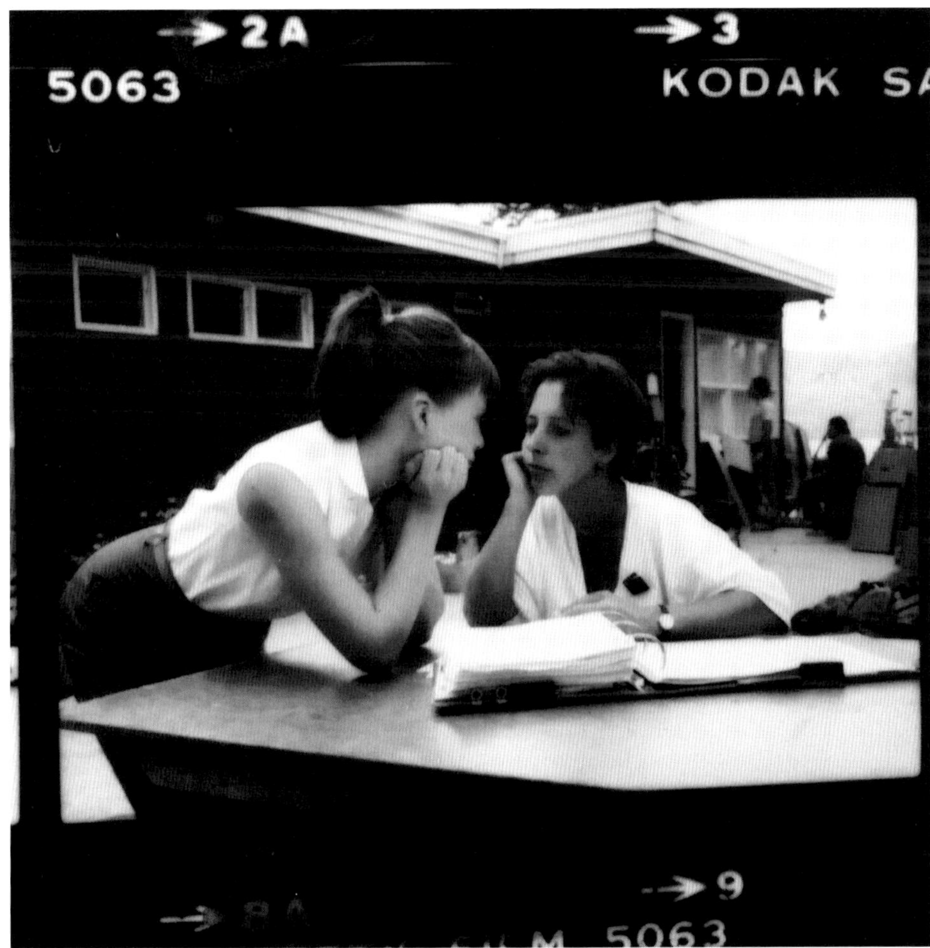

Filmmaker Sandy Wilson is on the left. *SFU Archives*

The Beginning of My Film Career at SFU

by Sandy Wilson

Hiking Up Skirts and Signing Up for Film

I was working as the switchboard operator in the SFU Transportation Centre at the entrance to campus when my friend Terri Nash told me there were some cute guys in the film workshop. So, I signed up.

It was September 1968, at the end of a long hot summer of protests, meetings, caucuses, conferences and endless debates on the SFU campus. We had been privileged to witness democracy in action at SFU, and guess what? It was work and it got boring.

1968 was not 1965.

In September 1965 SFU was a few concrete buildings, lots of steps and a vast muddy construction site. Cold, wet and remote. I was a charter student living on campus at Madge Hogarth House. I was planning to get my BA in English and history, be a virgin until I married a cowboy, and then we'd live on a ranch, have a bunch of kids and I'd be an elementary school art teacher.

By September 1968 I'd given up on virginity and marriage, gone on the pill, ditched the bra and stockings, hiked up my skirts, dropped out of modern dance and signed up for film.

Well, you didn't exactly sign up for film. There was no sign-up sheet or registration, or credits given or attendance taken. You just showed up Thursday evenings at seven down in the basement of the theatre.

The theatre was the only comfortable place for students to hang out. It had a carpet, chairs and a colourful abstract mural called *Theatres of the World*. Even guys from the sciences hung out in the theatre. You'd have to walk through this gauntlet of theatre people and down more concrete stairs to get to the basement. The place was buzzing.

Stan Fox was in charge of the film workshop by 1968, and as soon as we found a space to hold the workshop, Stan said, "We've been given these brand-new Super 8 cameras and they want to see what you do with them. They're the latest and the best. So go out and shoot your movies."

Everybody took turns taking out a camera. Well, the guys took turns anyway.

Marshall McLuhan had said "the medium is the message" and I looked at the cameras and wondered what he meant. I was afraid I'd break something expensive so I stood by the exit and waited to see what would happen next.

The guys liked to talk about f-stops (I still don't know what they are or how you get them), film stocks, cameras, camera speeds, ratios, chemical properties, colour density, definition, magazine loads, exposures and credits, and credentials and opportunities. I wasn't sure if girls even talked about those sorts of things.

I would never have admitted it back then, but I love fun, glamour, beauty, makeup, hair, wardrobe, jewellery—all the things commonly referred to then as "the girlie bits" or "the pretty department," and not in a good way.

The guys were crazy for European directors and the French New Wave.

I was crazy for French films too. Films like *A Man and a Woman* and *Belle de Jour*. I wanted to see girls like me, families and tribes like mine, up there on the big screen. My dad, Victor Wilson, took 16 mm home movies of us kids growing up at Paradise Ranch in the Okanagan Valley of BC. He'd rent a 16 mm projector and some documentary films from the NFB, and we'd watch NFB films and Dad's home movies. We loved Dad's home movies. I'd see myself and think, "So that is what I look like." And "I remember that coat and I remember that day too."

Dramatic Documentary and "Real" Drama

I was drawn to that fine line between dramatic documentary and drama that looks as real as a documentary.

In those days there was still a hard line between documentary and drama. It was the same with the dividing line between amateurs and professionals. Amateurs were frowned upon, and girls were considered a distraction, if they were considered at all.

Of course, these lines were all about to dissolve into the mists of time.

There were about a dozen guys and a couple of girls in the film workshop. Peter Bryant was shooting a feature called *Felix*, and J. Andrew de Lilio Rymsza Jr. was working on a documentary about Pierre Trudeau called *Reason Over Passion*.

I remember with affection most of the other guys: Bryan R. Small, David Scott (who changed his name to Zale Dalen), George Johnson (terrific producer at the NFB), Tony Westman (cameraman director), Mark Dolgoy, Trevor Whitford (a cowboy from Alberta) and Danny Singer (photographer of note). Several of the film workshop participants didn't even go to SFU; they came up from downtown: Tom Shandel, Al Razutis, Al Sens and Dave Rimmer.

And then there were the other girls—Terri Nash and Linda Johnston—but our paths didn't cross at the film workshop. There were so few of us compared to the guys. Like me, they got involved when and where they could but were mostly relegated to the sidelines.

Finally, Stan Fox said, “Sandy, everyone’s shot something but you. Here’s a camera. Go out and shoot something. Anything. Here. Take it. Go.” And so, I did.

Holding that little camera in my hands made me feel as if anything was possible. I wasn’t sure exactly what was possible, but I knew something was.

It was the Thanksgiving long weekend, and I went back to Paradise Ranch and shot Super 8 mm footage of my sister Nonie frolicking about under the autumn leaves, with horses, down by the lake on a sparkling sunny day. I loved framing the shots and following the action.

The important thing is what is in the frame and what is not in the frame. You choose what you want to focus on and put a frame around it. I began to dream with a frame around everything. My dreams would start with a small TV frame, then I would gradually make it go up to the size of a drive-in movie screen.

Stan would send our Super 8 film cassettes to Seattle for processing, and when we got the cassettes back, we’d all sit together and watch our rushes and make comments. So, there we were, back in the basement, watching our raw footage, and suddenly there’s Nonie and the horses back at the ranch! It looked almost like a Hollywood Western to me. It looked like my dad’s home movies. My heart leapt. Stan said, “Whoever shot this has a good eye and a steady hand.” And I was hooked. It was a moment of breathtaking joy.

Encouragement and Opportunities

That’s what Stan Fox brought to the film workshop.

He didn’t seem to notice that I was a girl, and the guys took notice of that.

Bryan R. Small asked me to be in his movie and I was tickled pink. Turns out they wanted me to show up in a bikini and lie on a row of sinks in one of the men’s bathrooms and some guy poured chocolate syrup all over my midriff to make it look like I had been gutted. I remember looking out at this lineup of guys around the camera looking at me. They said it was experimental and artistic, but I wasn’t so sure.

It felt spiritually degrading. But I didn’t want to be a bummer and come off as a plastic square, so I did as directed and pulled myself together again. Like a baby in the birth canal, if you’re flexible you don’t get bent out of shape.

We prepared our films for a noon show in the SFU Theatre. The noon-hour series, programmed by Nini Baird, was about the only game in town if you wanted to see class acts from all over the place. It was the heart of the university. The broader program featured evening performances, film series, poetry readings, serious lectures and lots of wonderful music. People came up to the mountaintop from downtown. Critics wrote reviews in the Vancouver newspapers. Artists, musicians, dancers and poets wanted to be there.

Rita Tushingham had been in town shooting *The Knack... and How to Get It*, Mike Nichols filmed some scenes for *Carnal Knowledge* in Vancouver, and Robert Altman was filming *That Cold Day in the Park* in Tatlow Park in Vancouver. Apparently, it was a tough shoot. I saw Jack Nicholson and Warren Beatty in a downtown movie theatre once. They giggled a lot and left halfway through, and no one paid them any mind.

All this to say it was a big deal to be in a noon-hour show at the SFU Theatre.

I selected a Donovan song to play along with my footage. Sound was not considered as important as the picture. That would come later. I called it something like *Feeling Groovy*.

It was nerve-wracking and thrilling to see *Feeling Groovy* up there in front of a real live audience in a real theatre. The audience applauded and I understood how addictive applause might become. Like respect, applause feels warm and wonderful. I wanted to take the audience home with me. But, of course, that was impossible.

Besides, it was bad manners for a girl to stand in the spotlight too long. She'd be labelled a show-off and considered self-centred and bossy. A young lecturer at SFU said that he didn't like women who got up and spoke on platforms; they turned him off. A woman undergraduate snapped back, "You're not supposed to be turned on. You're supposed to listen." The women's liberation movement had come to SFU.

Garbage

By the spring semester of 1969 I was in my final year at SFU.

I registered for a political science and anthropology course called urban studies. It was a five-credit course with no curriculum. You didn't have to do anything. Students would say what they were interested in and then go do something.

I proposed making a film about garbage and finally someone in authority said, "Go ahead. Show us a film about garbage and you'll get your five credits. Just be sure to tell us all about it." And so, I did.

I was concerned with the rampant consumerism I saw all around me. Credit cards had just been invented and people were buying all kinds of stuff. Shopping got serious. Garbage was increasing. I was curious to see if rich people treated their garbage differently from poor people. I shot 16 mm film using a hand-held Bolex spring-wind camera while riding around on the back of garbage trucks in the East End and then around Point Grey. The garbage in the East End was not that different from the garbage on the West Side—there was a lot of out and out trash, some treasures, some messy bits, some beautifully wrapped bits. It was amazing to see what was thrown out.

I went out to the dump. It was a sea of garbage with a flock of seagulls hovering above.

I shot *Garbage* on my own, but I needed to ask for help and learn about editing.

I remember asking Shelah Reljic how to edit, but she was in the middle of a "discussion" with Nini Baird about the green room and she just threw up her hands and told George Johnson to show me how to edit. George reluctantly took me to what must have been a cleaning closet. He said, "This is the edit room." The concrete walls were covered in strips of film. There were bins with garbage bags in them and heaps of film taped to the rim.

George showed me how to use the splicers. He said, "You treat film like you treat women! Rough!" I laughed and said, "George, really? You're such a sweet guy." He sort of laughed and left because he had more important things to do. He was working on Peter Bryant's film with the other guys.

I applied myself. I cleared a space and got to work splicing and taping my footage together and laying down the soundtracks. I think we were allowed two or three soundtracks: one for dialogue, one for music and one for sound effects.

It was like sewing a dress. You started with an image of what you wanted, selected all the little details and then stitched it together—*et voilà!* A dress. A film. An idea come to life. No problem. I animated letters to spell out the title *Garbage* and I got the five credits.

Garbage was selected for a screening on a national CBC program called *Take 30*, hosted by Adrienne Clarkson. The program was focused on the films coming out of the West Coast. I only heard about the broadcast after it had aired because I was off at a Canadian Union of Students conference at the time. Some of the guys in the film workshop were not happy about *Garbage*. They wanted their serious films to be chosen, not *Garbage*. Not mine.

I got an A in urban studies, and I finally had enough credits to graduate.

Penticton Profile

Anyway, Stan invited anyone from the film workshop who was interested to come to his house for a special meeting. There was talk of an SFU Film Workshop collaboration with UBC's sociology program and maybe even the NFB. The plan was to make a student film. A 16 mm half-hour documentary about something to do with the changing times.

So, there we were in this big old house in North Van, eating Stan's wife Janet's delicious cookies, and Stan looked at a letter and said, "It's going to be a study of a small town in BC. They'll provide the 16 mm film and equipment, and we'll go on location." The guys wanted to know all the details. Who would be the director? How much equipment would they give us? What was the shooting ratio? Someone wanted to know where the small town was. Stan looked at the letter again. "Ah… It says here, somewhere… Penticton."

I jumped and blurted out, "That's my town!" And Stan said, "Okay, you'll be the director."

The summer of 1969 found the SFU Film Workshop up in Penticton shooting *Penticton Profile*. But we were not working in a vacuum.

On August 9, Sharon Tate was murdered, and it was personal.

On August 15, Woodstock started, and everything changed again.

I'm not exactly sure what dates we were filming in Penticton, but I do remember the heat was intense.

I had no idea what a director did. The guys shot whatever they felt like shooting. One guy recorded all ninety-nine motel and hotel signs, another covered girls in bikinis, another the hippies hanging out. Lots of scenic work. Don Cummings shot slow-motion footage of Debbie Day with her long red hair floating out beautifully behind her as she went down a slide. Slow motion eats up the film footage, so there was some grumbling going on after that.

Stan made sure I interviewed the high school principal, the mayor, some teenagers (my sister Elaine and her boyfriend Pat and their friends). Stan told me to ask questions that could not be answered with a simple yes or no, and not to talk overtop of anyone because it would be hard to make a clean cut afterwards. We had a professional sound man, Don Young, to record sync sound on his Nagra tape recorder.

Shooting sync sound was a big deal back then. A clapper boy would hold up the clapper board with the scene number on it and announce the take number to be recorded on the magnetic sound tape. The sound and picture would be synced up when the diagonal lines on the clapper board visually lined up and made a clap sound on the magnetic soundtrack. In a pinch, someone could stand there and announce the take, then clap their hands, and visually when the hands came together that frame would be synchronized to the sound of the clap. Later, in the edit room, the sound would be transferred to 16 mm mag tape, and you would edit the sound and picture separately. It was all very hands on, measured out in frames and feet.

The star of *Penticton Profile*, I thought, was the playwright George Ryga. He talked about the restless young people wanting change and how important the arts were in shaping our society.

But there was no thread, no structure, no direction to all that footage shot in the Okanagan summer sunshine.

Don Cummings was supposed to be the editor when we got back to SFU. He was a professional. After he saw the raw footage, he said it was a mess and he didn't want to touch it. None of the guys wanted to touch it either. Some of them were already working in film downtown. In desperation Stan asked me if I would like to edit it and I said, "Yes please!"

That September I had been accepted as an animation film student at Vancouver School of Art (soon to be Emily Carr Art School), but I spent most of my time editing *Penticton Profile*.

I applied myself once again, transcribing all the audio Don Young had recorded. I listened and I wrote it all down, long hand, in exercise books—all the banter, the pauses, the reactions and the laughter. (Turns out Dad squirrelled away all these notebooks and now, when I look at them, they read like the script for *My American Cousin*.) I was learning that the pen is more powerful than the sword.

Because there was no room to properly edit films in the theatre at SFU, Stan set me up in an old storefront on Lonsdale in North Vancouver where Luke Bennett was cutting a Jack Darcus film. Darcus would go on to become a well-known artist. Luke was editing 16 mm film on an old double-system Movieola. I had a 16 mm movie scope and reels on a bench in another room. Luke had moved to West Vancouver from New York and LA to escape the rat race, and he loved to tell terrifying tales about egomaniacal directors and how mean and awful the film business was. How it's a superficial business that attracts all sorts of crazy people. People who tend to view each other as bargaining chips to be used in advancing your career. Or not.

But Luke was also very inspiring. He'd say things like, "More close-ups. Cut on a movement. Match the movement. Try a cross dissolve between those two scenes."

Editing allows you to create meaning by putting certain shots together, adding a voiceover or music. I was finding my groove.

That's when I learned what a director is supposed to do. Which is:

1. Have some sliver of an idea or a vision or something to say.
2. Go out and shoot stuff.
3. Go into the edit room and see what you have to work with.
4. Make a film people will want to look at and listen to.

With a PS that whatever trouble you had on set, it will resurface when it comes time to do the credits.

With a PPS that having an active imagination and a sense of humour really helps during the sticky bits. And there will be sticky bits.

When I finished editing *Penticton Profile* in the spring of 1970, it was handed over to disappear into the NFB's Challenge for Change program. Stan got a better job and moved to Toronto. We are still friends today. He pried open the doors to the old boys' club and introduced me to theatre owners, lab technicians, actors and other filmmakers.

The Real University

Leaving SFU was sort of slippery. My diploma says 1970 but I was long gone by then. SFU was referred to as "a university without walls." The real world became my real university after SFU.

Terri Nash chose an academic path and then worked at the NFB, where she went on to win an Academy Award for her hard-hitting short documentary *If You Love This Planet*. Tony Westman became a cameraman director, George Johnson was a producer at the NFB, Mike Collier worked at the Alpha Cine Lab then set up Yaletown Productions. Bryan Small and Doug White worked as editors at the CBC and CKVU.

And I got a grant to make a short drama called *The Bridal Shower*.

I cast my mom, my sisters and some friends to be in *The Bridal Shower*. Doug McKay shot it over an extended weekend, and I edited it. When we screened it at the first women's film festival in Toronto in 1971, people thought it was a documentary and I was thrilled. But the audience was split between boos and cheers. Half the audience thought I was betraying women by showing how funny and bitchy we could be when the guys were not in the room. The gay guys loved it.

The Bridal Shower came in handy when I was pitching *My American Cousin*, but that's another story.

I learned you could make home movies that would reach out to a world of strangers and touch them, and a part of you might live forever on the silver screen.

So, in the end, the SFU Film Workshop turned out to be the spark that lit the flame that dropped into a can of gasoline and took off.

That was over fifty years ago now and I like to believe it's not over yet.

Warm Memories

I saw *My American Cousin* when it first came out, but not again until August 31, 2023, when it was paired with Colin Browne's *Strathyre* in a screening at the Pacific Cinematheque. It was fascinating to view the ways in which these two stories from BC's Interior resonated with each other, still speaking to the audience with a freshness some fifty years after their creation. After the showing, Sandy Wilson discussed, among other things, the spirit of fun she conveyed in her film. "Making film," she said, "is terrifically exciting."

Wilson has warm memories of the mutually supportive atmosphere of the film workshops at SFU. She comments that her colleague Mike Collier was a "soft-spoken, very thoughtful and capable guy" who was "was crucial to the success of *Growing Up at Paradise*, the short documentary I made from my dad's 16 mm films of us kids growing up at Paradise Ranch. I had a Canada Council grant, and I took the original 16 mm footage back to the NFB lab, where they said they couldn't do anything with it. They said the film had shrunk and it could not be colour corrected. So, I took it to the Alpha Cine Lab, and Mike teamed up with Louie, who did the colour timing and made my dad's footage look gorgeous! It went on to win the best experimental prize at the Yorkton [Saskatchewan] Film Fest, and it was screened at the Orillia Film Fest in 1978."[25]

Wilson is grateful to Stan Fox for introducing her to the old boys' club at the Alpha Cine Lab on Davie Street.

CHAPTER 7: LITERARY ARTS

Climbing the Green Mountain

FIRST STEPS IN THE WRITING LIFE

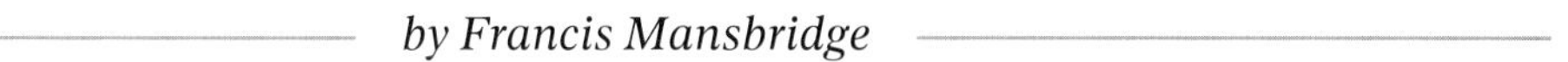

by Francis Mansbridge

Poems were open fields, portals to continual newness. Deep enchantment, the sense of embarking on a mystical journey, pervaded the syllabus and the lecture hall.
—Susan McCaslin (student of Robin Blaser)[1]

Creative Writing at SFU: A Western Canadian Avant-Garde

Creative writing was not one of the arts directly under the umbrella of the Centre for Communications and the Arts. The conventional wisdom was that creative writing could not be taught but was perhaps a manifestation of divine (or demonic) inspiration. Nonetheless, many writers responded to the same artistic ferment that supported the other arts at SFU. Readings and discussions by writers, both from SFU and elsewhere, contributed to the ideas and feelings that nourished the local aspirants. In many discussions, thoughtful and impassioned debates led to thoughtful and impassioned poems.

On the Canadian West Coast, Earle Birney, Dorothy Livesay and Phyllis Webb were by the early 1960s established poetic presences, but they still warmed their feet, or at least a couple of toes, in the inherited British tradition. Poets in Toronto and Montreal had established contacts with the Black Mountain poets in the eastern United States and later in California, especially Robert Creeley and Charles Olson.

A younger generation brought Canadian poetry into closer contact with recent developments in American poetry and poetics. Donald M. Allen's influential anthology *New American Poetry* (1960) included a broad selection of American poets whose work often reflected the natural rhythms of American speech, in contrast with the more formal cadences in British speech and writing. The vernacular of the New American Poets was often as much about lifestyle as poetics, especially for their Canadian followers. In the words of Brian Fawcett, who began his lifelong writing career while a student at SFU, "We wanted to write poetry, sure, but we weren't prepared to be tea-sipping aesthetes in a world of miniature aesthetic jewellery boxes."[2]

UBC's George Bowering, Fred Wah, Lionel Kearns, Frank Davey and others under the mentorship of American poet and UBC instructor Warren Tallman made up the first western outpost of the Canadian avant-garde. At SFU the second outpost, with Murray Schafer as mentor, was defended by Brian Fawcett, Sharon Thesen, Alban Goulden, Susan McCaslin, Allan Safarik, Brian Brett and many others, mostly students of Robin Blaser.

When Warren Tallman organized the Vancouver Poetry Conference at UBC in 1963, he brought in fellow American poets Allen Ginsberg, Charles Olson, Robert Creeley, Robert Duncan and Denise Levertov to read their poetry and evangelize the local audiences. Margaret Avison's close connections with Cid Corman and his Black Mountain periodical *Origin* had secured her an invitation as the only Canadian poet. Some of the American poets were dismissive of her presence—she was, indeed, responsible for several finely crafted sonnets, written in anything but the natural rhythms of American speech. Denise Levertov was less dogmatic and saw to it that a book of Avsion's splendid poetry (*Winter Sun*) was published in the US by W.W. Norton. But, in general, this was an American showcase for American men.

Make It New: Smashing Old Forms

The American poets wrote in response "to the political/cultural tyrannies of the first half of the twentieth century,"[3] calling for a greater specificity to confront the cruelty of the big lies that had inflicted themselves on the world. The formidable Charles Olson (he was 6'9") was the most influential American for the SFU poets; his voice was "overpowering in its vitality… powerful, high speed and rhapsodic."[4] His calls for "precise local knowledge" as the backbone for poetry met with a ready response from the SFU poets.[5]

With the threat of nuclear annihilation hanging over people's heads, and the raging war in Vietnam a more immediate backdrop, the necessity of a new language to express a new world took hold. The devastating atrocities of war may not have been new, but they were new to the young. As Stan Persky says in his introduction to Brian Fawcett's *Local Matters*, their intent was "to write in a way that took account of the totality and fragmentation of the world, and to achieve a new and intense quality of authenticity,"[6] or, in Ezra Pound's prescient words, to "make it new." As John Juliani did in the SFU theatre, the SFU poets smashed the old forms to create new ones from the resulting fragments. Many of these poets continued the bardic traditions of earlier times, with numerous public readings and the cultivation of a flamboyant personality and an unconventional appearance.

The young writers sought to transcend the limitations of rationalist thought that previous generations had often idealized. Syntax was frequently shattered as the more radical poets saw traditional grammar as closing off the most effective personal communication. Unfortunately, agreement on some common mode of language for effective communication was more difficult to find.

Models and Mentors

When Simon Fraser opened its doors in 1965, it generally hired faculty and graduate students from outside of Canada, particularly from England and the US—there were a limited number of academically qualified Canadians at this point in the country's history, so it seemed natural to invite an American to make the trek from San Francisco north to Burnaby. Jack Spicer was the first invitee, but he died in 1965 before his arrival at SFU. Robin Blaser, arriving in 1966, had better luck, becoming a much loved and respected teacher, mentor and friend, who had a lasting influence. Brian Fawcett recalls, "That first class with him was, I think, the most important moment in my entire education, both as a writer and as a human being."[7] Sharon Thesen, formerly married to Fawcett, also remembers the poet as a friend and an inspiration: "One early spring morning in Kitsilano when Brian (my then husband) and I had just gotten up there was a knock at the apartment door and there was Robin, with a huge bouquet of branches of cherry blossoms... He's been a significant influence in my life and writing. He encourages beauty, and laughter and the vitality of truth, as the best poetry also does.[8]

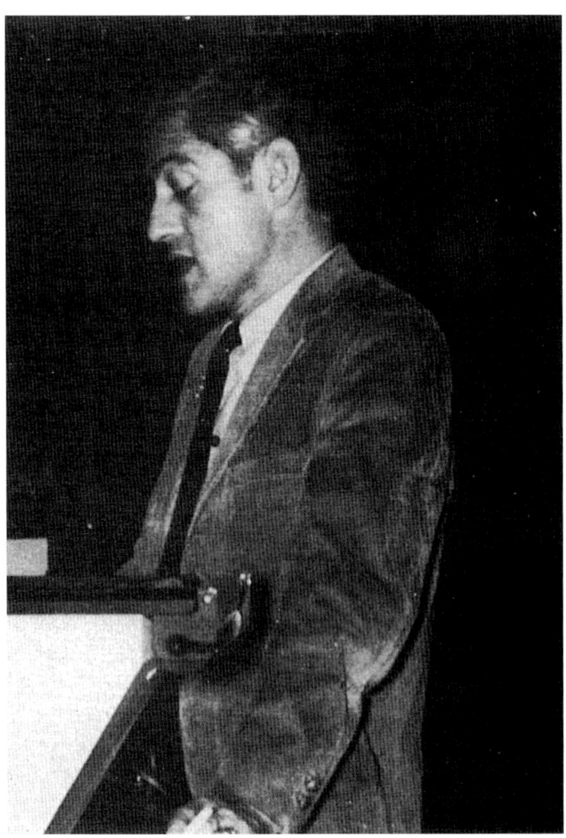

Robin Blaser was a much loved colleague and respected teacher, especially of poetry. *Fred Wong*

"BC students outside the Lower Mainland and Victoria had previously had little direct access to post-secondary education. The concrete towers of UBC were a formidable barrier for many from the Interior. The new colleges that sprang up in BC beginning in the late 1960s often had an energy and an openness to new initiatives that fitted more with the university that looked out over Burnaby than the hallowed halls of UBC. It took considerable courage and no small amount of money for eighteen-to-twenty-year-olds to uproot themselves from the friendly confines of their hometowns for the uncertainties of life at the coast, often demonized in small-town mythology as a place of danger and decadent morality. Many of the student writers at SFU arrived from places outside the Lower Mainland. Alban Goulden from Medicine Hat, Neap Hoover from Vernon, and Brian Fawcett, Sharon Thesen and Brett Enemark from Prince George brought a fresh iconoclasm to SFU. Perhaps the fact that some writing students were "mature" (in their early to mid twenties) gave them a greater confidence.

Diverse writers came to SFU to lecture and give readings from their work, giving student writers multiple yardsticks by which to measure their own. SFU faculty members such as John Mills and Frederick Candelaria combined with visiting fresh young talents like Seymour Mayne and Patrick Lane and older voices such as Earle Birney and Milton Acorn. Dialogue and controversies often sharpened their swords. In his anthology of SFU poetry, Stephen Collis notes that "a gradual shift occurs through the late 1960s and 1970s as Simon Fraser University came to replace her sister university as a key site of, and one of the standard bearers for, an avant garde poetics."[9] George Bowering, Lionel Kearns, Roy Miki and (later) Colin Browne were key figures in this transition, serving as models and mentors for following generations.

It doesn't take much research to realize women were rarely invited to read. Margaret Atwood, Gladys Hindmarch and a few other names turn up. Writers from ethnic backgrounds, whether women or not, were even rarer presences. The roads to broad acceptance were narrow and arduous, and the destination decades in the future.

During SFU's first ten years, many creative writers in the English department provided an ambience that stimulated their students' writing. Among the first hires were medievalist John Mills, whose first novel, *The Land of Is*, was published in 1972, and poet Fred Candelaria, who taught seventeenth-century literature and founded the *West Coast Review* in 1966. They were joined in 1969 by Stanley Cooperman, who had published several volumes of poetry before he arrived to teach American literature, and in 1972 by George Bowering, who would become one of Canada's most prolific and accomplished creative writers. Other faculty writers included poet Lionel Kearns, who had a twenty-year career teaching at SFU, and Betty Lambert, many of whose plays were produced on the CBC. All English students from the early years warmly remember Ken Conibear, who authored many books about the Canadian North before being hired as the department's student advisor.

Little Magazines

Improvements in the technology of cheap and rapid copying facilitated the growth of little magazines in the 1960s, which often ran counter operations to periodicals like English professor Frederick Candelaria's more conservative *West Coast Review*. The university's first literary journal, it appeared in the spring of 1966, aimed at a wide academic audience. Although Candelaria published in several of the more ephemeral SFU publications, such as *Ballsout*, he was omitted from Stephen Collis's anthology *companions & horizons: An Anthology of Simon Fraser University Poetry*. In Collis's view, Candelaria's poetry was more like a "well wrought urn" than an embodiment of an "intellectual and emotional complex," which he felt defined avant-garde poetry.[10]

Most of the little magazines that were generated by and for the SFU literary community had few connections with the wider literary world. The short-lived (one issue) *Literary Magazine*, presided over by SFU professor Jerry Zaslove, was published by the Creative Writers' Workshop under the SFU Literary Society. *Cheap Thrills* and *Maka* were other ephemeral student publications. *Ballsout: A Magazine of Unpleasant Verse and Impolite Prose*, first appearing in 1969, was emphatically engaged and political; in the second issue the editors quote with apparent relish the negative responses in *The Peak* to their first issue. Mike Rust had found some merit in Lionel Kearns's continuation of "The Cook's Tale" and David Marno's "After You Catullus," but was unmoved by the "pretentious" poetry of Ralph Maud and Frederick Candelaria.[11]

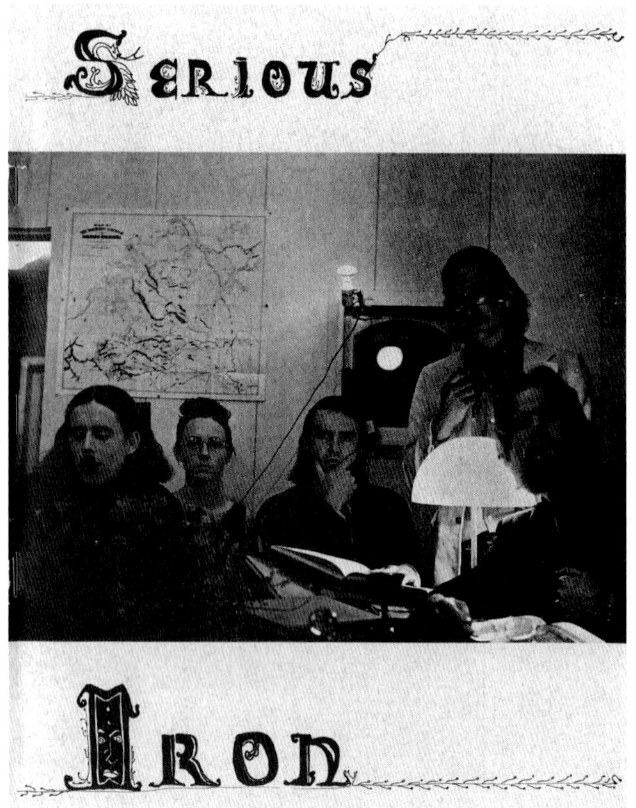

Cover of *Iron*, Oct 1971 (no. 12), the early literary periodical in which many young SFU writers first saw print. In this photo (left to right): Tom McGauley, Sharon Fawcett (later Thesen), Alban Goulden, Brian Fawcett and Brett Enemark are masquerading as canonical writers of the day, respectively Robert Lowell, Marianne Moore, Richard Wilbur, Karl Shapiro, and W.S. Merwin. *SFU Special Collections and Rare Books*

Iron Magazine

Iron, the most important of the early little magazines, ran for fourteen issues from 1966 to 1972, with another six ending in 1978. Brian Fawcett and Brett Enemark assumed most of the editorial duties, although colleague Alban Goulden mentions that if they felt the submitter had a clear idea of what they were doing, they would leave them alone.[12] Fawcett gives two accounts of the origin of the magazine's name. In a 1976 interview with Barry McKinnon, he remembered them saying, "Let's call this magazine Iron or Steel or something—anything but something that has meaning. The whole point about the title of *Iron* was that it didn't mean anything."[13] Later, in an article in his book *Local Matters*, he explained that "iron isn't gold or lead and it isn't refined enough to be called steel."[14] In any case, it was an expression of the tough ethos he brought to his writing.

Goulden stated the magazine grew out of "BS sessions" held by the aspiring poets:

> Well, we got to the point where we asked ourselves why we were just reading everyone else's stuff. We should do something ourselves... It kind of grew from some BS sessions at Brian's or my place with a few others. A guy named Bob Taylor, who was in history, he was very interested in the cultural dimensions of poetry, he was part of the group. Also Neap Hoover, who was in anthropology... All four of us—plus Sharon Thesen, who at that time was still functioning as a handmaiden. Thank God she got away from all that. Blaser's attitude was not female friendly particularly, although he would pick certain women, like Sharon, not at the beginning but later, and a few American female poets, like Denise Levertov and H.D. But mostly Blaser and Brian were very male-oriented. Oh, I have to here give a shout to Stan Persky, another escaped American, who for a time was Robin's companion and, though not a poet or fiction writer, had a strong political sense and that influenced us for sure.[15]

Indigenous Authors

While there were no dedicated writing courses at SFU at this time, students in English courses were often energized by their readings and courses to pursue their own writing. This was especially true in Robin Blaser's courses. The works of Ezra Pound, Charles Olson, Robert Creeley and others, which Blaser taught with creativity and passion, ignited poetic fire in many of the students. Other faculty poets also nurtured their students, as with English professor and poet Lionel Kearns's mentoring of Skyros Bruce, of the Tsleil-Waututh Nation, who would write the first book of poetry published by a BC-born Indigenous woman.

Bruce, a great-niece of Chief Dan George, grew up in North Vancouver, where her creative writing was encouraged by her teachers. Upon enrolment at Simon Fraser University in 1969 she began to contribute poems to local and campus periodicals, including *Blackfish*, the *West Coast Review* and *The Peak*. Encouraged by Kearns, she published *Kalala* with Daylight Press in 1972. Now known as Mahara Allbrett, she continues to write and present her poetry.

Student writing was encouraged in other sectors of the university, giving rise to writers who subsequently proved significant, such as author and Indigenous activist Lee Maracle. A member of the Stó:lō Nation and a granddaughter of Chief Dan George, Maracle was born Marguerite Aline Carter in North Vancouver. Her first book, *Bobbie Lee, Indian Rebel* (1975), synthesizing autobiography and fiction, grew out of an oral history project done for SFU professor Don Barnett's anthropology course. Barnett encouraged Maracle to do more with the story of her experience, and she became the main editor of the published version. This set her on the path to a career as an accomplished writer fighting the oppression of Indigenous people. Later novels *Ravensong* (1993) and *Celia's Song* (2014) unwrapped realities of Canadian racism; the latter was shortlisted for the $50,000 2020 Neustadt International Prize for literature. Other awards she received include the Premier's Award for Excellence in the Arts (2014), the Anne Green Award (2016) and the Bonham Centre Award (2017).

Fawcett recalled that the magazine was "ironic, playful and studiously disrespectful of authority."[16] It "didn't claim to be anything at all except basic student enquiry and insolence."[17]

Fawcett believed that one of the good things about *Iron* is that it did not outlive its usefulness.[18] By 1972, they had "sort of finished wrestling with our angels and there we were, out on the fucking street," and in hindsight he felt "it was necessary to go through that whole personal business to get to where we are now."[19] *Iron* provided a coherent focus for intellectual and emotional wrestling, like "belonging to a medieval college," in Jim Taylor's words—it moved most of them along to a fuller personal and intellectual development and acted as "the newsletter of our education at SFU."[20]

Murray Schafer's advice to the neophyte poets was down to earth and appropriate:

> When you're starting off, you learn best from your peers, people you can argue things out with in person. People your own age. So go off and make your own magazine. Use it to publish your own work while you're learning your craft. Don't send out your poems so strangers can judge how closely they resemble the ones they're writing, and never mind trying to impress the big shots. They're old, they're tired, and they'll always like you best when you're on their farm team... The best thing about being a student is that you get to be a student. Don't let anyone cheat you out of that experience.[21]

He provided an intelligent, more mature sounding board for his younger colleagues.

As Fawcett recalls, "A few weeks later we started *Iron* more or less directly on the basis of Schafer's advice."[22]

Alban Goulden is grateful for Schafer's mentorship: "He was very supportive of the mag, his spirit of experimentation and multi-disciplinary thinking was what we needed. Went to many of our parties and quietly stayed in the background, approached by the young as a kind of touchstone big brother. I found him unfailingly encouraging. He injected a spirit of maturity into a warren of so-called 'adult' profs and their student minions that was often sorely needed. He always left before we got so drunk we were impossible to talk to in terms of generating a meaningful conversation."[23]

Through his teaching and personality, Robin Blaser was a major force in encouraging his côterie to develop their talents. Susan McCaslin, who went on to become a lifelong poet, recalls first meeting him:

> It was one of the most blessed days of my life when I walked into Robin's course on classical backgrounds, team-taught with Romantics scholar Rob Dunham. Robin was impeccably dressed with silver hair, aquiline nose, dark brows and an elegant bearing. He seemed more European than American; yet he was, strangely enough, originally from Idaho [like Pound], later part of the San Francisco poetry Renaissance... Robin re-opened myth for me in a radically transformative way.[24]

McCaslin said he was always ready to meet, never intrusive or controlling, and was an inclusive, sensitive reader who helped her find her own voice. Recently she published an essay on Robin Blaser's libretto for Harrison Birtwistle's opera *The Last Supper* and completed a sequence of poems based on the libretto.

For Stan Persky, Blaser's "great gift to us was an ability to communicate his sense of wonder and appreciation of the meaningfulness of an expansive world." Allan Safarik describes him as "a flamboyant man in dress and style who lectured brilliantly... a marvellous poet with theatrical mannerisms and a bitchy attitude." Sharon Thesen recalls that Blaser "showed me that poems were essentially a sort of counterintelligence, and that I could rely on myself and my experience as a young woman from the working poor and from Prince George, to provide me with all I needed as a young poet." Christine Hearn took every course from him she possibly could.

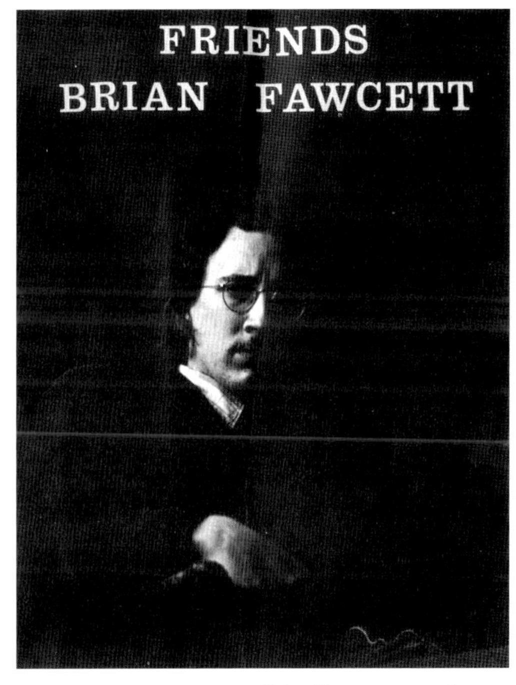

Brian Fawcett, one of the founders of Iron, on the cover of Friends, an early book of poetry issued by *The Georgia Straight* in 1971. His many accomplishments include winning the Pearson Trust Non-Fiction Memorial Prize. *SFU Archives*

Other students brought more distance to the relationship. While Brian Fawcett appreciated Blaser's salutary questioning of humanism, Jim Taylor cautions that this led the poet to sympathize with Ezra Pound's fascist leanings. While Blaser encouraged students to write about their locality and followed that to a limited extent, according to Alban Goulden, "his own writing was filtered through an American sense of a kind of overall destiny which was global, its heartland was an American unconscious desire to colonize everything."[25]

Brian Fawcett brought a northern feistiness to his poetic views. While the title *Iron* may not have been intended to mean anything, it fitted well with his rugged origins. Barry McKinnon says he heard Fawcett "once sat in a back chair at a poetry reading in Vancouver with a big rock in his hand and was poised to throw it on the stage if the reader's poetry didn't measure up."[26] No word if he did, although some said he could have. Fawcett also commented, "At that time, certainly myself and most of the people I knew didn't have any misgivings about why we were writing. We thought it was totally interesting to just simply be writers about writing as if that had no connection with, like, careers or fame."[27] And when it came to the objective of the writing, he was noncommittal: "I think I knew that what we were doing in the first place wasn't terribly important… it was going to be interesting to other writers because they might learn how to write better from it. If they think it's going to contribute to the Truth and Beauty in the world, they're a little bit abstracted about it and if they think it's going to effect [*sic*] anything they are out to lunch."[28]

Blackfish Press

In 1970 Brian Brett and Allan Safarik started Blackfish Press, which published broadside folios and literary books, including books by poetic heavyweights F.R. Scott, Earle Birney and Dorothy Livesay. In addition to local venues, Safarik recalls taking copies of the books they published to sell at bookstores in Toronto, Ottawa, Victoria and Edmonton. Blackfish Press spawned the periodical *Blackfish*, established in opposition to *Iron*. The dialogue between the two groups of poets was vigorous and often personal, with screaming matches that sometimes led to physical confrontations. Brett had a severe physical

Blackfish table of contents.
SFU Special Collections and Rare Books

BLACKFISH

No. 1, Spring 1971

Editors

B. T. Brett Allan Safarik

Manuscripts will not be returned unless accompanied by stamped self-addressed envelope. Subscriptions are $2.00 per year (three issues) Single copies 75¢. Send manuscripts and subscription correspondence to BLACKFISH, 1851 Moore St. Burnaby 2, B. C., Canada.

TABLE OF CONTENTS

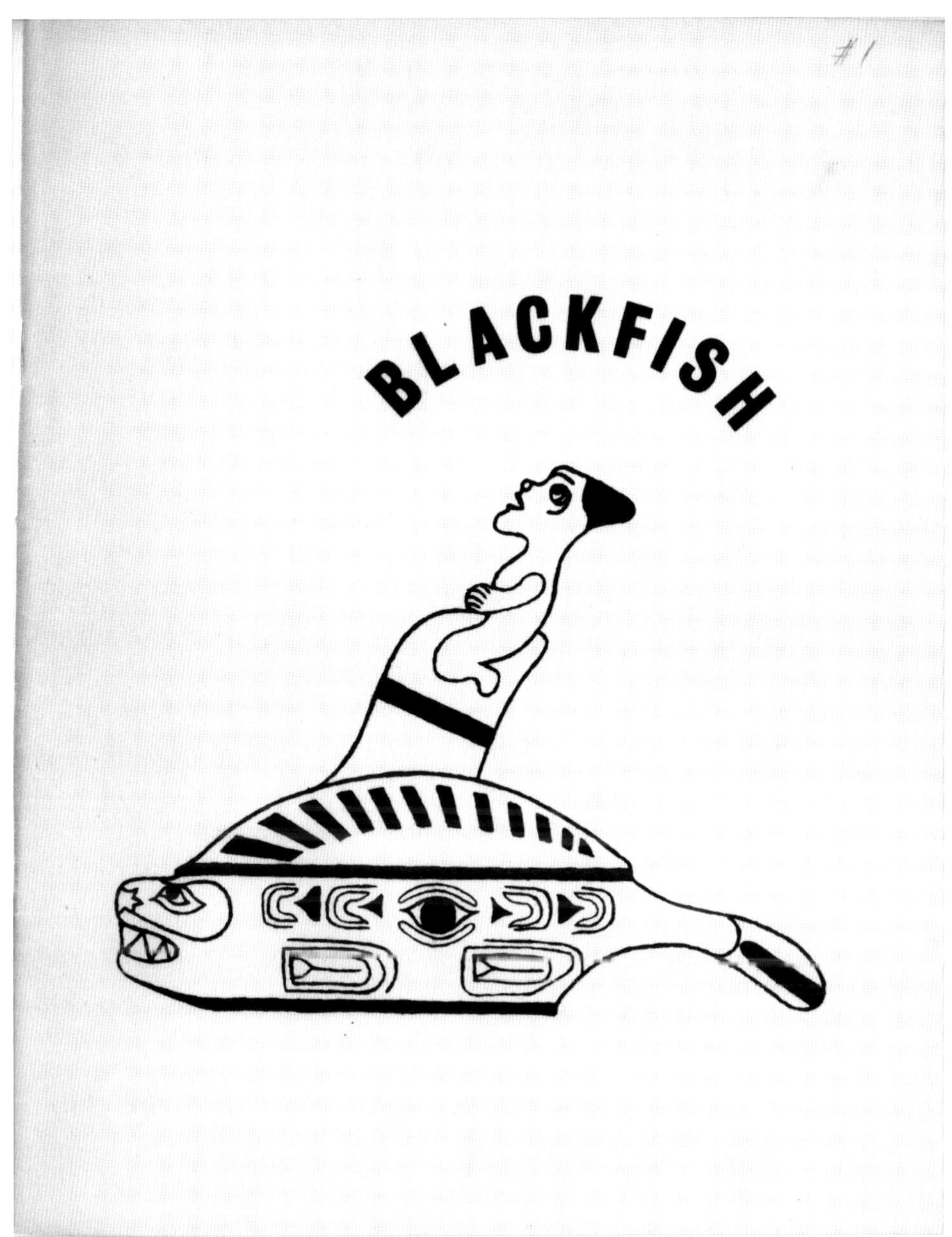

A cover for *Blackfish*, featuring the illustration used on most issues. *SFU Special Collections and Rare Books*

condition that caused delayed growth and physical maturation. While this was later corrected, Safarik states that, in the early days, Brian Fawcett bullied Brett. On one occasion, in retaliation, Safarik smacked the back of Fawcett's head—hard—against a door. Fawcett later responded by stabbing him in the back with a sharpened pencil. Safarik states that a rumour (untrue) that he was a Golden Gloves champion stalled Brian Fawcett's repeated calls to settle the matter outside.[29]

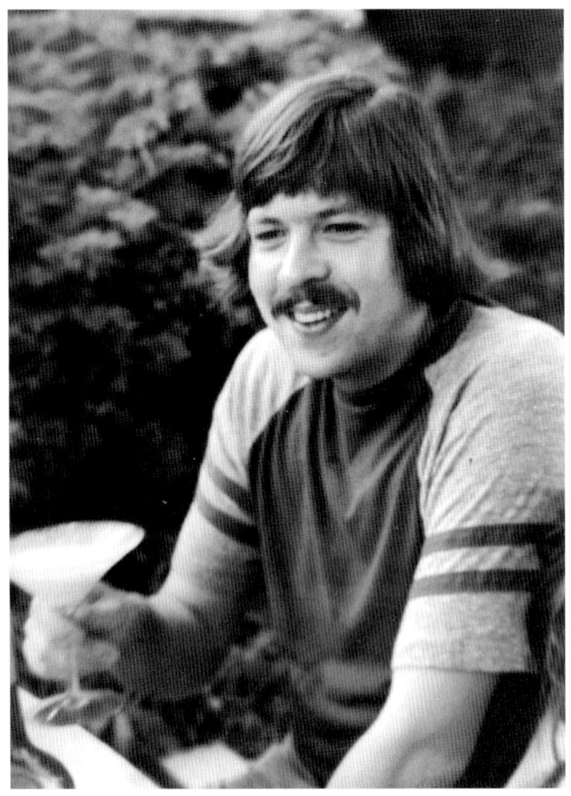

Allan Safarik.

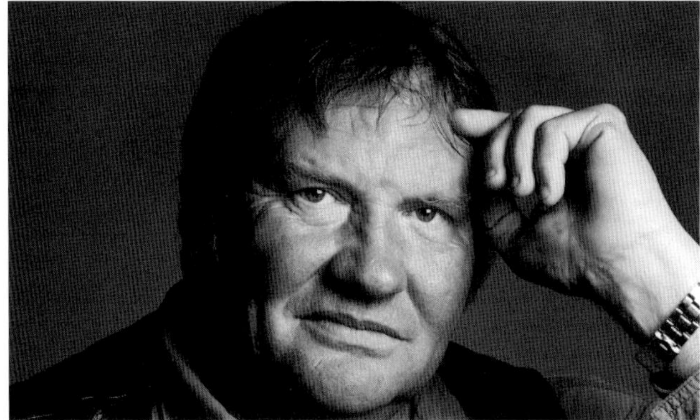

Brian Brett. *Michael Schoenholtz, Wikimedia Commons*

Brett and Safarik were founders of the student literary periodical *Blackfish*. While the general bent of *Iron* and its supporters was shaped by the experimental poetics of writers such as Charles Olson, Robin Blaser and George Bowering, the pages of *Blackfish* were more often home to the gritty social realism of Acorn, Al Purdy and others.

After the first issue, most of the poets in *Blackfish* were from outside the SFU community. They ranged from rising stars like Margaret Atwood, Susan Musgrave and Patrick Lane to established figures such as Earle Birney, Dorothy Livesay, P.K. Page and Al Purdy. The *Iron* folk were more than unhappy about *Blackfish*'s publication of Milton Acorn's lengthy article "Beware the Bad Mountain" (*Blackfish* No. 3). Acorn's often incoherent rant against Black Mountain poetry in general and George Bowering in particular occasioned a reasoned response by George Bowering in the next issue, which in turn provoked a twelve-page diatribe from Milton Acorn.

Mark Vulliamy reviewed the first issue in *The Peak* on June 9, 1971. While he found some merit in the poetry of Jody Conway, Christine Hearn and Simon Holwill, mostly he found that it "fails to distinguish itself."[30] A much more favourable review of No. 3 by John Simonitch appears in *The Peak* on July 19, 1972, although most of his praise was reserved for non-SFU contributors such as Milton Acorn, Thom Gunn and Margaret Atwood. Brian Brett wrote a scathing review of George Bowering's *Imago 17* in the March 7, 1973, issue of *The Peak*, in which he considered the energy that invigorated Black Mountain poetry to have largely dissipated. Brian Fawcett, in his view, was a "watered-down Blaser."[31]

The poets and their critics learned that no matter what their internal squabbles, there was a bigger world than Medicine Hat, Vernon or even SFU. Alban Goulden appreciated the new visions:

> I learned that the world was much bigger than the classical English literature with which I'd been presented at U of A... So it was a much

> wider purview, a liberating air of being able to read whatever we wanted to and make connections that we wanted to. That didn't come without a price. There was sometimes intense criticism, not all of it logical. A lot of tribalism. There was this American subculture of Olson, Creeley, Robin Blaser, Jack Spicer, Robert Duncan. It had its own behaviour and its own language. If you didn't use that language you were beyond the pale. [32]

Susan McCaslin agrees that the stimulation of the arts and integration of art with everyday life opened up her writing. That said, she had a few reservations, finding the "drug culture, experimentation with psychedelics, led to anxiety" on her part, and she tended to remove herself from that world. Still, she recalls her days at SFU well and says they gave her a "passionate preoccupation that has given my life both meaning and purpose."[33]

The image central to Canadian writer Sheila Watson's novel *The Double Hook* expresses the essential human truth that joy and pain are essentially intertwined in life experience. That was also true at SFU: the magic of the early days also generated its opposite. McCaslin experienced both the magic and the darkness during her time there. And when she applied in 1976 to do a PhD in English at SFU, she was refused admission in spite of high marks and solid recommendations. Michael Steig, head of the committee, "indicated they needed people to 'fit in' right away."[34] Later, in 1984, she completed her PhD at UBC, and she went on to teach for many years at Douglas College.

The anarchy of the late sixties and its untrammelled freedom created a great atmosphere for those with the strength and aggression to survive. For those who were more fragile, it was sometimes a different story. The first president, Patrick McTaggart-Cowan, along with CCA directors Bruce Attridge and Patrick Lyndon, and student Susan McCaslin were among those who, in Michael Bawtree's words, were simply "ground up."

While different cliques often engaged in vigorous combat with each other, nearly all recall these times with nostalgia. The support of a like-minded group alleviated the long, lonely periods gazing at an unresponsive blank piece of paper or into their own souls. It was nourishing to invite someone to have a few beers with and enjoy the collegial atmosphere that made SFU such a rewarding experience.

When the students left the friendly environs of SFU, relatively few continued to publish poetry. The lyric voice that fuelled most of their poetry had a short life, as it does for many poets. Fawcett writes, "In 1970 I believed that the road to poetic accuracy ran through the most rubble littered intersections of the self."[35] Perhaps a mistaken belief but getting beyond that is difficult. Fawcett himself gave up poetry and turned to publishing prose around 1983.

New Ideals: Taking the Writing Out into the World

The poets of this time would surely have agreed with William Wordsworth: "Bliss was it in that dawn to be alive, / But to be young was very heaven!" In many ways, Wordsworth's evocation of the euphoric time after the French Revolution parallels the 1960s and the hope that a new, ideal society can emerge from violence and chaos.

Many students went on to extensive careers as poets and writers. Brian Brett was widely published in poetry and prose, receiving both the Canada Writers' Trust nonfiction prize for *Trauma Farm: A Rebel History of Rural Life* in 2009 and the Matt Cohen Lifetime Award in 2016. Roy Miki, graduate student and then faculty, is a poet, scholar and editor. He has received the Order of Canada and the Order of British Columbia, the Governor General's Award for Poetry and the Gandhi Peace Award.

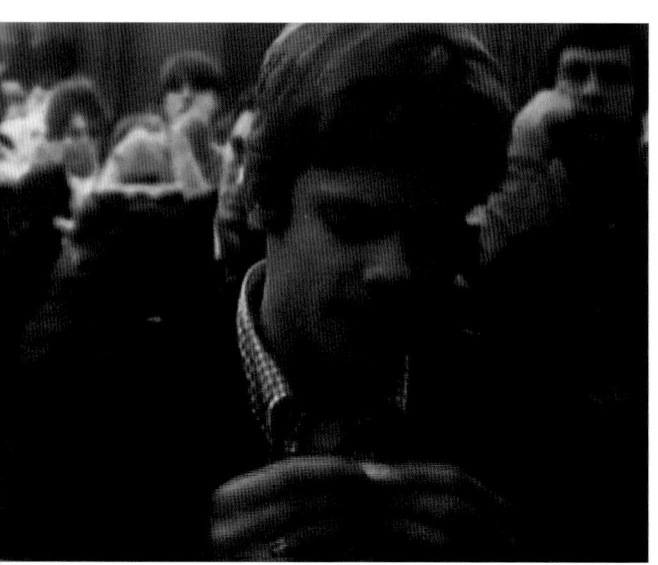

Karl Siegler, later owner of Talonbooks, devoted his working life to the promotion of Canadian literature. *SFU Archives*

Karl Siegler took a different literary path. He joined Talonbooks in 1974 and ran the press until 2007. He was a tireless lobbyist for the Canadian publishing industry; with Dave Godfrey he founded the Literary Press Group of Canada, and he was a founding member of the Simon Fraser Centre for Studies in Publishing. He was appointed a Member of the Order of Canada in 2014.

Sharon Riis developed many gifts through the SFU Film Workshop, co-writing, with John Juliani, the award-winning script for *Latitude 55*. Her second feature film script, *Loyalties*, was directed by Anne Wheeler. She is also the author of several novels and wrote for TV.

Other students who went on to become writers include Rick Antonson, his brother Brian, and Mary Trainer. The trio published their first book, *In Search of a Legend: The Search for the Slumach-Lost Creek Gold Mine* (1972), while still at SFU. Wayne Norton was energized by SFU's literary ambience but didn't start publishing until the 1990s. He has written several books on

BC history, including *Women on Ice: The Early Years of Women's Hockey in Western Canada.*

Although women were marginalized during SFU's first decade, a number emerged from those early years who continued writing and publishing poetry as they found their creative fuel in (among other things) feminism, environmentalism and spirituality. Sharon Thesen's deserved rise to the heights of the Canadian poetic pyramid is well known, but lesser-known poets like Susan McCaslin continue to explore their natures through poetry. Heidi Greco published in magazines such as *Waves*, *Carousel* and *Branching Out* during her student days (1971–1976), but with two young children she had little time for the dramas being played out in the literary community. Since 1994 she has written eight books and appeared in nine anthologies. She admires the simplicity of Rhona McAdam's poetry and the "beautiful, clean writing" of Sandra Djwa. "I hated poetry that obfuscates... I think it's important to be in and of the world. I have never intentionally been a snob."[36]

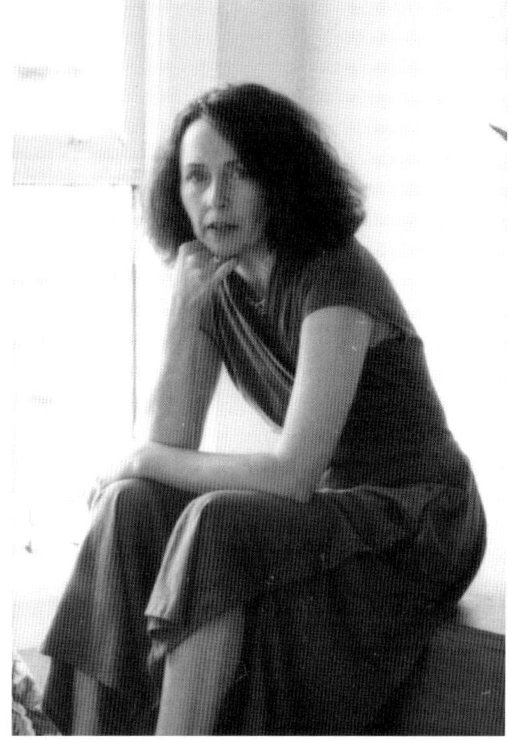

Sharon Thesen developed into a prolific and accomplished writer. Her many accomplishments include winning the Pat Lowther Memorial Award. *SFU Special Collections and Rare Books*

Alban Goulden sums up the experience aptly, deeply appreciative of his life-changing experience at SFU. "There was a tremendous sense of what could happen. Everything fluid, unfolding, uncertain. What was possible. Period. And that was so wonderful."

Chapter 8: Visual Arts

In the Beginning the Hill Was Without Form and Art Exhibitions Were but a Dream

by Bill Jeffries

VISUAL ART AT SFU HIT ITS STRIDE IN 1969 WHEN A SERIES OF THREE CONceptual art exhibitions were brought to campus via Iain Baxter's connections. Those shows, ephemeral though they were, put the university on the map of the international contemporary art world. SFU's other early exhibitions mattered, but only those three are cited in histories of contemporary art as resonating with artists in multiple countries. However, most of the now-famous artists whose work was shown in those late 1960s exhibitions never came to Vancouver. They never saw the urban sixties West Coast hippie energy of the city, which was also very present at SFU. As was the case at many a North American campus, the hirsute hippies mixed in with the suits, mainly recently appointed faculty in sports jackets and ties.

There is a paradoxical quality to SFU's historical fame in visual art. Not only did few of the artists come to Burnaby, but it is also very likely that almost no viewers saw these celebrated 1969 exhibitions—in the world of conceptual art, there is usually not that much to see anyway. Viewers accidentally coming upon the art may have thought they were seeing damage to a wall. In some cases, that art may never even have come to campus: it wasn't the physical presence but the intention, gesture and documentation that mattered to history. This ephemeral state resulted from art that was not an actual object (hence nonobjective) being "shown" on campus. As someone said about ephemerality, "What is short-lived may not be the object itself, but the attention we afford it."[1] With those SFU exhibitions it was very likely both.

So, as it turned out, SFU was known in global art circles for three almost-invisible exhibitions, attaining that fame perhaps before any of the university's academic disciplines gained a similar prominence. The similarity with academic papers being read by very few readers can help us understand why the lack of viewers is not cause for a revolution. The profile of SFU visual art in the period from 1967 to 1970 recalls the lyrics to Buffalo Springfield's "For What It's Worth": there might have been something happening here, but what it was wasn't exactly (or at all) clear. That is not the worst definition of conceptual art one could invent, and for five months in mid-1969 that was exactly what was happening at SFU.

However, before those brushes with art world fame came the slow process of sorting out what could be done. We didn't even have an art gallery! The first year of SFU's existence must have been wonderfully chaotic, in ways now lost to memory but perhaps still possible to imagine. In that first year, the course syllabus offered classes in four non-credit arts programs: dance, film, music and theatre. Visual art came a year later with the arrival of Iain and Ingrid Baxter in September 1966.[2] The creation of on-campus exhibitions over the ensuing nine years may have looked like a linear historical sequence, but at the time it was a collage of experimentation, opportunities seized and no small amount of serendipity. If SFU had no art gallery in its first years, the room repurposed in 1971 as a gallery was barely a gallery at all. It could have been called "The Nook," but it was better than nothing. That space was in the busy southwest corner of the academic quadrangle from 1971 to around 1983.

The Institutional Context

It is easy to assume that the riotous sixties were the result of a popular groundswell emanating from young people, mainly students, many of whom had by then read Jack Kerouac's *On the Road* or William S. Burroughs's *Naked Lunch* and were all too aware of protest as a rediscovered form of expression. You could say freedom of expression was taught by newspaper headlines. There was no shortage of things to protest about, and plenty of newly hatched universities from which the noises of youthful protest could be heard. Yet at SFU we glimpsed senior administrators subscribing to approaches that all had one thing in common: being open to new ways of doing things. This shift has been recounted in the collection *Utopian Universities: A Global History of the New Campuses of the 1960s*, where we discover that SFU was not unique in its sorting out of things. The one Canadian essay in that book, "The Other 60s: Academic Administrators as Agents of Change in Canadian Higher Education," by Paul Axelrod from York University, summarizes the role of the "higher ups" nicely, with a focus on SFU, Trent and York. Reading between the lines, in the history of the arts at early SFU, we can see signs of the very thing Axelrod describes—the university's *administration* catalyzing change, and at the very least going along with the cultural experimentation, even if their support was via benign administrative neglect rather than actual enthusiasm.[3]

SFU's faculty and administration in the 1960s were undoubtedly swamped with their task of inventing a new school. They may well have felt somewhat alone in grappling with the excitement of the times, but they were not really alone—just alone in the Greater Vancouver context. New institutions do have an aura simply owing to their state of newness; I felt that when visiting Trent in 1973, thinking, "Much of this wasn't here four years ago." There was also the energy of concepts finding their form, of ideas panning out as institutional successes, and all of it evolving via something akin to an experimental process. Through experimentation, some concepts settled in to become permanent; and once permanent, they became elements in the character and structure of the institution. A city on a hill may be a place "that cannot be hid," but it is also a concept that must go on to prove itself, which SFU seems to have done.

Iain Baxter Does Anything (N.E. Thing)

One of the first employees in visual art at SFU, if not the first, was Iain Baxter. Baxter's time started in late summer 1966, importantly also the time that Iain and Ingrid invented the N.E. Thing Co. as their quasi-corporate art world identity. Ingrid may have been hired in physical education, but she was an equal partner in N.E. Thing and contributed many of the ideas Iain used in his art. In my interview with Iain, he described their role in the arts at the time:

> I'm not a writer, but I like to play with language. If I wanted to do anything, it could be anything. In the art world, it felt good to be an entity that could do anything it wanted. We added to that then, in order to have the integrity of a major corporation, the setting up of this company. That's how all that got going. If you say you're a consultant, you can do anything. I was able to go to the Canada Development Corporation and ask for funding to run some ads. I could get in most places by having that corporation. It was another way of entering and being, and having doors open up and for me to play in the area called

> the art world as well as the normal world that we're all in. I guess that's kind of how the company got started. To me as an artist it was all quite amazing.[4]

As if to mirror that philosophy, workspaces for art (such as theatre stages) as well as the medium in which artists do their work (say paint on canvas) are essentially places or spaces where *anything* can happen. That is a cliché in art, but perhaps an important one. The Baxters' "anythingness" also sums up visual art at SFU in its first ten years. The SFU experiment may have been unique, but it was also of a piece with many other projects in the arts in the 1960s and 1970s. The exploration and experimentation, with unusual events and exhibitions at hundreds of other art departments, galleries and museums around the globe, provided the context for visual art at SFU. Very much in that mix, SFU was offering a collage of the expected and the unexpected, but in the first six years, all of it took place in the absence of a proper exhibition space.

Iain Baxter's hiring was the usual 1960s combination of luck, propinquity and word of mouth regarding positions that might be available. His landing pad in September 1966 was the Centre for Communications and the Arts. With no existing visual art department, it fell to Baxter to invent and create one. Within the CCA, many faculty—the residents—were multitasking, and that included Baxter. He was teaching non-credit classes, but also coming up with new designs for the university's logo, its letterhead, various university publications and then SFU's first-ever annual report.

Conceptual Art at SFU and Beyond

Visual art at SFU was born not just into a period of ferment, but into the aforementioned global shift away from art objects and toward art as concepts. This tendency, which many assumed was just a fad, became entrenched in the 1960s and 1970s as the conceptual art movement. University courses in philosophy and literary criticism played a major role in this shift to conceptualism, as did classes in twentieth-century art. When the Baxters first came to Vancouver in autumn 1964 to teach at UBC, their art already had a sense of play and irony, which retained a central place in their creations through this ten-year period at SFU and beyond. To that fertile mix they added parody, explorations into the weirdness of language, and their trademark versions of environmentalism. In their own artmaking, the Baxters were not 100 percent conceptual; their practice was more akin to conceptual sculpture.

Baxter's curatorial projects for the new campus were congruent with SFU's state of incompletion. He exploited the stark, minimalist town square agora of the mall, and the academic quadrangle itself. Conceptual art was not the only type of art presented at SFU, but I come back to it because it is what set SFU apart; there were probably more conceptual goings-on at SFU in 1969 than at any other North American university. Situations and materials were reduced to statements to be interpreted or instructions to be carried out. As art famously became "dematerialized" in the period from 1965 to 1975, the notion of "art as idea as idea" took hold.

Dematerialization in art is broadly defined as a sub-set of conceptual art in which the physical manifestations of the work of art is limited to the idea behind the art. The idea is primary, the work of art secondary and not even necessary. Its material form is commonly a text either describing the nonexistent art object or providing directions for its creation. The first major book on the subject was Lucy Lippard's *Six Years: The Dematerialization of the Art Object*. Lippard came to SFU in 1969 as part of the summer exhibitions.

In conceptual art practice there is a lot of shorthand for a thing that could exist but would not—for now. I like to think of conceptual art as a space-saving mechanism for art, as if it were the further extension of minimalist theatre or minimal sculpture.

I mention this web of connections because, of all the new Canadian universities built in the 1960s, SFU is the only one closely linked with what was arguably the most radical of all the new art movements prominent at the time. It was the place where a "radical campus" mirrored exhibitions of radical conceptual art on that campus.

This separating out of the ideas in art from any actual object, so that the work of art had its own dematerialized (often textual) and separate presence, raged on through the 1960s and very quickly spawned an important exhibition that merged "art as idea" with "idea becomes object." That 1969 exhibition in Bern, Switzerland, titled *Live in Your Head: When Attitudes Become Form*, came after SFU's conceptual art efforts. Its media release summed up the show as follows: "Works – Concepts – Processes – Situations – Information," prefaced by the admonition to live in your head.[5] In short, that landmark show was characterized by its abundance of "stuff," but stuff generated by a concept: "things," but things modified by shifts in our attitudes to them. In the 1960s, there was nothing new about the notion that "things" and "stuff," in both their flattened and three-dimensional forms, might be taken as art objects, but that did not deter artists from finding new ways to present old ideas; all it took was a change in attitude.

That was exactly what Iain and Ingrid Baxter brought to Simon Fraser University. This mattered because fully formed, diverse ideas about attitudes toward art were not exactly thick on the ground on Burnaby Mountain in the mid-1960s. The ideas the Baxters introduced at SFU would have been new and exciting anywhere, but the fact that SFU was still in its infancy made the Baxters' world view, and the view of their jobs at SFU, both easier to spring on the unsuspecting university, and also doubly exciting owing to the fact that their activities occurred in an institutional context that was changing and being reinvented month by month.

Exhibitions "Around Campus"

Conceptual art was not the only game on the hill in those first ten years. Without a proper gallery space, the theatre galleries (AKA the foyer) came to the rescue, providing theatre patrons with bonus access to an art show, much as happened decades later at Riverside Studios in London. Starting in 1966, the theatre galleries saw solo shows by Toni Onley, Edward Weston, Ken McAllister and Bryan Dyson, and an exhibition of "things" by Iain Baxter. In addition, there were shows tangential to art itself, such as shows of Polish theatre posters, photography from space and a 1970 exhibition titled *Computer Cartography*.

The library was another site pressed into service. Works by Corita Kent, Tony Westman, Honore Daumier and Joseph Albers were all exhibited in the W.A.C. Bennett Library in one-person shows.

■

There was also a show of pre-Columbian artifacts from Jim Felter's personal collection, and an exhibition titled *Bella Coola: Photographs and Artifacts*. Those shows came very early in the history of First Nations art exhibitions in the Vancouver area.

Ian Wallace and Duane Lunden exhibited works "around the campus" in May 1968, a precursor to the 1969 conceptual art exhibitions that were scattered about the campus a year later. Fred Herzog and Harry Stanbridge showed in Gallery West (in the theatre), where there was also an exhibition of William Blake's illustrations to the Book of Job.

The three conceptual art exhibitions in spring and summer 1969 began with *One Month* in March 1969. March has thirty-one days and this exhibition had thirty-one invited artists, alphabetically ranging from Carl Andre on

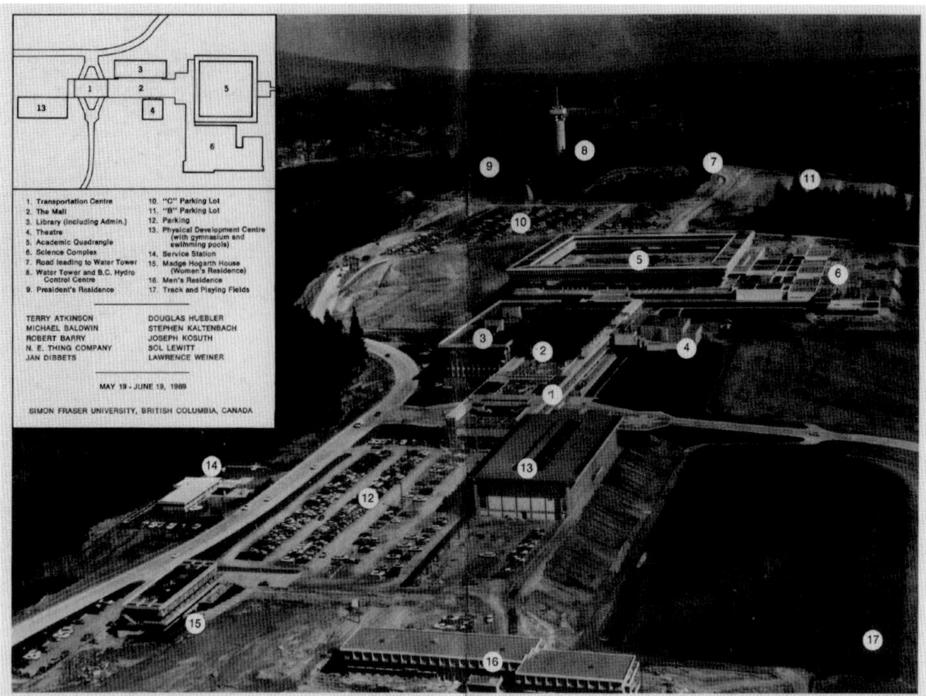

The cover of the catalogue for the exhibition *One Month*. The exhibition was at SFU from May 19 to June 19, 1969. The numbers on the aerial view of the campus correspond to the locations where the various works numbered on page 5 of the catalogue could be seen. *SFU Archives*

March 1 to Ian Wilson on March 31, very much in the style of an advent calendar. Curated by Seth Siegelaub, who directed all thirty-one artists to "kindly return to me, as soon as possible, any relevant information regarding the nature of the 'work' you intend to contribute to the exhibition on 'your' day." It goes without saying that the artist list is a who's who of the formative years of conceptual art. Only three or four of the artists invited have fallen off the map of art history; the rest are truly famous.

The second, an untitled exhibition, ran from May 19 to June 19, 1969. Its untitled status was raised to a higher power when the catalogue of the show was simply titled *Catalogue for the Exhibition*. Artists included were Terry Atkinson, Michael Baldwin, Robert Barry, Jan Dibbets, Douglas Huebler, Stephen Kaltenbach, Joseph Kosuth, Sol LeWitt, N.E. Thing Co. Ltd. and Lawrence Weiner. The problem of what to call this show was addressed by the symposium notice in *The Peak* for June 18, 1969. The purpose of the symposium is stated as, "To communicate with artists in '   ' exhibition [*sic*]." We might think of that as an orthographic solution to a conceptual art problem.

The third and final exhibition in SFU's summer of conceptual art, titled *18'6" × 6'9" × 11'2-½" × 47'11-3/16" × 29'8-½" × 31' 9-3/16*, ran campus-wide from July 7 to August 1. The show, curated by Eugenia Butler, was borrowed from the gallery at the San Francisco Art Institute; its title refers to the room

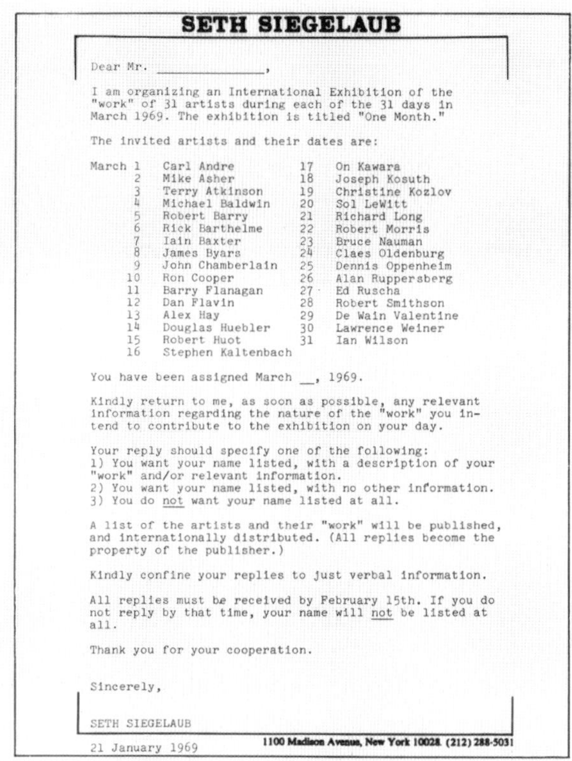

SETH SIEGELAUB

Dear Mr. ________,

I am organizing an International Exhibition of the "work" of 31 artists during each of the 31 days in March 1969. The exhibition is titled "One Month."

The invited artists and their dates are:

March			
1	Carl Andre	17	On Kawara
2	Mike Asher	18	Joseph Kosuth
3	Terry Atkinson	19	Christine Kozlov
4	Michael Baldwin	20	Sol LeWitt
5	Robert Barry	21	Richard Long
6	Rick Barthelme	22	Robert Morris
7	Iain Baxter	23	Bruce Nauman
8	James Byars	24	Claes Oldenburg
9	John Chamberlain	25	Dennis Oppenheim
10	Ron Cooper	26	Alan Ruppersberg
11	Barry Flanagan	27	Ed Ruscha
12	Dan Flavin	28	Robert Smithson
13	Alex Hay	29	De Wain Valentine
14	Douglas Huebler	30	Lawrence Weiner
15	Robert Huot	31	Ian Wilson
16	Stephen Kaltenbach		

You have been assigned March __, 1969.

Kindly return to me, as soon as possible, any relevant information regarding the nature of the "work" you intend to contribute to the exhibition on your day.

Your reply should specify one of the following:
1) You want your name listed, with a description of your "work" and/or relevant information.
2) You want your name listed, with no other information.
3) You do not want your name listed at all.

A list of the artists and their "work" will be published, and internationally distributed. (All replies become the property of the publisher.)

Kindly confine your replies to just verbal information.

All replies must be received by February 15th. If you do not reply by that time, your name will not be listed at all.

Thank you for your cooperation.

Sincerely,

SETH SIEGELAUB

21 January 1969

1100 Madison Avenue, New York 10028 (212) 288-5031

The invitation from Seth Siegelaub to the thirty-one artists invited to take part in the exhibition *One Month* which was 'at' SFU in March 1969. Not all of the invitees responded. *SFU Archives*

Duration Piece #8

Simon Fraser University

On the chart that accompanies this paper 32 rectangles have been drawn representing the 32 days during which this work will be a part of an exhibition at Simon Fraser University.

On the first scheduled day (May 19) of the exhibition the piece will begin to be formed and will continue to form until the final day (June 19). At that time the "information" that actually forms it will be synthesized into two final documents.

You are invited to participate by gathering some of that information through the procedures described below.

1. In the same manner that the "image" of a coin may be transferred onto paper (by rubbing a pencil onto paper that has been placed over the surface of the coin) rub one rectangle on the chart over one surface within your environment during each day of the exhibition's duration.
2. In the space beneath each rectangle briefly describe the kind of surface and its location.
3. At the conclusion of the exhibition mail the chart to

DOUGLAS HUEBLER
BOX 102
TRURO, MASSACHUSETTS 02666

The language of all charts received will be compiled to form a master chart (a copy of which will be returned to the art department at Simon Fraser to publish, or post).

The individual charts will be dissolved into a paper paste that in fact will merge all surfaces together. A second document will be made by curing and shaping that paste into an 8 1/2 X 11" chart whose thickness will depend on the number of original charts returned.

That document and the master chart will constitute the completed work by containing in present time and place all of the real surfaces, locations and duration of the Simon Fraser exhibition.

Douglas Huebler

April 20, 1969

Douglas Huebler's proposal to Seth Siegelaub for the exhibition One Month. Huebler asked the artists in the show to provide him one frottage (rubbing) per day with an eye to making a book from all the replies. The book was never produced. *SFU Archives*

sizes at their art gallery. The artists included the now famous Michael Asher, Robert Barry, James Lee Byars, Douglas Huebler, Joseph Kosuth and Lawrence Weiner. It was reviewed in the *San Francisco Chronicle* by Thomas Albright. He was not amused. "As a put on it's a tedious, warmed-over bean soup. As anything else, it's the biggest bomb since U.C.'s 'Air Art' show last winter." The 150-pound crate containing it was shipped to SFU via Emory Art Freight at a cost of $75 one-way and insured for $500. We don't know how the SFU community responded; we may assume that some were, at the least, confused by what they saw.

Other visual art exhibitions at SFU also showed work by artists who were famous then and who are now giants of the twentieth-century visual arts. One example is a group exhibition of actual art objects that were drawn from the SFU collection, including works by Robert Rauschenberg, Jasper Johns, Roy

Lichtenstein, Lee Bontecou, Frank Stella, Larry Poons, Robert Morris and Jim Dine, all in Gallery West. Brilliant purchases in each instance. Artwork by faculty was also exhibited, as was work by SFU Gallery curators Iain Baxter and James Felter. These shows were models of achieving much with minimal means. One can only imagine the budget constraints, often a great source of creativity in arts administration. It is also not surprising that some of the exhibitions were borrowed from local collections, this being yet another route to achieving significance on a miniscule budget.

During its first ten years, SFU also had a vibrant program of visiting speakers. These included Walter Hopps, David Rothenberg, B.C. Binning, Dana Atchley, Gordon Smith, Pat Martin Bates, Alistair Bell, Jack Shadbolt, Gathie Falk and Gary Lee Nova. The exhibitions and the speaker series were nothing if not eclectic; this was a very strong list of speakers, with Walter Hopps perhaps being the big catch (his link to SFU was Iain Baxter).

The guests from off campus came as speakers or as teachers who could demonstrate techniques, which was especially true in the case of printmaking. The Baxters were committed to bringing outside ideas and energy to SFU, and they seemed to enjoy the process of organizing visits from all sorts of artworld movers and shakers. Maurice Tuchman was a curator at the Los Angeles County Museum of Art at the time he was invited. Ken Tyler, the founder of what was arguably the most famous printmaking facility in the world, Gemini Ltd., later Gemini G.E.L. (Graphic Editions Limited), came to SFU. The Los Angeles connection was further explored with Ed Kienholz visiting as part of the Vancouver Art Gallery's exhibition *Los Angeles 6* in spring 1968. As Iain Baxter describes it, "I met Ed Kienholz in Los Angeles. He came up to Vancouver to help install a show of six LA artists. Four or five of the artists in that show came up, I hung out with them, had them over to my house."[6] The LA exhibition was curated by John Coplans; the six LA artists were Larry Bell, Ron Davis, Robert Irwin, Craig Kauffman, Ed Keinholz and John McCracken, all of whom became major players in the Los Angeles scene. Looking at the years 1968 to 1970 at SFU, one might think it was located south of the border given the number of American artists who passed through.

Conceptual Art at SFU: A Closer Look

The May 1969 conceptual art show (the one lacking a name) arrived via the presence of its curator, Seth Siegelaub, and his partner Lucy Lippard. Its catalogue, titled *Catalogue for the Exhibition, May 19–June 19, 1969*, demonstrates a form of conceptual art logic. Literally, call something what it is.

Iain Baxter initiated the project in the spring of 1969. It was scattered around campus and many works were so dematerialized that they hardly existed at all. Carrying out the project, the execution of the works in the show mainly fell to the newly hired Jim Felter, who was in process of succeeding Baxter as the director of SFU's visual art exhibitions. Seth Siegelaub worked out of New York. I'll briefly recount the works in the untitled show by Sol LeWitt, N.E. Thing Co. and Jan Dibbets, hoping that readers get the flavour of the idea of "art as idea as idea."

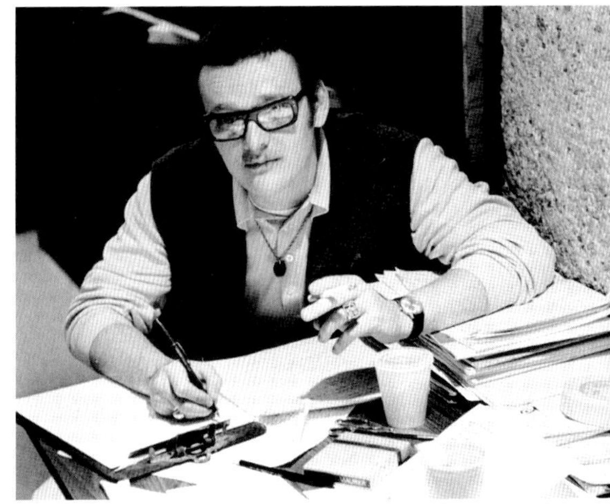

Jim Felter. *SFU Archives*

Sol LeWitt

The piece LeWitt submitted was executed in Library Room 5040, which no longer exists. I wonder, could one or two LeWitt drawings live on, sandwiched between the walls of Rooms 5039 and 5041?

LeWitt's instructions:

> On the north wall of a room, using a yard-stick as a straight edge, draw a line three feet long in any direction. Draw parallel lines (2) to this line until the end of the wall is reached, in both directions. The lines should be as close together as possible and still be distinct from one another, and as light as possible and still be visible. On the east wall, repeat as on the north wall, and then draw another three-foot line bi-secting [*sic*] one of the first sets of lines and perpendicular to them. Parallel lines are drawn to the first line until the end of the wall is reached. On the south wall the procedure of the north and east wall is repeated. A line is then drawn intersecting the right angle formed by the first two sets of lines. This line is also three feet long. Lines are drawn parallel to the first line in both directions, until the end of the wall is reached. On the west wall the procedure for the other three walls is repeated: a line is drawn perpendicular to and bi-secting the set of lines introduced onto the south wall. This line is also three feet long. Parallel lines are drawn to this until the end of the wall is reached.[7]

6. JOSEPH KOSUTH

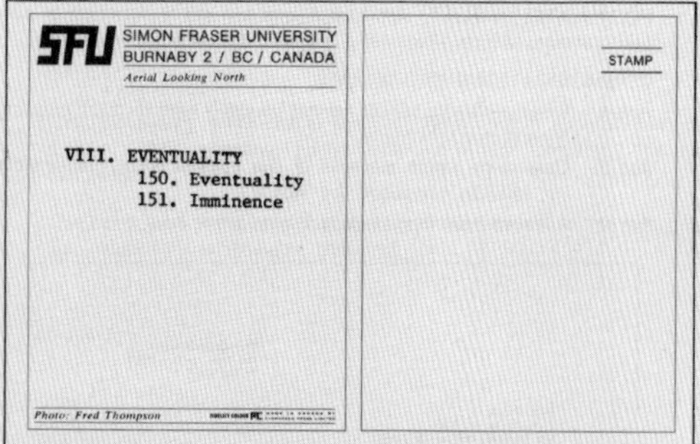

(Presentation of) "VIII. Eventuality (Art as Idea as Idea)," 1968.

(The information was printed on already existing Simon Fraser University postcards.)

The postcards were available during the exhibition at the information centre in the Theatre building.

7. SOL LEWITT

"On the north wall of a room, using a yard-stick as a straight edge, draw a line three feet long in any direction. Draw parallel lines (2) to this line until the end of the wall is reached, in both direction. The lines should be as close together as possible and still be distinct from one another, and as light as possible and still be visible. On the east wall, repeat as on the north wall, and then draw another three foot line bi-secting one of the first sets of lines and perpendicular to them. Parallel lines are drawn to the first line until the end of the wall is reached. On the south wall the procedure of the north and east wall are repeated. A line is then drawn intersecting the right angle formed by the first two sets of lines. This line is also three feet long. Lines are drawn parallel to the first line in both directions, until the end of the wall is reached. On the west wall the procedure for the other three walls is repeated: a line is drawn perpendicular to and bi-secting the set of lines introduced onto the south wall. This line is also three feet long. Parallel lines are drawn to this until the end of the wall is reached."

On June 9, 1969, in the SFU Week, it was announced that the Sol LeWitt project was located in the Communications Centre Room, 5040, Library Building.

"Simon Fraser University Wall Drawing", 1969 (4th Wall).

8. N. E. THING CO. LTD.

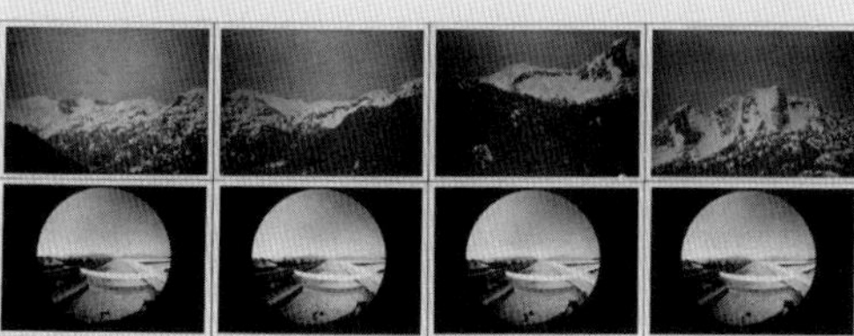

Frames 6°, 4°, 2°, 360°, 7°, 5°, 3°, 1° from "V.S.I. Formula 3".

Page spread from the catalogue with a conceptual work by Joseph Kosuth, Sol LeWitt's instructions for creating a multi-wall conceptual drawing in Room 5040 of the W.A.C. Bennett Library, and N.E. Thing's *V.S.I. Formula 3*. Room 5040 no longer exists; the LeWitt drawings executed by two SFU students may exist between the walls of the newly enlarged rooms formerly on either side of 5040. *SFU Archives*

One would hope that the two students tasked with following LeWitt's instructions, Rosemary Gagné and Malcolm Ramsey, were at least given credit for an undergraduate class in logic, simply for following LeWitt's instructions. Room 5040 was in use then, so its occupants got to live with four original LeWitts.

N.E. Thing Co.

Reading the N.E. Thing Co. text below, I am reminded of internet browsers, email and Zoom calls. The work in the exhibition was titled *V.S.I. Formula 3*. Iain Baxter summarized it in an article by David Bellman titled "Frameworks for an Intervention":

> N. E. Thing Co. Ltd. *V.S.I. Formula 3*. 1968/69. 35mm, Anti-halation Microfilm: 12' long x 1 1/16" wide. [180 photographs taken every 2º

> (0º – 360º) with a 1000 mm lens and 180 photographs taken every 2º (1º – 359º) with a fish eye lens. Alternately edited.]
>
> TRANS-VSI: Transmission of Visual Sensitivity Information": a term to denote the flow of Visual Sensitivity Information from place of transmission to place of reception—via any communications medium—like, telecopier, telex, phone, telegram, letter, videophone, conversation, Telestar, television, etc. A number of these transmission devices embody the possibilities of relay, cognizance and interplay. This is at the moment bringing into play the cultural impact situation we are experiencing and will experience more so when this flow of SI develops universal and provincial overtones. We shall then be experiencing global SI or "culture" through the ends of all our highly developed senses and along the lines and at the receptors of our electric systems.[8]

The work was available in the microfilm reading area on the second floor of the Social Sciences Library and could be seen during the exhibition from 8 a.m. to 1 p.m. daily.

Jan Dibbets

The one work in the exhibition that did not consist of texts, but resulted from one, was titled *Perspective Correction* (1969), by the Dutch artist Jan Dibbets. The art existed in two forms. The first was a patch of grass removed from the lawn in the middle of the academic quadrangle, such that it appeared to be a square rather than a trapezoid when viewed from a particular place. The second element was a postcard illustrating a square patch of ground in a lawn. That square was, of course, the trapezoid in the AQ.

The history of precisely how all this rampaging conceptualism came about is probably lost, but at some point in early 1969, these exhibitions were hatched by Iain Baxter. In my interview with James Felter, he said, "The Seth Siegelaub/Lucy Lippard connection resulted from Iain Baxter's contacts with the art world. But he referred them to me and when anything came up in which they might have an interest, I had the responsibility to carry it out. Now, this is before there was an art gallery. There was no gallery."[9] Coincidentally, the arte povera movement in visual art appeared around the same time; it was developed mainly by Italian artists, but the term is also an apt description of the visual art budget at SFU, "povera" meaning poverty. An easy way to trim art

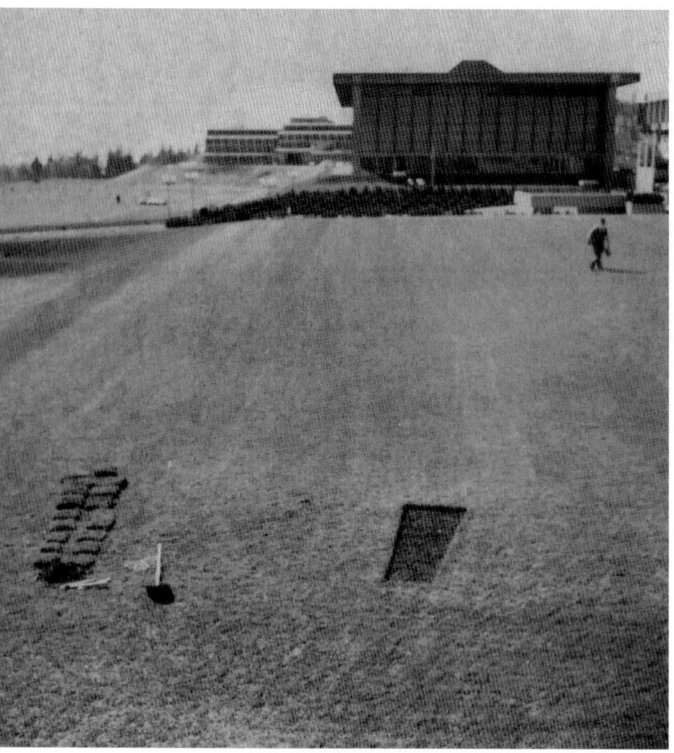

A view of SFU looking west in summer 1969 with Jan Dibbets' *Perspective Correction* in the foreground. The gym is at upper right. The catalogue of the exhibition seems to have the Dibbets in different location (see the catalogue cover, #3) and the work by Douglas Huebler (#4) at the spot where the Dibbets was actually located near the site of the Maggie Benston Student Services Centre. Visual proof that the Dibbets "rectangle" was indeed a trapezoid. *SFU Archives*

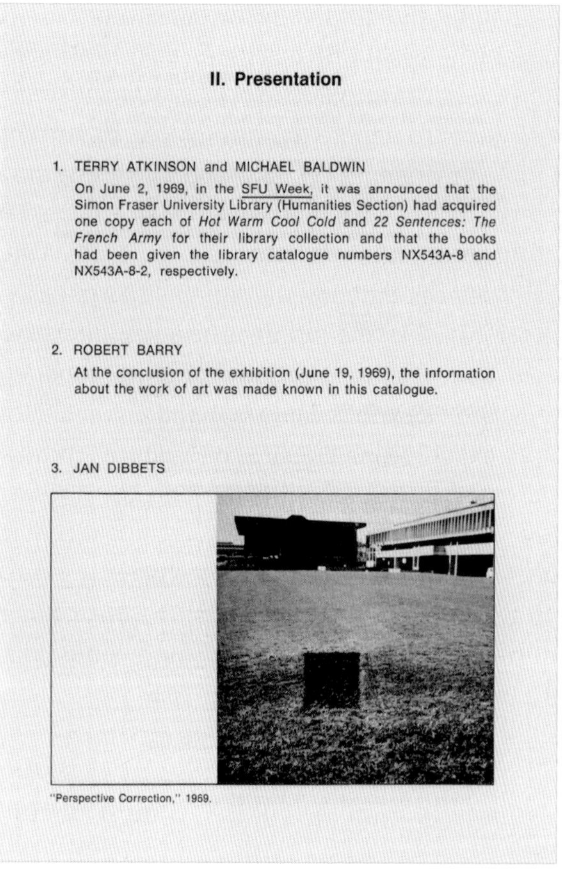

II. Presentation

1. TERRY ATKINSON and MICHAEL BALDWIN
   On June 2, 1969, in the SFU Week, it was announced that the Simon Fraser University Library (Humanities Section) had acquired one copy each of *Hot Warm Cool Cold* and *22 Sentences: The French Army* for their library collection and that the books had been given the library catalogue numbers NX543A-8 and NX543A-8-2, respectively.

2. ROBERT BARRY
   At the conclusion of the exhibition (June 19, 1969), the information about the work of art was made known in this catalogue.

3. JAN DIBBETS

"Perspective Correction," 1969.

The seventh page of the catalogue has self-explanatory work by Terry Atkinson/Michael Baldwin and Robert Barry, both taking the form of gestures. The Jan Dibbets Perspective Correction (1969) was executed by Jim Felter on the lawn in the middle of the academic quadrangle. *SFU Archives* exhibition budgets is to show conceptual art; usually there is neither shipping nor an object to be shown. A few words will often do. Siegelaub and Lippard were among the most important writers on conceptual art, and although they may not have been directly involved in the movement called arte povera, they were at the forefront of the curatorial ability to accomplish great exhibitions without breaking the bank. The word "dematerialized" was the basis of conceptual art. It was more widely known than one would expect owing to Lucy Lippard's book *Six Years: The Dematerialization of the Art Object from 1966 to 1972*. That book, written in the late 1970s, had its seed planted in and around the time that she was a visitor making things happen in Vancouver.

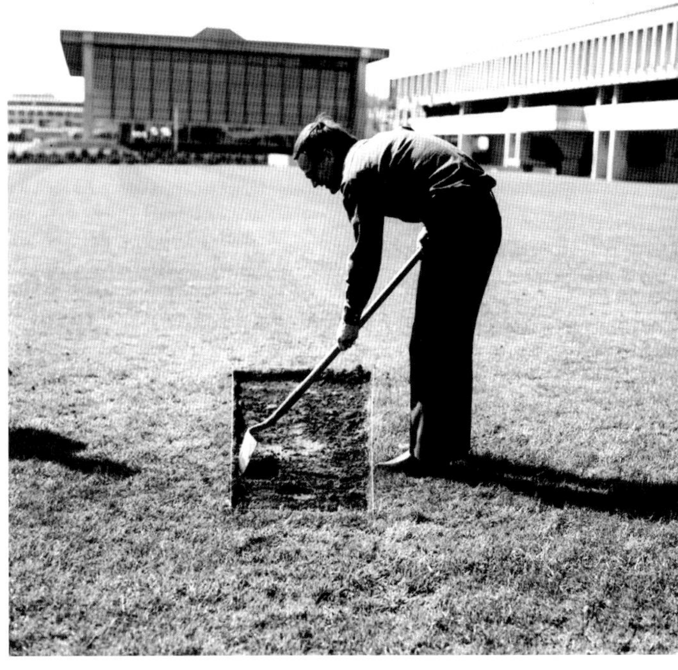

SFU Gallery curator Jim Felter digs the trapezoid that became the Jan Dibbets work *Perspective Correction*, 1969. The publication has the size of the card for the Dibbets piece rather than the size of the trapezoid excavation. *SFU Archives*

A University Course as Conceptual Art: The Twenty-Six-Hour Class

Another project Iain Baxter initiated at SFU was the condensation of a course meant to be two hours per week for thirteen weeks into a single twenty-six-hour extravaganza. A pedagogical theory of information density was transformed into an experiment in which the students traversed the Lower Mainland over a very long day, exposed to "experiences" both in the arts and outside of them. Baxter described the class for *The Tartan* in 2015:

> "I became aware of Marshall McLuhan and started to see art as information. With a twenty-six-hour class I thought maybe you'd learn just as much," he said. "I happened to be judging a fashion show, so the class went to that. The class met on campus at eight in the morning and had walkie talkies to keep in touch throughout the day. We went downtown. I took them to a sushi restaurant, way before they were on every block. There are a lot of visual aspects to Japanese food."[10]

According to *The Tartan*, the class visited many artists' studios, went to the Vancouver Art Gallery to see exhibitions, and eventually returned to SFU to watch movies. The end of the day was taken up with the students writing a report about that day's activities. "In the early days," said Baxter, "basically, it was your class. I decided to just do this idea I had."[11] You might wonder if this raised any eyebrows. "One dean said, 'Why don't we just hire you for one day instead of the whole semester?'" The class went from 8 a.m. the first day to 10 a.m. the second day.

This might be the place to clarify something by not clarifying it. Art and art history have their own battles. In the 1960s, a key fight was that between concepts and objects. Concept boosters, the conceptualists, maintained that art need not be a physical object. Others felt that all the historical media did the job well enough and should continue. To make this history more confusing, there were also conceptual artists who made gigantic objects, such as Robert Smithson's *Spiral Jetty* in Utah, often said to be the only artwork one could see from the moon. Yet it was conceptual owing to its basis in an idea. There exist thousands of other examples, forcing any definition of conceptual art to be about as elastic as a Theraband.

The conundrum that presented itself at SFU—the need for presentation and the absence of a place to present—was addressed in a few ways. Iain Baxter and James W. Felter were the key players in the evolution of the visual arts at SFU and both were well positioned to take on the exhibition challenges. As far back as June 1962, Baxter had written a paper for a class at Washington State University that explored alternative ways of teaching art; its title was "Art Education: Teaching Approaches and the Relationships to Creativity." Alternative approaches to pedagogy were part of the deal with many of the arts hires in the 1960s. In education, these were called teaching methods, but the methods being explored in the late 1960s were not part of any university course syllabus—not anywhere that I know of, anyway. For instance, James Felter's years in Ecuador with the Peace Corps truly informed his approach to the programming at SFU. While Baxter brought conceptual art and early fame, Felter brought a global awareness and openness to art from other cultures. This idea is now universal; SFU was an early adopter.

What Are We All About Here? Iain Baxter on Multimedia, Interdisciplinarity and the CCA

In July 2022, I found Iain Baxter at home in Windsor, Ontario, via Zoom. We began by discussing the situation in SFU's early years and the role that experimentation had in shaping SFU into the institution it became. I asked about experimental pedagogy and mentioned that I hoped he could describe what separated SFU from other universities at that time.

In his memory, the departmental meetings in the Centre for Communications and the Arts (CCA) were very cordial, with none of the internecine battles that characterized life in some other departments. Was the cordiality unique? It might have been. He summarized the meeting agendas as repeatedly exploring the question "What are we all about here?" This was on the floor for consideration by residents, associates and faculty in music, dance, theatre, visual art and film. The department meetings were interdisciplinary, so it was not a huge step for performances, exhibitions and plays to become interdisciplinary as well. As Baxter recalls, "This was in the early days of Intermedia and multimedia performances and all that. It really helped my thinking in a way, just to be surrounded by examples of other groups and individuals working on an interdisciplinary level."[12] The idea that SFU's Centre for Communications and the Arts resembled an outsized version of Intermedia is not that far off the mark.

Intermedia was an association of Vancouver artists working in a variety of media who collaboratively staged events. Founded in 1967 by Jack Shadbolt and Glenn Lewis, among others, it aimed to create a centre of community resources where Vancouver artists, architects, engineers, technologists and educators could come together and explore new models and formats for intensifying and expanding the effectiveness of creative sensibilities in the community.

Asked about the origins of both SFU's interdisciplinarity and the aura of experimentation, Baxter replied that he wasn't sure. "Regarding the idea that courses in the arts should be non-credit… it must have been somebody in the administration or someone from the liberal arts faculty who felt that non-credit classes were the way to go." Non-credit classes were yet another SFU experiment. Baxter gives then-SFU president Patrick McTaggart-Cowan full credit for setting the tone: "To hire faculty as 'residents' was a pretty smart idea. McTaggart-Cowan was really important in that he's the one who embraced that concept and really held it together." But, he said, "it wouldn't be my guess that the non-credit aspect would have been the thing that led to the aura of experimentation. Because it didn't matter, for instance, for getting a job or whatever."

When I mentioned that it was nice to hear kind words said about a former president of a university, Baxter replied, "It was awful what happened to him. I don't know what transpired, but it seemed awful at the time. I really got along with him. And he's the one who allowed me to look at the graphics of the university. I made the new SFU logo even though that was not my specialty. So, it was really great for me to get to work with him." And this generosity carried over to those who leapt in as caretakers of the SFU Gallery during the years when the budget was reduced to almost zero: "There's faculty like Ed Gibson from geography as well as others from other faculties who came in and were trying to help our area." I mentioned that Ed Gibson had passed away a few years ago and that he and his wife, Marianne, had donated a substantial sum of money to build a new art gallery on campus, to which Baxter replied, "That's really what's needed. And so they came up with that. That's perfect."

Baxter also clearly remembered SFU's then-culture of planning via endless meetings, planning in a pre-email world:

> It was interesting because you had everything you could ever think about in an SFU arts group: dance, film, music and visual art in one place. Back then we were all used to having so many meetings. That's what I remember, the meetings, which helped formulate a lot of my thinking. Again, it was because we would sit down and try to figure it out: "What are we all about here?"
>
> The faculty were trying to see if there were coordinates between and among the disciplines. Through Tyler at Gemini, I was able to get Bob Bigelow, who then came to SFU to teach printmaking. Bob did the Simon Fraser University Centennial suite of prints. I hired him and then we together picked out ten or twelve artists from Vancouver to make the prints for the suite. It was in an edition of about fifty, and people don't know that we shipped the suite to institutions worldwide. We sent it to the Tate and to many of the other major museums around the world. I think it's in all their collections to this day.

When I asked Baxter about the mix of art and business in his own practice, he described the efforts to merge the two realms:

> The arts faculty discussed Andy Warhol, who pioneered the contemporary merger between the artist and the artist as businessperson. He certainly came at it from a completely different direction, with his particular emphasis on the Factory [Warhol's studio] and all that. I appreciated how he had managed to invent his Factory, but I wanted to set this entity up as the N.E. Thing Company as a way to allow me to just do anything, and to tie it into the corporate world. Our lives were being controlled by these big corporations. So, I thought I could kind of jump in there and have fun playing with that whole thing.

The Baxters' prescience was undervalued back in the day, but the art business models invented by Warhol and N.E. Thing Co. are now the norm for most financially successful artists. In the 1970s, some artists had a studio assistant; in the 2020s, many have a team of employees, sometimes twenty or more.

Iain Baxter and N.E. Thing Beyond the University

Iain Baxter/N.E. Thing Co. made a lot of work during the decade from 1965 to 1975—so much that the best approach for the curious is to find a copy of the Art Gallery of Ontario's 2011 catalogue *Iain Baxter& Works 1958–2001*. The twenty-six-hour class and the May-to-June conceptual art exhibition on campus are salient Baxter projects, as well as the beginning of the solutions to the problem of having no art gallery at a university that was expanding and growing in stature with every passing year.

Some of Baxter's projects had short but interesting lives, especially the Eye Scream Restaurant at 2043 West Fourth Avenue in Vancouver. Founded in 1977, the restaurant was a huge success but continually ran into cash flow issues. It closed after two glorious years. I had my own cash flow problems at the time, but still managed to dine there occasionally. The Baxters' creditors were supportive; after closing Eye Scream, Baxter says, "I owed some people money and

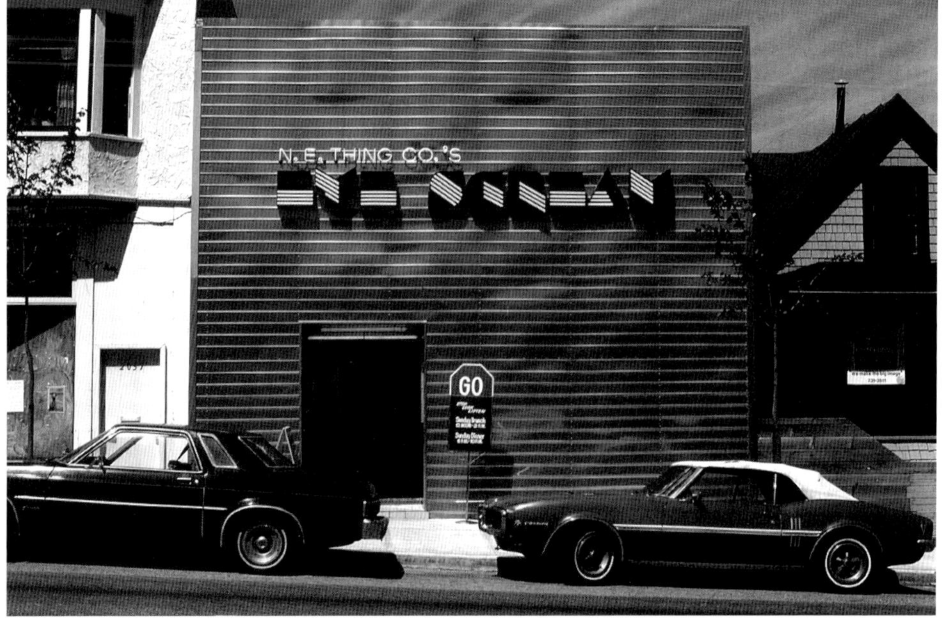

Years after leaving SFU, Iain and Ingrid Baxter opened the groundbreaking but relatively short-lived Eye Scream restaurant at 2043 West 4th Avenue in Vancouver's Kitsilano neighbourhood. *SFU Archives*

had to go to court to sort things out, where I said I could offer some drawings or prints [to settle the claims] and people agreed." At the time of writing, ephemera such as a single Eye Scream Restaurant business card can be found for sale on the internet for UK £65.

Baxter's work at SFU was significant enough to open many doors for him when he left. After Eye Scream, he taught briefly at Emily Carr College of Art and Design and then successfully applied for a Canada Council grant that provided financial support as well as a subsidized studio in Paris. He then moved to The Hague, again receiving studio space, this time in the Gemeentemuseum, and took part in many exhibitions in Europe as well as back in Canada. That was followed by access to Polaroid Corporation's photo equipment at their head office in Cambridge, Massachusetts, and travel around America to make some two thousand Polaroid images that comprised the exhibition *Instant America*. In autumn 1981, he accepted a teaching post at the Alberta College of Art in Calgary. On the side, he worked as a creative consultant to the Labatt Brewing Company for two years. In 1988, he received an offer to teach at the University of Windsor, where he continues to live, now as Professor Emeritus.

The Governor General's Award in Visual and Media Arts followed in 2004 and the Canada Council's Molson Prize in 2005. Somehow, in the midst of all this, Baxter took part in a hundred or more exhibitions. Other awards followed: the Order of British Columbia and an honorary doctorate from UBC in 2004, the Gershon Iskowitz Prize in 2006, and honorary doctorates from the University of Windsor and SFU in 2007 and 2008. The chronology in the Art Gallery of Ontario catalogue covers Iain's story up to 2010. Most extraordinary to me is his seemingly boundless energy, and the number of institutions to which Baxter gave that energy. SFU benefited from that creativity early on and has been the better for it. As far as the 1960s and 1970s, it may well be, as they say, that you had to be there.

The End of One Era, the Start of Another

Iain Baxter left SFU eight months after James Felter was hired in January 1969. They overlapped that summer, and by September Felter was in place, already planning *what* the SFU Gallery might be, as well as *where* a campus art gallery space could possibly go. SFU's administration saw the benefits of having a campus exhibition space, even if nothing resembling a truly proper space for exhibitions was to be had at the time. Felter continued in variously described positions as curator of the SFU Gallery until 1985—his sixteen years in the role remains a record.

Felter inherited an operating methodology from Iain Baxter, but he chose not to follow it. If the arts of the 1965 to 1975 period at SFU were exploratory and experimental, Felter explored and experimented in markedly different ways from those employed by Baxter. The rules were still few, and the templates for organizational structure could, and sometimes did, range across the entire history of experimentation in the arts as it had evolved in the previous half-century. The result, which continues to this day, is that the conventional wisdom that a gallery, or a theatre, is a space in which anything can happen, still holds. It was writ especially large in SFU's first decade, especially as Felter opened the programming up to art from other countries and to First Nations art.

James Felter's work history was an intriguing match for the imagined exhibition requirements on Burnaby Mountain. He was recently local, having arrived in Canada from the United States in March 1968. Prior to that, he had worked in Ecuador in the Latin American Regional Handicrafts Program run by the Peace Corps. Felter was posted to Ecuador in 1965, eventually running an art gallery in Quito. The gallery exhibited local artists, catalyzing good relations with the art community of Ecuador.

Felter was no stranger to life at a newly hatched university. He went to the University of South Florida (USF), which was in its second year of operation when he arrived in 1962. The small-world quirkiness of the SFU and USF acronyms being anagrams of each other was one of several similarities shared by the two institutions in their first years. At USF, Felter says, "I organized a statewide exhibition and competition of work from all of Florida's art schools. Almost everything I did there was the first time it had been done."[13]

The story of how Felter came to SFU was also not all that unusual in the human resources climate of the latter 1960s. As Felter described it to me, in summer 1968, he had an in at a sawmill in Castlegar, but before moving there he consulted an astrologer who advised him that he "might as well wait" in Vancouver until September because "nothing will be happening" during the summer. He waited, and during the wait, Alvin Balkind returned to his post as director of the UBC Fine Art Gallery and offered James the job of installing the exhibitions there. UBC's gallery was in the basement of the main library. "Then Alvin told me about the position as an associate in visual arts that was coming up at Simon Fraser in January 1969. He urged me to apply. That's how I found out about the job at SFU." He was the successful applicant and a year later, in January 1970, he was re-hired as "permanent, part-time curator-director of exhibitions, and also to be in charge of a new proper art gallery space."

This mountain utopia had its eccentricities, notably in the human resources area. Staff called residents performed certain tasks, and others, called associates, performed others. I doubt that the resident named Iain Baxter was tasked with organizing conceptual art exhibitions, but he did it anyway. Baxter was inclined toward pedagogical experiments as opposed to hanging pictures on gallery walls in a conventional manner. It fell to one of the associates, James Felter, to create and install the exhibitions from 1969 onward. Felter was hired by a resident named Joel Smith, who was from Chicago, and who at one point simply asked Felter if he'd be interested in teaching a non-credit course. So, teaching became part of Felter's SFU mix. January 2, 1969, was Felter's first day working at SFU. And on the mountain of Serendip, of course that was the day that he met his future partner, Iris Garland—at his new workplace.

The situation in which one person conceives of an exhibition and another carries it out is not rare; it happens every time a curator leaves a post. Shows are always booked far in advance (though less so at SFU in the 1960s and 1970s), with new staff inheriting contracted exhibitions and normally working on their own, without the project's initiator, to see the exhibition through. That is precisely what occurred. The conceptual art show may have been Iain Baxter's baby, but it was James Felter's to design, coordinate, program and execute.

In 1969, SFU was in no position to design and build a new art gallery. In Felter's view, this presented an opportunity and offered solutions to a problem he saw in a different area. Felter's assessment of SFU's architecture was that the building exteriors were wonderful but the public inside spaces were dark and drab. His initial effort involved appealing to then-president Ken Strand to reform the existing committee structure. Felter recalls, "Strand reformed three committees, the design committee and aesthetics committee and a works of art committee, into a single presidential works of art committee."[14] Felter sat on it along with Arthur Erickson, Gordon Smith and some SFU faculty members.

If the quantity of hallway art at SFU still seems pleasurably unusual today, the presence of those hundreds of works of now-public art can be traced back to a pitch Felter made to the administration:

> So, I wrote up a proposal for three things. A securable gallery with a lock and key; some funds for the building of the collection; and that the collection was to be used on a loan basis for the offices all around campus, not just sit in a vault somewhere. It would be in use, and I also had the vision of making the university as a whole into a museum. I designed the frames that are in the hallways. And I got SFU

> carpenters to install the larger works in the hallways. So that's how all that got started. I worked closely with physical plant staff to do that.

Those requests led to all three proposals living on into the present. Faculty and staff may borrow art for their offices, larger works of art are found on walls throughout the campus, and a small, secure gallery space was eventually carved out of the southwest corner of the academic quadrangle (AQ), later shifting down the hall to AQ 3004, a space that was still in use in 2024 pending the construction of a new free-standing gallery building to the east.

Beginning in the late sixties, SFU also acquired and exhibited First Nations and Inuit art. In 1967, two rooms on the east side of the AQ concourse were designated as a museum and lab space for archaeological and ethnographic materials, many of which are now regarded as artistically significant. The gallery was originally located in AQ 3144 and the lab space in AQ 3145. The first exhibit in the new museum featured Northwest Coast First Nations baskets borrowed from a private collector. (In 1969, stone tools and ceramics from Roy Carlson's Nubian excavations were featured.)

Carved Poles from Naheeno Park

The two poles by Tsimshian carver Ray Wesley that now grace the entrance to SFU's Office for Aboriginal Peoples were commissioned in 1973 by the SFU Alumni Association and originally mounted in Naheeno Park, with a plaque proclaiming that they were "for the enjoyment of all people." The park, on the south side of the campus, was the brainchild of student Mel Woolley and was developed in 1971 with the aid of grants from several sources, including the SFU Alumni Association. It was taken over by the SFU administration in 1973. Envisioned as a forest retreat from the stress of campus life, the park was christened "Naheeno," described by Woolley as an Indigenous name meaning "peaceful, tranquil" that was chosen to represent an escape from "the concrete jungle that traps us most of the time." The poles remained in place for several decades before being restored and moved to their present location on the third floor of the AQ.

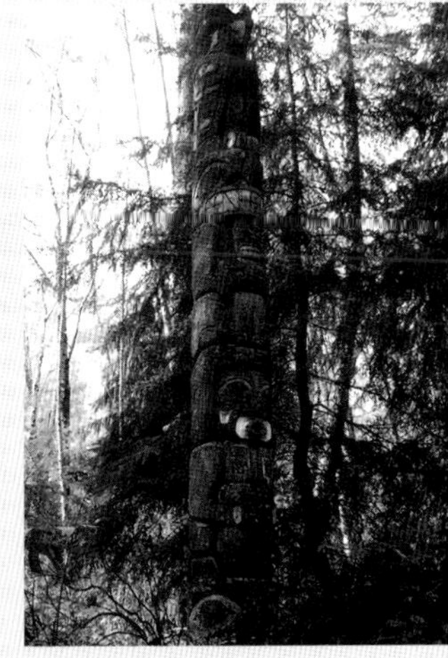

One of Ray Wesley's poles in its original location in Naheeno Park. *John Hebron*

In 1970, SFU hosted its first exhibition of work by Inuit artists (referred to as "Eskimo" art at the time). Curator-director James Felter subsequently built the university's collection of Inuit graphics and, by 1972, the university had acquired one of the largest collections of Inuit art outside of Ottawa. An article in *Comment* described the collection: "When Dr. John Ellis of the Faculty of Education heard that Dr. Donald De Nevi of California wanted his prized Eskimo graphics returned to Canada he suggested that Simon Fraser University would be an ideal home for the collection. The collection includes 96 Cape Dorset and Holman Island prints, three major soapstone carvings and three sets of miniature sculptures produced by artists such as Parr, Kiakshuk and Kenojuak."[15]

While so much work was going on behind the scenes to find display space, any visual art activity was forcibly moved out onto the campus, occasionally even to places where no viewer would ever find the art. For example, the artworks for the 1969 untitled conceptual art exhibition were scattered around campus. The concept of a gallery being a space where anything could happen carried into the art itself: a painting is a place where anything might be painted; a concept might be realized in any way imaginable, or never realized at all. All of these summary descriptors of the arts follow quite logically from the idea, current since 1900, that the arts were free to be anything, even if their subject was not freedom itself. Art remained a serious undertaking, but it also felt like a game— a game in which SFU, even with its limited means, was certainly a player in the 1965 to 1975 period.

Conceptual art was not just dumped at SFU and left for students and faculty to puzzle over. There were serious educational programs on offer, introducing "The New Art," which was the title of a lecture James Felter gave at the SFU Theatre on May 29, 1969. The May 23 media release announcing this lecture begins, "Visual Art Associate James Warren Felter will present a voice event dealing with Conceptual Art, a new movement in art that emphasizes the thinking process almost exclusively, in his lecture on 'The New Art' at 12:30PM."[16]

By 1971, the SFU Gallery had opened in the corner of the AQ, upstairs from the student-society-run second-hand bookstore. The gallery space had formerly been the Student Advice Centre. There was no budget for blacking out the windows, hence the first gallery at SFU had windows overlooking the mall and the SFU Theatre, which was not good—windows are a no-no in the museum world. It was in that modest space that Felter started working through the ideas he brought to SFU, some sounding as if he were designing an ecology of art for the campus. For instance, here is Felter describing what he terms "gaps," which are actually niches waiting to be filled:

> I played music in the gallery. My philosophy of university exhibitions was to look around and see what was available, as well as what other spaces were showing in the city, and fill in the gaps. I did what I think was the earliest First Nations art show at a public institution in Vancouver. Commercial galleries did them, but not public spaces. I did the first province-wide photography exhibit, as well as the first province-wide craft exhibit. I did Chinese art exhibitions that nobody showed in the downtown art galleries. As a result, the SFU Gallery was getting a lot of coverage in the media, especially in the *Vancouver Sun* and *Province*. One of the editors back then, who is now a friend of mine, told his bosses that they should stop covering so much at this university. But everything was different, you know, we did things that nobody else was doing and we were all so young and creative and perhaps a bit insane.[17]

When I asked James if he had a sense of how many people actually saw the shows he brought to campus, he said, "My assistant had a counter, so we kept track. We recorded everybody who came through the doors, but the numbers depended on press coverage. If we got good press coverage in the *Sun* or the *Province*, then people from off campus would come up." When I asked about any model he used for his shows, where the ideas came from: "I just dreamed them up. I still do. I have exhibition ideas all the time. The only thing I can say is that it was in my head. I should also say that I had no idea what conceptual art was, because I had been in South America. Iain Baxter was the introduction to that whole channel—and he had all the conceptual art contacts."

Dreamed-Up Exhibitions

If I were to say that the arts at SFU in its first decade were not very bureaucratic, that might be understating the situation. Here is James Felter's description of the major decision-making process on his very first day at SFU:

> I walked into the office of the Centre for Communications and the Arts, where Nini Baird was in charge of publicity. That's how I met Nini for the first time. And she says, "Well, what are you going to do?" I thought, if I don't tell her, she will tell me what to do. I just made up everything I could think of, pulled out of my head on the spot. I included an exhibition of my stuff from Ecuador and rattled off, I can

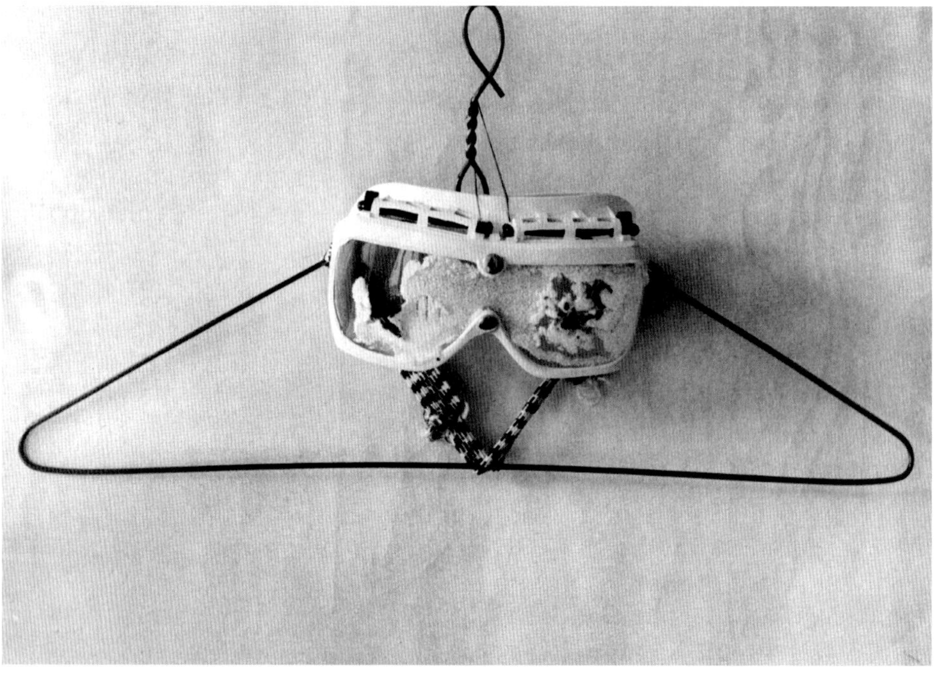

An experimental gesture by the Group of Non. *SFU Archives*

> do this and also that; I made up the whole program for that trimester on the spot. I would have to plan ahead of time, each time, the whole semester so that it could be promoted in the magazines.[18]

After the conceptual summer of 1969, Felter came up with some uniquely conceptual exhibitions. For instance, there was an exhibition titled *The Group of Non*, an ironic nod toward the Group of Seven. Why were the paintings and sculptures conceptual? Quite simply, none of the artists named in the show existed, and the works of art were all made by the exhibition's curator and a group of his friends. Today this might be somewhat questionable, but in the era of anything-goes experimentation, it was just another experiment, just another creative jab at the cultural status quo. Marcel Duchamp had taught us a lot about what might constitute a work of art, and this exhibition picked up where Duchamp left off. Felter describes the gesture in the spirit of the late 1960s: "You could make up anything and hang it in the gallery. I can exhibit anything if it's done properly. It doesn't matter what it is, but you set it up to be looked at, and it will be looked at. I did two or three things with coat hangers, and in one of them I set it up with Christmas tree tinsel. That hanging work was reproduced in a review in *Arts Canada* by a member of the Group of Non; we got lots of media coverage." It was a different time: one of the anonymous artists who helped create the show wrote a review of it that was published!

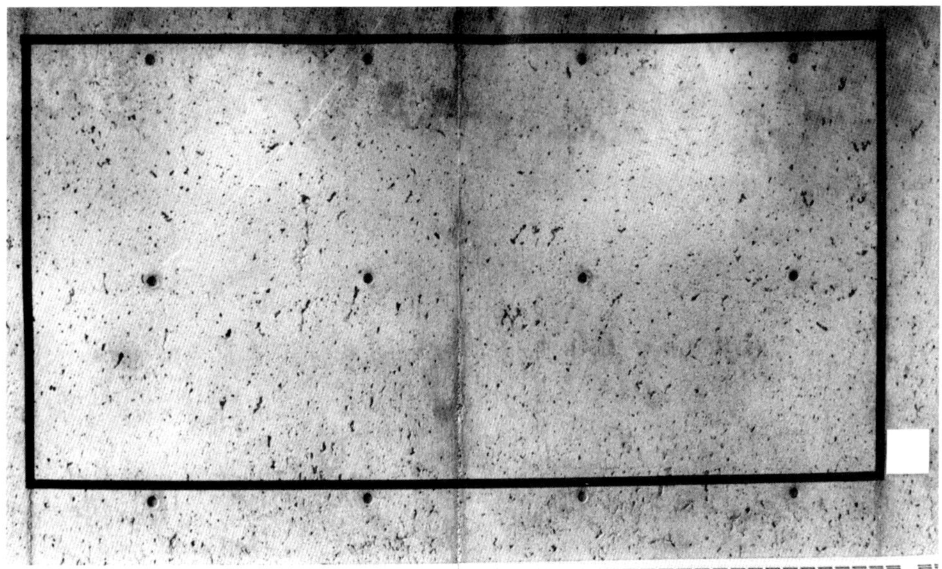

"The world's first completely conceptual work," created by members of the Group of Non. *SFU Archives*

FROM CENTRE FOR COMMUNICATIONS AND THE ARTS
SIMON FRASER UNIVERSITY
BURNABY 2, BRITISH COLUMBIA

GROUP OF NON

TO: You are looking at the world's first completely conceptual work. The individual members of the group of NON have spent many long years of investigation in this area and are now able to make Great Art Masterpieces with a single glance. They are at this very moment perceiving the world in their very special way and projecting mentally on this reserved wall space their fantastic images. "If you look long enough and with the proper dedication and frame of mind you will be able to be part of this totally new Art experience.

FEB. 17-MARCH 14, 1967

When I asked Felter how many artists were in the Group of Non exhibition, he said, "There may have been three of us. One of them was probably Walter Piovesan, another was a friend who emigrated from Seattle because she wanted to work with Iain Baxter. Joel Smith may have contributed something. However, Iain Baxter knew nothing about this bit of institutional subterfuge." Felter was not so much trying to undermine a system, which wasn't really possible anyway because the visual arts at SFU didn't have much of a system in

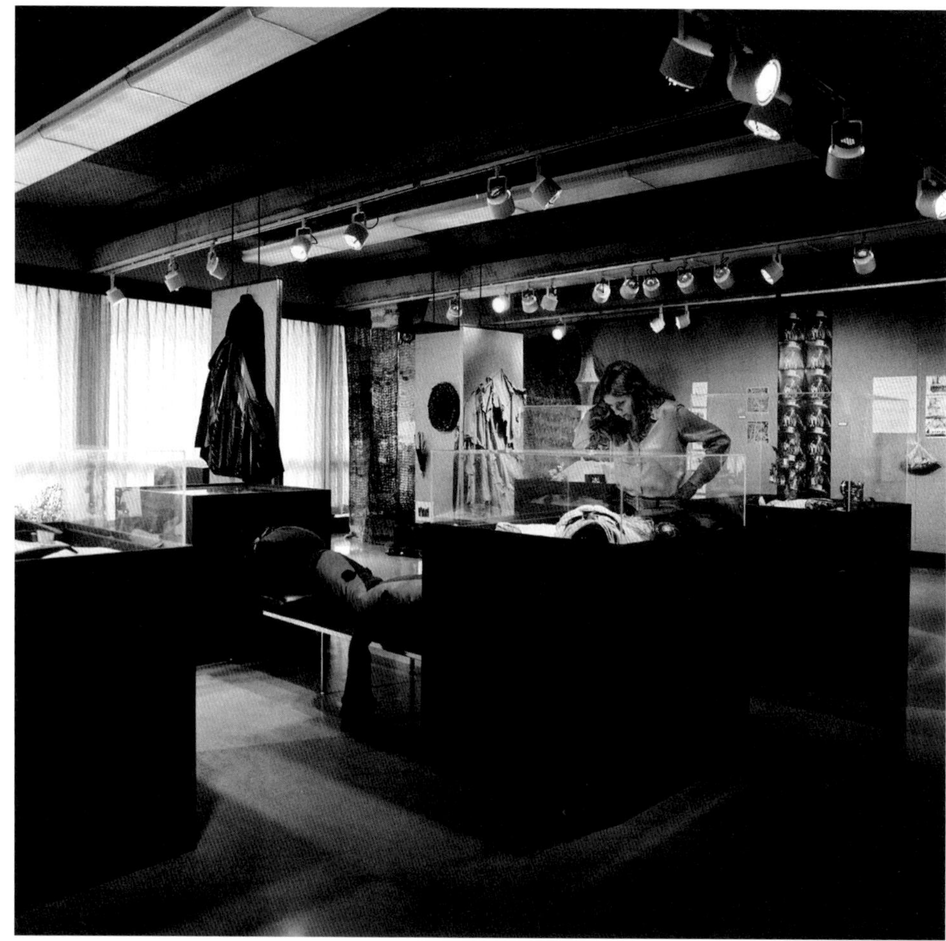

SFU Gallery assistant Wendy Newman looks over a 1971 exhibition at a time when the gallery was located at the southwest corner of the AQ on the main lecture room level. The work shown demonstrates curator Jim Felter's affinity for material from global cultures, whereas Iain Baxter's legacy was almost entirely in the realm of Conceptual Art. *SFU Archives*

those first ten years. Rather, he introduced a sense of play very different from the Baxters' idea of play, as a way of keeping things alive—and extending the notion of creativity outward, from the artist, out into the institutional context.

And SFU continued to receive visitors in the form of visiting artists. Visits might be as short as a one- or two-hour lecture or as long as an all-day or week-long workshop. Dana Atchley came in the early 1970s. He had a position at the University of Victoria from 1969 to 1971. At SFU for a single day, presumably he gave a talk on what became known as "digital storytelling," but he was also a good graphic artist, a performance artist and a pioneer in the video-by-artists scene. He had connections with the Western Front in Vancouver, the founders of which included UVic grads Eric Metcalfe and Kate Craig. Bob Fried from San Francisco was in town doing business with the *Georgia Straight* newspaper, for which he did several covers in the psychedelic style for which he was known. Fried and Atchley were both early advocates for stamp art, or artist-designed works in the form of postage stamps, and as guest artists they were both important to the history of art in Vancouver. James Felter developed an interest in artist stamps as well and brought works by several artists into the SFU collection in the 1970s.

Doing exhibitions with artists from other countries is expensive, from other cities less so, but still expensive. SFU was not awash with the kind of money needed to be internationally involved, so creative ways had to be found. Here is Felter describing the organization of an early exhibition of postage stamp art that was shown at SFU in the autumn of 1974:

> I eventually got enough material to make the first exhibition of artist stamps and stamp images. Nini Baird got the former postmaster general of Canada to open the exhibition. We couldn't afford a catalogue so I xeroxed a black-and-white catalogue with all the images and other stuff for the first exhibition. I had borrowed all the work from the artists. One day Nini told me that the Koerner Foundation had some extra money: "Do you have anything you want money for?" I thought, "OK, maybe we'll buy this collection." We wrote up the proposal to buy the collection and they accepted it and gave me the money, which was only two-thirds of its total value. I wrote each artist a letter saying, "Would you accept two-thirds of your asking price?" And they all accepted, including Donald Evans, who did these fabulous watercolours.[19]

That stamp art exhibition became a ten-year touring exhibition from SFU, going to Europe and across the United States as well as Canada. In New York, it was shown at the Museum of Modern Art's PS1 site in Long Island City. The saga of the catalogue also had a happy ending when the Canada Council awarded the SFU Gallery funds to produce it—designed to mimic the look of a postage stamp album.

Despite such successes in visual art at SFU in the early seventies, change was in the wind. Felter's description of the restructuring events immediately after 1975 make it sound as if some aspects of the ten-year golden age were coming to an end: "The Centre for Communications and the Arts was split—those who had chosen to be professors went to the communications department, including the painter Joel Smith. He continued under the academic line. Those who wanted to retain the title of 'resident' remained in the Centre for the Arts and were put on terminal contracts, as they were no longer part of the academic structure. The structural change took place in 1976 and was very traumatic."

The life of visual art continued in interestingly various ways in the post-1975 period. But then the financial crunch of the early 1980s hit and the university was looking for programs to cut and places to save money. Art galleries are always an easy target for those who see them as a frill. James Felter was bought out of his contract in 1984, but the gallery continued to have exhibitions organized by faculty seconded from other departments, especially Ed Gibson from geography. That arrangement continued until September 2005.

When we spoke in 2022, James Felter was cognizant of the fiftieth anniversary of the SFU artist stamp exhibition being the fall of 2024; one day, he said, he'd like to see that exhibition re-created, with the inclusion of additional material from what he terms his own "enormous collection of artist stamps" to create a museum-quality stamp exhibition on campus, and to offer for touring.

In the end, James W. Felter's legacy at SFU is immense. His idea of making the university itself into a museum/gallery is as relevant today as it was in the 1970s. And it is a concept that became policy during the post-1984 period, when Ed Gibson promoted Felter's idea that art should be part of every student's life—that students should see it every day on campus and absorb, by a kind of cultural osmosis, the idea that art belonged in their lives. That bit of educational aspiration lives on to this day at SFU and should be a focus at the new art gallery. *Plus ça change.* By the early 1980s, the Centre for the Arts became the School for the Contemporary Arts, a name that has survived for over forty years. One can only hope that the excitement of those first ten SFU years, back when digital still mostly meant using your fingers, continues—in whatever form it may take.

On a final note, this chapter would not have been at all possible without the time, effort and support of both Iain Baxter and James Felter. My thanks go out to them again now, some five years after the year of the interviews with them. As I said when asked if I'd take on the writing, "I wasn't there then." Iain and James helped me 'attend' SFU in its first years, and now they have helped their readers do the same.

CHAPTER 9

Legacy

by Ann Cowan

THE MAGIC OF SIMON FRASER UNIVERSITY'S FIRST DECADE TOUCHED FACulty, students, staff, visitors to campus, and the community that surrounded it. So many factors contributed to that magic: the vision of a new kind of university where thought was free-flowing and collaborative; the blurred lines between disciplines; the abandonment of hierarchies for a democratic approach to governance and learning; education that occurred inside and outside the classroom, on the campus and in the community, and was not hidebound by tradition and precedent. The established universities were not immune to this changing tide, but the new schools that opened in the 1960s, of which Simon Fraser was one, had a clean slate.

Utopian Universities

In the essay "The Other 1960s: University Leaders as Agents of Change in Canadian Higher Education," Paul Axelrod writes that at Simon Fraser University, "the year-round university and the inclusion of a diverse body of students, particularly mature students, or those who did not meet the usual high school graduation requirements, was important. Faculty and students alike were attracted to the 'promise of greater intimacy and inventiveness at Simon Fraser which had, early on, cultivated an image of innovation, academic excellence and openness.'"[1]

Axelrod further suggests that SFU and the other new "utopian universities" were "unable to sustain the idealism and experimentalism of their early days." As he describes it:

> Demographic and financial pressures, student unrest, faculty-administration conflict and public criticism pervaded these and other campuses in the latter half of the 1960's [*sic*]. University administrators

> who considered themselves educational reformers were suddenly on the defensive—attacked by radical students for being too timid and by bemused citizens for apparently losing control of their campuses. Still, the academic changes they did introduce in the early 1960's [*sic*]… should not be overlooked in the wake of cynicism that followed. This included the design and architecture of the new institutions, propelled, in interesting ways, by utopian academic concepts.[2]

The lively voices in this volume are those whose lives were changed by the vibrant arts scene created by the Centre for Communications and the Arts, the SFU Student Society and the flexible and engaged faculty in many departments who allowed artistic creation to be part of course work. These first-hand accounts give a picture of how experimentation, opportunity and youthful enthusiasm embedded the notion that anything and everything was possible. This small community of a few thousand students and faculty, in many cases close in age, challenged societal norms and artistic tradition. The legacy of these early students and faculty members underpins many cultural and artistic institutions today.

Rowland Lorimer, who came to SFU in 1968 and joined the Faculty of Education to teach behavioural science foundations in education, recalls the first ten years of his time at SFU as a period of experiment and exploration, with much discussion among the faculty of what should be taught and how, and what collaborations would advance the ideas underpinning this new university, with revolutionary notions about education and learning, interdisciplinarity and democracy. Soon Murray Schafer and Tom Mallinson would leave the CCA and, joined by some education colleagues, such as Bob Harper, Rowland Lorimer and Pat Hindley, move to a new interdisciplinary Department of Communication. Departments, faculties and programs were remarkably fluid in the early years of the "instant university," and interviews with faculty and students recount the hours of discussion and countless meetings seeking to establish a rationale for the curriculum. Democracy is very time consuming!

Pressures of Governance and Academic Power

From 1968 until the late seventies, when I arrived at SFU, the university was embroiled in very public conflicts among students, faculty and senior administration, as lines of authority were drawn and redrawn. The result, after a period of intense unrest, was a university tired of conflict, with a strong commitment to democracy among students, faculty, staff and administration. SFU had established a radical reputation that appealed to some and disturbed others. By 1975 SFU's transition was in progress: the Centre for Communications and the Arts was re-conforming into departments and programs and moving to various faculties, and sentiments along political lines profoundly affected Pauline Jewett's presidency, as did labour unrest on campus. It was an unsettling time. Filmmaker Colin Browne, who had studied at SFU and joined the faculty in the eighties, said that he found his colleagues in the School for the Contemporary Arts in a state of shock and grief after years of scarcity following the first ten years of exuberance and access to funds. It was a sobering time.

Hugh Johnston writes of the bold promise of a Centre for Communications and the Arts within the Faculty of Education and its dissolution and the eventual formation in 1975 of a Faculty of Fine and Performing Arts.[3] SFU Vice President Brian Wilson appointed Evan Alderson as director. Alderson was not an artist but rather a faculty member in the English department who was highly regarded for his ability to mediate among those with different priorities. He remained director until 1981 while the faculty transitioned into the School for the Contemporary Arts, with separate departments for the disciplines of dance, film, music and theatre. Alderson later became dean of arts and was the founding director of Graduate Liberal Studies.

This was not the vision of the early years. Schafer, with his wife, musician Phyllis Mailing, and education professor Tom Mallinson, had hoped for a small experimental institute modelled on the highly influential Bauhaus School in Germany, where there was interdisciplinary integration of art and craft. Murray Schafer left SFU in 1975, but Phyllis Mailing and Tom Mallinson stayed.

Nini Baird: Impact on Campus and Beyond

In her leadership role at the CCA, Nini Baird excelled as a facilitator and ambassador for the arts; her approach was always to figure out ways and means to get things done by knowing how to find resources and whom to engage. She was viewed as a friend to artists, a person who smoothed the way and made sure their efforts were funded and well attended and reviewed. At performances she always mingled with the artists and the audiences. It was not uncommon for her to host events in her home for visiting artists, senior university members and business community executives.

Prior to arriving at SFU she had worked in the private sector as a communications professional and for six years at Berkeley with the Committee for Arts and Lectures, during which time she became aware of the International Association of College and University Concert Managers. When she arrived at SFU in June of 1966, she brought this knowledge and expertise with her. She relates that she "had to hit the ground running because there were summer productions [including John Juliani's first] to promote and present. It was not only a question of getting to know the residents, but also the university, local media and the broader Vancouver area."[4]

Nini understood the importance of developing a wide network connecting artists across the university community with supporters of the arts in business and government. She knew how to raise the profile of SFU in the vibrant world of the performing and visual arts by fostering invitations and exchanges and finding the funding to do so once university funds for the CCA became scarce, as other priorities and new departments began to emerge.

Because Nini was involved with other national organizations, SFU became the facilitator and manager of the Arts Access conference on provincial arts policy in the fall of 1973, which emerged out of the lobbying work of the Canadian Conference of the Arts, to which Nini had been appointed in 1972. On that occasion, over 1,000 people attended from across the province. The event impressed provincial politicians, and the BC Touring Council was formed, in which Nini played a leading role. Nini was also appointed to the Canada Council in 1973.

Nini Baird was exceptionally talented at following the money and embodied what it meant to be an arts entrepreneur, a new concept in the sixties and seventies, but which became part of the arts community as presenters and impresarios found their way to Vancouver. Nini and many of the artists who were part of the scene in those early years have been honoured by the arts community and have been named to the Orders of British Columbia and Canada. Nini was awarded an honorary degree from SFU in 2012.

Aside from the departure of faculty and residents from the CCA to new departments, the departure of Nini Baird in 1977 to the newly configured Emily Carr College of Art and Design (formerly the Vancouver School of Art) prompted a reorientation of the arts scene on campus.

When Nini departed, many non-credit activities were left to the departments to generate, with the support of the new Office of Continuing Studies headed by Dean Jack Blaney. From 1979 until 1985, Murray Farr served as the public program consultant for the Centre for the Arts. In *Ask Around: The Larger-Than-Life Story of Impresario Murray Farr*, published thirty years after his death, his sister Maureen Farr-Egan writes:

> He brought a unique avant-garde combination of traditional and outrageous events to the mountain campus. These included theatrical, musical, and dance performances. The dance companies included the Anna Wyman Dance Theatre, Regina Modern Dance Works, Toronto's Dancemakers, La La Human Steps from Montreal, Laura Dean from New York, and the Pacific Ballet Theatre. Musical events included the acapella vocal group Sweet Honey in the Rock, folksinger Oscar Brand, bassoonist George Zukerman, percussion ensemble Nexus, and the Bill Smith Ensemble jazz trio... Among other events were Mike Absalom, the Quebec puppet theatre Theatre Sans Fil, Spiderwoman Theater from New York and *The Last Yiddish Poet* by the Travelling Jewish Theatre. Innovative musical events included Richard Teitelbaum on the Moog synthesizer, Robert Ashley with new electronics, Inuit throat singers, and Temba Tana on African Drums.[5]

Like Nini Baird, Murray Farr created many opportunities for visiting artists and groups to engage in the community and perform in several venues. He also promoted tours, supported by the newly formed BC Touring Council and the Canada Council, throughout British Columbia.

Visiting artists, writers and lecturers from other universities were invited by various departments and coordinated through the Office of Continuing Studies, and continued to appear in the noon time slot, when classes were not scheduled, so that students and faculty could attend. Santa Aloi joined the newly forming Faculty of Dance in 1975 at the behest of Iris Garland, who was determined to expand the open invitation to dance on campus to the opportunity to take credit courses in dance that would lead to a degree, if not a professional career in dance. The commitment to community connection and exchange was strengthened by summer workshops on campus and workshops held in the community.

In a 2017 interview with Emma Metcalfe Hurst, published in *Coming Out of Chaos: A Vancouver Dance Story* on the Karen Jamieson website (www.kjdchaos.ca/barbara-clausen), Barbara Clausen describes the effect of those days at SFU as follows:

> Well, I think it's worth mentioning the effect of Simon Fraser [University] as an institution, but also the individuals: Iris Garland, who held a very important place in making a dance department. She came out of Kinesiology and she formed a dance department. She

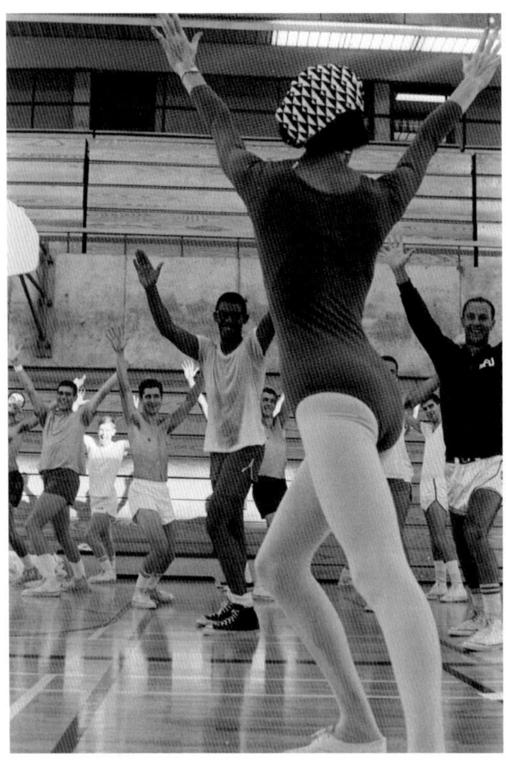

Iris Garland leads a dance workshop with the SFU basketball team. *Tony Westman, SFU Archives*

was very supportive of Karen and Savannah and those dancers. And then Grant Strate, who held a really important part in the development of dance in Vancouver. He was the first Chairman of the Board of The Dance Centre, then he was Chairman of the Department at Simon Fraser. He commissioned the [*Coming Out of Chaos*] work. He was a real player on a national and international scale, as well as locally. I think that can't be minimized. Then Murray Farr, who was presenting up at Simon Fraser. He was a colleague of Chris Wootten who started the Vancouver East Cultural Centre… Murray Farr was the presenter at Simon Fraser when all the really exciting work was being presented. He had been working in New York and had connections there. We had some special ingredients to contribute to the development of dance and in Vancouver. Murray Farr, Iris Garland, and Grant Strate were seminal in the creation of excitement.

The SFU Student Society also programmed campus activities, both during the day and in the evening, and both the pub and Images Theatre were popular venues. But the tide had turned, and the degree of spontaneity and informality that characterized the first decade was rarely achieved. I asked Donna Wong-Juliani, who was a charter student and active in the theatre, if she thought artistic engagement was part of the DNA of SFU, and she ruefully replied, "Well, maybe part of the myth of SFU."[6] Nonetheless, the openness to interdisciplinarity and new disciplines that included the arts remained an important element of the SFU culture.

An enduring legacy of the early arts at SFU is that collaborative thinking became well accepted in other academic areas. An example is offered by cultural historian Maria Tippett, who came to SFU in 1971 after travels and work in Europe from 1964 to 1966. She found that the young faculty members in the SFU history department were open to supporting her interest in the arts and politics and was encouraged by Warren Williams, Martin Kitchen and Richard Debo. She writes, "I was in my element at Simon Fraser University. Encouraged by my professors to combine my passion for the arts with my interest in history, I was making sense of the world through the things that I knew and loved best. Had I been at an older, more established, or larger university… I might never have been encouraged to pursue cultural history. Had I studied art, music, dance, and drama within their prescribed faculties, I might not have challenged the canon, but accepted it as a given. Nor would my consideration of a painting, a composition, or a play have gone very far beyond the picture frame, the music score, and the stage."[7]

Linda Johnston, a student during the 1960s, spoke of a similar openness on the part of faculty to accepting students' artwork as a fulfillment of course requirements. Professor Pat Hindley of the Department of Communication accepted Linda's work on the Bella Coola project, which resulted in the prize-winning film *Noohalk*, as part of her MA thesis.

Maintaining Space for Innovation through Transitions

If we want things to stay the same as they are, everything will have to change.[8] Tomasi di Lampedusa's often quoted words apply to times of transition and that, of course, has been the challenge at SFU: how to maintain the boldness and innovation of the early years as the university matured and grew and, as Axelrod also notes, pressure to conform was coming from government and granting agencies as well as from prospective students, parents and employers.

The continued attraction of SFU lies in the radical and innovative cornerstones (both literal and philosophical) that were established at the beginning. Over the ensuing decades both faculty and students have continued to choose SFU for that reason. At the same time, they value the rankings and research funding that come from meeting standards set by others.

In 2012, Sharon Procter interviewed French-born Philippe Pasquier—a composer, musician, performer, producer, artistic director and educator with a PhD in artificial intelligence—who had recently joined the faculty of the School of Interactive Arts and Technology at SFU Surrey. She asked him why, despite all the industry offers he had, he chose to be an SFU professor. He replied, "I love pure research that leads to new knowledge. Only universities offer that. As for SFU, it's a top-ranked university and Canada is as close to paradise as any place on Earth."[9]

The April 2012 issue of the SFU magazine *aq* also featured an article by Katherine Brodsky on young filmmaker Kelvin Redvers, who came to SFU in 2005 from Hay River in the Northwest Territories, where he had been making films with his school friends and his father since he was twelve years old. He chose SFU because he wanted to study English, anthropology and theatre, not just the technicalities of filmmaking. In the years since graduation, he has had a successful career in film and television. In 2016, he and his sister launched We Matter, a national online campaign to bring awareness to the struggles of Indigenous youth across Canada. The campaign collects videos and writings from Indigenous communities across the country while providing them with mental health resources. The emphasis on community connection continues to be a cornerstone of the SFU experience.

The Faculty of Education has maintained its commitment to a broad and experiential approach to teacher training and research and has been open to community collaboration, as has the Morris J. Wosk Centre for Dialogue. The association of dancer Judith Marcuse in various capacities over several decades is a good example. In 2000, in recognition of the impact of her work as a choreographer, producer and pioneer in the field of community-engaged art for social change (ASC), Marcuse received an honorary doctorate from the university. This led to teaching in the Semester in Dialogue program and the creation of an undergraduate course and two-year master's program in ASC.

Judith Marcuse's extensive and publicly available archive is housed at SFU.

In 2013, a national team of academic researchers and community partner organizations, hosted by SFU's International Centre of Art for Social Change, received a $2.5 million grant from the Social Sciences and Humanities Research Council of Canada (SSHRC) to run a six-year national collaborative study—the ASC Project—on the current state and future needs of ASC in Canada. The project included team members and collaborators from across Canada, employed some thirty-nine research associates and research assistants, and received more than $1 million in matching contributions. In addition to performances, exhibitions and diverse community events, outcomes from this project include numerous resources, as well as practical tools for the ASC sector, many of which are still available at icasc.ca.

The School of Communication, which also had its origins in the Faculty of Education's Centre for Communications and the Arts (CCA), has continued to embrace collaboration across the university through the development of joint majors such as communication and anthropology, communication and sociology, and communication and English, as well as a joint major with the School of Interactive Arts and Technology. Research projects and symposia are deeply rooted in community concerns. Recently a SIAT research initiative addressed the issue of "Cultural Industries in Times of Acute Crisis" in response to the disruption caused by the COVID pandemic.

These advances suggest that the value the university founders placed on experimentation and interdisciplinarity has not been lost during the years of transition from the 1970s to the twenty-first century, but that is not to say they were easy years for the arts.

Artistic Struggles in the Ensuing Decades

Colin Browne, who headed the film department in the School for the Contemporary Arts, told me in interviews in May/June 2021 that he believed that the creation of a BFA and then an MFA with diminishing resources and no new faculty had a devastating effect on the spirit of the school and inspired a siege mentality that dampened the artistic excitement of the early years.

Michael Stevenson joined SFU as president in September 2000. His first visit to the campus had been for his interview the previous year. I asked him if he was attracted to SFU because of his interest in the arts and if he was aware of the School for the Contemporary Arts. He responded that his knowledge of SFU's program was very limited.

When he arrived on campus on that occasion, he recounts, "I was swept away by the magnificence of the Erickson-Massey scheme. At the same time, I was struck by how miserable everyone was in it... It seemed to be an awful shame... I also found fascinating that it was the first university—and I've been to many—at which there was a profusion of public art."[10]

During the early days of his presidency, on visiting the SFU Gallery, Stevenson found an odd disjunction where something that seemed to be such a source of pride revealed deep wounds: "When you spoke to the people responsible, you felt they were suffering from exhaustion... that they had been stripped of resources and that their work wasn't really valued by the university... This led me to look a little bit more closely at the School for the Contemporary Arts... I did a bit of background before I ventured to approach the faculty in that unit, and of course read about the late sixties and seventies. I was amazed at what was described as a cauldron of innovation in the arts from music to dance, film and theatre, and I thought, 'This has to be one of the most lively places in the university.'"

Stevenson was further shocked by the physical state of the campus, most particularly by the crowded and rat-infested "temporary" but seemingly permanent huts that housed the School for the Contemporary Arts, and the conditions in the theatre, which by this time was used mainly as a lecture hall rather than a performance space.

Gibson Report Envisages Revitalization

In an early action to rectify the situation, Stevenson asked Edward Gibson in the geography department to write a report envisioning how the arts might be revitalized at SFU. Professor Gibson had been appointed by Vice President Jack Blaney to oversee the SFU Gallery after James Felter's departure during the budget crisis of the early eighties. "The Gibson Report" (2002) was broad-ranging and stressed the importance of a gallery/art museum that would engage every faculty in arts-based education. Bill Jeffries, having recently left Presentation House, was appointed full-time curator of the SFU Gallery with an increased budget and new priorities.

Jeffries began a vigorous program of exhibitions and events. Through his connections in the Vancouver art scene, he was able to entice people to come back up the mountain and to the Teck Gallery at the downtown campus. President Stevenson was encouraged by the success of this investment and placed improving the physical infrastructure for the gallery and the School for the Contemporary Arts as a priority in the university's capital program, although, as he observes, "I knew it probably would be nobody else's first priority in the provincial funding system." Nevertheless, "we nailed it up there."

Together with Warren Gill, also a geographer and a close friend of Edward and Marianne Gibson, who at the time served as vice president of external relations, and Milton Wong, the university's chancellor, President Stevenson began to explore sites off campus. He recalls a weekend spent with the Gibsons on their farm in the Cowichan Valley discussing their personal interest in art, including their long-time championing of Coast Salish art. While supportive of the building of a downtown site to house the School for the Contemporary Arts, Edward remained convinced that there should be a free-standing art museum on the Burnaby campus that would be a resource for every faculty and department.

Eventually the prospect of becoming part of the redevelopment of the Woodward's department store block became a possibility. Negotiating the

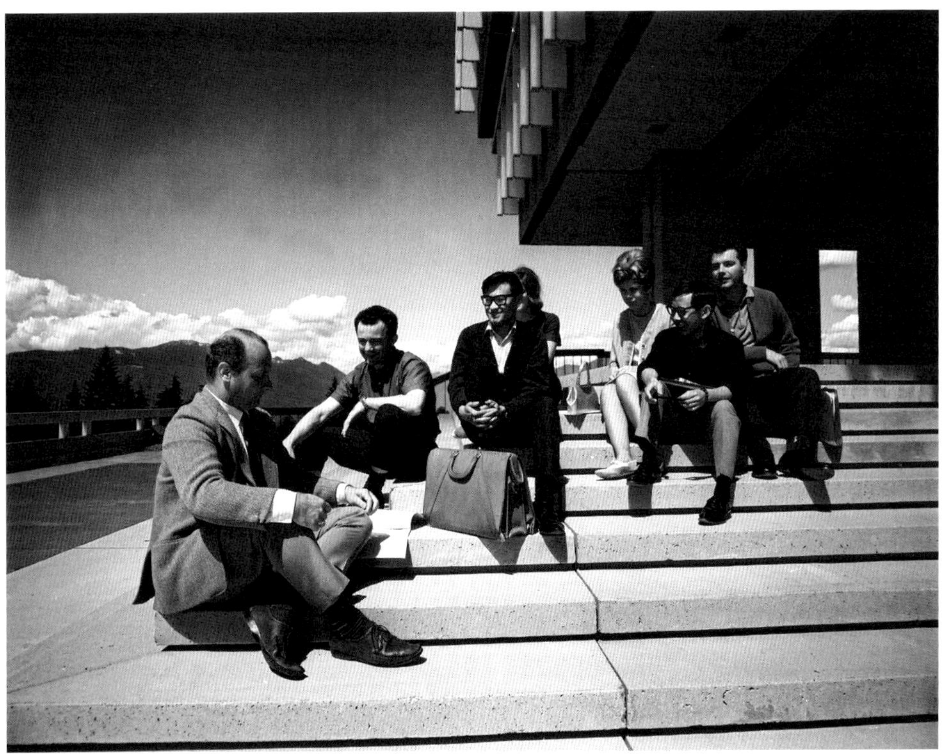

Edward Gibson and his geography students holding class in 1965 or 1966. He believed students and faculty should integrate the arts into their studies as part of university life. Throughout his career, Edward, with his wife Marianne Gibson, collected contemporary and Indigenous art. *SFU Archives*

funding for what would be a new building with social housing on the upper floors was a harrowing experience involving many meetings with the province, the community and the City of Vancouver, but met with eventual success.

Situating the SCA in a new building with teaching spaces, studios, modern theatres for public performances and a gallery open to the public was exciting. The downtown location held the promise that energy would come from the interaction of faculty and students with the broader arts community. The new building would also bring together the faculty who had been scattered across campus and in two locations downtown. It was hoped that the spirit of the early days of the CCA would be reinvigorated in these new surroundings. Consistent with the mandate of the Vancouver campus, the school would make its theatres and galleries available to the broader community for their productions.

The first event at Woodward's was part of the Winter Olympics entertainment program in 2010. In a bold move, artistic director Robert LePage was invited to bring his company Ex Machina to present the multidisciplinary, cross-cultural production *The Blue Dragon*. The production played to consistently sold-out houses in a building that was not to be open for students and faculty until the following September. On the opening evening, President Stevenson outlined the following credo:

> We are here because SFU is committed to the deepest engagement in the life of our community, and we are here because SFU embraces the arts as fundamental to our education and to our service to the community.
>
> We believe that the arts are integral to creativity, and therefore to the development of Vancouver as a truly creative city.
>
> We believe that the arts enable the imaginative capacity for empathy, for understanding those in positions quite different from our own, and therefore for overcoming the isolation of the poorest and least powerful.
>
> And we believe that the arts promote our critical capacity to imagine worlds and futures otherwise forbidden in the iron cages of the technological and political status quo, thereby empowering movements for progressive social change.[11]

That Michael Stevenson took on the challenge of building a new home for the School for the Contemporary Arts speaks to his passion for the arts and his determination that the university needed to return to the founders' vision, which saw the performing and visual arts as the heart and soul of the university. Together with his wife, literary agent Jan Whitford, he was a strong presence in the arts community during his presidency, and I believe his deep understanding and lived commitment were instrumental in beginning a renaissance of the arts at SFU.

President Andrew Petter arrived in the fall of 2010 when the School for the Contemporary Arts and its students and faculty moved into the Goldcorp Centre for the Arts, SFU's facility in the Woodward's project (SFUW). Situated between Chinatown, Gastown and the Downtown Eastside, where SFU had been working with the Carnegie Centre and other community groups for over twenty years, the new facility added studios, concert halls and theatre spaces to the downtown campus, with the promise of engaging the community deeply in campus life.

Michael Boucher, Director of SFU Woodward's Cultural Programs and Partnerships joined the SFU Woodwards Project to produce the opening shows, which began with *Blue Dragon* during the 2010 Winter Olympics. His office was responsible for fulfilling the commitment to partnership with community arts organizations that was central to the mandate SFU accepted in joining the redevelopment project, and key to securing funds from the Government of Canada to build the theatre. Since inception in 2010 SFUW commissioned, produced and presented over 200 events per year in partnership with over twenty-five professional cultural community partners, reflecting the diversity of the Lower Mainland.

Am Johal was appointed as director of the Vancity Office of Community Engagement to focus on creative engagement, knowledge democracy, and access to arts and culture through public programming, community partnerships and community-engaged research. Key programming themes include arts, culture and community, social and environmental justice, and urban issues. With the support of that office, jazz singer Vanessa Richards continued to build the community choir she created for students, staff, faculty and community members in anticipation of SFU's presence in the Downtown Eastside. The choir met in the new social housing units managed by the Portland Hotel Society on the top floors of the building. The repertoire required less training than the campus-wide group Phyllis Mailing had formed on the Burnaby campus in the first decade and maintained the spirit of welcoming anyone who wanted to sing. The community-building effect of singing together became evident, and the choir performed across the city.

When thinking of music and community, one cannot neglect to mention the pipe band, which has long been an ambassador for SFU and a presence on Burnaby Mountain. From its modest origins in 1966 in the basement of the theatre, the band expanded to its stature today as one of the foremost pipe band organizations in the world. Jack Blaney speaks of standing on the stage at Carnegie Hall in 1998 to introduce the SFU Pipe Band, the first ever to have performed there, as a high point in his presidency.

The organization attracts teachers and students from the local and international communities to participate in year-round and summer programs. It may, in fact, embody the spirit of community partnership more widely than any other arts program at SFU; and while the bagpipes and the repertoire include ancient tunes, the SFU band is remarkable and famous for its innovation both musically and as an organization. One collaboration that speaks to the wonderful variety of British Columbia is a collaboration with Uzume Taiko, Canada's first professional Taiko Ensemble. While there are no credit courses in bagpiping or drumming at SFU, there are scholarships for students who qualify to play in the band. There are highland dancing clubs on campus and performance opportunities with the Pipe Band.

The changing population at SFU over the past sixty years is reflected in the popularity of bhangra dance in many forms on all campuses, both as part of the credit curriculum and in student activities and clubs. SFU participates annually as a sponsor and on all campuses in the Indian Summer Festival, which is produced by the Indian Summer Arts Society. The mission statement, taken from the website, reads in part, "We strive to be loving and fierce, with an audacious curatorial punch that dismantles walls, plays with ideas and provokes necessary dialogue and debate. In doing this. We believe in the transformative power of the arts and their ability to offer society's renewable resource: hope."

Renaissance

Reflecting on the growth of SFU, I'm struck by the boldness with which new ideas and new disciplines have been embraced over the past sixty years. The founders had in mind a university that would address the needs of the times and celebrate creativity, developing teaching strategies that were fresh and student oriented. Student life would be enriched by exposure to the arts. Indeed, all the campuses remain remarkable for the public art that one encounters indoors and out, a collection that began in 1965 with the two monumental Gordon Smith mosaics that frame the entrance to the mall from the quadrangle. There are now more than 1,000 works of art on public display across the campuses. But does every student find an opportunity to participate in artmaking? Is there a vibrant cultural scene enjoyed by students and faculty together on every campus?

By all accounts, the movement of the visual arts program—first downtown to Jeff Wall's studio in the eighties, and then to 611 Alexander Street, and finally the whole school's move to Woodward's in 2010—removed encounters with artmaking and experimentation from the Burnaby campus. The first-year art project, in which students created site-specific projects around the campus, and the graduate shows no longer were part of the SFU Burnaby experience. And the SFU Gallery had not been part of the school since James Felter stepped down in the 1980s.

There are encouraging signs, however, of a new energy and a recommitment to cross-departmental cooperation. Professor Sabine Bitter, previously the coordinator of the Audain Visual Artist in Residence Program and curator of the Audain Gallery at Woodward's, recently collaborated with Kimberly Phillips, the director of SFU Galleries, to reinstate campus projects on all campuses. The experiment to bring congruence between study and experience and the inclusion of seminars and social media to amplify the project were very successful. Other faculty have begun to approach SFU Galleries to participate in projects related to chemistry and biology.

The Library has joined the Gallery in its mission to engage students, staff, and faculty in art making whether related to research, coursework or personal projects. The SFU Library Media and Maker Commons is a collaborative, hands-on learning space located in the W.A.C. Bennett Library in Burnaby which provides space, services, tools, and training to make, create, and play.

For the past fifteen years, in her roles as gallery director, curator and teacher at SFU and elsewhere, Kimberly Phillips has worked to amplify the voices of under-acknowledged artists and practitioners, and to create meaningful and unexpected ways for contemporary artists and their publics to find one another.

And Phillips will soon have another dedicated space in which to do that work. Nearing the end of his life, Edward Gibson, who had for decades been involved in reinvigorating the arts at SFU, told Michael Stevenson that he and his wife would leave a bequest to establish a new gallery on the Burnaby campus at SFU. The Marianne and Edward Gibson Art Museum is now (at time of writing in 2024) in the process of construction.

The 12,000-square-foot purpose-built space across from the First People's Gathering House, close to the anticipated gondola station, is planned to create dynamic possibilities for artist-led interdisciplinary research and exploration through a broad suite of all-ages public programming. The new art museum will unite the SFU founders' original intentions with Michael Stevenson and Edward Gibson's vision for a renewal of artistic energy on the mountain.

The Marianne and Edward Gibson Art Museum will also play an important role in achieving SFU president Joy Johnson's What's Next Strategy, which offers a framework of four pillars for action: "Uphold Truth and Reconciliation, Engage in Global Challenges, Make a Difference for BC, and Transform the SFU Experience." The new endowed curatorship of Indigenous Projects will deepen the gallery's ability to work together with researchers and faculty from Indigenous Studies, the Bill Reid Centre and the Bill Reid Gallery in Vancouver.

Artmaking is one way of sharing cultural experience and creating the dialogue that allows us to engage in global challenges. Art that looks outward has been part of SFU's practice since the early days of Murray Schafer and the soundscape projects, guerrilla theatre and social commentary through film. Art for social change creates understanding across cultures and can make a difference for BC as the province addresses increasingly complex challenges in the twenty-first century.

What remains from Johnson's list is to transform the SFU experience. If recent issues of *The Peak* and *The Tartan* are any evidence, SFU students still have a lively voice. They are experiencing many of the problems the charter students faced: busy lives, often the first of their family to attend university, carrying the weight of expectation on their shoulders, the need to work part-time to support their studies and housing challenges, not to mention an

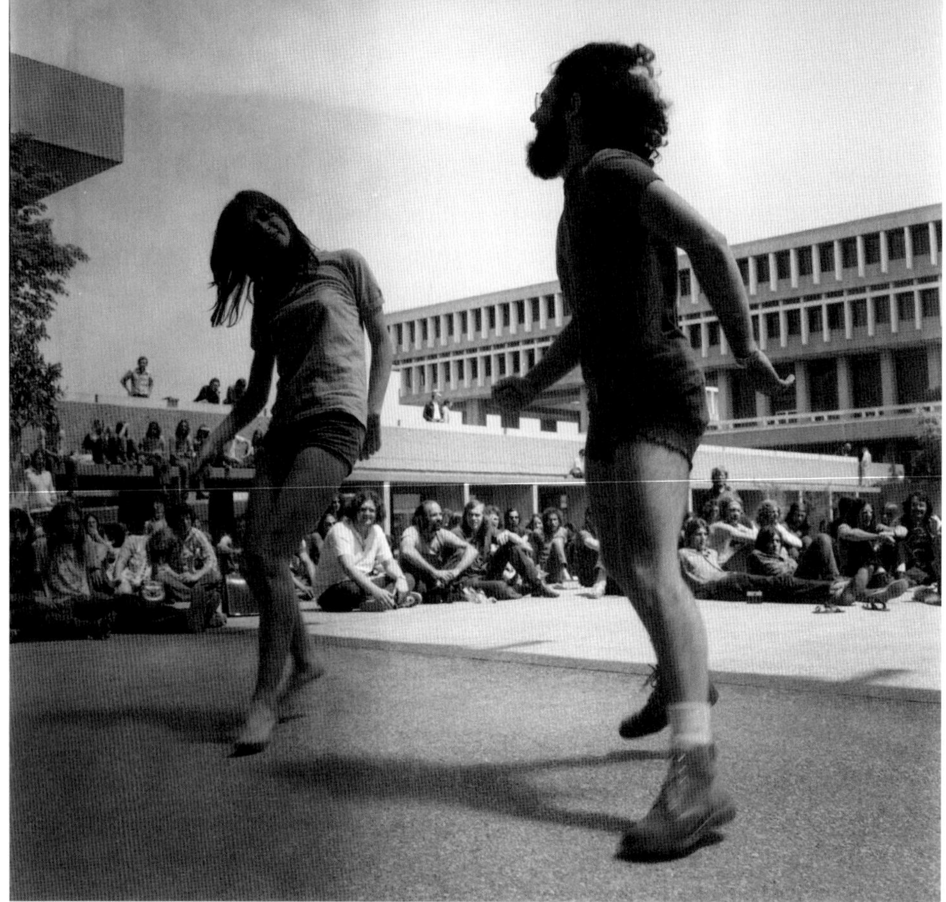

Students enjoying a noon show between classes. *SFU Archives*

increasingly complex world. And they want to make SFU better. Students recently stepped up to support the charge to get approval and funding for a gondola from the SkyTrain to the top of the hill. When completed, the gondola will take them right to steps of the Gibson Art Museum, where they will find a warm hearth and places to be quiet with their thoughts and be stimulated by their surroundings. As did the charter students in the theatre foyer in 1965, today's students will gather to build a better world and challenge the status quo.

At the groundbreaking ceremony on August 1, 2023, Kimberly Phillips expressed the hope that "the Gibson Art Museum will be a new hub for SFU Galleries, a new heart for this campus, from which extends a vast circulatory system of artistic initiatives."

She went on to say:

> But I feel a tremendous sense of humility and responsibility too. For taking on a project like this today, we must really reconsider who we are building these spaces for. Who feels welcome? Who feels they can contribute? How can we encourage learners of all ages and abilities to find one another through art, and catalyze ideas and forms across disciplines? How do we support artists to stretch and reach in their

research, to connect with new audience communities? How can the work of an art museum unsettle the conditions of colonialism, and how can our work in this new space properly honour the rightful stewards of the territories on which we operate? How can a space not just house a university art collection, but activate it so that it fosters new inquiries about the cultural life of this region, surfaces underacknowledged histories, and helps us imagine new worlds together?

I feel so fortunate to ask these questions with an incredible group of people here at SFU. And SFU, with its deep commitment to inclusivity, with its insistence on an irreverent and brave interdisciplinarity, its history of creative connectivity, feels like the exact right place to ask such questions.

What makes this project particularly special is that these questions are also fundamentally the same ones that Edward Gibson asked too, years ago. He understood the fact that art is deeply lodged in the fibre of this university and, as a geographer, how it can transform how we understand our environment and one another.

Flashback to 1965, the year SFU opened: What a time to be alive! Simon Fraser University benefited from a fertile period of post-war economic expansion, national confidence and overall optimism. But here we are, well into the twenty-first century, and it's one that many did not imagine—and one that needs a new vision.

There is perhaps a path we can follow to get back to the place we started. Despite current tensions and anxieties, we do speak a common language: the language of the arts, which arises from our experiences of nature, family, community—the ties that bind generations, and span cultures. I want to believe, as the founders of SFU believed, that sharing experience and creating new experiences through the arts will, as my mother would have said, "Carry us through."

Notes

Preface

1 Thomas J. Mallinson, "Brave New University." Simon Fraser University Archives. F-70 – Allan B. Cunningham fonds. F-70-2-0-0-8.
2 George Manuel, "A New Era," *The Peak*, April 5, 1967, p. 9.
3 "Dan George Speaks on Indian Injustice," *The Peak*, September 13, 1967, p. 3.

Introduction

1 Michael Bawtree, *The Best Fooling: Adventures in Canadian Theatre* (Cirencester, UK: Mereo Books, 2017), p. 102.
2 Bawtree, *The Best Fooling*, p. 103.

Chapter 1

1 Alexandra Griffith Winton, "The Bauhaus 1919–1933," The Metropolitan Museum of Art, October 2016, https://www.metmuseum.org/toah/hd/bauh/hd_bauh.htm.
2 Christine Hearn, conversation with Francis Mansbridge, June 2023.
3 David Stouck, *Arthur Erickson: An Architect's Life* (Madeira Park, BC: Douglas and McIntyre, 2013), pp. 198–99.
4 Linda Johnston, interview with Ann Cowan and Christine Hearn, 2021.
5 Tom Mallinson, "Brave New University," SFU Archives F-70-2-0-0-8.
6 Michael Bawtree, *The Best Fooling: Adventures in Canadian Theatre* (Cirencester, UK: Mereo Books, 2017), p. 95.
7 Nini Baird, interview 1 with Christine Hearn, Francis Mansbridge, Marcia Toms, Walter Piovesan, November 28, 2022.
8 Michael Bawtree, interview with Francis Mansbridge, Christine Hearn, and Walter Piovesan at Simon Fraser's Vancouver Campus at Harbour Centre, February 23, 2022.
9 Schafer, R, Murray. "The Future of Music in Canada," in *Proceedings and Transactions of the Royal Society of Canada*, vol. 5, 1967, pp. 37–43. Ottawa, ON: The Royal Society of Canada, 1968.
10 Nini Baird, interview 1, 2022.
11 Nini Baird, "Centre for Communications and the Arts," *Communications* 70 (Japan), April 1970.
12 Iris Garland, "Memorandum to Nini Baird," November 5, 1967.
13 Tessa Perkins Deneault, "The Only Escape: The Early Years of the SFU Theatre," *The Tartan*, September 7, 2015.

14 Tom Mallinson, "Brave New University," SFU Archives F-70-2-0-0-8.
15 Peter Hay, *Horse Sheet* no. 3 (June 1969), SFU Archives F-109-13-4-0-2.
16 *The Peak*, July 2, 1969, https://newspapers.lib.sfu.ca/peak-collection/peak.
17 Nini Baird, interview 1, 2022.
18 Christine Hearn, conversation with Francis Mansbridge, June 2023.
19 Bawtree, *The Best Fooling*, p. 193.
20 Perry Long, "Theatre For Whom By Whom," in *Jade* (Burnaby, BC: Peak Publications, 1969), pp. 6–7.
21 *The Peak*, March 8, 1972, https://newspapers.lib.sfu.ca/peak-collection/peak.
22 Bawtree, interview, 2022.
23 Donna Wong-Juliani, interview with Ann Cowan, Christine Hearn, Francis Mansbridge and Carole Gerson, May 17, 2023.
24 Bawtree, interview, 2022.

Chapter 2

1 *The Peak*, April 5, 1967, https://newspapers.lib.sfu.ca/peak-collection/peak.
2 Nini Baird, memo to staff, November 1972.
3 *The Peak*, October 25, 1967, https://newspapers.lib.sfu.ca/peak-collection/peak.
4 Douglas Patterson, email submitted to the project, March 25, 2022.
5 Heidi Greco, interview with Francis Mansbridge and Christine Hearn, White Rock, BC, July 11, 2022.
6 *The Peak*, October 27, 1965, https://newspapers.lib.sfu.ca/peak-collection/peak.
7 *The Peak*, June 26, 1968, https://newspapers.lib.sfu.ca/peak-collection/peak.
8 *The Peak*, June 1969, https://newspapers.lib.sfu.ca/peak-collection/peak.
9 *The Peak*, September 17, 1969, https://newspapers.lib.sfu.ca/peak-collection/peak.
10 Nini Baird, "CCA: SFU's Alternative Environment for the Arts" in *Remembering SFU*, by the SFU Retirees Association, p. 164.
11 Nini Baird, CCA News Release, May 30, 1969.
12 *The Peak*, October 27, 1971, https://newspapers.lib.sfu.ca/peak-collection/peak.
13 *The Peak*, February 15, 1967, https://newspapers.lib.sfu.ca/peak-collection/peak.
14 *The Peak*, November 23, 1966, https://newspapers.lib.sfu.ca/peak-collection/peak.
15 *The Peak*, March 4, 1970, https://newspapers.lib.sfu.ca/peak-collection/peak.
16 *The Peak*, March 4, 1970, https://newspapers.lib.sfu.ca/peak-collection/peak.
17 *The Peak*, October 30, 1968, https://newspapers.lib.sfu.ca/peak-collection/peak.
18 *The Peak*, February 12, 1969, https://newspapers.lib.sfu.ca/peak-collection/peak.
19 *The Peak*, February 12, 1969, https://newspapers.lib.sfu.ca/peak-collection/peak.
20 Gord Lansdell, ed., "Dr. Bundolo's Pandemonium Medicine Show," https://vancouverbroadcasters.com/drbundolo.html.
21 *The Peak*, December 1, 1965, https://newspapers.lib.sfu.ca/peak-collection/peak.
22 Nini Baird, "Centre for Communications and the Arts," *Communications* 70 (Japan), April 1970.
23 *The Peak*, July 12, 1967, https://newspapers.lib.sfu.ca/peak-collection/peak.
24 *The Peak*, October 4, 1967, https://newspapers.lib.sfu.ca/peak-collection/peak.
25 *The Peak*, October 18, 1967, https://newspapers.lib.sfu.ca/peak-collection/peak.
26 *The Peak*, September 25, 1968, https://newspapers.lib.sfu.ca/peak-collection/peak.
27 *The Peak*, January 24, 1968, https://newspapers.lib.sfu.ca/peak-collection/peak.
28 *The Peak*, April 5, 1967, https://newspapers.lib.sfu.ca/peak-collection/peak.

29 *The Peak*, February 1, 1967, https://newspapers.lib.sfu.ca/peak-collection/peak.
30 *Simon Fraser University Yearbook*, 1965–1966.
31 *The Peak*, November 15, 1967, https://newspapers.lib.sfu.ca/peak-collection/peak.
32 Smith, William Jay, transl., in *Dogalypse: Selected San Francisco Poetry Reading* by Andrei Voznesensky (San Francisco: City Lights, 1972).
33 *The Peak*, March 21, 1973, https://newspapers.lib.sfu.ca/peak-collection/peak.
34 *The Peak*, October 13, 1965, https://newspapers.lib.sfu.ca/peak-collection/peak.
35 *The Peak*, October 27, 1965, https://newspapers.lib.sfu.ca/peak-collection/peak.
36 *The Peak*, December 1, 1965, https://newspapers.lib.sfu.ca/peak-collection/peak.
37 *The Peak*, December 8, 1965, https://newspapers.lib.sfu.ca/peak-collection/peak.
38 *The Peak*, April 6, 1966, https://newspapers.lib.sfu.ca/peak-collection/peak.
39 *The Peak*, April 6, 1966, https://newspapers.lib.sfu.ca/peak-collection/peak.
40 *The Peak*, May 11, 1966, https://newspapers.lib.sfu.ca/peak-collection/peak.

Chapter 3

1 Michael Bawtree, interview with Francis Mansbridge, Christine Hearn, and Walter Piovesan at Simon Fraser's Vancouver Campus at Harbour Centre, February 23, 2022.
2 Michael Bawtree, *The Best Fooling: Adventures in Canadian Theatre* (Cirencester, UK: Mereo Books, 2017), p. 105.
3 Tessa Perkins Deneault, "The Only Escape: The Early Years of the SFU Theatre," *The Tartan*, Sept. 7, 2015.
4 Bawtree, interview, 2022.
5 Clifford Leech, in Michael Bawtree's *The Last of the Tsars* (Toronto: Clarke, Irwin, 1973).
6 Bawtree, *The Best Fooling*, p. 156.
7 Bawtree, *The Best Fooling*, p. 157
8 Bawtree, *The Best Fooling*, pp. 157–58.
9 Bawtree, *The Best Fooling*, pp. 159–60.
10 Overheard by Christine Hearn, n.d.
11 Bawtree, *The Best Fooling*, p. 132.
12 Ann Gerson, email to Carole Gerson, October 12, 2023.
13 Bawtree, *The Best Fooling*, p. 145.
14 Bawtree, *The Best Fooling*, p. 146
15 Michael Bawtree, in association with the Centralia Theatre Workshop, *Centralia* (New York: William Morris Agency, 1968), n.p.
16 Michael Bawtree, *Centralia*, 1968.
17 Jerry Zaslove, review of *Centralia*, *The Peak*, March 8, 1967, p. 7.
18 Malcolm Page, "Theatre at SFU: The First Ten Years," unpublished essay sent to Carole Gerson, September 2020, p. 3.
19 Bawtree, The Best Fooling, p. 193.
20 Bawtree, *The Best Fooling*, pp. 155–56.
21 Bawtree, interview, February 23, 2022.
22 Bawtree, The Best Fooling, pp. 132–33.
23 Page, "Theatre at SFU," p. 3.
24 Donna Wong-Juliani, interview with Ann Cowan, Christine Hearn, Francis Mansbridge and Carole Gerson, May 17, 2023
25 K.K. Ruthven, "The Savage God: Conrad and Lawrence," *Critical Quarterly* vol. 10, 1968, p. 39.

26 Interview with John Juliani, "Savage God and PEAK," *York Theatre Journal* no. 9, February 1975, pp. 16–17.

27 Renate Usmiani, *Second Stage: The Alternative Theatre Movement in Canada* (Vancouver: UBC Press, 1983), p. 80.

28 *The Peak*, October 2, 1968, https://newspapers.lib.sfu.ca/peak-collection.

29 Malcolm Page, "Savage God in Vancouver, 1966–72: A Documentary Account," *Theatre History in Canada*, Fall 1988, pp. 229–50. https://journals.lib.unb.ca/index.php/tric/article/view/7343/8402.

30 *The Peak*, October 2, 1968, https://newspapers.lib.sfu.ca/peak-collection.

31 Christopher Dafoe, "Juliani: Prophet of Unusual Theatre," *Vancouver Sun Magazine*, September 12, 1969, p. 6A.

32 *The Peak*, June 8, 1966, https://newspapers.lib.sfu.ca/peak-collection.

33 Jack Richards, title unknown, *Vancouver Sun*, n.d.

34 James Barber, "Music, Drama, Callboard," *The Province*, July 21, 1967, p. 15.

35 *The Peak*, August 2, 1967, https://newspapers.lib.sfu.ca/peak-collection.

36 Wendy Newman, Penticton interviews, October 16, 2021.

37 *The Peak*, January 31, 1968, https://newspapers.lib.sfu.ca/peak-collection.

38 Mark Leiren-Young, title unknown, *Vancouver Sun*, n.d.

39 John Juliani, "Savage Space," *Canadian Theatre Review* 6 (Spring 1975), p. 52.

40 Juliani, "Savage Space," p. 52.

41 Juliani, "Savage Space," p. 52.

42 Juliani, "Savage Space," p. 52.

43 Savannah Walling, email to Carole Gerson, June 17, 2021.

44 Shelora Fitzgerald, "John Juliani: Turbulent Times at SFU," *Conversation SnapShots*, https://www.youtube.com/watch?v=22uzJn7fOyM.

45 Juliani, "Savage Space," p. 52.

46 Fitzgerald, *Conversation SnapShots*.

47 Tessa Perkins Deneault, "The Only Escape: The Early Years of the SFU Theatre," *The Tartan*, September 7, 2015.

48 Wilfrid Mennell, interview, October 21, 2021.

49 James Barber, quoted in Nini Baird, "Cascando and Phases," *Jade*, p. 19.

50 Mennell, interview, 2021.

51 Mennell, interview, 2021.

52 Mennell, interview, 2021.

53 *The Peak*, November 9, 1966, https://newspapers.lib.sfu.ca/peak-collection.

54 *The Peak*, November 16, 1966, https://newspapers.lib.sfu.ca/peak-collection.

55 *The Peak*, October 24, 1973, https://newspapers.lib.sfu.ca/peak-collection.

56 *The Peak*, September 27, 1967, https://newspapers.lib.sfu.ca/peak-collection.

57 *The Peak*, September 25, 1968, https://newspapers.lib.sfu.ca/peak-collection.

58 Terry Hunter and Savannah Walling, Zoom interview by Carole Gerson and Tessa Perkins Deneault, Vancouver, January 26, 2022.

59 SFU Archives University Communications fonds F-61-4-3-0-3.

60 SFU Archives University Communications fonds F-61-4-3-0-3.

61 "Mime Troupe Invited to Ottawa," *The Peak*, January 20, 1971, p. 3.

62 "Mime Troupe Invited to Ottawa," p. 3.

63 Wendy Gorling, email to Carole Gerson, March 18, 2021.

64 Page, "Theatre at SFU," p. 3.

65 Page, "Theatre at SFU," p. 3.

66 *The Peak*, March 24, 1972, https://newspapers.lib.sfu.ca/peak-collection.
67 *The Peak*, July 8, 1972, https://newspapers.lib.sfu.ca/peak-collection.
68 *The Peak*, February 27, 1974, https://newspapers.lib.sfu.ca/peak-collection.
69 Perry Long, "A Backward Glance at Theatre," *Jade*, Peak Publications, April 6, 1969, p. 9.
70 *The Peak*, March 8, 1972, https://newspapers.lib.sfu.ca/peak-collection.
71 *The Peak*, March 8, 1972, https://newspapers.lib.sfu.ca/peak-collection.
72 Susan Baxter, "Snippets from the Underground," unpublished manuscript sent to Ann Cowan, August 18, 2023.

Chapter 4

1 Simon Fraser University Archives. Iris Garland fonds, F-197-4-0-0-3. "Developing Creative Dancemakers" by Raewyn White, *VanDance*, 1988.
2 Alana Gerecke, "Dance as 'Lead Card' in the Development of Simon Fraser University's Fine and Performing Arts," in *Renegade Bodies: Canadian Dance in the 1970s*, eds. Allana C. Lindgren and Kaija Pepper (Toronto: Dance Collection Danse, 2012), p. 142.
3 Marilyn Cairns, "A Strong Sense of Duty," SFU Archives 231-1-1-0-0-7.
4 Simon Fraser University Archives, Iris Garland fonds, F-197-4-0-0-3. "Seven Girls With Synthesizer" by Max Wyman, *The Vancouver Sun*, March 15, 1969.
5 Karen Jamieson, telephone interview by Tessa Perkins Deneault and Ann Cowan, January 2023.
6 Karen Jamieson Dance, *Mediums*, https://www.kjdance.ca/works/mediums-1969.
7 Simon Fraser University Archives, Iris Garland fonds, F-197-3-0-0-1. "SFU Medium Mixture Scores" by Max Wyman, *Vancouver Sun*, May 31, 1969.
8 Max Wyman, quoted in *Coming Out of Chaos: A Vancouver Dance Story*, an archival research and oral history project produced by Karen Jamieson Dance, https://www.kjdchaos.ca/chapters/1.
9 Simon Fraser University Archives, Iris Garland fonds, F-197-4-0-0-3. "Mediums Steal the Show at Workshop" by James Barber, *Province*, July 25, 1969.
10 Jamieson, interview, 2022.
11 Simon Fraser University Archives, Iris Garland fonds, F-197-3-0-0-2. "Hello No-Name Dancers" by Max Wyman, *Vancouver Sun*, October 29, 1969.
12 Simon Fraser University Archives, Iris Garland fonds, F-197-3-0-0-1. "Some Thoughts on the Arts Blossoming at SFU" by Max Wyman, *Vancouver Sun*, September 5, 1969.
13 Jamieson, Hunter and Walling resigned from Terminal City Dance Research in 1983; in 1986, Terminal City Dance Society officially changed its name to VDC Dance Centre Society, when the dance centre was founded as a resource centre for dance professionals and the public in Vancouver.
14 Savannah Walling, quoted in *Coming Out of Chaos*, https://www.kjdchaos.ca/chapters/1.
15 Savannah Walling and Terry Hunter, Zoom interview by Tessa Perkins Deneault and Carole Gerson, January 26, 2022.
16 Walling, quoted in *Coming Out of Chaos*, https://www.kjdchaos.ca/chapters/1.
17 Walling and Hunter, interview, 2022.
18 Terry Hunter, quoted in *Coming Out of Chaos*, https://www.kjdchaos.ca/chapters/1.
19 Walling and Hunter, interview, 2022.
20 Karen Jamieson, interview, 2022.

21 Alana Gerecke, "Dance as 'Lead Card' in the Development of Simon Fraser University's Fine and Performing Arts," in *Renegade Bodies*, eds. Allana C. Lindgren and Kaija Pepper (Toronto: Dance Collection Danse, 2012).
22 Karen Jamieson, interview, 2022.
23 Simon Fraser University Archives, F-109-7-3-0-10-5, news release, March 6, 1975.
24 Walling and Hunter, interview, 2022.
25 Simon Fraser University Archives, F-197-4-0-0-3. James Barber, "A 'Windmill' That Can't Be Ignored," *Province*, November 1967.
26 Simon Fraser University Archives, F-109-7-3-0-7-2, news release, May 19, 1972.
27 Simon Fraser University Archives, F-197-4-0-0-3. "Concert Mixture Served at SFU" by Max Wyman, n.d.
28 Max Wyman, quoted in *Coming Out of Chaos*, https://www.kjdchaos.ca/chapters/1.
29 Terry Hunter, quoted in *Coming Out of Chaos*, https://www.kjdchaos.ca/chapters/1.
30 Phyllis Lamhut, interview by Tessa Perkins Deneault, March 27, 2023.
31 Simon Fraser University Archives, F-109-7-3-0-8, news release, June 20, 1973.
32 Judith Newbergher-Renaud, *Art as Catalyst*, unpublished memoir, 2023.
33 Simon Fraser University Archives, Iris Garland fonds, F-197-3-0-0-1. "Save This Dance For Yourself—But Hurry," Max Wyman, *Vancouver Sun*, March 28, 1969.
34 Simon Fraser University Archives, *Public Programs*, F-109-7-1-0-9.
35 Simon Fraser University Archives, Iris Garland fonds, F-197-4-0-0-3. "Revolution Sweeps Through Dance," Max Wyman, *Vancouver Sun*, January 29, 1970.
36 Gerecke, "Dance as 'Lead Card.'".
37 Gerecke, "Dance as 'Lead Card.'"
38 Hugh Johnston, *Radical Campus* (Vancouver: Douglas & McIntyre, 2005), p. 247.
39 Simon Fraser University Archives, Iris Garland fonds, F-197-1-1-0-3. "Dance in the University... No Longer a Frill!" Iris Garland, *VanDance*, December 1979.
40 Gerecke, "Dance as 'Lead Card.'"
41 Gerecke, "Dance as 'Lead Card.'"
42 Santa Aloi, interview by Ann Cowan, Carole Gerson and Christine Hearn, Sylvia Hotel, Vancouver, February 19, 2024.

Chapter 5

1 Soundohm website product listing, https://www.soundohm.com/product/phases-and-other-pieces-e.
2 "SFU Composer Wins Award," *The Peak*, January 16, 1974, p. 10, https://newspapers.lib.sfu.ca/peak-collection/peak.
3 Mary Trainer, "Quartet in High Demand," *Comment*, March 1974, pp. 12–13.
4 David Skulski, emails to Carole Gerson, February 16, February 17, August 3, 2023.
5 Mary Trainer, "Phyllis Mailing: SFU Singer Who Reached the Top," *Comment*, October/November 1972, pp. 12–13.
6 Excerpted and edited from the report on *Dido and Aeneas* in the SFU archives, F-108-7-6-0-4.
7 Based on an interview by Susan Baxter with Ann Cowan and sent to her by Susan Baxter in August 2023 as "Snippets from the Underground."
8 Murray Schafer, *The New Soundscape* (Don Mills, ON: BMI Canada Ltd., 1969), p. 62.

9 Reprinted from Hildegard Westerkamp, "The Disruptive Nature of Listening: Today Yesterday Tomorrow," in *Sound, Media, Ecology*, eds. Milena Droumeva and Randolph Jordan (Cham, Switzerland: Palgrave MacMillan, 2019), pp. 45–63.
10 Westerkamp, "The Disruptive Nature of Listening," p. 49.
11 Westerkamp, "The Disruptive Nature of Listening," pp. 49–50.
12 "Ecology of Sound: Hildegard Westerkamp," CBC *Ideas*, February 2, 2017, https://www.cbc.ca/radio/ideas/how-opening-our-ears-can-open-our-minds-hildegard-westerkamp-1.3962163.

Chapter 6

1 Peter Bryant, "SFU Film Workshop: A Critical Look," *Cinema Canada* no. 20 (July/August 1975). pp. 42–43.
2 Zoë Druick, "Vancouver Cinema in the Sixties," in the online archive project *Ruins in Process: Vancouver Art in the Sixties*, www.vancouverartinthesixties.com/essays/vancouver-cinema-in-the-sixties.
3 Tony Westman, conversation and emails with Francis Mansbridge, September 2023.
4 Danny Singer, telephone interview with Francis Mansbridge, April 2023.
5 *The Peak*, February 9, 1966, p. 3, https://newspapers.lib.sfu.ca/peak-collection/peak.
6 Danny Singer, telephone interview with Francis Mansbridge, 2023.
7 Danny Singer, telephone interview, 2023.
8 George Csaba Koller, "Vancouver Independent Film-Making: Peter Bryant," *Cinema Canada*, April/May 1973, no. 7, p. 34.
9 David Rousseau, "Memories of SFU Centre for Communication [*sic*] and the Arts."
10 *The Peak*, September 21, 1966, https://newspapers.lib.sfu.ca/peak-collection/peak.
11 Zale Dalen, "Simon Fraser University, the Early Years," *Zale Dalen* (blog), April 4, 2023, http://www.zaledalen.com/zaledalen.
12 Dalen, "SFU, the Early Years," April 4, 2023, http://www.zaledalen.com/zaledalen.
13 Linda Johnston, interview with Ann Cowan and Christine Hearn, 2021.
14 Mary Trainer, "Vincent Vaitiekunas: The Film Man," *Comment*, December 1972, pp. 10–11.
15 Jaan Pill, "Simon Fraser Film Workshop," *Cinema Canada*, July/August 1975, no. 20, pp. 34–39.
16 Pill, "Simon Fraser Film Workshop," pp. 34–39.
17 Mary Trainer, "Guy Bergeron—a dedicated professional who puts the emphasis on ethics in the art of film-making," *Comment*, August 1975, pp.12–13.
18 Tony Westman, conversation and emails with Francis Mansbridge, September 2023.
19 Westman, email, September 2023.
20 Johnston, interview, 2021.
21 Johnston, interview, 2021.
22 Westman, conversation and emails, 2023.
23 Johnston, interview, 2021.
24 Due to space limitations, Tony Westman's full Bella Coola photo collection has not been included here. It can be found on the companion website www.sfu.ca/earlyarts.
25 Sandy Wilson, conversation and emails with Francis Mansbridge, September 2023.

Chapter 7

1 Susan McCaslin, "Trailblazing with Blaser," Cascadia Poetry Festival website and blog, July 28, 2015; https://web.archive.org/web/20160324151339/http://cascadiapoetryfestival.org/trailblazing-with-blaser.
2 Brian Fawcett, *Local Matters* (Vancouver: New Star Books, 2003), p. 139.
3 Stan Persky and Brian Fawcett. *Robin Blaser* (Vancouver: New Star Books, 2005), p. 100.
4 Persky and Fawcett, *Robin Blaser*, p. 84.
5 Persky and Fawcett, *Robin Blaser*, p. 88.
6 Stan Persky, "Introduction," in Fawcett, *Local Matters*, p. xii.
7 Persky and Fawcett, *Robin Blaser*, p. 70.
8 Sharon Thesen on Robin Blaser, *Capilano Review*, Spring 2008, p. 18.
9 Stephen Collis, ed., *companions & horizons: An Anthology of Simon Fraser University Poetry* (Vancouver: West Coast Line, 2005), p. 11.
10 Collis, *Companions & Horizons*, p. 16.
11 *The Peak*, March 5, 1969, p. 8.
12 Alban Goulden, interview with Francis Mansbridge, Vancouver, April 7, 2022.
13 Barry McKinnon, "Fawcett, Blaser & Simon Fraser," in "Chairs in the Time Machine," unpublished memoir, p. 32.
14 Fawcett, *Local Matters*, p. 138.
15 Goulden, interview, 2022.
16 Fawcett, *Local Matters*, p. 138.
17 Fawcett, *Local Matters*, p. 4.
18 Persky and Fawcett, *Robin Blaser*, p. 146.
19 Persky and Fawcett, *Robin Blaser*, p. 34.
20 Fawcett, *Local Matters*, p. 9.
21 Murray Schafer, quoted in *Local Matters* by Brian Fawcett, p. 137.
22 Fawcett, *Local Matters* p. 138.
23 Alban Goulden, email to Francis Mansbridge, April 25, 2022.
24 Susan McCaslin, "Trailblazing with Blaser."
25 Goulden, interview, 2022.
26 McKinnon, "Fawcett, Blaser & Simon Fraser," unpublished memoir.
27 McKinnon, "Fawcett, Blaser & Simon Fraser," p. 30.
28 McKinnon, "Fawcett, Blaser & Simon Fraser," p. 31.
29 Allan Safarik, interview with Francis Mansbridge, July 2023.
30 *The Peak*, June 9, 1971.
31 Brian Brett, *The Peak*, March 7, 1973.
32 Goulden, interview, 2022.
33 Susan McCaslin, interview with Francis Mansbridge and Christine Hearn, Fort Langley, BC, June 9, 2022.
34 Susan McCaslin, interview with Francis Mansbridge and Christine Hearn, Fort Langley, BC, June 9, 2022.
35 Fawcett, *Local Matters*, p. 25.
36 Heidi Greco, interview with Francis Mansbridge and Christine Hearn, White Rock, BC, July 11, 2022.

Chapter 8

1 Ronald Beiner, *Political Philosophy: What It Is and Why It Matters* (Cambridge University Press, 2014), p. 10.

2 At the time of the Baxters' appointments to their SFU positions in 1966, Ingrid Baxter was Elaine Baxter (she later changed her name). I refer to her as Ingrid throughout. She was fully half of the N.E. Thing Co., and any reference to or mention of their artmaking as Baxter or Baxters refers to them both.

3 Paul Axelrod, "The Other 60s: Academic Administrators as Agents of Change in Canadian Higher Education," in *Utopian Universities: A Global History of the New Campuses of the 1960s*, eds. Miles Taylor and Jill Pellew (London: Bloomsbury, 2020).

4 Iain Baxter, Zoom interview with Bill Jeffries, July 2022.

5 Media release for *Live in Your Head: When Attitudes Become Form*, a 1969 exhibition at the Kunsthalle Bern curated by the Swiss curator Harald Szeemann.

6 Baxter, interview, 2022.

7 *Catalogue for the Exhibition, May 19–June 19, 1969*, p. 10.

8 David Bellman, "Frameworks for an Intervention."

9 James W. Felter, interview with Bill Jeffries, May 2022.

10 *The Tartan*, Peak Publications, 2015.

11 Baxter, interview, 2022. (Additional comments from Baxter that follow are from this interview.)

12 Baxter, interview, 2022. (Additional comments from Baxter that follow are from this interview.)

13 Felter, interview, 2022. (Additional comments from Felter that follow are from this interview.)

14 Felter, interview, 2022. (Additional comments from Felter that follow are from this interview.)

15 Simon Fraser University Archives. University Communications fonds, F-61-4-3-0-3. *Comment* magazine article, 1972.

16 Felter, media release, May 23, 1969.

17 Felter, interview, 2022. (Additional comments from Felter that follow are from this interview.)

18 Felter, interview, 2022. (Additional comments from Felter that follow are from this interview.)

19 Felter, interview, 2022. (Additional comments from Felter that follow are from this interview.)

Chapter 9

1 Paul Axelrod, "The Other 1960s: Academic Leaders as Agents of Change in Canadian Higher Education," in *Utopian Universities: A Global History of the New Campuses of the 1960s*, ed. Miles Taylor and Jill Pellew (London: Bloomsbury, 2020), p. 291.

2 Axelrod, p. 291.

3 Hugh Johnson, *Radical Campus*, pp. 240–48.

4 Baird, interview 1, 2022.

5 Maureen Farr-Egan, *Ask Around: The Larger-Than-Life Story of Impresario Murray Farr* (Kingston, ON: Woodpecker Lane Press, 2022), p. 185.

6 Donna Wong-Juliani, interview with Ann Cowan, Christine Hearn, Francis Mansbridge and Carole Gerson, May 17, 2023.
7 Maria Tippett, *Becoming Myself: A Memoir* (Toronto: Stoddart, 1996), pp. 164–65.
8 Giuseppe Tomasi di Lampedusa, *The Leopard* (Milan: Feltrinelli, 1958).
9 Sharon Procter, "Composing to a Different Drummer," *aq*, April 2012, pp. 16–18.
10 Michael Stevenson, interviewed by Ann Cowan and Christine Hearn, February 2022.
11 Michael Stevenson, unpublished remarks at the opening of *The Blue Dragon* in 2010, used with permission.

Selected Sources

The following reference materials have been of help in the writing of this book.

General Works

Simon Fraser's student newspaper, *The Peak*, available online at https://newspapers.lib.sfu.ca/peak-collection/peak, chronicles much of SFU's history. The issues covering 1965–1975 are rich in information on the artistic scene.

Baird, Nini. Interview 1 with Christine Hearn, Francis Mansbridge, Marcia Toms and Walter Piovesan, November 28, 2022; Interview 2 with Marcia Toms, Walter Piovesan and Ann Cowan, March 9, 2023.

Bawtree, Michael. *The Best Fooling: Adventures in Canadian Theatre* (Great Britain: Mereo Books, 2017).

——Zoom interview with Francis Mansbridge, Christine Hearn and Walter Piovesan at Simon Fraser Downtown Harbour Centre, February 23, 2022.

Gibbons, Maurice, ed., Ron Long and Walter Piovesan, assoc. eds., *Remembering SFU* (Vancouver: Simon Fraser University Retirees Association, 2016).

Johnston, Hugh. *Radical Campus: Making Simon Fraser University* (Vancouver: Douglas & McIntyre, 2005).

Wong-Juliani, Donna. Interview with Ann Cowan, Christine Hearn, Francis Mansbridge and Carole Gerson, May 17, 2023.

The Centre for Communications and the Arts

Baird, Nini. "Background on the Centre for Communications and the Arts." Written for the University Services Retreat December 1–2, 1972, at Harrison Hot Springs.

——"Centre for Communications and the Arts." *Communications* 70 (Japan), April 1970.

——"SFU's Centre for Communication and the Arts 1965–1970." SFU Arts History Project, 1965–1970.

——"Transition from CCA to Centre for the Arts 1971–1976." SFU Arts History Project, 1971–1976.

"Public Programs Organized by or Presented in Facilities Managed by Centre for Communications and the Arts at Simon Fraser University 1965–66 through 1975–76." Unpublished report, n.d.

Warner, Gerry. "Theatre of Total Limbo," *The Peak*, March 8, 1972.

Theatre and Mime

Fitzgerald, Shelora. "Nuggets from Linda Johnston in Conversation with Christine and Ann." 0.91 Theatre, 2021, www.youtube. com/watch?v=22uzJn7fOYM.

Horse Sheet no. 1 (March–April 1969); no. 2 (May 1969); no. 3 (June 1969).

Okanagan Interviews with Wilfrid Mennell, Dorthea Atwater, Peter Hay and Wendy Newman, October 21, 2021.

Page, Malcolm. "Savage God in Vancouver: A Documentary Account, 1966–72." *Theatre Research in Canada* vol. 9, no. 2 (Fall 1988).

——"Theatre at SFU: The First Ten Years." Unpublished article sent to Carole Gerson, September 2020.

Perkins Deneault, Tessa. "The Only Escape: The Early Years of the SFU Theatre," *The Tartan*, September 7, 2015.

Dance

Gerecke, Alana. "Dance as 'Lead Card' in the Development of Simon Fraser University's Fine and Performing Arts." In *Renegade Bodies: Canadian Dance in the 1970s*, eds. Allana Lindgren and Kaija Pepper (Toronto: Dance Collection Danse, 2012).

Savannah Walling and Terry Hunter, Zoom interview by Carole Gerson and Tessa Perkins Deneault, Vancouver, January 26, 2023.

Karen Jamieson, phone interview by Tessa Perkins Denault, Carole Gerson and Ann Cowan, January 2023.

Iris Garland fonds. Simon Fraser University Archives, F-197-4-0-0.

Sound and Music

Truax, Barry. "The Sonic Environment: Archiving Soundscapes," www.sfu.ca/~truax/-.

Westerkamp, Hildegard. www.hildegardwesterkamp.ca/bio/.

——"The Disruptive Nature of Listening: Today, Yesterday, Tomorrow." In *Sound, Media, Ecology*, eds. Milena Droumeva and Randolph Jordan (Cham, Switzerland: Palgrave Macmillan, 2019), pp. 45–64.

Film

Bryant, Peter. "SFU Film Workshop: A Critical Look." *Cinema Canada* 20 (July/August 1975), pp. 42–43.

Hearn, Christine. "Canadian Graffiti." *Alumni Journal* (Summer 1986), pp. 16–17.

Johnston, Linda. Interview with Ann Cowan and Christine Hearn, 2021.

McKinnon, Ann. "Sandy Wilson: First Features, Canadian Wives, American Cousins, an Interview."

Pill, Jaan. "Simon Fraser Film Workshop." *Cinema Canada* 20 (July/August 1975), pp. 34–39.

Wilson, Sandy. "The Beginning of My Film Career at SFU." Unpublished essay, 2021.

Literary Arts

Blackfish, eds. Allan Safarik and Brian Brett. Burnaby, BC. 1971-75.

Fawcett, Brian. *Local Matters: A Defence of Dooney's Café and Other Non-Globalized Places, People, and Ideas* (Vancouver: New Star Books, 2003).

Goulden, Alban. Interview with Francis Mansbridge, Vancouver, April 7, 2022.

Greco, Heidi. Interview with Francis Mansbridge and Christine Hearn, White Rock, BC, July 11, 2022.

Iron, eds. Brian Fawcett and Brett Enemark. Port Moody, BC: English Department, Simon Fraser University, 1966-77.

McCaslin, Susan. Interview with Francis Mansbridge and Christine Hearn, Fort Langley, BC, June 9, 2022.

McKinnon, Barry. "Fawcett, Blaser & Simon Fraser." In *Chairs in the Time Machine*. Unpublished memoir.

Persky, Stan, and Brian Fawcett. *Robin Blaser* (Vancouver: New Star Books, 2005, 2010).

Safarik, Allan. Interview with Francis Mansbridge, Dundurn, Saskatchewan, July 24, 2022, and with Francis Mansbridge and Christine Hearn in Vancouver, August 25, 2022.

Visual Arts

Jeffries, Bill. Interview with Iain Baxter, July 2022.

——Interview with James W. Felter, May 2022.

Contributor Biographies

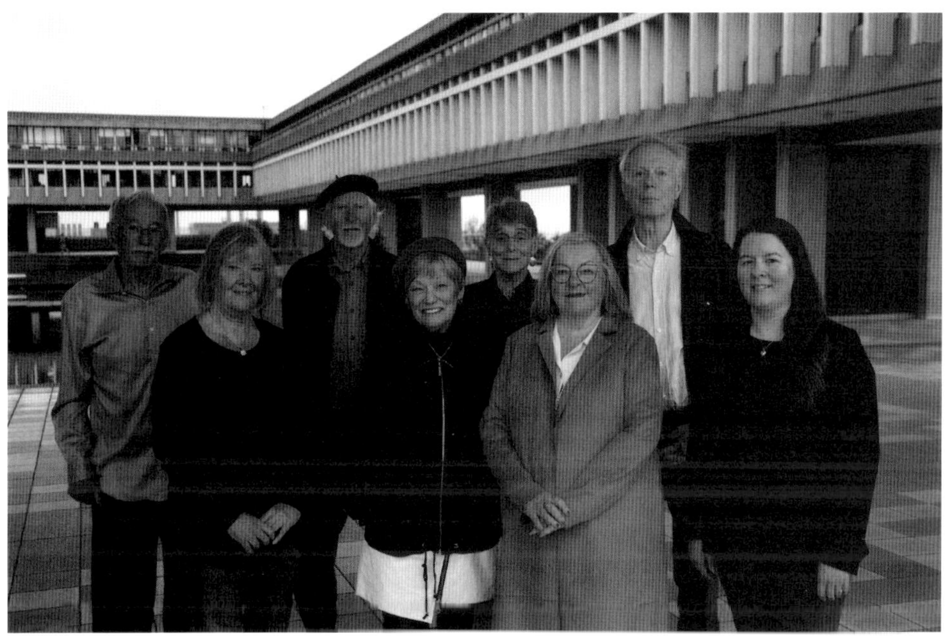

Front row (left to right): Frances Atkinson, Ann Cowan, Christine Hearn, Tessa Perkins Deneault. Back row: Francis Mansbridge, Tony Westman, Carole Gerson, Bill Jeffries.

Frances Atkinson was born in Northern Ireland and moved to London, England, in 1974, then emigrated to Canada in 1980. After completing a bachelor of science degree (BSc) in computing science, she received a master's in information science from City University, London. She worked for Imperial College, London, before joining Simon Fraser University in 1982 as a systems analyst, then as an IT director. When she retired from her IT career at SFU, she received a doctor of business administration (DBA) from the University of Bath for her study of major technology change in universities. She has extensive leadership experience implementing all generations of internet technologies, from the pioneering days of email and the web to the smartphone, social media and data-sharing age. For Frances, the inventiveness involved in delivering unknown new technologies is reminiscent of the experiments in new forms of artistic expression that marked the early years at SFU.

Ann Cowan was the executive director of Simon Fraser University's Vancouver campus until 2010 and previously director of program development with SFU's Morris J. Wosk Centre for Dialogue. She joined the university as the director of program information in continuing studies in 1977. In 1979 she was the founding director of the Writing and Publishing Program, and together with Rowland Lorimer built the Canadian Centre for Studies in Publishing. Before settling in Vancouver in 1976, she worked for the National Museum of Man (now History) as project director of Canada's Visual History. Her degrees are from the University of Toronto and Carleton University, and she is also a by-fellow of Churchill College, Cambridge. Her late husband Peter Buitenhuis joined SFU as chairman of the English department in 1975. Family members Paul Buitenhuis, Penelope Buitenhuis, Hugo Cameron, Adrian Buitenhuis and Juliana Buitenhuis all studied at SFU over the next forty-five years in a variety of disciplines. They are all artists and thrived in the bold, cross-disciplinary and outward-looking environment they found there.

Tessa Perkins Deneault recently published her master's thesis, "Iris Garland: Modern Movement." A freelance writer and arts journalist, she regularly contributes to publications including *The Dance Current*, *Dance International* and *Dance Central*. She is the associate director of marketing and communications for SFU's Faculty of Communication, Art and Technology, which is home to both the School for the Contemporary Arts and the School of Communication, whose beginnings can be traced back to the Centre for Communications and the Arts. She holds an MA in liberal studies, a BA in English and French literatures and publishing, a certificate of liberal arts and a post-baccalaureate diploma in communication—all from SFU. In her spare time, she takes dance classes at the Bez Arts Hub and spends as much time as she can watching live theatre and dance.

Carole Gerson (previously Carole Fainstat) was born in Montreal and transferred to SFU in 1968 after completing her first two years at McGill. While an undergraduate at SFU she avidly participated in Iris Garland's dance workshops and enjoyed the wide array of noon shows and other campus events. After graduating in 1970 with a BA (Honours) in English, she received her MA from Dalhousie and her PhD from UBC. She soon found herself back at SFU as an English professor specializing in Canadian literature and book history, until she retired in 2020. She has published extensively on Canada's literary and cultural history with a focus on early Canadian women writers, from well-known figures such as Pauline Johnson and L.M. Montgomery to more obscure figures. A member of the editorial team of the foundational *History of the Book in Canada / Histoire du livre et de l'imprimé au Canada* (2007), she was co-editor of the third volume (1918–1980). In 2011, she received the Gabrielle Roy Prize for Canadian criticism for *Canadian Women in Print*, 1750–1918, followed in 2013 by the Marie Tremaine medal from the Bibliographical Society of Canada. Her most recent book, co-authored with Peggy Lynn Kelly, is *Hearing More Voices: English-Canadian Women in Print and on the Air, 1914–1960*. Over the years, she has been a grateful recipient of research support from SSHRC as well as funding from SFU and the CFI, and a Killam Research Fellowship.

Christine Hearn was a student at SFU during most of the early creative period. She was active in literary circles, having poetry published in *Blackfish* and *40 Women Poets of Canada* and articles in *West Coast Review* and *The Peak*. She was involved in the English department, graduate studies, and SFU Alumni Association politics, and was the first alumni representative on the SFU Board of Governors. After graduation she was a reporter at the *Vancouver Sun*, established BCTV's Ottawa bureau, was secretary of the Parliamentary Press Gallery for several years, then was media advisor to a federal cabinet minister. After returning to Vancouver, she was director of the Writing and Publishing Program at SFU, developing the university's *aq* magazine and editing it during its sixteen-year history.

Bill Jeffries is from New Jersey. He taught the sciences in schools from 1967 to 1975. In 1976, he did a bachelor of fine arts degree (BFA) at UBC, and later a master's at SFU. In 1983 he opened the Coburg Gallery. From 1988 to 1991 he was director/curator of the Contemporary Art Gallery, then a registrar at the Vancouver Art Gallery and director/curator at Presentation House Gallery from 2001 to 2005, after which he ran the SFU Galleries until 2013.

Francis Mansbridge received his MA from the University of Toronto and his PhD from the University of Ottawa. He has taught at several colleges and universities, including a year at Foreign Affairs College in Beijing, China. In 1990 he left teaching and spent thirteen years as an archivist at North Vancouver Museum and Archives. He has published widely in both the academic and popular markets. His works include a biography of Irving Layton and a selection of his correspondence, and six books of local history.

Max Wyman was born in England and emigrated to Canada in 1967. He was a theatre, dance and music critic and arts columnist for the Vancouver newspapers and the CBC for many decades, and he has written several books on the arts, among them *The Defiant Imagination*, a manifesto placing the arts at the heart of the social agenda. He has just published a sequel, *The Compassionate Imagination*, which argues that engagement with creativity will be an essential means of post-pandemic healing and renewal. Wyman was a member of the board of the Canada Council for the Arts, president of the Canadian Commission for UNESCO and mayor of Lions Bay. He is an Officer of the Order of Canada and holds an honorary Doctor of Letters degree from Simon Fraser University. He and his wife Susan Mertens were members of the inaugural cohort of Shadbolt Scholars in SFU's graduate liberal studies program.

Index

TICKETS

Reservations are accepted at 291-3514 between 9 a.m. and 4:30 p.m three days. Reservations made within three days of the performance at the box office.

Mail Orders: Cheques should be made payable to Simon Fraser Un addressed, stamped envelope.

Box Office Hours: The Simon Fraser University Theatre Box Office 4:30 p.m. The box office opens one hour before curtain time on the

PARKING

Underground metered parking below the mall (entrance to right of to theatre patrons after 7 p.m. The cost is 25c. (The open air parkin time).

CENTRE FOR COMMUNICATIONS AND THE AR
SIMON FRASER UNIVERSITY
BURNABY 2, B.C.

CENTRE FOR COMMUNICATIONS AND THE AR

EVENTS IN T

S

The Centre for Communications and the Arts

presents

DA VITA

THE PREMIERE of

a new feature film by

DAN SINGER

whose **The Beginning**, the first film made at Simon Fraser University, was premiered at SFU last spring and has won for this young film-maker the Dorothy Burritt Award.

Thursday, January 19. Friday, January 20. 8 p.m.

$1.25 (Students $1.00) at door.

The Department of History
in co-operation with
Centre for Communications and the Arts

presents

PROPAGANDA AND VIOLENC

a film series of

contemporary history mirrored in British, French, C man, Russian, American and Cuban films since the F World War.

Wednesdays at 6:30 and 9:30 p.m.

January 18:	*To be announced
January 25:	**Ten Days That Shook the World**
February 1:	**Triumph of the Will; Night and Fog**
February 8:	**Germany Calling; Divide and Conquer; The Nazis Strike**
February 15:	**Battle of Russia**
February 22:	**Peace of Britain; They Also Serve; The Silent Village; World of Plenty**
March 1:	**War Comes to U.S.; Battle of San Pietr**
March 8:	**Heart of Spain** (excerpts)
March 15:	*To be announced
March 22:	**Cuba Si!**
March 29:	**Year of Lightning, Day of Dreams**
April 5:	*To be announced

*—Film bookings not confirmed at press time.

The Physical Development Centre
in co-operation with the
Centre for Communications and the Arts
presents
a concert by the

DANCE WORKSHOP

IRIS GARLAND, Director

Members of the SFU Dance Workshop performed during the Northwest Dance Symposium held at SFU in November and were also seen in concert on campus last spring.

Friday, March 17, 8:30 p.m.
Tickets: 75c each, on sale beginning March 1

BUCKMINSTER FULLER

Architect and Designer
Inventor of the Geodesic Dome

one of the visionaries
of the 20th century
will speak on

"Nature's Co-ordinate System"

Friday, January 27
12:45 p.m.

SFU THEATRE COMPANY

FRIDAY PRODUCTIONS

Staged Readings and Full Productions of contemporary one-act plays, original plays by SFU students in the playwrights workshop and other works.

Each Friday at 12:30 p.m.
January 13 through April 7

Scheduled: January 13—**The Dock Brief** by Mortimer
January 20—Playwright Jack Winter (See Poets and Writers)
February 3 —**The Tiger** by Schisgal

Projected: **The Lesson** by Ionesco
Krapp's Last Tape by Beckett

Michael Langham, Artistic Director, Festival Theatre of Stratford, Ontario, will speak Friday, February 24 at 12:30 p.m.

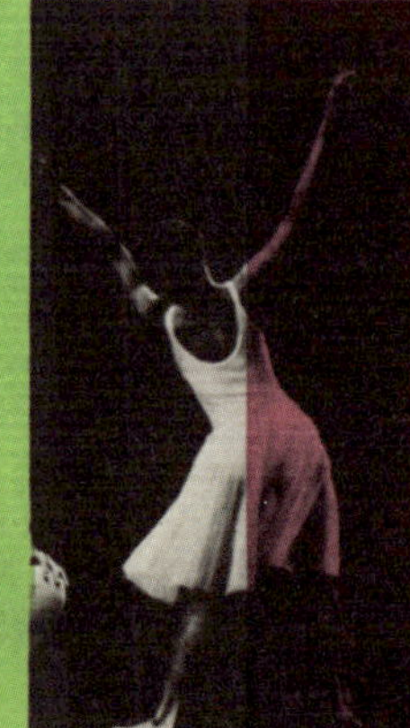

FILMING AND FILM-MAKERS: CANADA

Viewing and discussion of original films by Canadian film-makers.

Each Monday at 12:45 p.m.
January 23 through April 3

January 23: **Day of the Beginning**
a color film by John P. Fitzgerald
of Toronto based on Indian legends.